The Marine Aquarium Reference

Systems and Invertebrates

Martin A. Moe, Jr.

Green Turtle Publications
P.O. Box 17925
Plantation, Florida 33318

GREEN TURTLE PUBLICATIONS
P.O. Box 17925
Plantation, FL 33318

Library of Congress Cataloging in Publication Data:

Moe, Martin A.
The marine aquarium reference : systems and invertebrates / by Martin A. Moe, Jr.
p. cm.
Bibliography: p.
Includes index.
ISBN 0-939960-05-2 : 21.95
1. Marine aquariums. 2. Marine invertebrates. I. Title.
SF457. 1 .M64 1989
597 . 092'074—dc20   89-7554
                                       CIP

Printed in the United States of America

10 9 8 7 6 5 4 3 2

Dedication

Most authors include a dedication. It's a good way to acknowledge and pay respect to people who are important to the author. Books are usually dedicated to family, friends, supporters, mentors, heros, or pioneers. There are many people in these categories to whom I would love to dedicate this book. Instead, however, I want to dedicate the book to a group of people who are not only important to me, but to all marine aquarists.

This book was written as a source of information for those that enjoy the challenge and satisfaction of keeping marine aquarium systems. That fascinating but sometimes troubled path is often smoothed by those that begin and maintain marine aquarium societies. Great effort is put into organization and planning; long nights of sweat and tears are spent building a newsletter, managing funds and auctions, umpiring important and unimportant arguments—all to encourage, aid, and spread the enjoyment of the marine aquarium hobby. This is frequently a labor of love with little reward. I am happy to dedicate this book to the "spark plugs"—those individuals that have started and/or served as officers and have given freely of time, effort, money, and love in aquarium societies all over the world.

Acknowledgments

Professional and amateur aquarists and aquatic scientists, too numerous to mention, have contributed to this book through extensive conversations and correspondence. The essence of many books and articles by professionals and amateurs have likewise contributed to the information presented in this reference. This book, however, is the product of a very small publishing company, and much of the credit for the production of the book belongs to my wife Barbara Battjes Moe. We shared the tasks of layout, design, editing, and production. This book is truly a joint effort. It was developed and designed through use of modern computer and desktop publishing technology, with a great deal of help from Scott Moe. Andrea Moe contributed some of the drawings in Chapter 8. Charles Delbeek provided helpful editorial comments for the second printing.

TABLE OF CONTENTS

Contents

Contents

Part III. Marine Invertebrates — 391
The Organization of Life In the Sea

Contents

12   Contents

Introduction

First of all, something to think about. Is keeping a marine aquarium morally right? Is it ethically correct? You may think it strange that such questions are brought up in a book about how to keep marine invertebrates, or even that such questions are worthy of consideration at all. Times are changing, however. Thinking people are now very concerned about how our activities impact the environment. As citizens of the Earth, we are becoming more and more aware that the world does not "belong" to humanity, that we *share* this planet with all life, and that our quality of life, even our survival, depends on the survival of natural ecosystems. With the ability to change the ecosystem comes the responsibility to preserve it. I think there is hope for humanity. In the last three decades we have seen the development of a general understanding of the fragile nature of our world. T-shirts and bumper stickers that say "Save the Whales" and "No Forests—No Reefs—No People" and "Extinction is Forever" are pricking our collective conscience. In many instances, we are moving in the right direction. We have become aware that the sea is not a garbage dump, that its web of life is delicate and must be studied, understood, and carefully managed if we are to live in harmony with the mother of life, our oceans.

We who delight in the life under the sea and try to maintain a little bit of ocean bottom in our homes have been particularly troubled. It has come to our attention that the methods used to collect these fascinating creatures are, in some instances, very harmful to fish, invertebrates, and the coral reefs where many of them live. Coral reefs are delicate, slow growing ecosystems and are particularly vulnerable to the results of human activity in the sea and on nearby land areas. Coral reefs require our special concern. Maintaining a successful marine aquarium, however, is a rich and colorful thread in the fabric of our lives. We learn a great deal and gain much enjoyment and satisfaction from this hobby. We also spread knowledge and concern for life in the sea to those around us and this may well be the greatest legacy of our hobby. It is very important that we conduct our hobby with the greatest concern for the environment that is the object of our interest.

The extremes of environmental rights and wrongs are easy to determine. It is very wrong to destroy a coral reef with dynamite to collect a few stunned angelfish and wrong to use cyanide and other methods that kill far more aquarium fish then they capture in good health. It is wrong to kill whales threatened with extinction, wrong to pollute with toxic waste. On the other hand, use of fish, shrimp, and lobsters for food is right if the fishing is so managed that the populations are not destroyed and the ecosystems are not damaged. It is right to use fish and invertebrates in scientific research to learn about the nature of these animals and the effects our activities have upon the environment. However, as with birds and mammals, marine organisms are an aesthetic as well as a sustaining resource and this is where some conflict of opinion lies.

Fisheries for "food fish" such as grouper and lobster and fisheries for marine aquarium fish such as angelfish and starfish are both legitimate fisheries. It is not right to allow fishing for food and sport and prevent commercial collection of marine life for aquariums. Both provide employment and satisfy human needs. Stocks of angelfish and other tropicals that sustain commercial fisheries should be protected and managed when necessary, just as other fisheries.

Different cultures often have different ideas on the proper use of animal populations. One culture may not think it proper or right to use sea urchins, marine angelfish, whales and dolphins, or even dogs and cats as exploitable animal populations. Other cultures may consider them valuable food and industrial resources. Part of being human is the dominion over, and the use of, the mineral, vegetable, and animal resources of the

Earth. We do not always agree on how these resources should be used, but rational people are in agreement that the natural ecosystems and the productivity of earth and ocean must be protected and preserved. We are now trying hard to learn to cooperate with each other, to understand each other's point of view, and to use these resources in a responsible and proper manner.

Life in the sea is short and seldom sweet. Relatively few individual organisms survive to become adults and most of those that do seldom live more than a year or two. In nature, survival of the individual is rarely significant. It is the survival of the species that counts. An individual shrimp may be quickly inhaled by a grouper, scooped up in a shrimp net and frozen for market, or carefully collected and maintained in an aquarium for a few months. Whatever the fate of the individual animal and whatever, if any, human use is made of it, the loss of the animal to the environment is one thing and the meaning of its death in human terms is something else.

Take a quiet beach, a gentle breeze, a setting sun, and two 10 year old boys. One of these kids is catching fiddler crabs on the beach and carefully putting them on a fish hook to catch a flounder for the family cook out. The other is catching fiddler crabs, pulling their legs off, and gleefully watching them try to run down the beach on two legs. Then he pulls off the claw and slowly cuts the crab in half with its own claw. One of these kids is right and one is very wrong, and few of us have any problem determining which is which. As far as the fiddler crabs are concerned, however, attitude and intent is not a consideration—their fate is the same in the hands of either boy. The significance of this incident lies solely in the portent of human behavior, for the few individual crabs that are lost to these humans will not effect the survival of the species.

So, is it right or wrong to keep a marine aquarium? There is no one answer that is right for everyone. The morality of keeping sea creatures in aquariums should be carefully considered by the individual aquarist and a decision made based on individual beliefs and convictions. If it disturbs you to keep animals in captivity and to watch nature interact in your living room, then a marine aquarium is not for you. However, if the form, color, and behavior of these animals is fascinating, and the technical and biological maintenance of a marine aquarium system is an exciting challenge, then go for it.

In my opinion (since you ask), as long as we use the living resources of the sea for food and fishing, sustenance and enjoyment, keeping a marine aquarium will be a source of knowledge, achievement, and personal satisfaction—an activity to be commended and encouraged. If the ecology of the sea is not damaged and the intent of the aquarist is not cruel or sadistic, an aquarium is no more right or wrong than any other human endeavor that impinges upon nature. The lives of the individual animals that are collected and maintained in the aquarium may well be better and longer in captivity than in the wild, and those that are lost could expect no better in the sea.

Ofttimes, some aquarists feel that they have somehow failed if the creature that they bring into their tanks does not live for at least five years and get so big that a special tank has to be built when they finally donate it to the public aquarium that has been clamoring for it. Although we strive to maintain all the creatures in our tanks in health and harmony, the life and death of many marine creatures, particularly invertebrates,is often out of the total control of the aquarist. Life in the aquarium struggles to create its own ecological balance, and a large part of keeping an invertebrate aquarium is the observation and manipulation of the aquarium's ecology. Flowers and potted plants have a limited life, and there is no sense of failure when their time is done. Likewise, many invertebrates have a limited life, and if we enjoy and learn from them while they live with us, however long that may be, then we have been successful aquarists.

We do have a responsibility, however. Like everyone that uses the resources of the sea in any way, we must do everything in our power to preserve the vitality of the ecosystems we exploit. We must discourage the destruction of coral reefs and the taking of endangered species in any way we possibly can.

Good aquarists are concerned about the coral reef environment. They learn about efforts to protect coral reefs and support organizations such as International Marinelife Alliance (IMA) that actively strive to improve the fisheries for coral reef creatures. We must also do our best to sustain and nourish the creatures we maintain and care for them to the best of our ability.

Remember too, that our responsibility to the environment is far, far greater than any responsibility to an individual animal or plant. Never, never release any organism into an environment where it does not naturally occur. It is far better to dispose of an unwanted animal quickly and humanely and send it out with the garbage than to risk unknown damage to the environment through introduction of an exotic organism.

Why keep a marine invertebrate aquarium? Well, for one thing, not to develop an interest in invertebrates is to ignore 97% of all known animal species. True, a fish may be a better "pet" than a crab or a sea urchin, but one can not appreciate the complexity and diversity of sea life without learning about invertebrates. The vertebrates (chordates), the group of animals that includes marine tropical fish, as well as birds, alligators, horses, and human beings, are all the animals that have a dorsal nerve cord at some stage of their development. The invertebrates, however, are just as important to life on Earth (actually more important) than vertebrates and far more abundant. There are an estimated 20,000 species of fish, but there are over 35,000 species of crustacea alone, at least 120,000 species of mollusca, and over 6,000 species of echinoderms. Invertebrates can be just as interesting and colorful in an aquarium as fish, and their behavior even more varied and fascinating. Keeping marine fish is challenging and interesting, but to ignore the invertebrates is to miss out on the greatest abundance of life that the sea has to offer.

To really enjoy a marine aquarium dedicated to invertebrates, however, you have to know a little bit about them and have some idea of how to care for them in home aquaria. And as Shakespeare said in *Hamlet*, "Ay, there's the rub." A great

deal of information is available on the form, structure, behavior, and culture of marine invertebrates in the scientific
literature, but most of this information is not available in the
popular literature. There are a few hard-to-get European books,
some good encyclopedic picture books, a few highly technical
books for the advanced hobbyist, and a few good magazine
articles on care and keeping of invertebrate and reef tank systems now available, but there is a need to bring information on
the many recent advances in technology of small marine systems, particularly in filtration and lighting, and an overview of
marine invertebrates together under one cover. I hope that this
book will help fill this gap.

It is meant to be a companion volume to *The Marine
Aquarium Handbook - Beginner to Breeder*. That book came out in
1982 and now has over 110,000 copies in print. Like that book,
this one is not designed to be a picture book, although much
more effort has gone into the illustrations. The emphasis is on
scientifically accurate, understandable information that will
help the marine aquarist maintain and enjoy a successful
marine fish, invertebrate, or marine reef aquarium. Topics
covered in detail in *The Marine Aquarium Handbook* are mentioned only briefly and the reader is referred to this previous
book. (If you don't have it, it's worth getting that book also.)

Just like individual human beings, every marine aquarium
is unique. Even if one tried to establish two unconnected
marine tanks exactly alike, differences in microscopic life and
differences and changes that develop in the larger life forms
would soon create two obviously different captive marine
ecosystems. This is a large part of the excitement and fascina-
tion of the marine aquarium hobby, especially in keeping a
marine invertebrate tank. One never knows what strange creatures will appear, which animals and plants will grow and
flourish, which will fade away and, as in the natural ecosystem,
who will eat and who will be eaten. The invertebrate tank is, in
some ways, easier to keep than a marine tank devoted to fish;
yet in its diversity, the invertebrate aquarium also represents
the greatest challenge to a marine aquarist. Some creatures are

relatively easy to keep and others very difficult, yet they may live side by side in the natural environment. Only in a marine invertebrate aquarium can an individual keep such a vast assemblage of wild creatures so easily observed in such a small space, under conditions so closely controlled.

The challenge may be just to keep an assemblage of invertebrates and a few fish in a balanced, reasonably natural state or to maintain and/or reproduce certain species of particular interest. Many invertebrates may be kept quite well in the simplest of marine aquarium systems, while others require advanced techniques that almost duplicate the environmental conditions in tropical seas. Advances in popular marine aquarium technology have only recently brought the intricate world of coral reef and tropical sea invertebrates into the living rooms of marine aquarists. The world of marine invertebrates is so vast and the hobby is so new that undescribed species, still unknown to science, are occasionally found in the tanks of hobbyists. Much information on the technology and the creatures themselves is available, but widely scattered through the popular and scientific literature. This book will give the aquarist a basic knowledge of the technology and biology of keeping marine invertebrates and provide a framework for accumulating additional information on this most fascinating hobby.

To gain a general understanding of the essence of a marine aquarium, we need to ask three questions:

- What does a marine aquarium do?

- How does a marine aquarium do what it does?

- What are the basic types of marine aquarium systems and how do they function?

The first two sections of this book answers these questions. The third section introduces the aquarist to the world of marine invertebrates. Please note that I have tried to avoid complex technical explanations that include detailed chemical formulae and advanced scientific terminology. This is good because most aquarists without academic training in chemistry and biology can understand and use the information. It is also bad, however, because we lose the deeper understanding found at a detailed technical level. Those aquarists that require more detailed technical expositions are encouraged to refer to the literature cited at the end of this book.

There are walls of book shelves in marine science libraries devoted to the scientific study of invertebrates. Scientists have spent lifetimes studying only certain facets of the life history and classification of small groups of invertebrates, but even so, the gaps in our knowledge are still far greater than the blocks of factual information. A marine invertebrate aquarium allows us to explore this frontier and even contribute to its expansion.

A marine invertebrate aquarium can be kept as just a fun thing to do or as a serious tool to help learn about the way life works. Either way, this book should be of help. There are three questions that I hope this book will help the marine aquarist to begin to answer:

- What are the characteristics of the natural environment where coral reef organisms live and breed?

- How can these fantastic coral reef plants and animals be kept in a marine aquarium system?

- What are these invertebrates and how do they live?

To answer these questions in great detail would require many years and many volumes, as well as a good bit of original research. Thus, this book can be only an introduction, a jumping off place, to the vast and fascinating invertebrate world that lies just beneath the sea. So it's time we got started. Keep an invertebrate tank—learn from it and enjoy it. And if you have a mind to, observe your creatures closely, ask questions, find answers, keep notes and write articles for your local club newsletter or a magazine. Every contribution to our knowledge of marine invertebrates is important and worthwhile.

Part I

The Marine Environment

An aquarist's perspective

What does a marine aquarium do?

In essence, a marine aquarium provides an *adequate substitute* for the natural conditions needed by a marine organism to maintain life.

Now what may be an adequate substitute for the natural environment for one species may be woefully inadequate for another. A rock boring sea urchin may do quite well in the same tank where an anemone withers and dies. In nature there are many different marine environments (microhabitats), often within one small area. If one sets up a marine aquarium for the basic purpose of keeping marine fish, then there is only one habitat in the marine environment that is most important. This is the open spaces in the reef structure and the few feet of open water above the bottom. Most marine aquarium fish live in this environment and as long as they have proper food, light, and water quality, the composition and structure of the tank bottom is not critical.

The marine invertebrate aquarium, however, may include creatures from *all* marine habitats. These creatures may live under, through, on top of, and/or extend above or below the substrate; they may feed on plankton, microscopic algae, tiny animals, mud, detritus, sunlight, worms and other burrowing animals, or one or more of these. They may crawl about, swim rapidly, or remain attached to one spot for life. Thus many factors, such as type and depth of substrate, intensity and spectrum of lighting, presence or absence of algae and detritus, water quality detail, and patterns of water movement, become very important in the invertebrate aquarium.

Perhaps the best way to get a good idea of what it is we are trying to create in a marine aquarium is to look at all the different elements of the natural marine environment. Dissecting the marine environment is not a simple task. It is easy to be overwhelmed by a coral reef. The experience of floating in warm, calm, crystal clear tropical seas under a sky so wide and so blue, and to glide over and through coral formations so massive and yet so intricate, and to view life in such a vast array of form and color—can stir one's soul and make it seem impossible to understand such complex beauty.

To draw an analogy, think of a symphony orchestra. It creates a glory that is more than the sum of its parts. Everything works together so intricately that one can't separate its component parts and still produce the same result. Individual instruments, however, a violin, a cello, a trumpet and piano can still make beautiful music together even if they can't create a symphony. And so a marine aquarium is also a thing of beauty even though it is only a pale shadow of a coral reef. A symphony orchestra has major sections—the strings, the brass, the percussion—and all are made up of many different instruments. The coral reef environment has different sections also— water chemistry, physical elements, and the biological environment (life)—which are made up of many factors. Just as the symphony orchestra has a "center of power", the conductor, so does the coral reef and this is the sun. The sun provides the energy that powers the coral reef environment, as it does in almost all other earthly environments. (An exception, the deep sea vent communities that are powered by the chemosynthetic activity of bacteria that feed on sulfur compounds.) Now if you're into rock and roll rather than symphony orchestras, you may want to think of the sun as the lead singer. OK, OK, so this analogy is beginning to break down, but I'm sure you get the basic idea.

Let's take a brief look at the major natural elements that compose or affect a coral reef and nearby habitats—what they are, what they do, and how they are measured. Then we will see what happens to each of these elements when we try to capture a coral reef in a marine aquarium. Certain components of marine aquarium systems and methods of maintenance can substitute for the elements of the natural environment and these are also discussed.

Our dissection of the marine environment is grouped under three chapters.

Chapter 1, The Chemical Environment, includes factors associated with water and water quality.

Chapter 2, The Physical Environment, includes factors that pertain to the physical structure of the habitat, nonchemical characteristics of water, and environmental parameters.

Chapter 3, The Biological Environment, discusses the interactions of life forms that occur in, on, and around coral reefs.

Note that Part II, *Marine Aquarium Systems*, describes the structure, operation, and function of the life support systems of marine aquariums.

Chapter 1

The Chemical Environment

Seawater Composition

Water, seawater that is, defines the natural and the captive marine environment. In nature, seawater is both the most constant and the most variable element in the marine environment. Yeah, I know this sounds like a contradiction, but it's true. Seawater is a very complex, dynamic fluid. It is made up of pure water (about 96%), dissolved inorganic salts and gasses, dissolved organic substances, and various microscopic living organisms. Technically, perhaps, the bacteria and microscopic plants and animals always found in seawater are not a part of the water, but in life and death and metabolism they are so intimately associated with the organic structure of the water that they often define the life determining properties of the particular environment. Lifeless water is found only in theory and scientific laboratories.

The seven salts—sodium chloride, magnesium chloride, magnesium sulfate, calcium sulfate, potassium sulfate, calcium carbonate and potassium or sodium bromide—make up about 99% of the inorganic solids in seawater and are the conservative elements. They are called conservative because they are always in the same proportion to each other regardless of the total amount of dissolved solids. In other words, the percentage of sodium chloride in the total salt content of seawater is always the same even if the seawater is concentrated or diluted. So constant is the relative amounts of these salts, that measuring the concentration of one of these major elements, usually chlorinity, also provides the concentrations of all other conservative elements. The relative amounts of trace elements, organics, and other substances, including life, varies greatly in natural seawater, *but the major salts are always in the same proportion to each other*. Thus even though there are vast differences in seawater from a tropical coral reef, an arctic ice flow, a polluted harbor and a northern temperate estuary, it is still fundamentally the same even though temperatures, salinity, life, and chemistry may vary greatly.

The salts are present in seawater as ions, the individual atoms of their respective elements. Each of these atoms have an individual positive (cation) or negative (anion) charge. Thus sodium chloride, the most abundant salt, is present as sodium ions (Na^+) and as chloride ions (Cl^-), and when the water evaporates from seawater leaving the salts behind, the sodium and chlorine hook up together and form the white salt, sodium chloride ($NaCl$). The total amount of dissolved solid matter in sea water determines the "salinity" of the water. The basic stuff of seawater is listed in Table 1.

All the elements that compose the structure of our world are found, somewhere, somehow, dissolved in seawater. Most of the elements are found in variable, very tiny amounts, and are considered trace elements or microconstituents. Some are inorganic, such as sulphur, lead, silver, zinc, copper, iodine, aluminum, iron, silver, phosphorus, vanadium, cobalt, molybdenum, yttrium, germanium, palladium, indium, antimony, uranium, and promethium, to name just a few. There is also a vast array of organic trace elements in seawater. These include vitamins, pigments, plant hormones, orthophosphate carbohydrates, peptides, polypeptides, proteins and their derivative compounds, free amino acids, fatty acids, other aliphatic carboxylic and hydroxycarboxylic acids, humic acids, organic iron, and many other organic (carbon based) compounds. Some trace elements, especially zinc, copper iodine, vanadium, cobalt, manganese, molybdenum, arsenic, organic iron, and vitamins, are essential to life for many marine plants and animals, while others are nonessential or useful, depending on the organism. The composition of sea water over a coral reef is very consistent. Its physical and chemical properties (temperature, turbidity, salinity) may vary with season and tide but the major constituents that compose it are always the same. A detailed analysis of the structure of sea water can be found in many technical texts. Harvey (1963) and Spotte (1979) are good references.

Table 1. Constituents of oceanic seawater.

Constituent	grams per kilo (‰)
Sodium	10.77
Magnesium	1.30
Calcium	0.409
Potassium	0.388
Strontium	0.010
Chloride	19.37
Sulphate (SO_4)	2.71
Bromide	0.065
Boric acid (H_3BO_3)	0.026
(total salts)	(35.1)
Carbon (as bicarbonate, carbonate and molecular carbon dioxide, pH 8.2)	0.025
as dissolved organics	0.001 - 0.0025
Oxygen (in equilibrium with the atmosphere, temperature dependent)	0.006 - 0.008
Nitrogen (in equilibriumwith the atmosphere, temperature dependent)	0.013
Other elements	0.005

Source Harvey (1963)

The seawater or artificial seawater in a marine aquarium begins to accumulate waste products of plants and animals as soon as life is introduced. The amount of life relative to water volume and filtration capacity of the system is the biological load, and this determines what happens to the water and how fast it happens. As the water in a properly filtered marine aquarium ages, two things occur. First, the trace element composition of the water changes. The activity of life, bacterial and algal, removes some trace elements and may increase the amounts of others. Generally, inorganic trace elements decrease and organic trace elements increase. Second, dissolved nutrients and waste metabolic products increase. These changes lower the capacity of the system to support marine life. These changes do not occur in nature (polluted harbors and bays excepted) because of the balanced interaction of plant and animal life and the vastness of the marine environment.

Proper filtration can be very effective in slowing these changes, but replacement of the water is the only sure way to periodically renew the water quality of a marine aquarium. The general rule of thumb in water change is 10% per month. The system may require more if the biological load is high and filtration is barely adequate, or less if the biological load is low and/or filtration is very good. Figure 1 illustrates the relationship between biological load, effectiveness of filtration, and time before necessary water change. Miniature reef systems and other systems with exceptional filtration, i.e., trickle filters, protein foam skimmers, ozonation, strong algal growth, etc., may run for extended periods before water changes are necessary. Be sure to faithfully replace evaporated water and to monitor pH, nitrate levels, and if possible, redox potential and carbonate hardness on systems that seem to require little, if any, water change.

Trace elements tend to decrease in marine aquarium systems, especially systems that use ozonization and have effective protein foam skimming devices. Most trace elements are renewed through compounds added to the system in foods and through water changes and addition of trace element supplements. A shortage of iodine, however, may become a problem in some systems since algaes take up iodine readily and iodine is rapidly removed by protein foam skimming. Low iodine levels may cause molting difficulties for crustaceans and con-

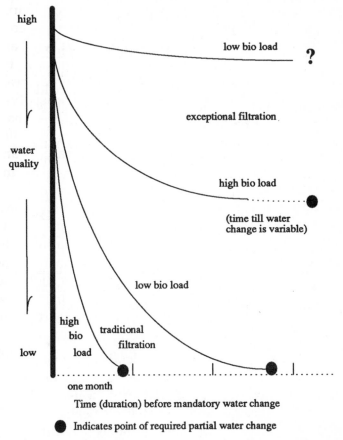

Figure 1. Theoretical relationship between filtration efficiency and the time between water changes for traditional and exceptional filtration over a range of biological loading.

siderably reduce activity levels for other invertebrates. Iodine occurs in concentrations of about .05 ppm in natural sea water. It is possible to increase iodine levels in a marine aquarium through addition of potassium iodide. Wilkens (1973) suggests preparation of a 10% solution of potassium iodide as a stock solution. One ml of this stock solution is then diluted in 100 ml of water and then one ml of this solution is added to the system for every 10 liters of aquarium system water. Iodine renewal should be done about every two weeks in systems that require this treatment. Don't add iodine unless it is necessary, however, for it is possible to overdose. Consider addition of iodine only if the system has both ozonization and protein foam skimming devices and/or if crustaceans have problems with molting.

Vitamin B_{12}, which contains considerable cobalt, is essential for the growth of bacteria and most algaes and is quickly diminished in marine systems, especially miniature reef systems, by the activity of bacteria and algae. This vitamin is found in concentrations up to 0.2 ppm in various natural waters. Many aquarists have reported that addition of a vitamin mix specially compounded to replace essential vitamins in marine systems has enhanced growth and survival of corals and other invertebrates.

For hundreds of millions of years, marine animals and plants have evolved with, and depend upon, the constant composition of seawater. Seawater is not magic, however, and all coral reef organisms do not necessarily require Mother Nature's formula right off the reef. Different animals, particularly invertebrates, have different tolerances for water that is not *exactly* of the same composition as seawater, and some algaes and lower invertebrates do better in water higher or lower in certain nutrients and essential elements. Scientists often put together artificial seawater formulas that differ from natural composition and are designed for propagation of specific animals or plants. With a home marine aquarium, however, we are interested in filling the aquarium with salt water that will support a wide variety of marine life. It need not be exactly the same as water right off the reef, but it must be an adequate substitute for this water.

There are two ways to put water in a marine aquarium. Natural seawater can be collected and used very successfully, or a package of artificial sea salts can be purchased and dissolved into fresh water to make up an artificial seawater that will support most marine life. Refer to Moe (1982), *The Marine Aquarium Handbook*, for methods of collecting and processing natural seawater and using artificial seawater salt mixes. Natural seawater carries many inorganic and organic trace elements and may better support many types of invertebrate and plant life than an artificial salt mix, at least initially. Many inorganic trace elements are now included in artificial salt mixes, however, and organic trace elements begin to accumulate in an aquarium as soon as life is introduced. After two or three months, differences between natural and artificial salt water in a marine aquarium are probably very minor. There are many brands available on the market these days and most of them are the product of a great deal of research and development. A good artificial seawater contains all the elements known to be essential to marine life, and the major elements are present in approximately the ratios and concentrations of natural seawater. The salts of a good quality artificial seawater dissolve easily and completely (or nearly so) in fresh water. If you don't have a particular personal preference for one brand, go with a major brand recommended by local aquarists or aquarium shops.

Salinity

Salinity is a measure of the total amount of dissolved solids in seawater. Salts, however, make up all but one or two percent of these solids, so the amount of salt dissolved in the water is usually all that is considered when the term salinity is used. In natural waters, salinity may be very constant or highly variable. On coral reefs, salinity is very constant. In coastal bays and estuaries subject to fresh water runoff or high evaporation rates, salinity may be very high or very low and usually varies considerably with season, tides, and weather. Salinity is measured in parts per thousand (ppt or ‰) of salt to water. Oceanic seawater runs right around 34 to 37 ‰, and this is the salinity in which coral reef organisms exist most of the time. Unusual current and weather conditions may increase salinity slightly or drop it a bit on coral reefs near large land masses. Average oceanic salinity is 35 ‰, but there are variations at different depths and between water masses. For example, surface salinity in the mid Pacific is 35.5‰, in the mid-Atlantic it is 37.0‰, and in the Red Sea, 40‰. This does not mean, however, that 35‰ is the best salinity for a marine aquarium. Marine fish and many invertebrates can do quite well at salinities slightly lower than normal oceanic levels, 28 to 32‰ for most organisms. This lower salinity allows for some evaporation of fresh water from the system without increasing salinity above normal levels and slightly increases the amount of oxygen dissolved in the tank water. Reef tank systems with live corals should be operaterated at near normal oceanic salinities of 33 to 35‰.

In typical marine aquarium practice, salinity is measured as specific gravity (sg). The proper salinity range for a marine aquarium measured in specific gravity units is 1.020 to 1.026. The true specific gravity of seawater at 35‰ is 1.026. Note that the specific gravity of seawater decreases as water temperature increases. *The Marine Aquarium Handbook* (Moe 1982) has a complete explanation of salinity, specific gravity, and methods of measurement in Chapter 5.

The Seawater Buffer System

Alkalinity, total hardness, carbonate hardness, pH, carbon dioxide, the carbonate-bicarbonate system, and calcium carbonate are all terms used to describe some component or process that is part of the complex buffering system present in seawater. This system is usually described in chemical terms and can be difficult for the average aquarist to understand. What follows is a simple, basic description of how the system works.

Seawater contains many mineral salts. These salts are present as ions of the elements that compose the salt, such as positive ions (cations) of sodium and negative ions (anions) of chlorine that form the salt, sodium chloride. Ions of various salts constantly move in and out of chemical reactions with many other elements, thus the sea is like a giant chemical square dance. Some dancers always stay on the floor and others enter and leave as the dance continues. Seawater also contains carbon dioxide gas. When dissolved in water, carbon dioxide reacts with the hydrogen of water to form a weak acid, carbonic acid (H_2CO_3). If excess carbon dioxide is in the water, carbonic acid levels increase beyond the point where it can be quickly utilized in the carbonate-bicarbonate system, and pH levels drop. If too much carbon dioxide is taken from the water, carbonic acid decreases and pH levels quickly rise. Addition or deletion of carbon dioxide beyond atmospheric equilibrium temporarily changes pH but does not change the alkalinity (carbonate composition) of the water.

Carbonic acid forms negatively charged carbonate (HCO_3-) and bicarbonate (CO_3^{2-}) ions. Carbonate in turn joins with calcium to form calcium carbonate ($CaCO_3$). The chemical reactions that form bicarbonate, carbonate, and calcium carbonate are equilibrium reactions; that is they can go back and forth depending on conditions, such as increase or decrease of carbon dioxide, pressure, and temperature. Under normal physical and biological conditions, the carbonate-bicarbonate ions act as a "bank" that automatically takes up excess carbonic or other acids, or forms more carbonic acid if carbon dioxide is lost. This is the buffer system that maintains the normal pH of seawater at about 8.2. Bicarbonate is most important in the normal pH range of seawater. Calcium is an important element present in seawater and is part of this system. Calcium, as you know, is important for building strong bones and teeth, also strong coral skeletons, mollusk shells, sea urchin tests, and algae supports and has numerous other biological uses as well.

As calcium carbonate is removed from seawater by chemical and biological processes (mostly utilized in the shells of tiny planktonic animals), more bicarbonate forms from carbonate, more carbon dioxide is assimilated into the buffer system, and pH remains constant. In the sea, carbon dioxide flows into the system in areas of high biological activity and water run off from land, accumulates in the great depths, and is released back to the atmosphere in areas where deep sea waters well upward to the surface. The carbonate-bicarbonate buffer system equilibrates back and forth and pH stays relatively constant. Gieskes (1974) is a good technical reference to alkalinity and carbon dioxide in seawater.

In a marine aquarium system, however, organic acids from decomposition of organic matter and animal metabolism are constantly being added to the water. These acids constantly withdraw carbonate and bicarbonate from the buffer "bank". Calcareous gravels can only add to the buffer bank by adding dissolved calcium carbonate if the pH falls below 7.5 to 7.8, which is too low to maintain a system in optimum condition. Thus the marine aquarist must battle to filter out organics before they make a "withdrawal" from the buffer "bank" and must add carbonate-bicarbonate through chemical addition or water change when a decrease in pH and/or redox potential indicates the need.

Alkalinity and Hardness

Alkalinity is not the same as salinity. Total alkalinity is determined by the amount of acid (free, positively charged hydrogen atoms) that is required to neutralize all the negatively charged bicarbonate, carbonate, and borate ions present in one liter of water. When these ions are neutralized by organic acids, they are no longer available and alkalinity drops although salinity has not changed. Alkalinity is measured in units termed millequivalents per liter or meq/l. Natural seawater has a meq/l of 2.1 to 2.5. One meq/l is equal to about 50 ppm calcium carbonate.

Hardness is a general term used to describe the total amount of minerals dissolved in water and is most generally applied to describe freshwater. If your tap water is hard, there are a lot of minerals in it, usually calcium carbonate ($CaCO_3$), which causes hard white precipitates to build up around your faucets. Soft water lacks high levels of dissolved minerals. Freshwater that has less than 75 parts per million (ppm) hardness is considered soft water. Distilled water has no dissolved mineral salts and is as soft as water can get. Sea water has 35 parts per thousand dissolved mineral salts (35 ‰ or S.G. 1.026), mostly chlorides, as described above, and is very hard. Carbonates exceed all other salts in freshwaters. Natural freshwaters vary greatly in hardness, and freshwater aquarists are very concerned with the degree of hardness that particular freshwater fish and plants require. Total or general hardness is a measure of all the dissolved minerals in the water, and aside from the concept of salinity, marine aquarists have little concern with total hardness. Carbonate hardness, however, the amount of calcium carbonate ($CaCO_3$) dissolved in the water, can be an important consideration to those who grow corals and algae.

Carbonate Hardness

The basic measure for carbonate hardness in marine and freshwater is parts per million (ppm). Unfortunately, different countries have different systems for defining calcium carbonate hardness, and the aquarium literature can be confusing on this point. The following information will make it possible to work with all systems. The most frequently encountered measurements of carbonate hardness and alkalinity are reported in German dKH, ppm $CaCO_3$, or meq/l.

Carbonate hardness in marine aquarium systems constantly decreases as biological processes, primarily biological filtration, produce acids that neutralize bicarbonate ions and remove them from the water. Many marine organisms also use carbonates and calcium in formation of tissues and hard skeletal parts, thus further reducing the carbonates in the system water. As calcium carbonate is decreased, it must be replaced to keep the animals that use carbonates—corals, echinoderms, mollusks, crustaceans and others—in good health. Normally, water changes and replacement of evaporated water with hard tap water is adequate for replacement of calcium carbonate in conventional systems. In miniature reef systems, however, particularly when corals and algae are growing well, water chan-

ges are few, and evaporation is made up with soft or distilled
water, addition of calcium carbonate may well be necessary.
Thiel (1988, 1989) recommends a carbonate hardness of dKH 15
to 18 and Wilkins (1973) mentions working with dKH of 15 to
20. Good success has also been obtained in reef tanks operated
at total alkalinities of 2.5 to 3.5 meq/l (7 to 10 dKH)—only
slightly higher than the normal seawater alkalinities of 2.1 to
2.5.

Table 2. Hardness equivalents.

Unit	Equivalents in ppm CaCO$_3$
1 meq/l	50.0
ppm CaCO$_3$	1.0
1 grain CaCO$_3$ per US Gal.	17.1
*Clark, English, 1 grain CaCO$_3$ per Imp. Gal.	14.3
10 ppm (France), 10 ppm CaCO$_3$	10.0
dKH, *KH, KH or dH, German, 10 ppm CaO	17.9
To convert meq/l to ppm CaCO$_3$	multiply by 50
To convert meq/l to dKH	multiply by 2.8
To convert dKH to meq/l	divide by 2.8
To convert dKH to ppm	multiply by 17.9
to *Clark	multiply by 1.25
To convert *Clark to ppm	multiply by 14.3
to dKH	multiply by 0.8
To convert ppm to *Clark	multiply by 0.07
to dKH	multiply by 0.05

Test kits are now available that will give carbonate hardness values in dKH, and tablets, powders and liquids are also
available that will raise carbonate levels. Test kits that measure
alkalinity in meq/l are also available. Carbonate hardness can
also be increased by the addition of sodium carbonate (soda
ash), 1 gm per 25 gallons at a time. A better addition to the
buffering system results from a mix of one part sodium carbonate to six parts sodium bicarbonate (baking soda). A

teaspoon of this mix for each 25 gallons of system water will increase carbonate hardness by about 90 ppm (5 dKH). Sodium carbonate has a tendency to greatly increase pH during the first few hours after addition to the system and sodium bicarbonate has the opposite tendency. Adding both sodium bicarbonate and sodium carbonate at the same time provides a better buffering action with less initial pH variation. Calcium is added to the water when calcareous gravels, chalk, or calcite dissolve in the system. Note that unstirred calcareous gravels quickly build up coats of organic and inorganic matter and stop releasing calcium carbonate. Calcium is also added when hard tap water is added to make up for evaporative loss, or can be added directly as a solution of calcium hydroxide (limewater or "*kalkwasser*").

It really is not necessary these days to prepare a home made solution to buffer the water in marine systems. There are a number of commercially available buffers that do more than just increase carbonate and bicarbonate. Better buffers also adjust sodium, magnesium, borate, and potassium as well as add calcium. They protect against great high and low immediate swings in pH that may occur with addition of pure sodium carbonate and sodium bicarbonate. A specially prepared commercial buffer solution is strongly recommended for use in reef tank systems. Measure the carbonate hardness of the system and add the product as recommended. These products are available at aquarium shops that have a strong marine interest.

pH

pH, *pondus hydrogenii*, is the abbreviation for "Power of Hydrogen". It is a measure of the relative amounts of positively charged hydrogen ions (H^+) and the negatively charged hydroxyl ions (OH^-). A pH of 7 is neutral, meaning that an equal number of each ion is present and the solution is neither acid nor basic. The solution becomes more acid as the scale drops toward 1 and more basic as the scale climbs toward 14. The pH scale is logarithmic, so each point represents a 10 times greater concentration than the previous point. The pH of natural sea water is normally constant, but can vary considerably under certain conditions. The pH of coral reef environments is almost always between 8.1 and 8.3. The pH of natural sea water is in large part determined by the chemistry of carbon dioxide.

Carbon dioxide (CO_2) is very soluble and is normally present in higher concentrations in seawater (45 - 55 ml/l total CO_2) than in air (0.3 ml/l). It enters seawater, from land run off, through the surface from the atmosphere, and is released by aquatic plants and animals during respiration. Decay bacteria also release CO_2 as they metabolize fecal particles and dead tissue. Most of this CO_2 combines with water (hydration) and forms a weak acid—carbonic acid. Less than one percent of the CO_2 present in seawater at the pH and salinity of a tropical marine aquarium system is in the form of free carbon dioxide. The carbonic acid then dissociates into carbonate and bicarbonate ions. These compounds are in an equilibrium with each other, that is the chemical reactions shift back and forth with changing conditions and retain the same ratio or chemical "balance" with each other. This is the buffering effect that keeps the pH of surface ocean waters at about 8.2, rarely dropping below 8.0 or rising above 8.3. In the coral reef habitat, a pH of about 8.2 is one of the great environmental constants. Increases in temperature and water pressure decrease pH, but these factors have little effect on the pH of coral reef habitats.

The *rapid* increase or decrease of dissolved carbon dioxide has the greatest immediate effect on the pH of sea water. Removal of carbon dioxide lowers the amount of carbonic acid and pH increases. Addition of carbon dioxide increases the amount of carbonic acid and pH decreases. Eventually, carbon dioxide will equilibrate with the atmosphere, the bicarbonate-carbonate buffers will catch up with changes in CO_2 content, and pH will stabilize at about 8.2. But this takes time and if CO_2 is being added or subtracted more rapidly or more extensively than the carbonate-bicarbonate bank can handle it, or if acids have reduced the amount of available bicarbonate, then pH changes will occur.

Sunlight, shallow still water, and abundant algae—natural conditions that occur in some isolated rock pools or shallow, enclosed bays—tend to decrease dissolved CO_2 and increase pH. Coastal upwellings, darkness, and cool waters are conditions that tend to increase dissolved CO_2 and decrease pH. Under natural conditions, changes in pH due to changes in dissolved CO_2 are temporary. As soon as dissolved carbon dioxide equilibrates with atmospheric pressures, the pH returns to the sea water standard of about 8.2. The situation is different in captive marine systems, however. It is possible for pH levels to rise during the day to 8.3 or perhaps even 8.5 in a brightly lit marine aquarium with extensive algal growth. A rise in pH under these conditions is not particularly detrimental since pH will quickly drop when the lights go out or algae is removed, but it is an indication that water movement and gas exchange are not adequate. Systems with inadequate biological filtration may face another problem. The percentage of free ammonia (the most toxic form of ammonia) rises as pH inceases (Figure 19). If ammonia is present in system water, the increase of free ammonia with pH rise can cause additional stress on fish and invertebrates. Addition of CO_2, when pH has increased due to exceptional algae growth, brings the pH down to normal levels and enhances the growth of the algae.

The main problem, however, is that pH levels usually drop in marine aquaria. Once free carbon dioxide shifts to carbonic acid in a marine aquarium, especially when aeration is not adequate, more free carbon dioxide is retained in the water, the total CO_2 level increases, and the pH of the system drops because excess CO_2 is not vented from the water. Thus the pH remains lower than normal because inadequate aeration does not release excess CO_2 to the atmosphere.

The pH trend is also downward in marine systems because of the accumulation of acids. Organic acids and phosphate compounds that are quickly cycled and kept at low levels in natural waters tend to accumulate in conventional closed marine systems. Organic acids tie up the bicarbonates and calcium carbonate and reduce the capacity of the buffer system of the sea water to maintain a high pH. Phosphate also combines with magnesium and calcium and forms compounds that precipitate out of solution, thus removing magnesium and calcium from the buffer system of the sea water. A drop in pH due to the accumulation of organic acids can not be corrected by just an increase in aeration and removal of dissolved CO_2. This decline in pH is due to a decline in alkalinity rather than accumulation of excess CO_2. Excess withdrawals from the buffer bank by the accumulation of organic acids are only corrected by water change or additions of bicarbonate and carbonate. It is important to the well being of marine fish to maintain a pH of at least 7.8, although a minimum of 8.0 to 8.1 is far better for invertebrates.

Incidentally, it is easy to determine if a drop in pH is due to accumulation of excess CO_2 or due to accumulation of organics that permanently degrade the sea water buffering system. First, take the pH of the aquarium water directly from the tank. If it is above 8.0, don't worry about it; just monitor the pH reading about every two weeks until it begins to drop. If it doesn't drop, you have adequate aeration and good filtration for the biological load in your system. If your pH is below 8.0 or drops to 7.8 in couple of weeks, the system may be accumulating CO_2. If the pH drops to 7.7 or 7.6 within two weeks to a month, accumulation of carbon dioxide is a very strong possibility. Now after you know the pH of the tank water, take a sample from the tank in a pint jar or large glass and aerate it vigorously for at least 30 minutes, an hour or two is better. Put an air stone in the jar and bubble it fiercely. This will allow any excess CO_2 to escape from the water. Without aeration, it may take several days for excess carbon dioxide to escape. After aeration, take another pH reading. If this reading is at least one tenth of a pH point (7.8 up to 7.9 for example) above the tank pH, then CO_2 is accumulating in your system and an increase in tank aeration is necessary.

Factors that aid maintenance of proper pH levels are good aeration, the mixing of air and water through wet/dry (trickle) filtration and abundant air release in the aquarium, protein foam skimming, algae filtration, regular water change, and if necessary (when a water change can't be made), addition of sodium bicarbonate (baking soda). The presence of calcareous material, coral sand, crushed oyster shell, dolomite, and crushed coral gravel, in biological and mechanical filters does not assure maintenance of proper pH. Bower (1983) describes laboratory experiments done with crushed coral, dolomite gravel, crushed oyster shell, and silica gravel to determine the buffering capacity of these substrates in marine systems. Silica gravel had no buffering capacity, of course, and pH dropped below 7.0 after 90 days. None of the other substrates, however, could maintain a pH above 7.8 after about two months of operation under a considerable biological load. Oyster shell performed best (It is high in the most soluble forms of calcium carbonate, high magnesian calcite and aragonite.) and kept the pH between 7.8 and 7.9, followed by crushed coral, 7.7 to 7.8, and dolomite, 7.4 to 7.5. These calcareous materials, crushed oyster shell in particular, may keep the pH of the system from dropping below 7.5 to 7.6, but this is far too low anyway.

The important thing is not to depend on calcareous filter media for pH control, although they do provide a "pH floor" of about 7.5 for the system. The buffering capacity of calcareous media is further diminished over time by the accumulation of organic coatings. These organic coatings can be cleaned from the media by washing, tumbling, and grinding to expose fresh surfaces. A greater problem, however, is the bonding of free phosphate ions into the crystal structure at the surface of the media. This forms insoluble calcium phosphate (apatite), and prevents the release of calcium carbonate over time. Magnesium also crystalizes as magnesium calcite and further seals the surface of the media. The limited buffering capability of calcareous media is mostly gone after about a year in a marine system, although it can be restored by acid cleaning, drying, and tumbling.

Strong aeration and removal of excess organics and nutrients are the keys to keeping a proper pH level. Replacement of water lost through evaporation with hard fresh water will replace some of the bicarbonate lost to organic activity. With attention to pH control, marine aquariums can be run very well with course silica sand or fine river rock as an undergravel filter media, or with a plastic filter media in a trickle type external filter.

If you find that the pH drop is not due to excess CO_2 in the system, and a water change is not feasible at the time, pH can be artificially increased by addition of sodium bicarbonate (pure baking soda). Take a glass of water from the tank and add one (1) teaspoon of baking soda for every 20 gallons of water in the tank. Stir it well and pour it slowly back into the tank. This should raise the pH about one tenth (0.1) of a pH point after the bicarbonate becomes part of the buffer system of the water. Wait a day, test the pH and do it again if necessary. Stop when the pH of the system tests at 8.0. The section on carbonate hardness also mentions two other formulas for increasing carbonate hardness, which also raises pH. Note that there are also several commercial buffering products on the market that maintain a high pH in a marine system. One of the best ways to prevent accumulation of excess organics and nutrients that lower pH in a marine system is installation and proper operation of a protein foam skimmer.

Dissolved Gasses

The gasses present in the atmosphere of Earth are also dissolved in oceanic waters. There are two categories, the conservative gasses and the nonconservative gasses. The conservative gasses are the biologically inert noble gasses, including helium, argon, neon, and krypton. They are present in seawater at concentrations determined by their equilibrium values between the atmosphere and seawater. The concentrations of the nonconservative gasses including oxygen, carbon dioxide, nitrogen, carbon monoxide, methane, nitrous oxide, hydrogen sulphide and hydrogen, are determined by biological and chemical processes. The interaction of these gasses in biological and chemical cycles are quite complex and are essential to life in the sea and life in a marine aquarium. Four of these are important to marine aquarists as dissolved gasses.

Oxygen (O2)

Oxygen is essential for almost all life. The biological "combustion" of oxygen releases the energy that makes life possible. It is present in nature as molecular oxygen (O_2), two atoms of oxygen bonded into a molecule. The outer electron shell, the L shell, of an atom of oxygen is two electrons short of a full complement of eight, so the valence of oxygen is -2. A single atom of oxygen is so hungry to fill this outer electron shell that it can not exist for long as a single atom. Two oxygen atoms, however, can share their outer electron shell and form the stable, molecular oxygen gas, O_2. Ozone, discussed in Chapter 4, is an unstable molecular form of oxygen gas made up of three oxygen molecules (O_3). A molecule of ozone is quick to lose that third atom of oxygen. This free oxygen atom has to hook up with something else *right now*, and it tears up a lot of complex organic molecules to do so. This gives ozone a very high oxidation potential.

Oxygen is present in the air (20 percent) and is dissolved in all the waters, even in the greatest ocean depths. The amount of oxygen that can be dissolved in water, the saturation level, is dependent on temperature, salinity and, to some extent, atmospheric pressure. The amount of oxygen dissolved in water is measured in parts per million (ppm). In warm, tropical, high salinity, coral reef environments, the range of dissolved oxygen is about 4 to 6 ppm. The amount of oxygen that can dissolve in water decreases as temperature and salinity increase. This variation can be quite significant because warm salt water doesn't hold much dissolved oxygen. Many fish and invertebrates suffer when the DO (dissolved oxygen) drops below 3.5 ppm and few survive DOs below 2 ppm, so there isn't a lot of excess oxygen in a marine aquarium. Dissolved oxygen can drop to the danger or even lethal point in marine aquariums with high salinities, high temperatures, dirty filters (high oxygen demand), low or no lighting, and poor aeration. An atmospheric low pressure area moving slowly through town could also release a little more oxygen from the water and compound the problem, especially at night when aquarium lights are off.

Table 3. Oxygen concentrations in ppm at various temperatures and salinities.

°C	°F	0‰	20‰	25‰	30‰	35‰
10	50	8.0	7.1	6.9	6.7	6.4
15	59	7.2	6.4	6.2	6.0	5.8
20	68	6.6	5.9	5.7	5.5	5.3
25	77	6.0	5.4	5.2	5.1	4.9
30	86	5.6	5.0	4.8	4.7	4.5

Every environment has a certain "demand" for oxygen that is created by the life that is present. This is termed the "Biological Oxygen Demand" or BOD. The BOD is high when a large amount of organic material is present that serves as food for bacteria and other microorganisms. BOD is low when organic material is absent or has already been digested and stabilized by biological activity. Coral reef environments do not have a lot of free organic matter and have low BOD's. High BOD's in natural areas are an indication of organic pollution. Organics can accumulate in some coastal estuarine areas and marine aquaria, however, and these environments generally have higher BOD's. Note that the BOD of a biological filter is high. If chemicals are present that use oxygen in a purely chemical reaction, then a COD or "Chemical Oxygen Demand" is present. COD's are not a feature of most marine environments unless chemical pollution is present and are not a factor in the operation of a marine aquarium.

Oxygen enters the water through the air-water interface at the surface and through the activity of photosynthesis during the day. (Photosynthesis, of course, is the process by which plants with chlorophyll use light, carbon dioxide, and water to create carbohydrates or "food". Oxygen is a released as a product of this reaction.) Turbulence on either or both sides of the air-water interface is of great importance in gas exchange. A strong, dry wind blowing across the sea soon brings oxygen levels in surface waters up to saturation. The photosynthetic activity of algae on a bright calm day can create a super saturation of oxygen in enclosed areas and in brightly lit marine aquaria, especially aquaria that receive some sunlight. The activity of algae is a two edged sword, however, because algae use oxygen at night during respiration when the lack of light makes photosynthesis impossible. Supersaturation of oxygen in marine waters is no problem, but the same factors that permit supersaturation during the day will work to deplete oxygen levels at night. Good aeration of a marine aquarium is essential to maintain high oxygen and low carbon dioxide at stable levels. Active turn over of the surface water layer through a free air stone or two in the tank is always a good idea since most of the gas exchange occurs through the water surface of an aquarium. A trickle filter, or any of the "wet-dry" filter systems, is also a good way to enhance gas exchange, especially if there is a counter current of air and water through the filter media.

Oxygen levels in a marine aquarium system with a trickle filter and strong circulation of water throughout the tank will always stay near saturation, perhaps a bit above saturation during times of active photosynthesis. A traditional system with an undergravel biological filter is more likely to suffer from reduced oxygen concentrations, especially if the filter is thick, filled with detritus and organics, and water circulation through the filter and about the tank is weak and creates areas of slow and stagnant water. A simple test kit for oxygen is now available for marine and freshwater aquarists. This allows an aquarist to take samples from different areas in the system (surface, bottom, in the filter, under the filter, etc.) and determine the pattern of oxygenation in the system. Although the rapid movement of oxygen from the atmosphere into aerated aquatic environments usually keeps the oxygen content of the water at near saturation levels, use of an oxygen test kit removes the guess work from this important environmental parameter.

Carbon Dioxide

Like oxygen, free carbon dioxide is dissolved in surface seawater. Carbon dioxide enters the sea in rain and river run-off. It also enters and leaves seawater through the atmospheric air/water interface and is cycled in seawater as a result of biological activity. The carbon cycle illustrated in Figure 6 shows the movement of carbon dioxide through the natural environment. The processes of photosynthesis, biological calcium carbonate formation, deep water upwellings, temperature changes, evaporation, and precipitation control the concentrations of CO_2 in surface waters. The chemistry of carbon dioxide in seawater is very complex. After dissolving in water, carbon dioxide first forms carbonic acid, which then becomes part of the carbonate and bicarbonate buffering system. Free carbon dioxide forms carbonic acid and causes the pH of marine systems to drop, but bicarbonate and carbonate, the main buffers in seawater, function to maintain a high, stable pH. See the sections on seawater buffering and pH for more detailed information. Free carbon dioxide is essential for photosynthesis, and bicarbonate formed from carbon dioxide and water also eventually combines with calcium to form calcium carbonate. The carbonate minerals (calcite and aragonite) are used by corals and other marine animals to form the skeletal structures that are the building blocks of coral reefs.

Carbon dioxide (CO_2) is a product of the biological combustion of oxygen and carbon and is a waste product of animal metabolism and plant respiration. There are many factors that modify the amount of free CO_2 dissolved in seawater, and although CO_2 concentrations are always moving toward equilibrium, unlike oxygen, actual equilibrium with atmospheric partial pressure is rare. The actual amount of dissolved CO_2 in sea water depends upon atmospheric pressure, water temperature, salinity, pH, and biological activity. In the sea, carbon dioxide is usually between 10 to 30 times over saturation. Compared to other marine areas, warm waters and high salinities keep concentrations of free CO_2 in waters over shallow coral reefs low and stable. Carbon dioxide is highly soluble in water. Seawater supersaturated or under saturated with oxygen quickly releases or gains O_2 when aerated by wind and waves or through air injection and surface turnover. Carbon dioxide, however, moves rather slowly between air and water and it may take many hours to remove excess CO_2 from seawater through moderate aeration. This is very important to the marine aquarist because the animals and biological filters in a marine aquarium use oxygen and produce carbon dioxide. This free CO_2 is metabolic waste and it must be removed from the aquarium. Unless the system is devoted to algal growth, **it is just as important to remove excess carbon dioxide as it is to replace oxygen.** A modest algal growth can not be totally depended upon to remove CO_2 because algae itself produces CO_2 at night during respiration and when it decays after death. Strong aeration and circulation of tank water is essential for exchange of O_2 and CO_2 with the atmosphere.

Although the general trend in most marine systems is toward accumulation of excess carbon dioxide, systems with extensive algal growth may deplete the water of free carbon dioxide and cause the carbonate/bicarbonate buffer system to release carbon dioxide. Under these conditions, it may be advantageous to add carbon dioxide if exceptional algae growth is desired in a brightly lit tank. Free carbon dioxide should be maintained in the range of 3 to 5 mg/l for systems with strong algal growth. Equipment is now commercially available that injects regulated amounts of carbon dioxide into marine systems designed for lush algal growth. Automatic systems that add CO_2 only when pH rises are also available. Carbon dioxide should be added only during the day when algaes are in active photosynthesis. Adding CO_2 increases the amount of carbonic acid and lowers pH, so be sure to monitor pH and do not let it drop more than two tenths of a unit before cutting back on the injection of CO_2. Thiel (1988, 1989) is a good reference on addition of CO_2 to marine systems.

Nitrogen

Nitrogen is one of the most abundant elements on Earth. It makes up about 80 percent of the atmosphere and, as the base of proteins in plant and animal tissues, nitrogen is the foundation of the structure of life. Nitrogen, incidentally, was discovered in 1772 by Daniel Rutherford, a Scottish physician. It was first called "azote" from the Greek "no life", because, when oxygen was removed from the air, what was left would not support life. It later got the name nitrogen because it was found in sodium nitrate, which was known as "Niter" in those days.

Despite the fact that nitrate (NO_3) is the thermodynamically stable (in the presence of oxygen) form of nitrogen, the most abundant nitrogen compound in the marine environment is pure nitrogen gas, N_2, also known as dinitrogen. This is so only because biological denitrification continuously converts nitrate, NO_3, through various steps back to N_2. Although nitrogen in the compounds nitrite and nitrate is an essential nutrient, nitrogen gas is not directly available to plants or animals. Thus the concentration of nitrogen gas in marine waters is conservative, a function of its solubility at a given salinity, temperature, and atmospheric pressure. Seawater usually contains about 10 to 15 ml/l dissolved nitrogen. (In nature, free nitrogen is broken. Fortunately many species of bacteria and blue green algaes have been issued tiny tool kits and go around repairing nitrogen atoms. This amazing phenomenon is known as nitrogen fixation.) As long as oxygen is present, biological processes do not create detectable changes in concentrations of nitrogen gas in marine waters; thus shallow marine waters are almost always at saturation with nitrogen gas. There are other dissolved gaseous nitrogen compounds in marine waters: ammonia gas, nitrous oxide, nitric oxide, nitrogen dioxide and nitrous acid, but these are not of particular importance to the marine aquarist.

As in the coral reef environment, nitrogen gas is at equilibrium with atmospheric pressure in a marine aquarium and is not of concern to the marine aquarist. There are some situations, however, where nitrogen gas can become supersaturated in an aquatic environment. When this happens, fish and invertebrates can ingest or absorb the supersaturated nitrogen and then, under normal atmospheric pressures, nitrogen gas slowly bubbles out of solution and creates bubbles within the tissues. The animals affected by this develop a case of the "bends", and usually die. This may occur in nature in cold, freshwater pools located just below highly turbulent rapids where air is compressed into the water by cavitation.

Nitrogen gas supersaturation can also occur, rarely, in a captive marine environment if air and water are mixed in the high pressure side of the pumping system. The most likely possibility is an air leak on the intake side of the pump. Bubbles in the tissues of animals and cloudy water caused by very, very tiny bubbles are signs of this condition. Small systems without high pressure water pumps are not subject to this situation. Tiny air bubbles in the tank water may become a problem in some reef systems, however, if water loss from evaporation is not regularly replaced. This water loss may cause the surface level in the sump tank to drop close to the pump intake and air can then be sucked into the pump system. The result is supersaturation of air in the tank water and a fine cloud of very tiny air bubbles throughout the tank. Gas reactors also cause slight nirogen supersaturation, but not enough to cause problems.

Hydrogen Sulfide

Hydrogen sulfide (H_2S) is a soluble, poisonous gas with a strong, unpleasant, rotten egg odor. It is formed by the activity of bacteria on organic matter (bacterial reduction of sulphate ions) in environments where oxygen is very low or absent. Buried sediments, muck, and deep still water are natural sites where hydrogen sulfide may form. It is not generated in coral reef environments and it is toxic to most coral reef organisms. Hydrogen sulfide should never be present in a marine aquarium. It is possible, however, for hydrogen sulfide and other noxious gases, such as methane, to form in a marine aquarium system wherever water circulation is low or absent. Every effort should be made to find the source if a rotten egg smell is detected in or around a marine aquarium system. Some possible trouble spots are a power or container type filter that has been turned off for a day or two or longer, a dirty, compacted undergravel filter that has developed areas where water does not circulate, or an improperly operated denitrification system. Denitrification systems are new to the marine hobby and the possibility of hydrogen sulfide formation should be kept in mind if you run one of these units. A denitrification system may produce a little hydrogen sulphide during operation if nitrate in the system is low and the water flow through system is too slow. Increasing flow through the system and decreasing the amount of nutrient for the bacteria decreases formation of hydrogen sulphide.

All filters that have been out of service for a day or more should be emptied and cleaned, or at least flushed well into a waste drain, before being put back into service in a marine system. Of course this can not be easily done to an undergravel filter. If an undergravel filter has been out of service for day or two, and if it has a large amount of organic detrital accumulation, the tank and filter may already be dead. If the undergravel filter has been off for more than a day or two, and the fish and invertebrates are still alive, the best thing to do is to remove the live animals and put them in a separate tank. Then get the filter systems going and let them run a day or two before putting the animals back into the tank. If the filter is started up again without removing the fish, watch them closely for the first hour and be prepared to move them if stress is noted. A persistent rotten egg smell around a marine aquarium system is a sure sign of trouble. Very low levels of hydrogen sulfide can be detected by smell, but the olfactory sense is quickly desensitized to H_2S; so after a strong initial whiff, one may no longer be able to smell the source of the hydrogen sulfide.

Dissolved Organics and Nutrients

I'm going to apologize in advance for the introduction to this section. It may be a bit gross, but I'm trying to make a point.

Suppose you're out to sea on a fishing trip. It's a beautiful day but the sea is a little rough, you're not used to the motion of the boat, and you get sea sick. A horrible feeling. There are two possibilities: one, you rush to the rail and discharge the remains of your lunch into the sea, or two, you're so sick that you can't even move and you deposit these nutrients into a nearby bait bucket half full of sea water. Now, if these nutrients go into the sea, they are quickly diluted and consumed and soon become part of the vast nutrient cycles of the ocean. The composition of the ocean water is changed not a whit. But, in the bait bucket, Oh, what a mess. The concentration of organics overwhelms the capacity of the water in the bucket to deal with organic matter, and bacteria bloom, free oxygen is consumed, carbon dioxide and methane are produced, bait fish die, vile odors are given off, and the contents of the bucket is no longer "simple" sea water and a few fish.

A marine aquarium is somewhere in between the ocean water and the bucket contents described above, hopefully much closer to the ocean than the bucket. Fish, other animals and plants, and fish food all produce organic matter in the aquarium system that must be either removed or broken down through bacterial activity (mineralization) and then oxidized (nitrification). The primary difference between the organic/nutrient composition of sea water and marine aquarium water is concentration and not kind.

When we discuss organic compounds and nutrient cycles in the sea and in marine aquariums, we're talking complex chemistry. I won't go into technical detail, but some of the basics are discussed below and the interactions of nutrient cycles in a marine aquarium are described in Chapter 3.

Organic compounds are, by definition, compounds that contain carbon and, when dissolved in sea water, they are lumped under the term "Dissolved Organic Carbon" or DOC. Nutrient elements, including carbon, are elements that are necessary for the growth of plants and animals. Major nutrients in sea water are carbon, nitrogen, and phosphorus. Silicon and calcium are required in considerable amounts in the skeletal structures of animals and some plants but are seldom considered major nutrients. Minor, but essential, nutrient elements include zinc, copper, iodine, vanadium, cobalt, molybdenum, and arsenic. Dissolved organics (DOC) are generally composed of large molecules that incorporate nutrient elements. The basic kinds of organic compounds found in sea water are carbohydrates, mostly sugars and starches; a vast array of proteins and amino acids; organic acids including fatty, lauric, palmitic, stearic, oleic, linoleic, acetic, lactic, glycolic, malic, citric, and carotenoids; biologically active compounds including organic iron, B vitamins and plant hormones; humic acids including "gelbstoffe" (also termed "gilvin") a yellow, melanoidin-like substance; various phenolic compounds; and some hydrocarbons.

Dissolved organics are present in natural sea waters in variable amounts. Coastal waters may have high amounts of DOC in certain places at certain times, but coral reef waters are almost always very low in DOC. The waters of a marine aquarium may accumulate DOC at a rapid rate, especially if biological loads are high and filtration is limited to an undergravel filter and perhaps a supplemental mechanical particle filter. Regular water changes are necessary in this situation to keep a healthy marine aquarium. A protein foam skimmer, activated carbon and/or resin filtration, denitrification, and ozonation are all helpful in reducing DOC in a marine system.

Dissolved nutrients are essential for the growth of plants, both large macro algaes and the tiny, extremely abundant, microscopic algaes that are the foundation of marine food chains. Carbon is present as free carbon dioxide, in buffer system compounds, and in dissolved organics. It is cycled relatively quickly in the processes of photosynthesis and respiration and in the buffer system of sea water as described in previous sections. Phosphorus is dissolved in sea water as inorganic phosphorus, orthophosphate, and as organic phosphate, tied up in various organic phosphorus compounds, phosphoproteins, nucleo-proteins and phospholipids.

A great deal of the phosphorus in the sea is present in particles of detritus and in the living cells of planktonic organisms. The activity of bacteria on detritus releases phosphorus as orthophosphate, and in this form it is available to plants and is quickly utilized. Phosphorus levels in the sea are variable. Levels are higher in deep water and coastal areas, but the clear, nutrient poor waters of coral reef areas contain little dissolved phosphorus. As with other nutrients, phosphorus tends to accumulate in marine systems. It can be removed through the growth of algae, through removal of detritus, through aeration (orthophosphate can be adsorbed onto air bubbles and released into the atmosphere when the air bubbles burst) and protein foam skimming, and, of course, through water change. Note, however, that if your fresh water supply contains high levels of organic phosphate, adding tap water to make up for evaporation loss constantly adds this nutrient to the system, and this stimulates growth of blue-green and other detrimental algae.

Nitrogen, as the gas N_2, has been discussed in a previous section. As dinitrogen gas it is relatively inert and not of great interest to the aquarist. But in biologically active compounds it is an essential nutrient and is an integral part of the protein structure of plants and animals; and as ammonia, nitrite, and nitrate, it is one of the primary concerns of marine aquarists. Early in the history of life, when prokaryotes (bacteria and blue-green algae) first ruled the Earth, an enzyme system evolved that was based on nitrogenase. This enzyme enabled these tiny organisms to "fix" nitrogen, that is make it biologically available for protein synthesis. This requires considerable oxygen and energy, but once the bacteria have fixed nitrogen, it is then also available to eukaryotic (organisms with nucleated cells) plants and animals.

Nitrogen fixation takes place in the marine environment in many areas: in marine sediments, on the leaves and rhizomes of marine grasses, and to a great extent, in mats of blue-green algae found on flats near coral reefs, even in bacterial faunas associated with sea urchins, sponges, and some marine worms.

Nitrogen fixation, however, is not an important contributor to waste nitrogen compounds in the marine aquarium. Waste nitrogen (nitrate) in the aquarium comes from metabolism of organisms, mostly animals, and from decay (mineralization) of protein compounds in food, feces, and dead tissue.

Plants and animals use a great deal of nitrogen just to live. Proteins form most of the physical and biochemical structure of an organism and nitrogen is constantly being built into and broken out of the cellular structure of every organism. When the organism dies, its nitrogen compounds are incorporated into the structure of the animals that feed on the carcass and are also liberated in solutions that diffuse into the environment. These organic compounds are consumed by heterotrophic bacteria, and inorganic nitrogen compounds, primarily ammonia (NH_3), are produced—a process known as **mineralization**. Ammonia is also produced directly by marine fish and other animals as a highly soluble waste product of protein metabolism.

Ammonia is very toxic to marine and other organisms, but fortunately, ammonia is quickly oxidized into nitrite (NO_2) and then into nitrate (NO_3) by two genera of nitrifying bacteria. *Nitrosomonas* oxidizes ammonia into nitrite and *Nitrobacter* oxidizes nitrite into nitrate. Nitrate is the basic nutrient form of nitrogen and is quickly utilized by plants. Inorganic nitrogen in the form of ammonia, nitrite, and nitrate are found in extremely small amounts in the waters around coral reefs as it is rapidly cycled in nature. Natural levels of NO_3 in the waters about coral reefs are below 1 ppm. In a marine aquarium, however, nitrate can accumulate relatively rapidly to concentrations never found on coral reefs. Unlike ammonia and nitrite, nitrate is relatively nontoxic, and although some organisms are sensitive to moderate concentrations, the average marine aquarium can accumulate about fifty parts per million of nitrate without obvious stress to fish and some large invertebrates. Biological filtration, which changes toxic ammonia to nitrite to nitrate, is the heart of all marine aquarium filter systems. The components of a filter system that function in biological filtration or otherwise aid in waste nitrogen reduction are trickle filters, undergravel filters, protein foam skimmers, denitrifiers, ozonators and algae filters. Of course, water changes must be used to reduce waste nitrogen and excess organics in simple systems.

Redox Potential

The redox potential of salt water in a marine aquarium system, along with pH, nitrate, and when possible, dissolved oxygen levels, is a valuable indicator of the status of the life support capacity of the aquatic system. Few American marine aquarists measure redox potential, but serious European aquarists have used this technology for more than a decade. In order to understand redox potential we have to briefly and simplistically refer back to atoms and electrons. Atoms, as you know, are little packets of matter composed of positively charged protons and neutral neutrons that form the nucleus. Negatively charged electrons surround the nucleus and are distributed in "shells" at various distances or energy levels from the nucleus. The more protons and neutrons, the heavier the element. Hydrogen is lightest with only one proton and lead is one of the heaviest with 207 protons. Elements interact with each other in different ways mainly by sharing the electrons in their outer shells, thus joining together and forming various types of molecules that compose compounds with different physical and chemical properties.

The term "redox" in the language of chemistry is a contraction for "reduction-oxidation reaction" and "potential" refers to the electrical charge on a molecule that has been formed in a reduction-oxidation chemical reaction and is dissolved in an aqueous solution. When two elements combine in a reduction-oxidation reaction, one is said to be oxidized and the other reduced. Although oxidation originally meant "to combine with oxygen", the term now has a much broader meaning. Any chemical process that includes either a partial or complete transfer of electrons is an oxidation-reduction reaction.

Such reactions do not necessarily have to involve the element oxygen, although oxygen is far and away the most abundant and important oxidizing element in our environment, including marine aquariums. Hydrogen is the most common reducing agent. Oxidation means the apparent loss of electrons by a molecule or atom and reduction means an apparent gain of electrons. Electrons are not actually gained or lost in these reactions, the atoms only change the way they share the electrons of their outer shells. The results of oxidation-reduction reactions are common chemical compounds such as water (H_2O), salts such as sodium chloride (NaCl), and oxides such as iron oxide or rust. Nitrogen, for example, is oxidized in a molecule of nitrate (NO_3) and reduced in a molecule of ammonia (NH_3).

Atoms of elements such as chlorine and oxygen "need" very badly to give up electrons and are strong oxidizing agents. Atoms of elements like iron and hydrogen "want" to gain electrons and are reducing agents. Whenever one element is oxidized, another must be reduced. If a molecule is a product of oxidization, it has a positive electrical charge or potential, a cation. A molecule that is a product of reduction has a negative electrical potential, an anion. The redox potential of sea water is a measure of the relative amount of the positive and negative charges on the oxidized and reduced molecules that are present. An equal amount of positive and negative charges results in a redox potential, measured in millivolts, of 0.0. An aquatic environment that is dominated by reduced molecules has a negative redox potential, and when oxidized molecules are more abundant, the redox potential is positive. In the sea, and especially in marine aquariums, more than one redox system is working, but since oxygen is the most important single oxidizing agent, the presence of free oxygen always keeps the redox potential in the positive range.

A negative redox potential only occurs in the absence of free oxygen. However, the accumulation of reduced molecules—the result of the addition of organic matter—will diminish the redox potential, even if oxygen is at saturation levels. Addition of strong oxidizing agents such as ozone, hydrogen peroxide, or potassium permanganate will oxidize more of these reduced molecules and increase the redox potential of the solution. The higher the redox potential, the more "pure" the solution. Thus knowing the redox potential of the water in a marine aquarium system at a specific pH can provide a relatively precise measure of system's capability to support organisms that require "pure" water. A high redox potential is important for optimum respiration in living cells, especially in animals with limited circulatory systems where the function of each cell is more intimately connected to the outer environment.

The classical method of measuring redox potential is with a platinum indicator electrode immersed in the water against a reference electrode of calomel or silver chloride. The results are expressed in millivolts. Breck (1974) reports the redox potential of natural sea water, at a pH of 8.0 measured by an equilibrium method with a graphite cell, to be about 0.5 volts (500 millivolts). Measurements of the same system taken with a platinum electrode ranged from 40 to 270 millivolts lower and averaged about 100 millivolts lower than the consistent standard of the graphite cell. Thus the redox potential of natural sea water over coral reefs measured with a platinum electrode should range somewhere around 350 to 400 millivolts. Because of the variations in results that are often obtained with redox meters, it is wise to take several measurements at any one time and to watch for any consistent upward or downward trends over periods of days or weeks. It takes considerable time for the probe to stabilize so it should be immersed in the water for 60 minutes or more before the reading is taken.

Different parts of the system, the tank and various areas of the filter, may well have different redox potentials. Cycles of light and dark and feeding cycles also effect the chemistry of the system and can be reflected in readings of redox potential. Temperature and pH also have an effect. Redox potential goes down as pH and temperature rise. The best way to use redox potential as an aquarium management tool is to take the reading at the same time each day, a couple of hours after feeding or before the first feeding of the day, and graph the readings over time so that trends in the system can be easily observed.

Use of ozonizers, UV sterilizers, trickle filters, and protein foam skimmers tend to maintain a high redox potential in a marine system. Overfeeding, lack of water changes, and low aeration tend to decrease the redox potential. Meters that measure redox potential are still rather expensive and not yet familiar to most American hobbyists.

Redox potentials of marine aquarium systems should range between 200 and 350 millivolts. Levels lower than 200 to 250 indicate an unacceptable accumulation of poisonous, reduced organic compounds. Levels above 400 to 450 millivolts indicate a too active oxidizing environment with *possible* damage to delicate plant and animal tissues and cells. Over treatment with ozone is the most likely cause of redox levels that are too high. Aquarists with considerable experience in observation of redox potentials, Wilkens (1973) and Paletta (1988), report differential growth of algae at various redox potential levels. Mat forming blue green and red algae do well at low levels of 200 to 250 mv, filamentous greens, *Enteromorpha*, grow well at levels of 250 to 300 mv, and the large macroalgae, *Ulva, Gracilaria, Caulerpa, Hypnea*, and *Halimeda* seem to grow best at redox potentials above 300 mv. A system that supports good algal growth and healthy invertebrates probably does not suffer from redox potentials that are too high or too low. It is not necessary to measure redox potential to run a good, high oxygen, low organics system, but it does provide another measure of control, especially if ozone is used in the system. Thiel (1988, 1989) presents an in depth discussion of use of redox potential in reef tank systems.

Chapter 2

The Physical Environment

Light

Along with water and oxygen, light is of critical importance to the marine environment and we should know something about it. Actually light is just as important as water and oxygen, it's just that marine organisms can live a little longer without light than without water and oxygen. So, just what is light anyway? Well, light is radiant energy that travels through space and is selectively absorbed by various substances. The fundamental unit of light is the photon, a massless particle of spin 1. When an atom absorbs energy (heat, light, electricity, nuclear reactions), the electrons move away from the nucleus of the atom and the atom gains energy. The atom is unstable in this energized or "excited" state, however, and the electrons quickly move back to the stable state of their original inner orbital shells. Excess energy is then released as a photon that shoots away at the speed of light. Under constant stimulation, the atom bounces back and forth between energy states and pumps out photons continuously. The human eye can detect as little light as a single photon, but usable light levels are only produced when billions and billions of atoms release photons.

Nuclear reactions, fission and fusion, release tremendous amounts of energy, much of it in the form of light. The nuclear fusion of hydrogen in the sun produces the abundant radiant energy that we perceive here on earth as sunlight. Scientific experimentation has shown that light waves travel at 186,000 miles per second in a vacuum (the precise figure is 186,281.7 mps) and drops to 140,000 miles per second when traveling through the dense medium of water. As well as speed, the composition and direction of light changes to some degree when it passes through any medium, including glass, plastic, and water, depending on the characteristics of the medium. For example, ordinary glass absorbs ultraviolet waves (UV), which is why the glass tube of a UV sterilizer must be made of a special quartz rather than ordinary glass.

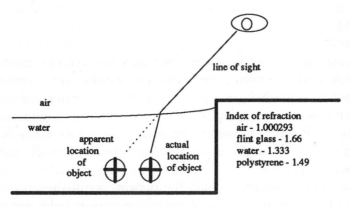

Figure 2. Effects of light refraction.

Light is also refracted (bent) when it moves between air and a dense medium such as water or glass because it travels more slowly in a more dense medium. If it enters or exits exactly perpendicular to the surface, it just changes velocity with no change in direction. But if it passes from one medium to another at an angle, then the light waves move more slowly on the outer edge as they "go round the bend" and the direction of the light beam is slightly altered. The difference in the ability of each medium to transmit light (refractive index) determines how much the light is refracted when it enters a different medium. Refraction is why an object on the bottom of a swimming pool appears closer to the edge than it really is and why an object in an aquarium appears to be in a slightly different place when looked at through different sides of the tank, Figure 2. Also, the more salt in the water, the denser the liquid and the greater the refraction of light, and this is how a refractometer, which measures degree of refraction, can determine salinity. Refraction also bends light entering the sea into a more perpendicular downward path. Except for the scattering effect (light waves bouncing off floating particles) there is little oblique light in the open sea. The brightest area is always upward toward the surface.

Blue light is absorbed less and scattered more than red light. Blue light is scattered upwards as well as in all other directions, which is why clear, offshore waters appear blue. Coastal waters appear green because the greater number of particles scatter more light of longer wavelengths, thus green becomes the dominant color. Particles and organic dyes in the water also absorb light, and since coastal waters contain many more of these than offshore waters, organisms in coastal waters and at depths greater than a few feet live at relatively low light intensities.

Scientific experimentation has demonstrated that photons of light (quanta) have the characteristics of both particles and waves, a phenomenon called the "wave-particle duality". Although difficult to comprehend, the proprieties of light are undetermined until it is measured. If particle-like properties are measured, light is composed of particles; if wavelike properties are measured, then photons behave as waves. Light is both particle and wave until it is measured, and then it is one or the other depending on the method of measurement. If you are confused, welcome to the wonderful world of quantum mechanics. For our purposes, however, considering light as waves of radiant energy is most practical. Figure 3 illustrates the range of wavelengths and the types of radiation that make up the electromagnetic spectrum.

In the natural environment, the sun is by far the greatest source of radiation. We don't get very much of it, however. The Earth only receives about one half of one *billionth* of the total output of the sun. Most of the sun's radiant energy that enters

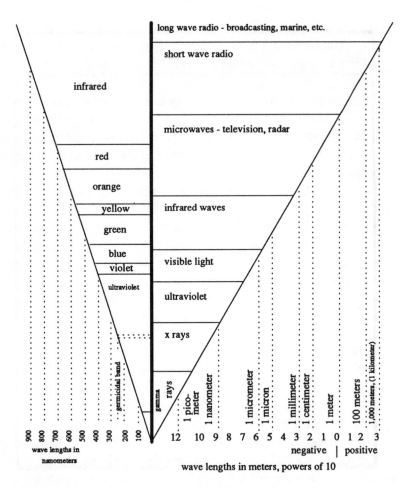

Figure 3. The visible and electromagnetic spectrum.

the marine environment is in the very narrow part of the electromagnetic spectrum that consists of visible light, although the infrared and ultraviolet wavelengths that bracket the visible spectrum are also present. Visible light is that part of the electromagnetic spectrum that ranges from deep red at a wavelength of about 700 nm to violet at a wavelength of about 400 nm. This visible radiant energy has two very important functions in the marine and terrestrial environment. One, it provides information about the environment by allowing

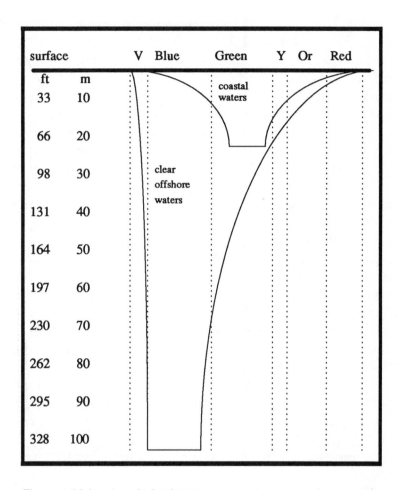

Figure 4. Light transmission in water.

animals to form images (sight). And two, it provides the energy that allows plants to manufacture food (photosynthesis), the very basis of life. Figure 4 illustrates the variation of light transmission in the marine environment.

If we are only concerned with providing enough light to allow fish and sighted invertebrates to find their way around an aquarium, then there is little to consider. An ordinary fluorescent light of whatever color and brightness is most pleasing is all that's needed. However, if we are concerned about the growth of algaes, the well being of animals that contain algaes in their tissues (primarily corals and anemones), and the subtle effects of intensity and quality of light on animals in general, then we must carefully consider the nature of the light we give to our captive marine environment.

The properties of light that are measured are wavelength, energy, and intensity. Wavelength is simply a measurement of the distance from crest to crest or trough to trough of a particular wave. The metric meter (100 centimeters or 39.37 inches) is the fundamental unit of measurement of electromagnetic wavelengths. There is an astounding variation in the length of waves of the various types of radiant energy that make up the electromagnetic spectrum. Waves that are in the range of one meter include microwaves, television, and radar. The longest waves include long wave radio waves at 30,000 meters (almost 19 miles) in length to waves that are about a million km, 620 miles long. The shortest are gamma rays at wavelengths as short as one tenth to one hundredth of a nanometer (nm), which is a billionth of a meter.

Visible light is only a small section of the electromagnetic spectrum. Wavelengths of visible light are usually measured in **nanometers** (nm), billionths of a meter, or in **angstroms** (Å), a unit that was developed by the Swedish physicist Anders Jonas Angstrom and is equal to one tenth of a millimicron. There is only one decimal point difference in these units, 7200 Å is equal to 720 nm. Just to give you an idea of how short a nanometer is, the thickness of a page in this book is approximately 125,000 nanometers.

The colors of light have different wavelengths and different frequencies (energy levels). This makes it possible to separate the colors that make up white light and create rainbows with glass prisms, diffraction gratings, and the natural prisms of raindrops. The wavelength of red light ranges from 700 to 650 nm; orange, 650 to 590; yellow, 590 to 575; green, 575 to 490; blue, 490 to 425; violet 425 to 400. Infrared waves are longer than 700 nm and ultraviolet waves are shorter than 400 nm.

Note that the boundaries of the wavelengths of the colors are not precise and wavelength color boundaries from different references may vary. The different wavelengths of light are important to marine aquarists for two reasons. One, water absorbs the longer wavelength, lower energy end of the spectrum rather rapidly. Red light is 90% absorbed within the first 15 feet of water. Blue and violet light, however, penetrate hundreds of feet in clear water. The wavelength of maximum light intensity in the underwater environment is 475 to 500 nm, green with a rapid shift to blue as depth increases (Dawes, 1981). And two, the various types of chlorophyll present in different algaes use certain wavelengths of light more efficiently than others, so we can enhance the growth and survival of algae, corals, and anemones by controlling the wave lengths of light that illuminate the aquarium.

The energy of an electromagnetic wave is a property of its particulate nature. The energy of a light wave varies with wavelength and long, red waves have less energy than short, violet waves. Ultra violet light has enough energy to alter the genetic chemistry of microorganisms, create mutations, and even kill viruses, bacteria, and other microscopic life. Ultra violet light kills bacteria at 220 to 300 nm with the greatest bactericidal effect at about 260 nm (2600 Å). The tanning effect on human skin occurs at 280 to 300 nm.

Visible light has relatively low energy. Orange light, for example, with a wavelength of 600 nm has an energy content of only one third of a billionth of an erg (an erg is a centimeter-gram-second unit of energy, a very small unit of work energy). The energy of light is important because different substances give off different types of light at different energy states, which are measured by the temperature of the substance. Everything above the temperature of absolute zero, $0 °K$ or $-273 °C$, (add $273°$ to any centigrade temperature to change it to the absolute temperature Kelvin scale) emits energy called "black body radiation". A warm sidewalk, for example, is radiating low frequency infrared energy as heat that can be felt but not seen, except with special infrared sensing devices. When a temperature of 950 °K is reached, the frequency of radiant energy released is high enough that dull red, visible light is released.

As the temperature of a radiating substance increases, the frequency of the light that is emitted also increases. Low temperatures produce low frequency light in the red end of the spectrum and high temperatures produce high frequency light in the blue end of the spectrum. The temperature of the surface of the sun is 6000 °K and its peak light emission is in the yellow orange range at 509 nm. Normal daylight, filtered through the atmosphere, has a color temperature of 5500 °K and it is at this color temperature that most colors appear normal and that the **color rendering** of a light is best. Light bulbs of various types often give their output in color temperature, from 2800 °K for ordinary tungsten light bulbs to 10500 °K for certain types of fluorescent bulbs. According to Lundegaard (1985), fluorescent light sources with color temperatures of 5000 °K to 7000 °K provide an excellent color appearance to marine aquariums.

Another aid to selecting bulbs that will give good colors to an aquarium is the "Color Rendering Index" (CRI). This is the standard for comparison of the colors of objects lit by artificial light. The CRI of sunlight is 100, and the nearer an artificial light comes to replicating the colors revealed in sunlight, the higher its CRI. Most fluorescent bulbs that give a natural appearance to marine aquariums have a CRI of 90 or higher. A high CRI index, however, does not mean that the light will supply all the wave lengths that a marine aquarium requires. It only means that the human eye will see the colors in the aquarium close to the way they appear in natural sunlight.

The intensity, the amount of light or "brightness", is also very important. Light intensity is measured as the amount of light per unit area and is usually expressed in units called lumens and lux. To understand what these units measure, however, we have to go back to the standard measure of light intensity or brightness, the candlepower. The original measure of one **candlepower** is the total light produced by a single candle of specific form made from the wax of the sperm whale. Candlepower or candles is the original standard measure of light intensity, the basic unit for measurement of the output, the brightness, of a light source. The light output of a lamp is usually given in candlepower.

Science is now more precise in the measure of light intensity. The Candela (cd), a very precise measure of light radiation, was adopted in 1979 as the standard scientific unit of luminous intensity. A candela is a measure of luminous intensity, in the direction of normal, of a black body surface 1/600,000 of a square meter in area, at the temperature of solidification of platinum (2042°K) under a pressure of 101,325 N/M2. Although it is a far more precise measure of luminous intensity, one Candela is basically equal to one of the old Candle units. Candlepower is still the expression of this unit in common use.

Candlepower, however, does not measure the amount of light actually reaching a particular area, thus a different type of measurement is also necessary. One **foot-candle** (fc) is a unit measure of the illumination over an area of one square foot at a distance of one linear foot from the candle flame. Light spreads outward in all directions, thus the further we are from a light source, the less light we see and the dimmer the source appears. Expressed mathematically, the intensity of light decreases by the square of the distance from the source. Since area also has to be taken into consideration, the **lumen**, a unit of luminous flux, is the amount of light that falls on one square foot of area with all points located one foot from the flame of a standard candle. Flux, incidently, means that the energy is in continuous flow. One lumen per square foot is the light of one foot-candle. The inside surface of a sphere with a radius of one foot has a surface area of 12.56 square feet, so one candlepower is equal to 12.56 foot-candles or 12.56 lumens. A lumen, then, is a measure of particular amount of light incident upon a surface of a specific size. Since it is a specific measure of a particular amount of light (one foot-candle), light intensity can also be expressed in lumens and the output of most fluorescent and incandescent bulbs is listed in lumens.

Lux, the International Standard unit, is the same type of measure in the metric system and is also termed a metercandle.

One lux is defined as one lumen falling perpendicularly on a surface of one square meter. One lux is equivalent to 0.0929 footcandles (lumens) and one lumen is equal to 10.76 lux. Multiply lumens by 10.76 to convert to lux and multiply lux by 0.0929 to covert to lumens. Sunlight falling on a particular surface is measured as energy per unit area. The basic measure is gram calories per square centimeter (gm.cal./cm^2) which is equal to the **langley**, a common measure of electromagnetic radiation incident upon a surface. One gm.cal./cm^2 per hour is equal to about 770 foot candles, which is about 8288 lux. (You know, of course, what happens to the critters in your marine aquarium when the lights go out. They run out of lux! I know, I know, but it's my book. I can put that in if I want to.)

In the natural environment, there is great variation in the amount of sunlight that strikes the water's surface in different seasons, from day to day and even hour to hour as weather changes occur. Time of day is very important because the smaller the angle between the sun's rays and the water's surface, the more light is reflected off the surface and the amount of light entering the water is reduced. Thus light intensity is much lower under water than at the surface in early morning and late afternoon. The angle of the sun's rays and the number of daylight hours vary with season and distance from the equator. The winter sun is low in the sky and less light penetrates the surface at any time of day. Maximum light intensity in the aquatic environment occurs near the surface on a calm summer day when the sun's rays are perpendicular to the surface and only a few white clouds dot the sky. On such a day over tropical seas, the intensity of light just above the surface may exceed 130,000 lux.

Light intensity under the surface is decreased to a greater or lesser extent by factors other than the angle of the sun's rays and cloud cover. Due to reflection and absorption, only about 100 gm. cal./cm^2/hr (77,000 lux) penetrates the sea surface when the sun is at zenith. Surface turbulence increases reflection of light off the water's surface. Only about 4% of the light is reflected on calm days and up to 25% is reflected when the surface is disturbed by moderate winds. Once light enters the water, it is absorbed and scattered by water molecules and by particles and organic dyes in the water. Light penetration in turbid coastal waters is severely restricted due to these conditions, while light transmission through clear, offshore waters is much greater. The water soluble yellow pigments (Gelbstoff or Gilvin) common in marine coastal waters are most responsible for the extinction of the blue end of the spectrum in coastal waters.

Under the most favorable of conditions (clear, offshore waters), only about 20% (up to 15,000 lux) of total incident energy penetrates 10 to 15 meters below the surface. Light intensities at depths of 5 to 10 meters in temperate coastal waters at noon are only about 7500 lux, dropping to lower levels at other times of the day. Thus, since average daily illumination is more important than peak noontime levels, many algae adapted to low light levels typical of coastal areas (including many microscopic red and blue-green algae) can live in aquariums with only 5000 lux per hour for 12 to 14 hours per day. Coral reef algae require more light. According to Homes (1957), maximum production from photosynthesis occurs at about 10 meters in tropical seas, and light saturation in these algae occurs at about 35,000 lux; which means that many tropical algae, especially green macroalgae, and corals are adapted to very intense lighting. A marine aquarium usually gets too little light for growth and survival of the desired algae and corals. Red and some brown algae often grow to the exclusion of the desired green algae. The light may include the proper wavelength and color temperature for growth of macroalgae and the *zooxanthellae* of corals and anemones, but the intensity may not be great enough even if the proper water quality is present. More information on light and algae can be found in the section on algae in Chapter 3.

Individual opinions and purposes will vary, but the following specifications should provide adequate lighting for most marine invertebrate aquariums. Light intensity is the most important factor in lighting an aquarium providing wavelength peaks and color temperature are reasonably proper. An intensity of about 12,000 to 16,000 average lux at the water's surface should maintain most organisms that utilize light for photosynthesis. Some reef tanks may require a higher surface level of 18,000 to 20,000 lux. This light intensity will decrease with passage through the water, only about 10,000 lux may be present at 12 inches and perhaps 5,000 lux may remain at the bottom at 18 to 22 inches deep. Given proper intensity, light with a color temperature of 5000 to 7000 °K and a wavelength pattern with peaks in the 475 and 650 nm wave length ranges will provide the right quality of lighting.

It's good to understand and have for reference all this information about light, what it is, how it works and how it is measured, but the important question to most marine aquarists is: What kind of bulbs and how many of them are necessary for my particular aquarium system? The section on lighting in Chapter 4 will provide more specific information on the types and numbers of lamps that can be used.

Photoperiod

Basically, **photoperiod** refers to the number of consecutive hours of light that occur within one day, a 24 hour period. This is also know as the diel periodicity. Except for cave dwellers, animals and plants do not live in nature under constant dark or constant light. They do not survive well in captivity if reasonably natural cycles of light and darkness are not provided. In nature, intensity and periodicity of lighting is not consistent. Sunlight intensity and day length vary with season and weather conditions. Night lighting varies not only with season and weather, but also with the phases of the moon. Nighttime is not absolutely dark on the reef. Bright moonlit nights provide considerable light for sighted creatures in shallow waters and even starlight and the light generated by some marine organisms (bioluminescence) keep the nights from being totally dark. A dim night light somewhere in the room is a good thing for a marine aquarium, but it is not absolutely necessary.

The number of daylight hours varies with latitude and season. This variation is most pronounced above the arctic and antarctic circles where the sun does not set in mid summer and does not rise in mid winter. Night and day in the tropics on the other hand are almost equal the year round. If animals and plants from temperate waters are kept, 8 to 10 hours of light per day is good, and if tropical organisms are kept, 12 to 14 hours is good, although they will also do fine with fewer light hours. There are two things that are important to consider under the general topic of photoperiod. One, it is not always noontime on the reef, and two, the sun does not go on and off with the flick of a switch. Light levels on the reefs slowly increase during morning hours and slowly decrease during afternoon hours. The crepuscular periods, dawn and dusk, are slow transitions between light and dark in the natural environment.

Dawn and dusk can be simulated in a marine aquarium with an incandescent bulb or two set up on a timer that will turn these bulbs on 30 minutes before, and off a few minutes after, the main tank lights come on in the morning. The same timer turns these crepuscular period lights on just before the main lights go off at night and then turns them off 30 minutes later. Such a lighting set up provides a more natural environment and reduces the shock between light and dark, but most typical marine and reef aquarium systems seem to get along well enough without a dawn/dusk period.

Temperature

The temperature range of a particular environment rather broadly determines what forms of life inhabit that environment. Tropical organisms can not withstand the cold winters of temperate zones, and temperate organisms are not adapted to survive the constant high temperatures of tropical areas. The body temperature of poikilotherms ("cold-blooded" animals including all invertebrates) is controlled by their environment, and cold blooded aquatic animals are the same temperature as the water that surrounds them. Their metabolism, the chemical reactions in their bodies, progress more slowly when the water is cold and more rapidly when the water is warm. Generally, the speed of metabolic activity doubles for every 10°C rise in temperature. The animals in an aquarium kept at 82°F (27.8°C) will generally be more active, eat more, and grow faster than those kept at 72°F (22.2°C).

Coral reef organisms live within a rather narrow temperature range. Shallow reefs experience a greater range in temperature than deep reefs, but even so, shallow reef temperatures seldom dip below 18°C or rise above 32°C (65°F to 90°F). Coral reef animals can generally adapt to temperatures within these extremes, but sudden temperature changes of significant magnitude can cause thermal stress, and even death. Unusually cold temperatures are sometimes experienced on coral reefs as a result of upwelling of deep, cold waters. This occurs when strong, persistent winds blow warm, coastal waters far offshore and cold water from the depths flows up to replace it. Depending on severity and duration, this phenomena can cause the death of many fish and invertebrates. More often, however, unusually high water temperatures in late summer cause stress and some mortality in the coral reef community. Although these elevated temperatures seldom directly cause high temperature death, they increase the susceptibility of fish to bacterial disease and place severe survival stress on corals.

Corals often release the *zooxanthellae* from their tissues during times of high temperature stress and they will eventually die if they can not reestablish these algal symbionts; which most of them do when water temperatures cool. Clouds of yellow water surround the reefs when the corals release their *zooxanthellae*. Some corals and algaes are adapted to the shallow waters of the grass flats and are able to withstand seasonal and daily temperature extremes, but the same extremes severely stress the deeper coral reef community. For basic information on temperature, Gunter (1957) presents an in depth discussion of the role of temperature in the marine environment.

Temperature is measured in degrees Fahrenheit, or degrees Celsius, or degrees Centigrade, or even degrees Kelvin. These different scales frequently create frustration for those of us without workaday experience in scientific laboratories. Celsius is the scale used by Europeans and most scientists, thus it often pops up in aquarium literature. Unfortunately, if one grew up thinking in Fahrenheit degrees, a temperature given in Celsius may not mean much.

The least I can do is provide a little background information. In 1714 the German physicist Gabriel Daniel Fahrenheit invented the sealed mercury thermometer. After he demonstrated that the mercury rose and fell in the sealed tube according to the amount of heat in the environment, he then had to create a temperature reference scale so that everyone could refer to the same points on the thermometer. The story goes that he set 0 at the lowest temperature he could achieve in his laboratory with ice and salt, a point well below the freezing point of pure water. He then wanted the distance between freezing and boiling of water to represent 180 degrees, half the degrees of a circle. This put the freezing point of water at 32 °F and the boiling point at 212 °F. We've been saddled with this unwieldy system ever since.

Anders Celsius developed a different system in 1742. He set the freezing point of water at 0 degrees and the boiling point at 100 degrees. Because each step in the scale was one part of a hundred, the scale was called Centigrade, the Latin word for "hundred steps". In 1948 this scale was renamed the Celsius scale to honor its developer, and the C symbol can refer to either name although it is officially the symbol for the Celsius scale. Most of the world, with a few exceptions, measures temperature in degrees Celsius. The Kelvin scale is based on absolute zero. A French physicist noticed in 1787 that the volume of a gas decreased by 1/273 for every degree C that it was cooled below 0 °C. Then Lord Kelvin came along in the 1860's and developed the idea that the molecules of the gas were actually losing energy and that the loss of volume was only a shrinkage due to this energy loss. He predicted that gas would lose all energy at minus 273 °C (as would everything else), and that this was as cold as anything could possibly become. So the Kelvin scale starts at absolute zero (-273.16 °C), and is the fundamental temperature scale of science.

A marine aquarist, however, needs only to be able to convert one scale to another to understand the relationship between °F and °C. The back of the book has a table on useful data for aquarists that contains the conversion formula and a conversion scale. The optimum temperature of a tropical marine aquarium is around 78 °F (25.6 °C), and an acceptable temperature range is from 75 °F to 82 °F (24 °C to 28 °C), although fish tanks can stray a bit on either side of this range. Most marine aquariums need some heating and/or cooling to stay within the optimum temperature range. Methods for maintaining proper temperatures are discussed in Chapter 4.

Turbulence

Marine waters are seldom, if ever, still. The sources of water motion are wind generated surface waves, tidal and oceanic currents, and microturbulence. Shallow waters often receive great turbulence from wave action and strong tidal currents, while turbulence in deep waters results more from oceanic currents. Wave generated surges extend deep into the reefs. It is not unusual to find strong surges between reef structures induced by three and four foot waves 20 feet above the reef. Strong tidal currents sweep the reefs daily and oceanic currents may pass through the reefs as conditions change from week to week and season to season.

Microturbulence occurs in small, local areas from eddies formed by currents sweeping around and through reef structures and from the movement of fish and other local disturbances. A marine aquarium, especially one with water movement generated only by air lifts and fish movement, seldom has enough turbulence. Strong water movement is essential for the well being of most invertebrates, especially those that are sessile (attached to one place). Water movement brings food organisms and detritus, removes waste particles, exchanges oxygen and carbon dioxide dissolved in the water immediately surrounding the organism, and stimulates movement and interaction with the environment. Some marine organisms are adapted to still, silty environments of muddy bottoms in protected bays and deep waters, but most coral reef creatures live with the surge and flow of wave action and oceanic currents. A reef tank, in particular one that is well planted and contains corals, anemones, tube worms, tunicates and sponges, requires a good pattern of strong water movement to maintain the organisms in good condition.

A great deal of attention is paid to the amount of water that passes through the filter systems of marine aquariums, but the distribution of the water flow through the tank is often ignored. Water from the filter system is discharged on the surface and allowed to find its way through the tank structures without thought to direction, force, and pattern. Even a gentle flow directed to a specific area may allow some creature to thrive in a spot where it could not live without an active water flow. Strong water movement throughout the tank can be achieved by placement of air releases in strategic spots, directed flows from powered filter returns, and directed placement of small "powerhead" pumps whose purpose is only to move water actively about the tank. Many corals and other organism in reef systems do better if exposed to water movement that simulates water surge on the reefs. Water that moves first in one direction and then in the other washes and stimulates these organisms in a natural manner. Surge systems in large reef tanks should not be operated continuously. A period of quiet currents during the night hours and/or part of the day is typical of the natural environment.

Depth

The importance of depth in the marine environment is found in light, water movement, and pressure. Water temperature is also important, but not within the depth range that is of interest to marine aquarists working with tropical systems. As previously discussed, light diminishes in intensity and spectrum as depth increases. The change in the character of light as depth increases is the single most important factor in the distribution of life forms in the upper 200 feet of oceanic water. Life at depths also adapts to other changes, however. The chaotic turbulence of wave surge is markedly diminished as depth increases and is replaced by the relatively constant flows of oceanic currents. The structure and growth of corals, algae, and some sponges changes markedly as depth increases, and the need to withstand wave surge diminishes while the need to collect light increases.

Pressure, of course, increases rapidly with depth. Pressure increases at the rate of one atmosphere (14. 7 psi, lb/in^2) for every 10 meters (33 feet) of depth. The pressure at 30 meters, (98.4 feet) is 4 atmospheres (58.8 psi). Few of the organisms we keep in marine aquariums are taken from depths greater than 100 feet. Most of the organisms from the deeper areas of this range do well in one to three foot deep aquariums if care is taken in their capture and acclimation to shallow waters. Thus within the depth range from the shallows down to at least 100 feet, there does not seem to be any factor associated with pressure alone that prevents these creatures from surviving in only a few feet of water.

Certain species of fish and invertebrates often occur in deep water within relatively narrow depth ranges even though they are quite capable of long term survival in the shallow waters of a friendly aquarium. Most of these deep water animals are not naturally found in shallow water, so their settlement and/or survival must depend on environmental factors other than depth—such as light, substrate, associated organisms, and predation. Although not commonly attempted, it is now possible to create and maintain a marine reef tank that simulates the deep reef environment. Light and temperature are the key environmental factors to control in building a system that simulates the deep reef. This type of system is further discussed in Chapter 5.

Substratum

The bottom of the sea is the substratum. It is made up of many different types of substrates, and life grows in it, on it, and above it. The composition and structure of the substratum determine, within the bounds of light, temperature, depth, and water movement, the kind of organisms that live in that place. A rocky shore and a sandy beach support very different types of marine communities, as does a flat muddy bottom, a hard sand plain, and a rugged coral reef, all under 20 feet of clear tropical sea. The physical stability of the sediments is also important. Some bottoms, such as sandy tidal areas, shift and move easily and regularly, while deeper deposits of silt and mud and hard reef bottoms are more stable. Patterns of water movement have a great effect on the nature of the substratum. Fast flows tend to create hard bottoms with few soft, organic filled sediments; while slow water flows allow soft sediments and light organic matter to accumulate. Generally, deep water sediments are finer than those in shallow water locations. Sediment particles are graded according to their size. Clay particles (0.001 mm diameter) are the finest. Fine silt (0.005 mm) and coarse silt (0.03 mm) are the next largest particle size. Sand catagories begin with fine sand (0.1 mm) and grade up to medium, and then to coarse sand, which blends into gravel at particle size of above 1 mm. Pebbles go up to about 25 mm and then cobbles run up to 200 mm. Bolders and blocks are larger.

Outcroppings of hard rock and deposits of stones and gravel allow attachment and colonization of certain corals, sponges, and algae above the surrounding sediments. Over centuries of time, massive reef structures can grow from such small beginnings. There is little organic matter in coarse, well washed sediments, and animals that live in such habitats—fan worms, anemones, mollusks, and others—must capture food from the water above the sediments, thus they are mostly filter feeders. Animals living in fine sediments with little wash are adapted to feed on the organic detritus that accumulates in such sediments. Amphipods, some tube dwelling worms, and some mollusks are commonly found in such habitats. We keep organisms in our aquariums that originate from many types of substrates. Rocky reefs organisms are most common, but many creatures are found on bottoms composed of silt, clay, mud, sand, shell, gravel, rubble, sea grass, and algae flats. Sponges, corals, algaes and sea grasses are associated with various types of inorganic substrates and these living substrates all support various communities of marine life.

Some invertebrates, such as many worms, some echinoderms, various crustacea, and a large number of mollusks, are a part of the **infauna** and live within the sandy or muddy sediments of the sea bottom. These animals can have a great effect on the nature of the sediments as they feed and live within them. One effect is to stabilize the bottom sediments by cementing small particles together as they construct tubes and shelters. Some species of marine worms, *Sabellaria*, can create extensive, hard reef-like structures from sandy sediments. The sediment invaders, worms, mollusks and burrowing echinoderms, also bring oxygen rich water into the sediments and create a habitat for aerobic bacteria, which are very efficient in breaking down organic matter and releasing minerals.

Other invertebrates—corals, sponges, many crustaceans and mollusks, tunicates and most echinoderms—live on the surface of the substratum, some attached and some mobile. Most of these live on hard bottoms, but many prefer the surface of soft sediments and feed on small organisms and organic material trapped in the sediment. Most fishes and some invertebrates, squid, jellyfish and many planktonic crustacea, live relatively independently of the bottom and are not intimately associated with any particular bottom substrate. The coral reef environment encompasses a great variety of bottom substrates. These include hard rock surfaces, soft rock, coarse coral gravel of sorted and unsorted particle size (natural sorting of particle size occurs from wave surge and currents), soft sediments in protected areas within the reef structure and on the grass flats surrounding the reefs, areas of shifting sand and occasional hard clay deposits, and living substrates such as grasses, algae, sponges, live hard coral formations and gorgonians. Organisms from all the varied substrates that compose a coral reef find their way into our aquariums. The substratum, the composition of the bottom, is just as important to the survival of many invertebrates as is food and water quality. Just as we provide the proper food, temperature, lighting, and water quality for the invertebrate aquarium, we should also consider the bottom substrate we provide for various invertebrates.

The traditional marine aquarium system is based on an undergravel filter composed of a 2 inch (5 cm) layer of some type of calcareous gravel with a particle size of about 2 to 4 mm or a layer of washed shell hash. This type of media forms a good base for the biological activity of an undergravel filter. Very course silica sand is also a good substrate for a biological filter and is not uncommon. Although some invertebrates can live comfortably with this type of substrate, many are unable to live within it. With the recent development of the reef type invertebrate aquarium, another type of substrate has become functionally important to many marine aquarists. This is the so called "living rock" that is the base substrate for life in the reef tank. Biological filtration (bacterial transformation of nitrogenous waste), which was the major function of the media of the undergravel filter, is performed by an external filter in a reef tank system. Although the rock substrates in the tank harbor extensive bacterial colonies, the main purpose of the rock is to introduce and to support reef life. The rock itself is not alive, of course. It is collected from the sea bottom and the term "living rock" refers to the marine life that is still alive on the rock when it is placed in the reef tank.

Fortunately, most of the invertebrates we keep in aquariums are creatures of rocky reef substrates and can survive without access to the soft sediments that normally surround the reefs. It may be quite interesting, however, to provide a small section of soft substrate in a reef tank and observe the invertebrates and algaes that colonize this area. It may even be possible to grow certain sea grasses such as *Halophila* in this area. Care must be taken to provide for water circulation through the soft sediments, however, to prevent development of anaerobic conditions.

Suspended Particulate Matter

Seawater, even the clearest offshore water, contains a great deal of particulate matter. One of the most fundamental differences between the sea and a sea water aquarium is that the aquarium usually has very little suspended particulate matter. Most of the particles in the sea are alive, and these minute plants and animals compose the plankton, which is part of the natural biological environment. Marine aquarium systems have almost no planktonic organisms aside from bacteria and perhaps a few floating algal cells. Suspended nonliving particles can be organic or inorganic and range in size from less than a micron to objects the size of tree trunks. Leptopel, as the tiniest particles are called, are inorganic particles composed of tiny needles of aragonite and calcite, tiny pellets of silicates, phosphates, etc., and organic particles of proteins, lipids, and carbohydrates. These very tiny particles, a fraction of a micron in size, usually originate from compounds dissolved in seawater.

Larger inorganic particles such as grains of silt and sand and shell bits picked up by wave surges remain suspended only as long as sufficient water turbulence exists. Organic material is lighter and remains in suspension more easily, but even organic particles eventually fall, especially when they aggregate with inorganic particles of clay and silt. There is a constant rain of large and small particles through the sea that eventually become part of the bottom sediments. Some of these are the castings and remains of planktonic creatures, but most organic particles are in the form of detritus. Most suspended particles, tree trunks and the like, are filtered from the water before it becomes a part of a marine aquarium, but the sea and the aquarium have detritus in common.

Detritus

There are a lot of scientific names that refer to detritus in the marine environment: particulate organic carbon (POC), organic and inorganic particles, leptopel, aggregates, marine dirt or dust, mud, yucky stuff, guck, gunk, and a few other terms inappropriate for inclusion in this book. All are in current use by scientists and laymen alike. Detritus is very important to the marine environment. The production of organic material through the formation of detritus is ten times the annual value for phytoplankton productivity (Fox 1957).

The same mechanisms that work to form detritus in nature also produce detritus in the marine aquarium. In most marine systems, detritus is that dark brown to grey green, soft, flocculent material that accumulates underneath and on the surface of undergravel filters and in the bottoms and crevices of various filter boxes. It starts off as dissolved organic and inorganic compounds. These dissolved compounds are attracted to the surfaces of small bits of solid material, silt, sand grains and the like, and also to the surfaces of air bubbles. When the air bubbles rise through the tank they accumulate a "coating" of inorganic and organic compounds. Small air bubbles leave the water and enter the atmosphere, but leave behind the now insoluble "skin" of compounds that surrounded the bubble. This little microscopic package of organic and inorganic particles attracts other compounds and becomes a larger aggregate of particles. As these aggregates clump together they become particles of detritus and accumulate wherever water flows deposit light, flocculent particles. Other organic particles—fecal pellets from fish and invertebrates, worm castings, molts from crustaceans, bits of vegetable matter, and dead microorganisms—become part of this detritus base. All sorts of animals, macro and microscopic, make use of detritus as food and habitat. A look at this "marine dust" under a microscope will reveal round worms, flat worms, ciliates, bacteria, algae cells, diatoms, filamentous algaes, tiny crustaceans, and many other life forms.

Detritus quickly becomes part of the organic cycles in the sea and eventually part of the sediments that build up on the sea bottoms. It also accumulates in marine aquarium systems and adds to the organic load in the system. It should periodically be removed from the system to reduce phosphate, organics, and the organic substrate available for bacterial growth. There are a number of ways of removing detritus. Filter cleaning is important and stirring gravel and siphoning off the dirt that accumulates above the gravel removes most of the detritus. Tanks that have external biological filters and do not have an undergravel filter can have the entire bottom siphoned and any gravel or sand that is removed can be rinsed and replaced. Detritus that accumulates between and under rocks can be flushed out and siphoned or picked up by the filter intake. Mechanical filtration, usually a floss or pad filter, picks up extensive detritus and should be cleaned and/or replaced as necessary, daily, weekly or monthly depending on the individual system. Moe (1982) has a good section on cleaning tanks and filters in Chapter four.

Chapter 3

The Biological Environment

Concepts and Definitions

The **biosphere** of the sea, a term for the collective presence and interaction of marine life, has two great divisions or zones that are quite separate and yet, indivisible. These are the **pelagic zone** (the water column that extends from surface to bottom), and the **benthic zone** (the sea bottom). The science of marine ecology is the study of the interactions of life in the marine environment.

Life in the pelagic zone consists of the nekton and the plankton. The **nekton** are the swimmers that can control their own movement, the fish and squid, the whales and turtles. The **plankton** are the drifters, and, despite some limited swimming capability, their destiny is controlled by the flow of currents. The macroplankton are the big drifters, such as jellyfish and *Sargassum* weed. The microplankton may be animals, **zooplankton**, or plants, **phytoplankton**, but the largest of them are barely large enough to see without magnification. The planktonic world is of great importance in the sea, in fact, life on the bottom is almost an afterthought.

The phytoplankton is the base for most of the food chains in the sea, and the larval stages of most animals, large and small, pay their dues in the fierce planktonic environment. The plankton also has a strong influence on the physical structure of sea bottom sediments and land based rock formations. Planktonic organisms, Foraminifera and Coccolithophorids in particular, create many of the sediments that form the habitats of the benthic zone and even the structure of vast land areas such as nummulitic limestones (the blocks of the Egyptian pyramids were quarried from such deposits) and chalks (like the White Cliffs of Dover).

There are many ways to classify plankton. The holoplankton are those organisms that are planktonic throughout their lives, permanent members of the planktonic community. Meroplankton are those organisms that are only planktonic during the larval stages of life, temporary plankters. **Bacterioplankton** are the bacteria that are free floating and they are among the smallest of the planktonic organisms. Plankton is also classified by size. The **macroplankton** is the largest group. These organisms, mostly zooplankters, can be taken in a net with a mesh size of one millimeter or larger. The **microplankton** is made up mostly of phytoplankton and are those organisms captured in nets with a mesh size between 0.06 mm and 1 mm. The **nanoplankton** is made up mostly of tiny flagellates, tiny phytoplankters, and bacteria that are smaller than 60 microns. The very tiniest plankters, those smaller than 5 microns (0.005 mm), are termed the **ultraplankton** and are mostly very tiny flagellates and bacteria.

The benthic zone is loosely defined as the sea bottom. It is composed of the **substratum**, the rock, sand, and sediments that form the sea bottom, and the **benthos**, the life forms that live on and in the bottom. The organisms that live attached to, or that crawl or swim right on the substratum, make up the **epifauna,** and those organisms that live within the sediments are the **infauna**. Corals, crabs, and algaes are typical of the epifauna and worms, clams, and burrowing sea urchins are members of the infauna. Figure 5 illustrates the major life zones in the sea.

These three great spheres of marine life—the plankton, the epifauna, and the infauna—are intimately associated and interdependent even though they occupy very different environments. The very structure of the plankton is often determined by the benthos it bathes; for both epifauna and infauna depend

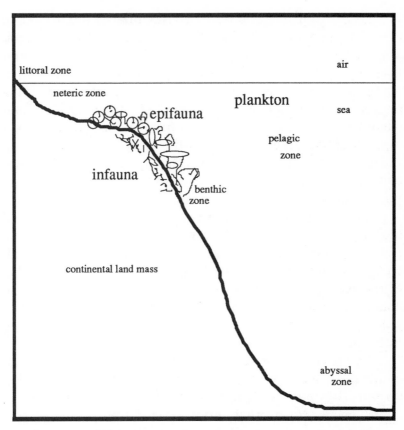

Figure 5. Major zones and habitats in the sea.

on the plankton for food and dispersal of eggs and larvae. A coral reef with its millions of planktonic predators can effectively filter most of these tiny organisms from a plankton laden current and, at other times, contribute vast numbers of larval forms to the currents that sweep through the reef.

The concepts of habitat and ecological niche are very important to marine aquarists. A **habitat** is a place where an organism lives. This is often described with a general term such as a coral reef, a grass flat, a muddy bottom, or the plankton. A broad description is adequate for animals that move extensively or algaes that grow in many different areas; but a specialized habitat description within the broad term is usually necessary for most organisms. The term **microhabitat** is often used to describe a specialized habitat. For example, certain plants and animals live only on the blades of turtle grass, *Thalassia*, and these epiphytes and epizooites live in the microhabitat of the surface of a grass blade. A microhabitat may be type of living organism—a sponge, a coral, even the internal organs of sea cucumber—or a particular type of area—in the sun on the reef top, under the ledges near the bottom of the reef, or in a hole in the rock. A knowledge of the microhabitat of a particular plant of animal is a great help in learning how to keep it and where to put it in an aquarium.

The term **ecological niche** refers to the role or function of the particular species within the community or ecosystem. Thus terms like predator, grazer, borer, filter feeder, and symbiotic are descriptive of the ecology of the species. A knowledge of the ecology of the species is also helpful in setting up an aquarium. A sea urchin that feeds on algae, for example, may not be a wise addition to a tank where algal growth is a prime intention.

Despite our efforts to create a natural coral reef environment in the modern reef tank, there are vast differences between the natural environment and the aquarium environment. We create a very restricted, specialized ecosystem in a marine aquarium. Perhaps the greatest difference between the biospheres of a coral reef and a marine aquarium is that *the marine aquarium has no plankton*. The infauna is also very limited in a marine aquarium, and only organisms from a varied but restricted epifauna, the rocky reef, are usually supported in the ecology of a marine aquarium system. Even if we supply the light and the water quality that coral reef organisms require, we must still compensate for the loss of the plankton to maintain many of these life forms. Fortunately, for many coral reef organisms the planktonic environment is critical only for reproduction, and we can keep them successfully during their juvenile and adult stages. When it comes to culture and propagation, however, we must find substitutes for the planktonic environment required by the larval stages of many coral reef creatures. We must also take the absence of plankton into consideration when planning the food and feeding of a coral reef aquarium. There are ways to provide some sub-stitutes for planktonic food for some organisms and this is addressed in Chapter 6.

Primary Productivity

The production of organic matter is the "responsibility" of plants. It is through photosynthesis that plants are able to take elemental carbon and "fix" it for use in organic compounds. This is the process that is at the base of food chains and ul-timately determines how much life can exist in any environ-ment powered by light. Primary productivity is the rate of fixation of carbon by photosynthetic organisms. It is dependent on many factors such as temperature, light, oxygen, carbon dioxide, and availability of any of the basic plant nutrients. It is limited when any of these essential factors are in short supply. In most marine waters, especially nutrient rich, life-filled coas-tal waters, phytoplankton are the major primary producers. In nutrient poor, clear tropical seas that flow over coral reefs, however, the major primary producers are the *zooxanthellae*, the algal cells that live within the tissues of corals and a few other animals.

As mentioned above, a marine aquarium has little, if any, phytoplankton. Plant growth must occur in the form of macro-algae or encrusting growths of green, red, and blue-green algae. Factors limiting plant growth in marine aquariums are usually lack of light and/or an imbalance of essential nutrients. Undesirable algae often displace desired macroalgae growths as nutrients increase. Usually, nutrient levels are diluted by water changes, but in those tanks where the growth of macroal-gae can meet or exceed production of nutrients, periodic har-vesting of the algae is necessary to maintain the balance of plant and animal life.

Natural Cycles

The elemental raw materials of life in the sea are constantly cycling between the atmosphere, the water, the sediments, and the land. It is life, in many varied forms, that drives these cycles. The round trip for these elements may be relatively rapid, such as nitrogen moving from the atmosphere to bacteria to plants to animals to bacteria and back to the atmosphere. The cycle for silicon, on the other hand, may take eons as it moves with the wash of sediments from the land down to the sea, into the shells of diatoms, and then down into the sediments again to await the uplift to land before breakdown, dissolution, and wash back to the sea once more. These cycles in a marine aquarium don't take eons but the they are just as important in the aquarium as they are in the natural environment. In some instances, element cycling in the marine aquarium results in accumulation of toxic compounds and, in other situations, removal of important nutrients. It is important to know a little bit about how these cycles work in nature and what happens to them in the marine aquarium system.

Carbon

Carbon, in the gas carbon dioxide, is exchanged between air and water at the surface interface. Free carbon dioxide in the sea quickly becomes part of the buffer system of seawater, and although free carbon dioxide lowers the pH of seawater, it works to maintain a high, stable pH when it is part of the buffer system (see Chapter 1). Plants use carbon dioxide during photosynthesis to manufacture sugars, starch, proteins, and fats. These complex organic compounds manufactured by plants are then consumed by animals and bacteria to power their own metabolism. To complete the cycle, carbon dioxide is released back to the environment during the respiration of bacteria, animals, and also plants.

Carbon tends to accumulate in a marine aquarium system in the form of dissolved and particulate organics. Development of a yellow color in the aquarium water is a result of the

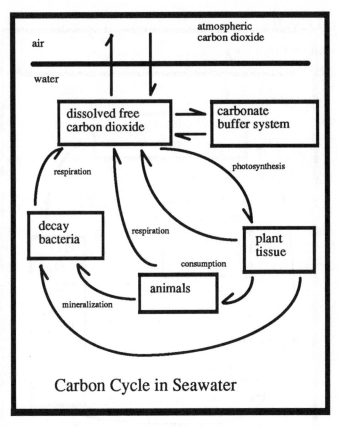

Figure 6. The carbon cycle in seawater.

accumulation of DOC, Dissolved Organic Carbon. Particulate Organic Carbon (POC) also accumulates as part of the structure of detritus. Detritus should be periodically removed by siphoning out dirty gravel and tank bottoms, cleaning mechanical filters, and cleaning filter boxes. Accumulation of DOC can be controlled by water exchange, protein foam skimming, denitrification, ozonators, and activated carbon filtration. Figure 6 illustrates the cycling of carbon in the marine environment.

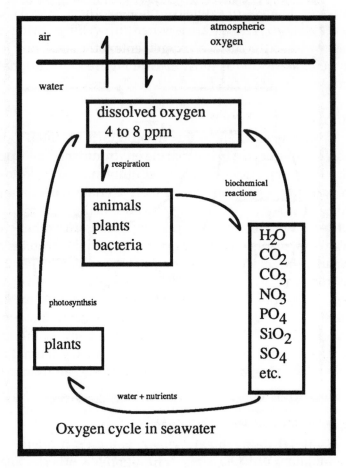

Figure 7. The oxygen cycle in the sea and in marine aquariums.

Oxygen

Oxygen is highly reactive with many substances in biological and purely chemical reactions, and it is difficult to chart a simple cycle for this essential element. It represents 21% of atmospheric gas, but is present in seawater at only 4 to 8 parts per million, less than 1%. Like other gasses, it is exchanged between air and water at the surface interface. The direction of movement depends on the degree of saturation of the gas in seawater. In areas of extensive photosynthetic activity, oxygen leaves the sea, and in areas where upwellings bring oxygen poor water to the surface, oxygen enters the sea. The cycling of oxygen in seawater is illustrated in Figure 7. Additional information on oxygen can be found in Chapter 1.

Nitrogen

Nitrogen, as a component of protein, is essential to life and has a complex cycle in the marine environment. Dinitrogen gas (N_2) is present in seawater at equilibrium with atmospheric pressure. As a gas, nitrogen is inert. Certain bacteria and blue green algaes can "fix" nitrogen and make it available as a nutrient to plants. Through photosynthesis and other chemical pathways, plants incorporate nitrogen into the proteins of their tissues. This protein bound nitrogen eventually reenters the environment as ammonia (NH_3) through two paths. Animals feed on the plants and convert the plant protein into animal protein, then as part of animal metabolism, the protein is broken down and ammonia is excreted back to the environment as either urea, uric acid, or ammonia. Bacterial activity quickly changes any urea and uric acid into ammonia. On the other pathway, nitrogen moves from plant and animal protein into ammonia through the process of bacterial decay after the death of the organism.

Bacterial decay breaks down complex proteins and organics into basic inorganic compounds, a process known as **mineralization**. Ammonia, a nonorganic mineral, is the end product of both metabolism and mineralization and is a toxic compound to most marine life. Fortunately, ammonia does not last long in the marine environment. Nitrifying bacteria quickly oxidize ammonia into first nitrite (NO_2) and then nitrate (NO_3). Nitrate can then be used by plant life as a nutrient (as can nitrite and ammonia in many instances) or can be reduced to dinitrogen gas (N_2) through the activity of denitrifying bacteria.

In most marine aquarium systems, proteins from plants grown in the tank are not sufficient for the nutritional needs of

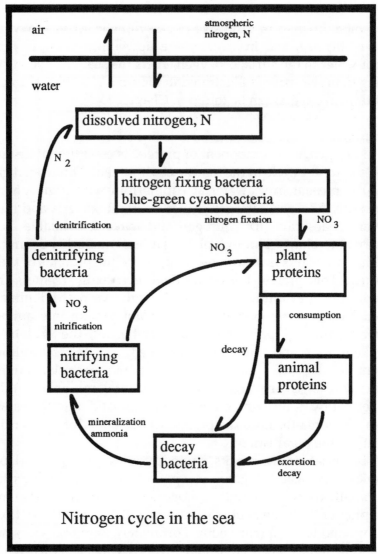

Figure 8. The nitrogen cycle in seawater.

the animals in the system. Additional protein must be added in the form of food to nourish the animals. Without mechanisms to facilitate the nitrogen cycle in marine systems, the water would soon be loaded with toxic compounds—ammonia, nitrite, organic compounds, and bacterial toxins—and most animals would die. Also, there is seldom enough plant life to

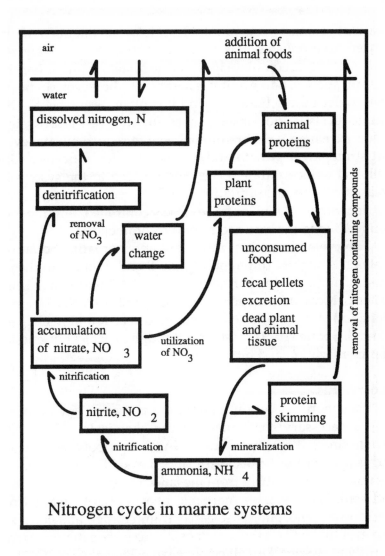

Figure 9. The nitrogen cycle in marine aquarium systems.

utilize the nitrogenous compounds that accumulate within the tank. Fortunately for marine aquarists, Mother Nature can pack an awful lot of nitrifying bacteria into a very small area. All she needs is a substrate for the bacteria and a supply of oxygenated, ammoniated water, and the bacteria quickly oxidize the ammonia to nitrate. The biological filter of a marine system accomplishes this function. Nitrate is relatively non toxic and can accumulate in a marine system without harm to tolerant species. Some animals and plants, however, do not do well under nitrate build up, and it is often desireable to keep nitrate levels low or absent, especially in a reef tank system. Water exchange is the traditional way to reduce nitrate levels, but strong algal growth and/or use of a denitrification filter will also reduce nitrate levels. Food added to the system increases nitrate accumulations and in reef systems, where nutrient accumulation must be closely controlled, limiting food and feeding to the bare necessity is recommended.

The cycle of nitrogen in the sea and in marine aquarium systems is slightly different. Figures 8 and 9 illustrate the cycling of nitrogen in marine waters and in marine aquarium systems. More information on nitrogen in the marine environment and in the captive environment can be found in chapters 1 and 4. Spotte (1979) presents a through, technical discussion of mineralization and nitrification.

Phosphorus

Phosphorus is very important in the marine environment. It is a necessary component of the chemicals of life, ATP (Adenosine TriPhosphate) and DNA (DeoxyriboNucleic Acid), and is also part of bones, teeth, and shells. Phosphorus enters the marine environment from the land. The breakdown of rock and sediments releases inorganic phosphorus to wash from land to sea. Phosphorus released from sewage and fertilizer also eventually finds the sea. Phosphorus occurs in three forms in marine waters: Dissolved Inorganic Phosphorus (DIP) as orthophosphate and phosphate, Dissolved Organic Phosphorus (DOP) as part of dissolved organic compounds, and as Particulate Organic Phosphorus (POP) in organic particles, including components of detritus. Phosphorus is not a part of the atmosphere and there is no exchange toward equilibrium with atmospheric gas. However, dissolved inorganic phosphate (DIP) readily leaves seawater incorporated in tiny droplets of

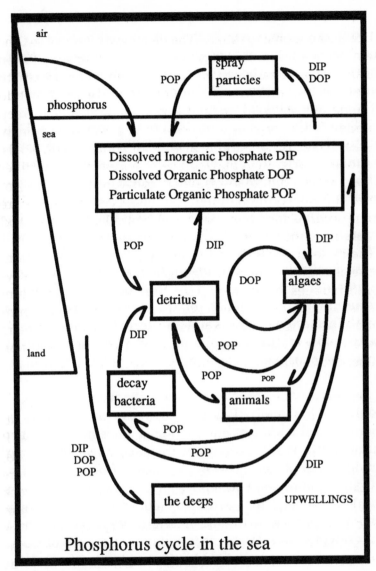

Figure 10. Phosphorus cycle in seawater.

salt spray along with other organic and inorganic compounds.
DIP coats air bubbles in seawater, travels with the bubbles to
the surface, and leaves the water with the transport of salt
spray. This mechanism for phosphate loss from seawater is
more of a factor in marine aquariums where spray particles are

lost from the system than in the natural environment. In fact, these "aerosol particles" composed of phosphate and organic compounds form particles that are an important food source to planktonic organisms. DIP is converted to POP though air/water interaction at the sea surface.

Algae readily take up dissolved organic phosphate (DOP) and dissolved inorganic phosphate (DIP), and in the natural environment, the amount of phosphate present is often the limiting factor in the bloom of microalgae. Phosphate levels are higher in coastal areas near rivers and near oceanic upwellings of water from the deeps. It is in these areas that phytoplankton blooms are most common. Phosphorus moves from algae as DOP and POP when the algae decompose and also into the tissues of animals when consumed. A great deal of phosphorus becomes part of the detritus in the form of particulate organic detritus (POP). Were it not for the legions of bacteria and animals that feed on detritus and transform POP into DIP in the process, most marine phosphorus would be lost in the sediments. The phosphorus cycle in seawater is illustrated in Figure 10.

In the natural environment, especially over coral reefs, the amount of DOP and DIP is very low, less than 30 parts per billion in most coral reef environments. Phosphorus tends to accumulate in marine aquarium systems, however, through excretion from plants and animals, decay of plant and animal tissues, and animal and bacterial processing of detritus. Excess phosphorus, over 1 to 2 parts per million (mg/l), vigorously encourages plant growth, and interferes with calcification in coral growth; and unless there is a luxuriant growth of macroalgae, growth of undesirable blue-green algae and encrusting red algae are stimulated. Aside from algal growth, phosphorus accumulation can be controlled by water exchange, protein foam skimming, and removal of excess detritus. Reduction of the animal loading of the aquarium and/or increasing the total water volume of the system are other methods that will improve the balance of plant and animal life and reduce nutrient accumulation.

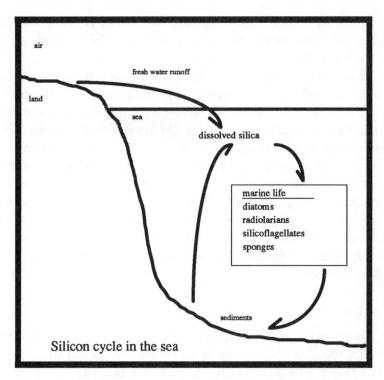

Figure 11. The silicon cycle in sea water.

Silicon

The silicon in the sea, like phosphorus, originates from the land. Silicon (Si) is the element. When combined with oxygen, it becomes silica (silicon dioxide, SiO_2), the stuff of sand, flint, quartz, glass, and the skeletons of some tiny planktonic protoctists. Silicone (with the "e") is SiO that is combined with various semi-inorganic polymers (R groups) to form adhesives, lubricants, and coatings.

Some silica is dissolved during the breakdown of rocks and sediments and is washed into rivers and out to sea. Silicon is an essential element to animals that use it in development of skeletal supports such as diatoms, radiolarians, silicoflagellates and sponges. In the marine environment, silica is obtained from the water by the organisms that utilize it, and some is returned to solution when the organism dies. Silica that is not dissolved accumulates as sediment on the ocean floor. The cycle of silicon in the sea is illustrated in Figure 11.

Silica in the form of sand, rock, and glass is not very soluble and is not a chemical concern to marine aquarists. Silica in the soluble form of silicic acid is another matter. Very few animals are kept that require dissolved silica in any significant amount; however, excess dissoloved silicic acid may stimulate growth of unwanted diatoms and certain red algae. Silicic acid does not usually accumulate to problem status in marine systems. In fact, if anything, it is gradually depleted from aquarium water. However, if fresh water supplies contain high levels of silicic acid, constant addition of tap water to make up for evaporative loss may cause excessive diatom growth if other nutrients are also available.

Bacteria

Who runs the world? Human beings? Naw, we use the world, we don't run it. Animals? Naw, the world uses them! Plants? Naw, they make the world work, but they don't run it. Bacteria run the world—that's who! They've owned it ever since life first started over 3.5 billion years ago, and they're not about to turn it over to the cute little humans that were born only yesterday. Bacteria control the ebb and flow of the major chemical elements of life in all environments—with oxygen, without oxygen, with and without light, and even in the guts of humans, termites, whales and cows. Were it not for the chemoautotrophic bacteria, all the nitrogen, carbon, and sulfur of the world would be tied up in gasses and salts and unavailable to life. The only reason we don't stand in awe and wonder of bacteria is that we can't see them; thus we take what they do for granted.

We didn't even know bacteria existed until 1683 when Antony van Leeuwenhoek took a small glass bead, ground it into a tiny lens, mounted it between two metal plates, and looked through it at a drop of water on the head of pin. This opened the door to a whole new world. Everything moist teems with bacteria—soil, mud, leaves of trees, fresh and marine waters, marine sediments, the gut of all animals, even the surface of your teeth. We constantly fight the negative effects of bacteria: decay, disease, and infection. We also work to enhance the positive aspects of bacterial activity: nitrogen fixation, digestion, yogurt production, tools for genetic engineering, and, for the marine aquarist, biological filtration.

Nutrient cycles in the marine environment depend on bacteria, and bacteria are important participants in marine food chains. Free-floating bacterioplankton feed on dissolved organic matter and are eaten by filter feeding planktonic animals. Coastal waters and surface ocean waters support large populations of many species of bacteria. Bacteria also control the sanity of marine aquarists. Note carefully that a marine aquarium system will not support life until an astounding number of bacteria call it home. A successful marine aquarium is more the result of a careful balance of bacterial populations than the selection, care, and feeding of marine life. Chapter 8 lists all the phyla of bacteria recognized by Margulis and Schwartz (1988) and additional information and scientific names of many important groups of marine bacteria are listed in that chapter.

The most important bacteria in a marine aquarium system are those that deal with nitrogen. There are four general types.

- Decay bacteria. These are the bacteria that break down food, feces, and dead tissues and release ammonia and complex organic compounds to the aquarium. This process is termed mineralization and is performed by a wide variety of bacteria called heterotrophic bacteria.

- Nitrifying bacteria. These organisms oxidize ammonia into nitrite and nitrate, the basis of biological filtration.

- Denitrifying bacteria. These chemoautotrophic bacteria work best in the absence of oxygen and, with a carbohydrate substrate, reduce nitrate into free nitrogen gas. This process does not occur in a marine aquarium unless a denitrifying filtration device is established.

- Nitrogen-fixing bacteria. These bacteria are present in relatively small numbers in marine aquariums. Although very important for plant growth in the natural environment, this part of the nitrogen cycle, production of fixed nitrogen from free dinitrogen gas, is not a factor in marine systems and is not a consideration in aquarium management.

Marine Plants

Marine botany is essentially the study of algae. There are only a few true plants (angiosperms) that are totally marine. These are the marine grasses that cover vast areas of shallow bottoms. With this exception, all marine plants, excluding those that are shoreline inhabitants, are relatively primitive algae. Algae are very different from the true plants. Their structures are not leaves, stems, trunks, and roots. The body of a large macroalgae such as the brown algae, *Padina*, and the green algae, *Caulerpa*, is known as the **thallus**, which is composed of a **holdfast** (equivalent to the root of true plants), **stipe** (stem), and **blade** (leaf). Algae may also have air bladders that provide buoyancy and hold the algae up off the bottom. The thallus may take the form of a flat flexible sheet, a rigid branched structure, a bulbus mass, a long thread, or even an encrusting growth.

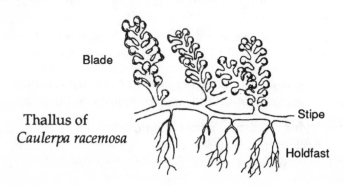

Blade

Thallus of
Caulerpa racemosa

Stipe

Holdfast

Marine aquarists are most familiar with four major groups (phyla or divisions) of algae. These are the Cyanophyta or the **Cyanobacteria**, the blue-green algae (now considered a bacteria rather than an algae); the **Chlorophyta**, the green algae; the **Phaeophyta**, the brown algae; and the **Rhodophypta**, the red algae. Marine algae are either single celled **microalgae** (or chains of a few cells), tiny forms that make up the phytoplankton; or many celled forms that grow on a substrate as filaments and crusts; or large complex growths, the **macroalgae**. These algae live with the epifauna and could be considered the epiflora. Plants and animals are generally more intimate in the sea than on land. Some animals, such as some nudibranchs, feed on algae and transfer their chloroplasts to their own tissues where they continue to manufacture food, but now for the nudibranch and not the algae. Animal/plant associations such as the *zooxanthellae* in corals are common in the marine environment. Although we are most familiar with the big, spectacular marine algae—like the macrogreens *Caulerpa, Penicillus, Udotea,* and *Ulva,* and the biggest brown algae, the giant kelp—there is a whole world of smaller greens, reds, and browns that inhabitat the rocks and reefs and often turn up in marine reef aquariums. These algae grow well when good conditions for the growth of the big greens exist, and it is quite interesting to watch these small plants appear around the rocks.

Algae are in great demand by many types of grazing animals, and they have developed many physical and chemical defenses that offer protection from grazers. The place of growth for an algae in nature depends on light, nutrients, and, to a large extent, freedom from grazing. Marine algae are not easy to identify (most require microscopic examination), and one must study marine algae diligently before developing a proficiency in identification. Dawes (1981) is an excellent text on general marine botany and Taylor (1960) and Dawson (1956) are helpful in algal identification.

Plants, including algae, respire in darkness and photosynthesize in light. Photosynthesis, of course, is the unique capacity of plants to use the energy of light to manufacture food (complex carbohydrates) from the raw materials of water, carbon dioxide, and various inorganic salts. Respiration uses up the plant's stores of food and photosynthesis increases them. This is not an on/off phenomena, however. The two processes occur simultaneously, but at different rates. As light intensity increases, photosynthesis and the production of oxygen also increases. There is a level of light intensity, called the **compensation point**, where oxygen production from photosynthesis is sufficient for production of carbon dioxide during respiration. Since light intensities diminish as water depth increases, there is a depth for each species of algae where respiration and photosynthesis are equal, and this is the compensation depth. This depth, of course, varies with the light absorption characteristics of the water.

Increase of light intensity above the compensation point results in increasing photosynthetic activity up to the point of **light saturation**, also different for different algae. Light saturation occurs when light intensity reaches the point where all the chloroplasts are at maximum photosynthetic activity and oxygen production can not be increased by additional light intensity. If light intensity increases too far beyond the point where the plant becomes light saturated, chloroplasts retract, and, over time, growth inhibition and possible tissue damage may result. Plants can adapt to some degree to the light intensity they typically receive by increasing the number of chloroplasts, and the number of thylakoids within the chloroplasts, under consistent low light levels and decreasing them in high light levels. This adaptation is a gradual process, but it does help algae and corals adjust to aquarium conditions.

Light intensity must exceed the compensation point for the metabolism of the plant to be on the positive side of growth and production. It is not enough for light intensity to exceed the compensation point for only a hour or so each day. The algae must receive enough light so that the total production of photosynthesis exceeds the losses from respiration over the daily cycle of 24 hours. Homes (1957) reports the compensation point of green algae at between 17 to 45 lumens (183 to 484 lux), two species of brown algae at 34 to 40 lumens (366 to 430 lux), and three species of red algae at 27 to 30 lumens (290 to 323 lux). Reported light saturation in marine algae ranges from a low of 1076 lux to a high of over 30,000 lux. This gives us quite a range of light, between a minimum of 1000 and a maximum of 30000 lux (93 to about 3,000 lumens) that actually reaches the algae (not the water surface), to work with in setting up a marine aquarium for macroalgae growth. It is important to have a range of light intensities in the aquarium to serve the varied needs of different types of algae and light requiring invertebrates. Note that algae contained in animal tissues (*zooxanthellae*) usually require more light than exposed algae.

Algae that never or seldom receive light intensities above their compensation points do not do well and eventually die, and if these algae are present in the tissues of animals such as the *zooxanthellae* of corals and anemones, the animals eventually die as well. Light intensity levels do not have to reach the point of light saturation for algae to survive, but light intensity should be well above the compensation point for most of the day for algae to survive and grow. Photosynthesis is also inhibited by low temperatures in that utilization of carbon dioxide, but not of light, decreases as temperature decreases. This is generally not a consideration for marine aquarists, but one might try increasing temperature a few degrees if particular algae are not surviving well.

Different species of algae have different requirements for intensities and wavelengths of light. These differing needs are demonstrated by the usual occurrence of red algae in deep water, down to 125 meters (low light levels); brown algae at mid-depths, to 26 meters (moderate light levels); and green algae near the surface, only down to 10 meters (high light levels). Intensity and wavelength of light vary considerably at different depths and in different water quality, thus the occurrence of different species of algae varies with depth and placement (light or shadow) on the reef.

In non-technical language, the general term chlorophyll refers to the chloroplast pigments that allow a plant to capture the energy of light and use this energy in the reduction of carbon dioxide for the manufacture of carbohydrates. Things are not quite this simple, however. There are over 30 different pigments in four main classes: chlorophylls (types a, b, c, and d), biliproteins, carotenes, and xanthophylls that function in various ways in photosynthesis in algae. They are present (in different amounts) or absent in various algae. It is the types and amounts of pigments present in each algae that determines the intensity and wavelengths of light that are best suited to that particular algae. Table 4 presents a summary of pigments and light requirements of the major groups of algae.

This information is useful to the average marine aquarist in only a general way. There is a wide variation in the light requirements of the different species in each major group, and possibly even more important, plants of the same species may be adapted to different light intensities and different spectra depending on their place of origin. Some red algae, for example, reach light saturation at lux levels above 20,000 lux, although most others are light saturated at less than 2,000 lux. Various blue-green algae grow under a broad range of light levels. Some brown algae are often found in shallow tropical waters, less than 5 meters, where light intensities are quite high. Species of brown algae from shallow waters, in genera such as *Sargassum, Dictyota, Laminaria,* and *Padina,* should be interesting in marine aquariums when we learn to grow them properly. When it comes to propagation of marine algae in modern marine aquariums, we have barely scratched the surface of a vast and fascinating world.

Padina vickersiae

Table 4. Algal Pigments and Light Requirements in Artificial Culture

Taxon	Chlorophylls	Carotenes	Xanthophylls	Phycobilins	Light
Cyanophyta (blue-green algaes)	a	B	8 types	phycocyanin phycoerythrin	low to high
Chlorophyta (green algaes) Acetabularia Caulerpa Penicillus Ulva Halimeda Boodlea Valonia Codium	a, b	A, B	Astaxanthin Lutein Neoxanthin Violaxanthin Zeaxanthin		high, 13,000 to 20,000 lux
Bacillariophyta (diatoms)	a, b	A, B	Diadinoxanthin Diatoxanthin Fucoxanthin		variable
Phaeophyta (brown algaes) kelp Padina Dictyota Sargassum	a, b	A, B	Flavoxanthin Fucoxanthin Lutein Violaxanthin		moderate 5000 to 12,000 lux
Rhodohpyta (red algaes) Chondrus Euchema Rhodochorton	a, d	A, B		Phycocyanin Phycoerythrin	generally low, 2000 to 10,000 lux

Sources: Bogorad (1962), Homes (1957), Spotte (1979).

In the general practice of keeping a marine aquarium, especially in keeping corals, anemones, and algaes, the important thing is to provide lighting that will suit at least the minimal needs of a wide variety of organisms. Even though surface light intensities over coral reefs and other tropical areas are very high, underwater light intensities rapidly decline as sunlight is absorbed and scattered down through the water column. Except for some organisms collected on shallow flats in only a few feet of clear water, most marine plants and animals, even those from clear tropical seas, are adapted to light intensities far below surface incident sunlight and well within reach of the modern marine aquarist. Getting the proper light levels for a particular type of marine system does require some thought and planning, however. Keep in mind that as far as growth of algae and corals is concerned, it is more meaningful to consider average daily illumination rather than peak noontime light intensities. As long as light intensity is above the compensation point and not too far below the point of light saturation, 12 to 14 hours of lower light intensity is more useful to the algae than a just a few hours of high intensity light.

Growing and maintaining marine algae is new to most marine aquarists. Once lighting is correct, there are other water quality considerations, which include presence and quantity of nutrients, calcium carbonate, trace elements, and carbon dioxide, as well as the better known parameters of salinity, temperature, and pH. The most commonly grown marine algae are in the genus *Caulerpa*. The caulerpas are green algae in the family Caulerpaceae. The thallus consists of erect green blades (also called assimilators), horizontal green stems (stipes), and transparent rhizoids (holdfasts) that serve as roots. Fragmentation is the principal method of reproduction, although gametes (male and female sex cells) are also produced. The gametes are formed throughout the plant rather than in specially modified structures such as the flowers of higher plants. The plants often "self destruct" when sexual reproduction occurs. Tiny colorless hairs, superficial gelatinous papillae, form on the stems and blades; and gametes and cytoplasm are ejected leaving a transparent husk behind. Although not all portions of the plant are affected at the same time, it is possible for most of the *Caulerpa* algae of the same species in a marine aquarium system to undergo sexual reproduction at the same time.

Algae of *Caulerpa* sp. occasionally die back from time to time in the natural marine environment as well as in marine aquarium systems. The stems and blades turn white and begin to disintegrate, a condition that brings out the worries in many a marine aquarist. There is no one particular cause for this condition. White portions of plants should be removed from the system as noticed and strong growths of *Caulerpa* should be trimmed frequently. The diebacks may be associated with reproduction, nitrate increase, depletion of trace elements (organic and inorganic) or certain nutrients, and in nature, changes in temperature. In the Florida Keys, many species of *Caulerpa* occupy the same areas in spring and fall, but are not present as observable growths in the cold of winter or the high heat of summer. Calcareous algae in the genus *Halimeda* are

Halimeda discoidea

also popular in reef tank systems. These small, green, disk shaped algae contain large amounts of calcium in their structure and require constant high levels of calcium carbonate in the system water. They are an excellent algae for marine reef systems.

Many macroalgae assimilate nitrogen in the form of ammonia rather than as nitrite or nitrate, and elevated nitrate levels are generally detrimental. Lack of carbon dioxide in the water may also cause dieback, but more likely may bring on sexual reproductive activity or retard growth. Conditions that occur periodically and retard growth are often indicated in patterns of uneven growth displayed by the algae. A high redox potential is important, and decrease in redox potential and pH indicates accumulation of organics that can trigger algae dieback. A partial water change is also usually beneficial when growth problems are evident.

Marine Animals

Animals are the most important occupants of marine aquariums, at least as far as most marine aquarists are concerned. When most folk think of marine animals the ones that come to mind are whales, sharks, tuna, tropical fish of course, lobsters, crabs, octopus, and other big, "animal-like" creatures. The invertebrate aquarium expands a lot of our ideas about the nature of marine animals. On land, we are most familiar with animals that crawl, walk, run, and fly. In a marine aquarium, however, we also have animals that slink, squirm, wiggle, bloom, and even those that just sit and grow. Eyes and legs, and

Eucidaris tribuloides
The slate-pencil urchin.

fins and tails are not all that important to many of the animals found in marine aquariums. The diversity of life on Earth is nowhere so apparent in so small a space as in a marine invertebrate aquarium. Refer to Part III of this book to begin the process of classification and identification of the invertebrates that may occur in marine aquarium systems.

In nature, the animals that inhabit a specific area are the animals that can survive there by adapting to the physical and chemical parameters of the particular environment, that can find adequate food, and that can avoid predation. They occur in that particular area because of larval transport and settlement, juvenile or adult movement, or as a result of colonial growth or *in situ* reproduction. In captivity, the animals that inhabit a marine aquarium system are the animals that can survive there by adapting to the physical and chemical parameters of the environment, that can find adequate food, and that can avoid predation. They occur there as a result of colonial growth or *in situ* reproduction, or because an aquarist purposely or inadvertently placed them in the tank. In an invertebrate tank, especially a reef type tank, many animals are placed in the tank without the direct knowledge of the aquarist.

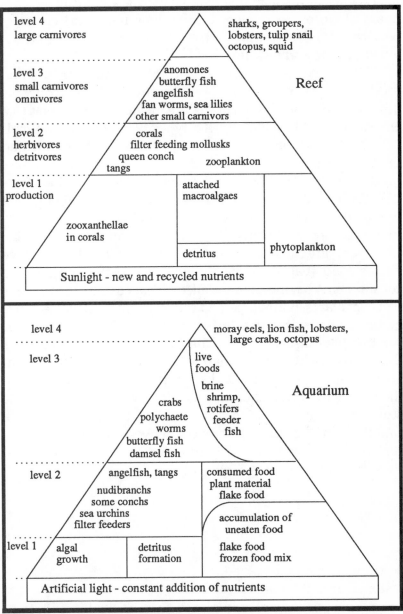

Figure 12. The trophic structure of coral reefs and marine aquarium systems.

Real appreciation of an invertebrate marine aquarium requires hours of close observation to learn how these odd creatures behave, to find new, unexpected occupants, and to figure out what they are and how they live.

Marine ecologists often refer to the trophic structure and food webs of a particular environment. These concepts describe the relationships of the organisms that inhabitat that environment. They identify the types of plants and animals that live within an environment and describe the kind and numbers of plants at the base of the food chain (the **primary producers**); the herbivorous animals that feed on the plants (the **primary consumers**); and the carnivorous animals that feed on the herbivores (the **secondary and tertiary consumers**). In natural environments, the primary producers determine how much life can exist in that environment, for they produce all the food that is ultimately available to the animals, the consumers. A balance, the so called "Balance of Nature", exists between plants, herbivores, and carnivores. This delicate dance of populations is orchestrated by availability of nutrients, weather patterns, biological evolution, and, relatively recently, the activity of humans. A marine aquarium is an artificial environment. It is created and controlled by an aquarist. Although each marine aquarium has its own particular trophic structure, dependent on the care and intent of the aquarist, we can illustrate the major differences between the trophic structure of a coral reef and a marine aquarium with a typical trophic energy pyramid, Figure 12.

Part II

Marine Aquarium Systems

Techniques and technology

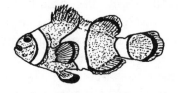

How does a marine aquarium do what it does?

Basically, a marine aquarium is a container of sea water, including associated filters and other water processing mechanisms, that provides life support for a finite number of living marine organisms.

A marine aquarium is subjected to the accumulation of metabolic wastes released from these organisms and can maintain them alive without water change for only a certain period of time. All things considered, there are two basic factors that determine the length of the closed system period (time between water changes) of all marine aquarium systems. It is the relationship between these two factors, controlled by the aquarist, that determines the success or failure of every marine aquarium. These are **BIOLOGICAL LOAD** and **FILTRATION**. Figure 1 illustrates the general relationship between these basic factors. As the amount of life, the biological load, in the system increases, the length of time that the system can support that life decreases.

Given proper food, light, temperature, and a *constant* exchange of clean, oxygenated seawater, life in an aquarium could theoretically exist indefinitely. In the absence of continuous water exchange, however, the life span of the system is controlled by filtration. The better the water filtration, the lower the biological load; and the broader the balance between plant and animal life, the longer the system can exist without a water exchange. As the biological load increases, the life span of the system decreases. A bucket of sea water with an air stone may keep two small fish alive for a week, but fifty fish may live for only a day. With filtration, the life span of the system can be greatly extended, and the more effective the filtration and the lighter the biological load, the longer the time between water changes. Eventual water exchange, even under conditions of extraordinary filtration, careful maintenance, trace element adjustment, light biological loads, and strong plant growth, is a requirement for almost all closed marine aquarium systems.

Some carefully balanced and maintained systems may be able to exist for a number of years without removal of old salt water and addition of new salt water, but eventual water exchange benefits the system. Note that addition of fresh water to replace water lost to evaporation has some of the salubrious effects of water change—replacement of some minerals lost in biological activity, for example.

Filtration is the fulcrum of a balanced marine aquarium system. Balanced means that the filtration systems of the aquarium are able to maintain the essential chemical parameters of water quality within a range that allows the organisms in the aquarium to continue to live. There are now many systems, techniques, types of filtration, and water processing devices available to the marine aquarist, and all have a place depending on the design and purpose of the particular marine aquarium system. Note that it is not neces- sary to spend hundreds or thousands of dollars to create a successful and satisifying marine aquarium. Although expen- sive, commercially available equipment makes it fairly easy to create and care for a miniature coral reef in your own home; the horizons of a marine aquarist are more limited by imagination and dedication than by money.

Part II of this book will not tell you exactly what you need for your particular system. Only you can determine this. Neither will it evaluate various designs and brands of aquarium equipment; there is far too much on the market to take on such a task. It will, however, provide information on the basic functions of the equipment found in many modern marine aquarium systems so that you can design or choose a system that will suit your particular purpose and budget.

Is this a great hobby, or what? A marine aquarist is part scientist (marine biologist, ecologist, taxonomist, algologist, chemist, nutritionist, physicist), part engineer (hydraulic, electrical, construction), and also part craftsman, part artist, part interior decorator, part poet, and part plumber. In addi- tion, other interests such as diving, boating, shell collecting, and beach combing often find a focus in a marine aquarium.

One can work with all of these facets of the hobby, or specialize in just one area. One can personally construct much of the equipment associated with a marine aquarium system or buy it all ready made. A system can be simple and basic or complex and high tech, off the shelf or custom throughout. Either way, all observant aquarists have the opportunity to push back some of the frontiers of the hobby and even contribute in many ways to marine science.

One of the most interesting things about keeping marine aquarium systems is that the aquarist is dealing with dynamic, ever changing, miniature marine ecosystems. The subtle responses of these ecosystems to the manipulations of the aquarist vary from system to system and time to time within the same system. So when all is said and done, the aquarist has only knowledge of the fundamentals and personal experience to guide him or her through the development and maintenance of a marine aquarium system. So beware of inflexible attitudes and "always" statements, for your experience may be the exception to the rule.

The first thing is to understand how the basic elements of marine systems work. Chapter 4 looks at the individual elements that can be a part of a marine aquarium system and describes how they function. Chapter 5 looks at types of entire systems, their design and the elements that compose them. Food and feeding methods and techniques for invertebrates are covered in Chapter 6. For those that construct and customize their equipment and maintenance tools, Dewey (1986) has compiled a very useful volume titled *For What It's Worth* that contains detailed tips on construction and maintenance gleaned from hobbyist's contributions to *Fresh Water and Marine Aquarium Magazine* over many years. A wealth of practical tips for the marine hobbyist is contained in that volume. And for the advanced, high tech reef aquarist, the recent books by Albert Thiel (1988, 1989) contain valuable technical detail on operation and maintenance of marine reef system equipment.

Chapter 4

Elements of Marine Aquarium Systems

Back in the 1950's and early 60's, setting up and running a marine aquarium was sort of like giving a blood transfusion in the days before discovery of the Rh factor. Sometimes it worked, often it didn't, and the aquarist never really knew why it was or wasn't successful. Nevertheless, the basic tools for successful marine aquarium keeping were under development during this period. Marine aquariums were very unusual during the 50's and early 60's. The popular books at that time, Axelrod and Schultz (1955) for example, had only a few paragraphs or a page or two on marine aquariums and made no mention of biological filtration. Simkatis (1958), one of the first modern books exclusively on marine aquaria, vaguely mentioned biological filtration in connection with use of sub-sand (undergravel) filters and gave it faint praise while recommending more strongly the newly developed box type, power filters that were located within the tank.

Of course, a power filter alone can not successfully maintain marine fish until nitrifying bacteria are established on the tank and filter substrates. Straughan (1964), praised the technique of undergravel (biological) filtration, but presented no technical understanding of why it worked. Good quality artificial sea salts were also beginning to be available about this time, and all glass tanks built with silicone sealer were soon manufactured commercially. R.P.L Straughan (1969) claimed to be the first to build an all glass aquarium with silicone sealer and this may well have been the origin of the all glass tank. At any rate, the vast superiority of silicone all glass tanks was demonstrated in the mid 60's. Popular literature began to catch up with scientific information on nitrification during the 60's, and as the nitrogen cycle within marine aquaria became common knowledge and simple test kits for ammonia and nitrite were developed, the stage was set for the marine aquarium explosion.

The techniques developed during the 60's and 70's became the basis for the "traditional" or "conventional" marine aquarium system as it exists today. Spotte (1970, 1973 and 1979), de Graaf (1973), Kingsford (1975), Moe (1982), Bower (1983), Melzak (1984) and Lundegaard (1985) along with two or three good magazines were, and are, a few of the important references to this technology for the hobbyist.

One can easily keep many marine fish and invertebrates with these traditional methods and equipment and achieve success beyond the wildest dreams of the hobbyists of the 50's and 60's. (Well, maybe not the wildest dreams of the wildest hobbyists, but certainly beyond their realistic expectations!) Now, in the late 80's, new technologies are emerging that are fueling a new explosion in the marine aquarium hobby. It is possible to keep, and even grow, macroalgae and some corals in a home marine aquarium system. These organisms and some other species that require a "pure" water quality and light intense enough to power photosynthesis can be maintained in marine systems that include the new techniques of filtration and lighting. Advanced hobbyists and professional aquarists are learning the particular water quality requirements demanded by corals and other reef invertebrates and how to supply these requirements in small marine systems. Other species that can be easily maintained by traditional methods are stronger and healthier when kept under these new systems.

Aquarium System Structures

Aquariums

This is also called the "tank", and it is the structure that defines the entire system. The size, shape, and construction can be standard or custom. Most custom systems use a standard aquarium and modify it to suit the requirements of a specialized filtration system, a particular environmental display design, and/or custom installation. Tanks are almost always constructed of plate glass, occasionally from acrylic plastic resin (Plexiglas® and Lucite® are acrylic resins), plywood, fiberglass, and concrete. I have built and used tanks in all these categories, and each medium has its applications. Before the all glass tank came into use in the mid 60's, most aquariums were constructed of four glass sides, a slate bottom, and a metal frame. The glass sides and slate bottom were held into the metal frame with a resilient aquarium putty. These were acceptable for fresh water use, but were often toxic and corrosive when used as salt water aquariums. There are many different types of marine aquarium systems available to build or buy these days. Note that building one's own marine aquarium system from the tank up is not a task to begin without careful planning and critical assessment of one's skills as a construction engineer. The following comments may be of help in the decision to build or buy various types of tanks and aquarium systems.

Glass

Most marine aquarium tanks are made of glass plates held together with silicone sealer. This sealer has an amazingly strong adhesion to the smooth, hard surface of glass and remains pliable when cured so the flexing of the tank as it is filled and emptied does not disrupt the seal. Tanks so constructed last many years. All glass aquariums that I built 17 years ago are still in commercial service. Most homemade tanks have a bead of silicone sealer filling the corners of the tank. Most commercially made tanks have little, if any, silicone fill in the internal corners of the tank. In a homemade tank, where the lay of the silicone sealer on the edge may not be a smooth, bubble free bead, and the glass sides and ends may not be cut exactly square, the corner fill is extra insurance against a leak. In a good commercially made tank, the glass is exactly square and exactly the proper amount of sealer is applied in exactly the proper place, and no corner fill is necessary to prevent leaks. The joint between the end of one side or bottom and the flat side of another pane should be smooth, clear, tightly together along the entire length of the joint, and show no bubbles or separations.

When buying an all glass aquarium, especially a large one, check all the joints to make sure that all glass cuts are absolutely square and that all seals are clear and complete. Also check to make sure the seals at the joints have not been disrupted by breaks and chips along the glass edges. It isn't hard to build an all glass aquarium, especially one 50 gallons or less. All glass tanks are also not particularly expensive so the saving on building rather than buying is not very great, unless you get an exceptionally good deal on the glass. If building your own tank is an important part of your marine aquarium experience, then refer to Moe (1982) and Dewey (1986) for instructions on how to build all glass tanks.

One important modification to glass tanks that is quite commonly done for reef type filtration installations and multi tank systems is drilling a hole in the side or bottom for a drain fitting. This task requires skill and experience and unless you are willing to acquire the tools—electric drills, silicone carbide grit, and brass glass drilling bits—and are willing to practice to acquire the skill, it is best to put an expensive piece of glass in the hands of a professional glass worker. Dewey (1986) and Birdsill (1988) discuss the process of drilling holes in glass aquaria in detail.

Acrylic plastic (Plexiglas®, Lucite®)

Large and small tanks can be constructed from acrylic plastics. The advantages are that the material is lighter and can withstand shock without breaking much better than glass, and it can be easily worked with drills and saws. It is, however, more expensive, and it can be more difficult to build a water tight container unless one possess considerable skill in cutting and bonding these plastics. Acrylic plastic can also be scratched more easily than glass, and care must be taken to clean it carefully without abrasive cleaners before and after it is put in use. Acrylics are used extensively for intricately constructed commercial systems that are subjected to hard public use or for aquariums in service in public bars and restaurants.

Acrylic plastics can also be formed into unusual shapes—bubbles, tubes, cylinders, hexagons, octagons, pentagons, and spheres—and can be used to install aquariums into bars and tables where glass could be dangerous. Acrylics have also found wide use in construction of trickle filters and other system components because they can be worked so much easier than glass and construction is lighter and safer.

Plywood

Many a large homemade tank and commercial system has been made of plywood. Properly constructed and sealed, plywood tanks can provide years of service. When built into a wall or cabinet by an accomplished craftsman, a custom installation constructed of plywood can be a polished and spectacular marine display. Plywood construction is probably the easiest and most inexpensive way that a handy hobbyist can construct a large (100 to 500 gallon) tank. Properly joined and braced, plywood can support a large volume of water, and drilling and fitting drains, filter boxes, and compartments are no problem. Dewey (1986) presents two articles that describe the construction of plywood tanks in great detail and Neelon (1987) also gives detailed instructions on construction of a 240 gallon plywood tank. I have used large plywood tanks for many years in commercial operations with great success.

Marine grade plywood and an epoxy based glue make a strong tank that will not deteriorate in a moist environment. The most important consideration in construction of plywood tanks, after making sure that it is braced well enough to support the weight and pressure of the water, of course, is to keep the water from any contact with the wood. A good, food grade (non-toxic) epoxy paint usually provides a proper seal. The epoxy paint must be the type that mixes two volumes, a resin and a hardener (activator or catalyst). Apply at least three coats for best results. Fiberglass resin can also be used to seal the wood, but when used without fiberglass mat or fiber, it has a tendency to crack and allow water to seep behind it into the wood. If the tank is to be a display aquarium, an oval or rectangular cutout is made in one side (before painting, of course) for the glass, which is sealed in place on the inside of the tank with silicone sealer (after painting, of course). The silicone seals well against the epoxy painted surface. The interior of the tank can be left with just the epoxy paint surface or, for greater protection against water penetration and leakage, the interior can be finished with laminated plastic (Formica®), or Plexiglas® sheets sealed at all joints with silicone sealer.

Fiberglass
A lot of amazing things can be built from fiberglass. As with acrylics, special tools and skills are necessary. Fiberglass tanks are usually built over a mold. The mold is carefully and specially built, and can be used to fabricate many identical tanks. In fact, the expense of constructing the mold is not recovered unless many tanks are made from it. Most fiberglass aquariums are made from tanks that were fabricated for another purpose. A cutout is made on one long side, a piece of glass set in place with silicone sealer, and a functional aquarium is quickly created. These are usually not tanks for the living room, but they have uses as commercial and supplemental tanks.
Coral replicas, simulated rock walls, ledges and caves can all be made from fiberglass. Spotte (1973) describes how to make rubber molds from coral and then make fiberglass casts

from these molds. Mixing sand with fiberglass resin (wear rubber gloves) also allows one to make various types of structures that can enhance an aquarium. I have seen fiberglass structures built inside onto the back glass of small glass tanks (30 to 100 gallons) that simulate ledges, cliffs, and caves. These structures allow anemones to reside near the surface where light intensity is highest, give other organisms a shaded environment and, in general, create an unusual and functional depth to an ordinary aquarium.

Concrete

Now we're talking big tanks, 1000 gallons or more, and rather stationary structures. Put a 3000 gallon concrete tank in your garage, with a skylight above it, that views from your living room, and you have a really spectacular display and, quite possibly, a real estate agent's nightmare. Small tanks can also be made of cement. I made a 30 gallon tank once by filling a framework of chicken wire with cement. It was cheap, strong, sturdy, and quite heavy! Planning is important when working in concrete. Drains and sloped floors can't be decided upon after construction. Either cement block masonry or poured concrete construction can be used. When completed, the interior surfaces must be protected. The food grade, epoxy paint also works well on concrete. Three or four coats are required. If you want to build a tank like this, I suggest that a good bit of research into construction techniques and the experiences of public aquariums is in order.

Water

There are two sources of saltwater for a marine aquarium system, natural seawater or artificial seawater. Refer to Chapter 3 in Moe (1982) for detailed descriptions of collection and processing of natural seawater and the makeup of artificial seawater from tap water and a commercial synthetic sea salt mix. Natural seawater works very well in captive marine systems, but there is always the risk of industrial and organic pollution, parasites, and a salinity that is too high or too low at the time the water is collected. Unless one lives quite close to the ocean, the preferred source of saltwater will be tap water and a sea salt mix. The brand your dealer recommends will probably be quite satisfactory. Always use plastic, never metal, containers and buckets when mixing and storing seawater for use in a marine aquarium.

A most important consideration in the makeup of artificial seawater is the quality of the tap water. In most situations there should be negligible contamination from heavy metals, detergents, and other pollutants. If there is any question on the quality of the tap water, however, check it out, especially if you draw from a well and there's a landfill in the area. Call the municipal water supply and ask for an analysis of the tap water. If they can't, or if they refuse to give you this information, there may be a larger problem than just what will happen to captive fish and invertebrates. The amounts of everything from antimony to zirconium plus organics should be below the Maximum Acceptable Concentrations (MAC).

The Environmental Protection Agency (EPA) has set upper limits on heavy metals in drinking water: lead, 50 ppb; copper, 1 ppm; and zinc, 5 ppm. High levels of these heavy metals can cause serious problems with freshwater and marine fish. Also, never use lead weights in a closed marine system, especially systems that receive few water changes and house delicate fish and invertebrates. Lead will erode over time in seawater and increase the lead content of the water, especially in systems treated with copper. Perhaps the easiest thing to do, whether or not there is a problem, is to run the tap water through an activated carbon filter. If the water is exposed to activated carbon for a long enough period of time, it can remove chlorine, chloramine, and many other compounds.

Further treatment may not even be necessary, but this depends on many variables such as the type and age of the activated carbon, the condition of the water, and the flow rate. The best quality fresh water can be made from tap water by using a reverse osmosis process to prepare the water for the marine system. Using reverse osmosis to prepare the evaporation make up water prevents repeated introductions of any nutrients or toxins that may be present in very low levels in the tap water.

It's easy to make an effective, inexpensive carbon filter from PVC pipe that can be hooked up to a tap. Figure 13 illustrates one possible configuration for such a filter. The more slowly the water runs through the filter, the more effective the filtration. Running water at a rate of about one gallon per minute through a volume of activated carbon of about two liters (2.2 pints or 62 cubic inches or a 20 inch long, 2 inch diameter pipe) will clean almost all tap water.

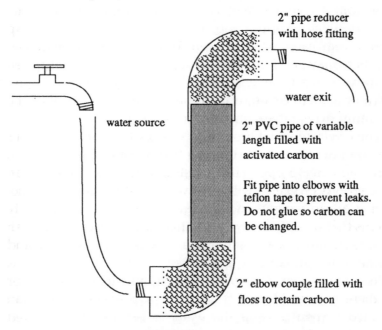

Figure 13. Carbon filter for tap water. Fill the bottom elbow with fiber floss. Fit the pipe section tightly into the bottom elbow. Fill the pipe with activiated carbon. Place floss into the upper elbow and filt it onto the pipe. Secure the pipe in an upright position. Attach hoses and flow water slowly through the carbon filter. Do not glue elbows to pipe so that carbon can be changed. Control water flow with valve on inlet side of filter.

Chloramine, however, may be a very persistent problem. Many community water supplies began switching from just chlorination to chloramination of water in the early 80's. This is complex chemistry (chloride ions, hypochlorous acid, trihalomethane, monochloramine, dichloramine, and trichloramine), but very important to aquarists. Moe (1982) has a brief discussion on chloramination of tap water and Blasiola (1984) presents a detailed account of the chemistry, toxicity, and removal of chloramines from tap water. The important points, however, are that water companies are now adding ammonia as well as chlorine to the water supplies. The ammonia combines with the chlorine to form chloramine. Chloramine may be a better water treatment than just free chlorine because it keeps a more stable level of germ killing hypochlorous acid in the water, reduces chlorine odor, and prevents formation of suspected cancer causing trihalomethane. Although this may be good for human use of the water, the stable chloramine is toxic to fish and other aquatic life as well as to bacteria and viruses. Since chloramine does not readily leave the water, concentrations may increase as tap water is added to systems to make up for evaporation, although a significant increase is unlikely in indoor systems with limited evaporation.

Removal of chloramine is not difficult and should be done when the system is set up with fresh water before the salt mix is added. Passing the water through the activated carbon filter described above may or may not solve the problem. It depends on how much chloramine is in the water and the condition and amount of the activated carbon.

The recommended procedure is to first treat the water with an effective dechlorinator, a solution of sodium thiosulfate. This breaks up the chloramine, removes the chlorine, and liberates the ammonia. It takes a good dose of dechlorinator to do this, so be sure to use the amount recommended by the manufacturer of the dechlorinator. Then test the water with an OTO chlorine test kit after 10 or 15 minutes to confirm that all the chlorine is gone from the water. If not, retreat with dechlorinator and test again. It is important to keep the water under aeration during this procedure. When the chlorine is gone, the ammonia remains. Ammonia will escape from the water over time if the water is aerated. A quicker, better way to remove the ammonia is to filter the water through zeolite, a natural clay that can remove ammonia from *fresh* water. It is particularly important to remove ammonia from water intended for marine aquariums since more of the ammonia (almost 10% at pH 8) is in the toxic un-ionized form at the higher pH of marine systems. After filtering the water through zeolite (available at aquarium shops), remove the zeolite from the filter and replace it with activated carbon. Run the water through activated carbon overnight or for a few hours, test again for chlorine and ammonia, and then add the salt mix.

Synthetic salt mixes come in packages in amounts designated to make up a particular number of gallons of salt water at a salinity determined by the manufacturer. When doing a partial water change, an aquarist may not wish to make up an entire package of 10, 20, or 50 gallons and store the surplus as a salt solution in a plastic container. The following simple mathematical procedure is detailed for those of you that still haven't recovered from 8th grade general math story problems.

First of all we have to determine how much water to remove from the system. Unless you have an exceptionally large reservoir in the system, this can be done from the tank. Ten or, at the most, twenty percent is usually all the water change necessary unless nitrate is very high (80 to 100 ppm). If water changes haven't been done in some time and nitrate levels are high, several 10 percent changes over a period of a week or so is easier on the invertebrates than one 50 percent change. The volume of water in external filters is usually not enough to be considered, but a percentage of any external tank volume can be added to the amount removed.

First top the tank off with fresh water if there has been evaporation loss. If you know the volume of water in the system, determine how many gallons represent 10 percent, remove this amount and then replace it with pre mixed salt water. If you don't know the volume of water in the tank

system, or want to place a mark on the tank side to show the
drain down point rather than measure the number of gallons
removed, then this can be done with a ruler. Measure the distance from the normal water level to the bottom of the tank.
Let's say this is 20 inches. Then multiply the height by 0.20 if
you want a 20 % change (4 inches), 0.10 for 10% (2 inches) or .25
for a 25% change (5 inches). Then measure down the tank from
the top to the inch that marks the percentage change you desire,
4 inches in a tank that is 20 inches high. A small permanent
mark on the back of the tank at the 10 percent point will save
time and trouble on future water changes.

Now we have to figure out how much water is removed
when the tank is drained down to the mark. There are two
ways. One, siphon the water from the tank and measure it in a
marked bucket. If a marked bucket is not available, use gallon
jugs to fill a bucket and mark each gallon level with a permanent felt marker pen. The number of gallons removed from
the tank will be known to at least the nearest half gallon. Two,
if the tank is square or rectangular, measure the length and
width and multiply to get the square inches of surface area.
Then multiply by the number of inches of water you plan to
remove to get the volume of water in cubic inches that will be
removed. Then divide the cubic inches of water by 231 to
calculate the number of gallons that will be taken from the tank.

$$\frac{\text{tank length x tank width x depth of water removed in inches}}{\text{divided by 231}} = \text{gallons removed}$$

If you have a 40 gallon tank, one that measures about 36"
long by 12.5" wide by 21" high, and 4 inches of water is
removed, this will be a total of 1,800 cubic inches or about 7.8,
rounded off to 8, gallons that must be replaced with new salt
water.

This formula does not work on tanks that are round,
hexagonal or half hex. In these cases you have to use the formula for the area of a circle or calculate the volume of the
missing triangles in a hexagonal or half hexagonal tank and
subtract them from the total. (The easy way is to just measure

the amount of water removed from the tank.) The weights and measures page in the back of this book has a formula for calculating the volume of hexagonal tanks with sides of even width.

Now all we have to do is calculate how much salt mix to add to the volume of water we have to replace in the tank. In the example above, we have to add 8 gallons of new saltwater to exchange 20% of the tank. We may have a package of salt mix that makes up 10, 25, 50 or even 150 gallons of salt water. If the weight of the package is not listed on the label, the first thing to do is to weigh the entire bag. Then divide the weight of the bag by the number of gallons of saltwater it is designed to prepare. The result of that calculation will be the number of pounds of salt required to make up one gallon of saltwater. This should be somewhere between 0.25 and 0.3 pounds. Assuming that 0.27 pounds per gallon is required, 2.2 pounds of salt must be dissolved in 8 gallons of water for this particular water change. Weigh out 2.2 pounds and dissolve it in a bucket of water. After it is completely dissolved it can be added to the tank along with enough water to make up the total 8 gallons required. It is best to make up the new salt water the day before the exchange and let it aerate in a container overnight. It is also wise to use a hydrometer to make sure that the salinity, measured as specific gravity, in the system is within the proper range for the tank, usually 1.020 to 1.026. Refer to Chapter 1 for additional information on seawater and see Moe (1982) for a complete discussion of salinity and specific gravity of seawater.

Water Quality

A marine aquarium system, especially invertebrate tanks and reef type systems, must have and maintain high water quality to keep marine plants and animals in optimum condition. Sure, that's easy to say, but just what does "high water quality" mean? Obviously, "high water quality" is a relative term. What is high or adequate for one environment or one

system may be poor or unacceptable in another situation. The
important thing is to have an understanding of the elements,
units, and values that are used to define water quality; for then
one can move the system toward the water quality standards
that are acceptable to the purpose of the system. The following
table provides an information capsule on marine system water
quality. Listing an "acceptable" value or range may be a point
of some contention.

Table 5. Water quality trends and values

element	natural trend in system water	optimum value	acceptable value or range
salinity	increase	1.024 SG (32 ‰)	1.020 - 1.026 SG (28 - 35 ‰)
temperature	variable	78°F (25.6°C)	75 - 82°F (24 - 28°C)
redox potential	decrease	325 - 350 mv	250 - 400 mv
alkalinity	decrease	4 meq/l	2 - 6 meq/l
carbonate hardness	decrease	12 dKH	5 - 20 dKH
pH	decrease	8.2	7.8 - 8.4
oxygen	decrease	5.5 ppm	4.0 - 7.0 ppm
phosphates	increase	1.0 ppm	0.0 - 3.0 ppm
ammonia	increase	0.0 ppm	0.1 - 1.0 ppm
nitrite	increase	0.0 ppm	1.0 - 3.0 ppm
nitrate	increase	0.0 - 5.0 ppm	5.0 - 50.0 ppm
copper	decrease	0.2 - 0.3 ppm, fish treatment only not for use in invertebrate tanks	
trace elements	decrease	variable, timed replacement	
turbidity	increase	low turbidity, high water clarity desirable	
carbon dioxide	increase	value tied to pH, 8.2 indicates acceptable CO_2 level for typical marine systems. 3 to 5 ppm for algae systems.	
total organics	increase	no common inclusive measure, total nitrogen could be used.	
bacteria	increase	usually TNC (too numerous to count) In aquarium water, species more important than number.	

What is acceptable to one aquarist for a particular system may not be acceptable to another. The intent is not to pontificate optimum and acceptable values that are always right in all situations, but rather to provide a general guide until actual experience gives the aquarist the operating values that best suit a particular system. The natural trend is the direction, increase or decrease, for the particular element in the water of a marine system when no effort is made to counteract the natural tendencies of a closed system. The proper trend, the movement toward a healthy system, is usually the opposite of the general or natural trend.

Aeration

Aeration, the mixing of air and water, is very important to marine aquariums. In many systems it powers the movement of water through biological filters and provides the turbulent turnover of water in the aquarium itself. This exposes a constantly changing air/water surface interface through which the major exchange of gasses, primarily oxygen and carbon dioxide, takes place. Air lift tubes, protein foam skimmers, free air releases in the tank, tiny divers, and treasure chests are also powered by aeration. In the early days of keeping aquaria, before electrically powered pumps, aeration was accomplished by occasional dipping of hands and cups into the tank and manually stirring the water around. Aquarists were severely limited in those days.

We now have three basic methods of mixing air and water:

- Injection of air into the water by pumping air under pressure—an air pump.

- Drawing air into pumped water—a venturi apparatus.

- Mixing air into water as the water tumbles or sprays over a structure—a trickle filter.

Air pumps

If an aquarium system does not utilize a water pump, compressed air is solely responsible for water movement and gas exchange. Most systems, however, have an undergravel filter powered by compressed air and an external filter system powered by a water pump. Either way, the air pump is a very critical part of the system. The two types of air pumps generally available to the hobbyist are the vibrator pump and the piston pump. Good brands of each type are reliable and will do a good job.

There are two measurements on output from an air pump, volume and pressure. Generally, high volume is achieved with large diameter air system tubes at lower pressure while higher pressure means a lower volume delivered through smaller pipes. In most hobbyist applications, the size of the tubing from the pump to the release is determined by the standard size air tubing, so pressure alone determines the volume of air that moves through a single length of tubing. If a strong pump produces inadequate air from one or two air diffusers (air stones), addition of another air stone may be the best way to increase the air flow to a deep tank, although raising the release in the tank lessens the back pressure and allows a greater air flow.

High pressure is important for pushing air though restricted air diffusers (clogged and/or wood or fine air stones) and for releasing air in deep tanks. High volume is important for providing air to many relatively shallow tanks and/or providing enough air for air hungry applications. Once the proper air pressure is attained for a particular application, then the volume produced becomes very important. The output in volume and pressure and the size, quality, and price of vibrator pumps is highly variable. Pressure in pounds per square inch (psi) may range from about 3 to 10 and volume in cubic inches per minute (cpm) may range from 50 to 800. Air flow is also measured in liters per hour (lph). The volume of one liter is equal to 61.024 cubic inches, so 400 cpm is equivalent to 393 lph. A cpm of 800 will run 10 to 30 tanks depending on air line plumbing, tank depth, and type of air diffusers. Pressure and volume of piston pumps varies with the size of the cylinder, the speed of the piston, and the condition of the piston seal. Output from a single, typical small piston pump is about 200 cpm. For most typical aquariums in the 50 to 75 gallon range, an output of 300 to 400 cpm at a pressure of 5 to 7 psi is adequate.

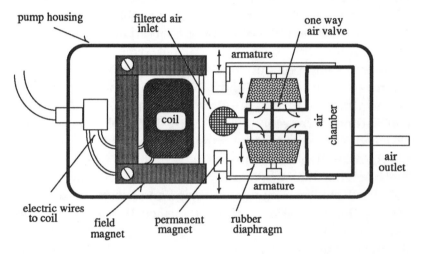

Figure 14. Internal structure of a typical, double diaphragm, vibrator air pump.

Vibrator pumps do not have a revolving electric motor that requires bearings, thus they can be made rather inexpensively. The better vibrator pumps, however, are made with high quality diaphragms, coils, and armatures and may cost as much as a piston pump. The diaphragms and armature springs are the only moving parts of vibrator pump, and if these are of good quality, the pump will provide many years of service. If the intake filters are clean and the air lines and air stones unobstructed, little or no output from a vibrator pump is usually caused by a weak or broken diaphragm or one way air valve, and these can be replaced relatively inexpensively. A good vibrator pump will put out almost as much air as a piston pump and operate with less maintenance, less heat, and less noise. When you buy an inexpensive vibrator pump be sure that the one way air valves work properly. Gently try to draw and blow air through the air outlet as you would through a straw. The one way valves in a good pump will let you draw air easily through the pump and prevent air from being blown back through the pump. Pumps that fail this simple test have faulty or inadequate valves. Figure 14 illustrates the operation of a typical, double diaphragm vibrator pump.

The coil of the vibrator pump is charged by the 60 cycle per second alternating household current. This means that the north and south poles of the electromagnet created by the coil are reversed 60 times a second. Thus, the permanent magnets on the armature springs are attracted to and repelled from the coil 30 times each second. Thus the flexible rubber diaphragms attached to these armature arms also move inward and outward, expanding and compressing, cycling 30 times a second. Although the total area of compression of the diaphragm has a very small static volume, compression and expansion occurs so rapidly that a great deal of air is pushed through the pump. One way valves on the intake and outlet of the air pump keep the air moving in only one direction. The volume of air the pump produces is dependent on the size of the compression chamber created by the movement of the diaphragm, and the air pressure is dependent on the strength of the armature springs and flexibility of the diaphragm. A good quality pump has strong springs and a sturdy diaphragm that work harder against the back pressure to maintain a strong air flow in a deep tank. Guard against too much back pressure, however, as this can deform valves and diaphragms and shorten the life of the pump.

The pistons in piston pumps move fast, but not as fast as the diaphragms in vibrator pumps. The volume of air that the piston pushes through on each stroke, however, is far greater than one compression of a diaphragm. A piston and cylinder are also strong, ridged structures and as long as little or no air leaks from the piston washer seal, a piston pump puts out a lot of air under constant high pressure. The electric motor of the piston pump revolves and a mechanical linkage pushes the piston back and forth in the cylinder. An oiled leather washer seals the air chamber between the cylinder and the piston, and one way valves regulate the flow of air in and out of the cylinder. A piston pump is a good choice for applications that require a constant high volume of air in a relatively deep water tank. Low output from a piston pump, not caused by clogged air stones, usually means that the leather washers must be reoiled or replaced.

On a piston pump, the motor whirrs and the pistons go "thucka, thucka, thucka". It's a little louder than the "buzzzz" of a vibrator pump. Both are quite noticeable in a quiet living room, but the piston pump is a little louder. Placing the pump on a 1 to 2 inch foam pad helps to considerably reduce noise from vibration, more so for a vibrator pump than a piston pump. If the vibrator pump has the air inlet on the bottom, the foam pad also acts a prefilter for the incoming air. For most installations, a good vibrator pump is quite adequate, but the choice is really the preference of the aquarist. Air pumps are not expensive and are so important to most systems that an aquarist should keep a spare pump on hand for emergencies. Even if the system relies only on water pumps, a spare air pump hooked up to a few air stones can save the tank if the water pump happens to die on a Saturday night.

Air diffusers

An air diffuser receives the output from the air pump and releases the air into the aquarium or a specialized structure. The most common of these diffusers are small cylinders or spheres of a compressed sand-like material, "air stones", although they may also be wands, blocks, rods, plates, and tubes of various porous materials as well as plastic shipwrecks, clams, and skeletons. For many applications, protein foam skimmers and large bore air lift tubes, for example, a great volume of very tiny bubbles is highly desired. High pressure and great volume of compressed air (meaning a good air pump) and an air diffuser with tiny pores is required to produce many fine bubbles.

A very good diffuser for tiny bubbles is a wooden air "stone". These are usually made of basswood, silver birch, oak, or limewood—hard woods with very fine, very straight, porous grain—and cut so that the end grain is the largest flat surface. A hole is drilled in the end of the block that extends all the way through the block almost to the other end, Figure 15. A section of rigid air tube fits tightly in place at the opening of the drilled hole. The rigid tube can not extend very far into the drilled hole or it will block the air release from part of the block. One can purchase a block of basswood and make them up with a fine saw if they can't be found in an aquarium shop. There are also air stones available made of various sizes of glass beads bonded into small cylinders that are designed to release bubbles of various sizes. These high quality stones produce a reliable air flow and do not break apart after some use. Air releasers can also be made of natural porous stone, such as pumice, by drilling a hole in a block of the stone as with a wood block. An effective air diffuser that seldom clogs but produces large bubbles can be made by sealing one end of a small section of rigid, plastic tubing and drilling a series of very fine holes around the tubing. A type of ceramic air stone is also available that can be cleaned by heating the stone (minus the plastic tubing, of course) with a propane torch and burning out organic clogs.

Sometimes, depending on the air pump and the water depth, a stone that releases medium or course bubbles is more effective than a fine bubble release. The quality of inexpensive stones often varies considerably. One may be almost blocked while another flows too freely. Good "disposable" air diffusers are also available these days.

Perhaps the greatest air thief is the clogged air diffuser. Always check the air diffuser first when working with an air release problem. Minerals are deposited on surfaces in all aquariums where air and water meet, but especially in marine aquariums. The extremely high mineral concentrations and alkaline pH of saltwater combine to deposit a hard mineral cake wherever there is an air/water interface. These mineral deposits very effectively clog up air diffusers in marine aquariums in a month or two.

Often a clogged high quality air stone can be returned to service. Sometimes just drying out the stone or wood block is enough to open the pores for additional service, but this is usually not very effective. A good stone or wood block can also be soaked in hot water and scrubbed with an old toothbrush to restore air flow. Soaking in a light solution of acid or bleach (one part liquid bleach to four parts water) and scrubbing, rinsing, and then drying them well restores high quality stones and most wood diffusers. Inexpensive stones usually break up under such treatment. Soaking in a baking soda solution before scrubbing can also be done with wooden air diffusers. Wood diffusers must be well dried before reinstallation in a skimmer or tank since the wood is swelled when wet and many pores will not reopen until it is dry.

Air scrubbers

In most situations, the filter pad or sponge that filters the intake of the air pump is quite sufficient to process the air supply for the aquarium. Under some conditions, however, it may be helpful, even advisable, to clean the air before it is pumped into a marine aquarium system. Some of the problems that can be introduced into a aquarium system through the air supply are nicotine (highly toxic) from tobacco smoke, insecticide fumes, oil particles from the atmosphere or the air pump, and fumes from paints and other chemicals. If these or other atmospheric pollutants are common in the area of the marine system, an air scrubber device that cleans the air before it enters the system is recommended. Air can be filtered by passing it through one or more of the following filters. These are a very fine particulate filter (0.02 to 1.0 microns), a column of distilled water, and a column of activated carbon. The particulate filter will remove dust, bacteria, and other fine particles. The distilled water can remove water soluble compounds such as ammonia and some fine particles, and the activated carbon removes many organic pollutants, insecticides, oil, perfumes, and solvents from the air.

A simple air scrubber that will be adequate for all but the most polluted atmospheres can be built from a one foot length of 1 to 2 inch PVC pipe and two end caps. Drill a hole in the top of each end cap and glue a short length of rigid air tubing into each hole. Fit the pipe firmly onto one cap. Don't glue it together. Fit it so that it can be tapped apart and the carbon changed every six months or so. Pack about 2 inches of filter floss into the bottom of the capped pipe; fill the pipe with activated carbon up to an inch or so from the top; fill the top of the pipe and the last cap with floss; and fit the top cap firmly on the pipe. The carbon should be packed tightly between the floss layers so that it will not slump and create an air space along the top if the filter is horizontally mounted. Air should pass through the floss and carbon with little restriction, and most pollutants will be filtered from the air as it passes through the activated carbon.

Air driers

One may wonder why anyone would want to dry the air before pumping it into a wet aquarium. Well, the only reason for drying the air is if ozone is used in the system. Ozonation greatly increases the efficiency of protein foam skimmers, increases redox potential in reef type systems, and provides a sterilizing effect on system water. High humidity, however, such as found in the air around aquarium installations, greatly decreases the efficiency of ozonizers. In fact, running an ozonizer without an air drier is like filling the gas tank of an automobile every day instead of fixing a leaky fuel line. Ozone production may drop up to 30 to 50 percent when humidity goes from 0 to 50 percent.

An air drier is a simple acrylic plastic contact tube filled with silica gel desiccating beads. An air line fitting on both ends allows air to flow freely through the tube and the silica gel beads remove the moisture from the air. The beads turn color from blue to red when they are saturated with moisture. They can be regenerated by removing them from the contact tube, placing them in a metal pan, and baking them in 200 to 250 degree oven until they turn blue again. The air drier can be constructed just the same as the activated carbon air scrubber described above; however, a transparent tube rather than a section of PVC pipe allows observation of the condition of the beads without pulling the device apart.

Venturi

A venturi is basically a tube with a one way valve that allows air to be drawn into a pipe through which pumped water is flowing, Figure 15. A great deal of air can be drawn into the water and broken up into very tiny bubbles through the action of a venturi. Most powerhead pumps have a venturi option that allows the water drawn up from beneath the under-gravel filter to be strongly aerated as it is released into the aquarium. Protein foam skimmers can also be operated by venturi and when properly designed and adjusted, their efficiency is considerably enhanced through the strong mix of air and water created by the venturi effect.

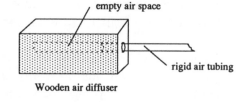

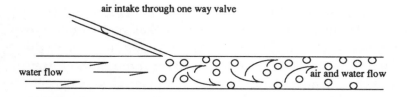

Figure 15. A wooden air diffuser and the principle of venturi operation. Both sources of fine air bubbles.

Water Movement

Like a living organism, the life of a marine aquarium system depends on its circulation, which is the flow of water through its filters and around the tank. This water flow is created by air lift and/or electrically powered water pumps. The typical pattern of water movement in a traditional marine aquarium system is to draw water slowly through the undergravel filter, lift it up the air lift tubes, and deposit it at the surface of the tank. Water movements through the tank are slow and diffuse. There are no strong currents to stimulate sessile invertebrates and distribute oxygenated water through the tank. Reef systems and powerhead powered undergravel systems produce stronger currents and provide much better circulation and water movement throughout the tank. Constant currents, however, do not produce the reciprocal surge and wave action of the reef environment. This type of water movement is very important to some types of corals and a few companies are developing new systems that provide a surge action to reef tank systems. Surge systems can be produced with "dueling powerheads" by a creative hobbyist with a timed, electronic switching apparatus or even by an automatic filling and rapid emptying of a container placed above the tank.

It is often very important to know how much water is actually being pumped through the system and how many times the volume of the system is circulated through the filters each day. The rating of a water pump in gallons per hour (gph), gallons per minute (gpm), or liters per hour (lph) is usually quite a bit greater than the actual flow that goes through the filter system. The "head" on a pump is the back pressure that the pump must overcome to push water through the system. This head is created by pushing water upward against gravity, by the friction of water passing through the pipes, and by the resistance of the filter media. Dense, small pored filter media creates a greater resistance to flow than open, large pored media. A pump that pushes water several feet upward through small pipes and dense, pressurized filter media works against a considerably greater head and pumps much less water than the same pump pushing water horizontally through large pipes and then flowing it over an open bed of filter media.

Table 6. Conversion of timed 16 oz. water flows to flow rates measured in gpm, gph, lph, and 24 hour system volume turnovers.

| seconds | | | | number of turnovers per gal. volume in 24 hours | | | | |
	gpm	gph	lph	50	75	100	125	150
1	7.50	450.0	1703	216	144	108	86	72
2	3.75	225.0	852	108	72	54	43	36
3	2.50	150.0	568	72	48	36	29	24
4	1.88	112.5	426	54	36	27	22	18
5	1.50	90.0	341	43	29	22	17	14
6	1.25	75.0	284	36	24	18	14	12
7	1.07	64.3	243	31	21	15	12	10
8	0.94	56.3	213	27	18	14	11	9.0
9	0.83	50.0	189	24	16	12	10	8.0
10	0.75	45.0	170	22	14	11	8.6	7.2
11	0.68	40.9	155	20	13	10	7.9	6.5
12	0.63	37.5	142	18	12	9.0	7.2	6.0
13	0.58	34.6	131	17	11	8.3	6.6	5.5
14	0.54	32.2	122	15	10	7.7	6.2	5.2
15	0.50	30.0	114	14	9.6	7.2	5.8	4.8
18	0.42	25.0	95	12	8.0	6.0	4.8	4.0
20	0.38	22.5	85	11	7.2	5.4	4.3	3.6
25	0.30	18.0	68	8.6	5.8	4.3	3.5	2.9
30	0.25	15.0	57	7.2	4.8	3.6	2.9	2.4
35	0.21	12.8	48	6.1	4.1	3.1	2.5	2.0
40	0.19	11.3	43	5.4	3.6	2.7	2.2	1.8

The actual amount of water moving through the system can be easily measured by counting the number of seconds required to fill a two cup measure at the output of the filter. Hold a plastic 16 oz kitchen measuring cup at the out flow of the filter system where it enters the tank and time the number of seconds it takes to fill the cup. Table 6 converts the number of seconds required to fill a 16 oz measuring cup to gph, gpm, or lph and also gives the number of daily turnovers for the volume of five typical systems for flow rates between 11 and 450 gph. Numbers of system volume turnovers per 24 hours are rounded to tenths of a volume only for turnovers of less than 10 per day. If the pump pushes water through a mechanical filter, flow rates will diminish over time as the filter clogs. Actual decrease in flow rates can be determined and the condition of the filter can be accurately determined by measuring flow rate.

Air lift pumps

An air lift pump is simply a tube that extends down into a body of water. Air is injected near the bottom of the tube and rises to the top within the tube. The mixture of air and water within the tube is lighter than the surrounding water so water enters the bottom of the tube trying to displace (float) the lighter air/water mix within the tube. As long as air enters the bottom of the tube and water can flow out of the top of the tube, a constant flow of water moves through the tube. This is the most efficient way to move water from bottom to top or to just above the surface.

The factors that affect the efficiency of an air lift pump are the diameter and length of the tube, the height of the discharge above the surface, and the volume and size of the air bubbles. The more air that is mixed with the water, the lighter the column of water and the faster the water moves upward through the tube. Bubble size and air flow volume control the amount of air in the column. Within limits, finer bubbles and greater air flows increase the efficiency of the air lift pump. This is why air lift tubes in marine aquariums that pull water through an undergravel filter must be large, one inch minimum diameter in tanks over 20 gallons, and air flows must be strong with numerous small bubbles.

The maximum flow from an air lift pump with a one inch diameter lift tube is about 90 to 95 gallons per hour, 1.5 gpm. The average flow, considering clogged air stones, filter restrictions, and an air pump operated at the limit, may be only 40 to 50 gallons per hour. Although the air lift pump operates most efficiently when the air release is near the bottom of the tube, it is better to position the air stone higher in the tube if air pressure is not great enough to provide an adequate air flow at the full depth of the tube. Figure 16 diagrams a working air lift pump. Spotte (1979) presents a thorough technical discussion of the design and workings of air lift pumps.

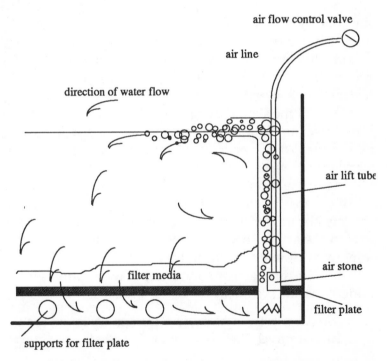

Figure 16. The function of an air lift pump operating with a typical undergravel biological filter. Water is pushed up the air lift tube and returns to the aquarium. Water flows through the undergravel filter to refill the air lift tube.

Water pumps

Water movement in marine aquarium systems can be produced solely by air lift pumps and this is adequate for small tanks. Air lift pumps, although they can move a great deal of water, do not provide as much water flow as electric powered water pumps. They also operate at very low pressures and the gentle water flows do not produce strong circulation currents within the tank. Most marine aquarium systems over 30 gallons have some type of electrically powered water pump that is either the sole power for system water movement or powers an auxiliary filter for a tank with an air lift, undergravel filter. This pump is either a sealed submersible pump or an air cooled, open motor pump. Either type must be specifically designed for salt water use. No metal, except for stainless steel, can come in contact with the water. All pump parts must be of plastic designed for salt water contact.

Neither type should be run dry, that is without water in the pump housing. Submersible pumps should also always be totally immersed in water. The internal motor depends on the surrounding water to remove excess heat through the sealed housing. If the pump is partly or totally exposed, it will often overheat and burn out. Both types of pumps should be protected by a float switch that turns the pump off if the water level in the system drops below a safe point or rises above a point that threatens an overflow.

There are three general categories of water pumps for use in modern marine systems.

- Small, mostly submersible pumps designed for use on undergravel filter tubes, usually called "powerheads".

- Small water pumps, submersible or air cooled, that are a built-in, dedicated part of a specific filter unit.

- Relatively large submersible or air cooled, general use pumps that return water to the tank from a separate filter installation, usually the sump tank of a trickle filter unit.

Comparison of submersible and air cooled pumps

Topic	Submersible	Air cooled
Noise	Generally quiet	Noticeable hum
Heat	Adds heat to water	adds heat to cabinet
Deterioration	Pump wear, leak in housing	Rust, salt creep on motor, pump wear
Shock hazard	Only if cord seal or housing is broken. Entire system may be charged	Salt creep can effect brushes and wires. System or just pump may be charged.
Repair	Only pump parts can be repaired	Motor and pump can be repaired.
Maintenance	Occasional replacement of pump parts	Periodic cleaning and oiling, occasional replacement of motor and pump parts.
Cost	Relatively high	Relatively moderate

The pumping capacity of small water pumps are rated in gallons per hour (gph) or liters per hour (lph). Large capacity pumps may be rated in gallons per minute (gpm) or liters per minute (lpm). Don't confuse these ratings or you might wind up with a pump for a swimming pool instead of an aquarium system pump. Small pumps for marine systems, i.e., power-heads, have capacities of about 100 to 400 gph while larger pumps used in reef type systems have pumping capacities in the range of 500 to 1500 gph and sometimes up to 2400 gph in large systems.

Powerheads

These small pumps are very useful to the marine aquarist. They operate undergravel filters at high flow rates and can direct strong currents in any direction about the tank. This greatly increases water flow through undergravel filters and improves the function and efficiency of these filters. A number of companies are now manufacturing these useful little pumps and a variety of models are now available with varying features and pumping capacities. Most of these pumps are now equipped with a venturi that provides aeration of the water that is pumped, which is especially valuable if the unit is used with an undergravel or tube type filter. This is a very important feature for even though powerhead pumps move much more water than air lift pumps, gas exchange problems can develop when these pumps are used with undergravel filters. Undergravel filters require a great deal of oxygen and the air lifts typically used with these filters aid oxygenation and carbon dioxide removal. Without the venturi feature, powerhead pumps do not provide for much gas exchange. Unless the pumped water is mixed with air by venturi and/or is strongly directed across the surface of the tank, gas exchange is limited and accumulation of CO_2 and loss of oxygen occurs. Some new powerhead models also have built in flow rate control and flow meters, which are very useful in adjusting the pump to the system. The visual flow rate scale on a powerhead pump allows a quick check on the condition of the filter since flow rates decrease when the filter clogs.

These small pumps can also provide strong in-tank circulation even if undergravel filters are not used in the system, thus are very useful in reef type aquarium installations. If used with a tube extension on the intake, they can draw water from beneath rock formations, and increase water circulation in restricted areas. They can also be used to create a surge effect in large tanks by automatically turning one or more powerhead pumps, aimed in opposite directions, on and off every few minutes.

Most powerheads are true submersible pumps with sealed motors and can be placed anywhere within the tank. Like all water pumps they can not be run dry and like other sealed submersible pumps, they should be submerged for optimum cooling of the motor unit. Dewey (1986) has an article on the repair and maintenance of powerhead pumps.

Like all electrical devices used in a marine system, powerheads introduce the potential for electric shock through damage or faulty manufacture. If a powerhead or any electrical device charges a marine system and a shock or tingle is felt when the water or tank structure is touched, the offending device must be replaced immediately. It's a good idea to buy an inexpensive neon electric circuit tester at a hardware store. This device is made up of a small neon bulb attached to two insulated wires with exposed metal ends. The neon bulb glows when the exposed ends of the wires complete a circuit with an active electric current. Only enough electricity to light the bulb goes through the device. Holding the end of one wire and touching the end of the other wire to the surface of a charged tank will cause the bulb to glow, and this informs you that the tank is charged without giving you an electric shock. One can then selectively disconnect electrical devices to determine which one is defective.

Filter unit pumps

Most powered filter units—internal and external box filters that hang on the tank top, and canister filters that mount under the tank—contain their own electric motor. It may be a sealed submersible or an open, air cooled motor. In most instances the motor and its housing are carefully designed to provide the power that the unit needs to accomplish its intended task. The cause of problems that develop with the motors in these units can almost always be traced back to poor maintenance of the unit and the system. For example, running the motor against a clogged filter medium for weeks or months, totally failing to perform recommended cleaning and lubrication, running the motor dry for extended periods, not noticing an obstruction in the pump vanes or an air lock in the plumbing, allowing salt creep to build up and actually enter the motor, and other horrors of neglect. These units do a really remarkable job of keeping a marine aquarium operating, but the motors that power them will not run forever without maintenance.

Large system pumps

Most commercially available reef type systems and large trickle/wet-dry systems are supplied with the pump that the manufacturer feels is best for the operation and the economics of construction and sale of the system. It may or may not be the absolute best pump for the system, but it should do a proper job if the manufacturer produces good quality equipment. The water pump in reef systems performs two major functions. It moves water through the filter system and it circulates water through the tank itself. The greater the capacity of the pump in gallons per hour (gph), the faster it moves water through the system and the more forcefully it circulates water about the tank. The gph flow rate of the pump should be 3 to 6 times the volume of the system. A 100 gallon tank with only a small reef section can get by with a 400 gph pump, while a 100 gallon tank heavy with rocks and invertebrates will function better with a 600 gph pump.

Lighting Systems

The sections on light and algae in Chapters 2 and 3 contain information pertinent to the selection of a light source. A review of these sections is worthwhile when one is considering the lighting system for a marine aquarium. Lighting is a very important factor in maintaining a successful marine invertebrate aquarium and many authors have discussed it at length. Additional information on lighting can be found in Burleson, J. (1987), Burleson, P. (1988), Lundegaard (1985), Osborne (1982, 1983), Spotte (1979), Thiel (1988, 1989), and Weast (1987). Generally, a marine aquarist is in one of three rough categories when it comes to lighting an aquarium, thus this section is broken up into three parts to address the needs of each of these categories.

- The off-the-shelf standard fresh/salt water aquarium system with an undergravel filter, usually an external filter of some sort, and a tank cover (hood) with a fluorescent light included as part of the hood. This system provides enough light to keep marine fish and most larger, sighted mobile invertebrates. Algal growth is usually limited to encrusting browns and reds although some filamentous greens may also grow.

- The custom or semi-custom salt water system designed for the installation of free standing fluorescent bulbs where the aquarist has more control over type and intensity of lighting. Given good water quality, this systems will maintain most macro green algaes, most filamentous red and green algaes, and many of the light requiring anemones and corals.

- The "super lighting" system over a reef tank, large or small, where the aquarist strives to simulate natural light conditions on a coral reef and is not particularly concerned with expense. The system consists of metal halide and/or mercury vapor lighting and may also include full spectrum or special spectrum fluorescent bulbs. The limits of this type of lighting system in maintaining reef life is not well defined. Most likely, almost any creature of the shallow, coral reefs can be maintained in a home marine aquarium system if enough effort is expended to understand and provide the elements it requires. (Wow, a few years ago who would have thought we could say this so soon?)

There is one very important factor to consider when planning the tank display under any type of lighting. Light on the reef is not uniform. The light intensity any organism receives is greatly dependent on its depth and placement on the reef. A coral or algae on the top of the reef in only a few feet of water receives far more intense light than one in deeper water or in the shade of other reef structures for all or most of the day. Therefore, whatever type lighting is placed over the tank, it is important to have areas of varied light intensity in the aquarium. Overhangs and shaded areas are important for some invertebrates and should be provided.

Some organisms such as anemones and algaes can move to, or grow toward, areas where the lighting suits them, but others such as corals must be placed in the right areas. Learning where the organism is usually found on the reef—shallow with high light intensity, or in shade or deep water with low light intensity—is a good start for finding out where it should be placed in the aquarium. Each tank is different, however, and information on the place of natural occurrence of the organism may not be available, so some experimentation on the part of the aquarist will be necessary for proper placement of various light requiring organisms.

Standard Light Hood

With this setup, the aquarist's control of above tank lighting is limited to selection of the type of fluorescent bulb to place in the fixture. The fixture usually holds only one bulb over a small tank and two bulbs over a large tank. The basic specifications of the bulbs in these standard fixtures are usually either 18 inch, 15 watt, about 800 mean lumens; 24 inch, 20 watt, about 1200 mean lumens; or 36 inch, 30 watt, about 2100 mean lumens. These units also usually come with bulbs selected by the manufacturer already in place. These are bulbs manufactured for use with aquaria and usually have a spectrum designed to stimulate the growth of fresh water plants and enhance the colors of fresh water fish.

The bulbs one finds in these fixtures are probably actually made by a major manufacture such as Osram, Sylvania, Westinghouse, or General Electric expressly for the aquarium company and are labeled with the hood manufacturer's trade name. The "Gro-Lux WS®" wide spectrum bulb manufactured by Sylvania is a good example of this type of bulb. There is a broad spectrum peak in the orange/red range of 600 to 675 nm with a much sharper peak in the violet 440 nm range. Although Sylvania's "Grow-Lux WS®", Westinghouse's "Agro-Lite®" and GE's "Plant and Aquarium Wide Spectrum®" bulbs are fine for well planted fresh water aquariums, they tend to give an unnatural look to a marine aquarium.

There are a number of bulbs made expressly for marine aquariums, however, that have a spectrum closer to natural sunlight with an additional stronger peak in the violet/blue range. Some of the trade names for these bulbs that I have seen in the literature or on store shelves are "Sun-glo®", "Aquarilux®", "Sealux®", "Naturalux®" and "Vibran-Sea®". These bulbs should have strong spectral peaks in the violet/blue and red wave length range and generally give a good, natural light to a marine aquarium. Full spectrum bulbs (not to be confused with the wide spectrum bulbs that emit an extended red light) are also available that emit light in the full range and colors of natural sunlight. "Colortone®", "Chromaline®", "Verilux®", and "Vita-Lite®" are trade names of the more common full spectrum bulbs. The Vita-Lite® bulb, and probably the others as well, is made in the standard 24 inch size as well as the 48 inch length. These bulbs also give a good color appearance to a marine aquarium.

I would recommend using the bulbs that come with the light hood at least during initial set up and "run in" of the marine aquarium. Then, if you are displeased with the general appearance of the tank, look for a bulb type that will provide the color rendering that is desired. Remember that a conventional aquarium set up is limited in the type of invertebrate life that it can support. One or two fluorescent bulbs, even with a "high-tech" filtration system, will not allow survival of corals and most macro algaes. These "off-the-shelf" types of light hoods contain the ballast in the fixture with the bulb. The ballasts are heavy metallic electrical equipment and generate considerable heat. They also have to be protected from salt water and salt spray. This means that the bulb and fixture should be separated from the water surface by a glass plate and that the aquarium cover hood should be strong enough to support the weight of the light fixture.

The light and ballast must also be well ventilated and the plastic very heat resistant to avoid warping. The glass plate that separates the light from the aquarium surface quickly accumulates salt build up and even algal growth. The encrusted salt and algae growth decrease and change the quality of light that enters the aquarium. If you notice that the light in the aquarium is not as bright as it used to be and has a peculiar greenish hue, then the glass plate is probably coated with a green algal growth and needs to be cleaned.

A marine aquarist with an interest in invertebrates may feel a bit discouraged or even intimidated by the recent development of "reef tanks" and the explosion of high technology in lighting and filtration that is changing the language of the hobby. If you don't want to make the investment of time, space, and money that such systems require, don't let it bug you. While it is true that these developments make it possible for the home aquarist to keep certain invertebrates more successfully then ever before, they have not driven the traditional marine aquarium into obsolescence. Not all invertebrates require the reef tank environment, and a traditional marine aquarium can support many, many invertebrates that do not require high intensity lighting and super water quality. Also, inexpensive modifications to traditional aquariums systems in lighting and additional filtration often greatly increases the numbers and kinds of invertebrates that can be maintained. Time and effort spent in acquiring and observing invertebrates suited to the traditional marine aquarium will be well spent.

Custom Light Hoods

Assuming an adequate filtration system, even if frequent water exchanges are necessary, one of the most important custom additions to a marine tank to help support more invertebrate and algal life is improved lighting. The easiest and most inexpensive way to accomplish this is with fluorescent bulbs. Incandescent bulbs may find some uses on a marine aquarium, i.e., a spot of intense light in a small area for an anemone in an otherwise poorly lit tank, but incandescent (tungsten light) has a low color temperature (2800 °K) and generates far too much heat for the amount of light produced (low efficiency) to be generally useful for aquariums.

Fluorescent bulbs are glass tubes coated on the inside with various types of phosphor power. This phosphor is made to glow with emitted light by passing an electric current through a mercury vapor inside the tube. (Don't breathe the fumes if a bulb breaks!) Electrodes at each end of the tube generate the electric current for the bulb. A choke coil, condenser, and starting switch make up the ballast that accompanies each lamp and this transforms the household electric current into energy the bulb can use. The bulb and ballast can be designed to emit particular intensities and spectrums of light, which gives this type of lighting great variability at reasonable cost.

A general estimate of the effective life of a fluorescent bulb is 20,000 hours, which figures out to about three and half years if it's on 15 hours a day. The initial lumen output of a standard fluorescent bulb is 10 to 15 percent higher than its output after about 4000 hours of use. Therefore one should use 85 percent of the initial lumen rating to get the mean lumen rating and this will provide a more accurate estimate of the light the aquarium will receive over the life of the bulbs. A 40 watt, cool white fluorescent bulb is rated at a light output of 3000 to 3200 lumens. The light output of a fluorescent bulb is related to wattage, but different bulbs of the same wattage may produce a different amount of lumens. For example, a standard 40 watt cool white is rated at 3150 lumens and a standard 40 watt Vita-Lite® is rated at 2400 lumens. Generally, however, the higher the wattage the more lumens produced.

It is possible to get high output (HO) and very high output (VHO) bulbs that double and triple the initial lumen output of a standard bulb, but these brighter bulbs require more watts, higher amperage, and a *special, more expensive ballast,* than standard bulbs. Four of the high output bulbs can take the place of eight standard bulbs, so if you want the most light intensity possible from fluorescent bulbs, it's worth the greater expense for the HO or VHO lighting setup. It's a good idea to replace the bulbs after one year of service to make sure that the intensity and spectrum are always as intended for the aquarium. Table 7 presents the characteristics of various bulbs of all types for general reference.

Construction

The purpose of the custom fluorescent light hood is to provide the most optimum light quality possible for the marine aquarium at a reasonable cost. Since the quality and intensity of light in the aquarium is the primary consideration, concessions have to be made that favor the life in the aquarium over ease of maintenance and construction. Different materials (wood or plastic) and methods of construction can be used to build a light hood, but the following design elements should be included.

1. No metal should be used in construction, certainly no metal of any type should be exposed to salt spray or condensation. Also, all plastics must be non toxic. Polyethylene is about the only flexible plastic that can be safely used in and over a marine aquarium, but most rigid plastics are safe. Paints on any wood surfaces must also be nontoxic.

2. The bulbs should be only a few inches from the water surface and there should be no glass or plastic between the bulbs and the water (except for narrow braces). Although some transparent plastics are said not to change the character of the light that is transmitted through them, the need to use the full spectrum and as much emitted light as possible, takes precedence over a condensation and spray shield between the bulbs and the water. If the tank has an open air lift that releases air bubbles in a relatively restricted area of the surface, a small transparent plastic spray shield can be placed over this area, but it should be cleaned frequently as salt spray and algal growth will reduce light transmission over this area. The bare bulbs should also be cleaned frequently so that any build up of salt will not diminish the light from the bulb.

3. The bulbs need not be contained in a rigid fixture but may be loosely supported by plastic or glass bars above the tank or by supports attached under the hood. The electrical connections on the end of the bulbs must be waterproof plastic

caps that seal tightly on the end of the bulbs. The open plastic clips that hold the ends of fluorescent bulbs in typical fixtures will soon accumulate salt and create an electrical shock and fire hazard and must not be used when the bulb is exposed over the tank water. If professionally made, waterproof end caps can not be obtained, it is possible to make a waterproof connection for the ends of fluorescent light bulbs. Get a 1¼ inch PVC pipe cap and about a 2" length of 1¼ inch thin wall PVC pipe. Thin wall PVC pipe of this diameter fits very closely over a standard fluorescent bulb. Glue the short section of PVC pipe into the PVC cap with PVC glue and then drill a small hole through the end of the cap and pass the plastic coated electrical cord through the hole. Attach the cord to the pins on the end of the light bulb with strong clips or solder. Put about an inch of silicone sealer into the bottom of the cap/pipe assembly and push it slowly over the end of the bulb while gently pulling the electrical wire from the hole. Once the bulb is seated in the end of the cap, make sure the hole in the end of the cap is well sealed around the wires and that the pipe around the edge of tube is also well sealed. Clean up the excess silicone sealer and put the assembly aside for a day or two until the sealer has set. Note that this method is not much less expensive than commercially available water tight caps, considerably more trouble, and the caps can't be removed and used on another bulb.

4. The ballasts for the bulbs must be remotely located from the light hood, far away from any exposure to salt spray and salt water and where the heat from the ballast will not affect the tank. The wires leading from the bulbs to the ballast should be carefully installed so that water can not condense on the wire and then run down to the ballast.

5. The top of the aquarium need not be totally enclosed; however, the bulbs must have a white or silver curved plastic reflector above them along their entire length. White, plastic rain gutter material is good for this purpose. Plexiglass mirror, ⅛th inch thick mirrored plexiglass, can be cut and attached to the hood above the light with silicone sealer to make a very efficient reflector. Without a reflector, most of the light from the

bulb does not enter the aquarium. A total enclosure constructed with a nontoxic, white or mirrored surface over the aquarium is possible because fluorescent bulbs without the ballast do not create much heat, and beneficial because it will reduce evaporation and spray and reflect additional light down into the tank. Be sure to provide a few slits or holes to allow venting of whatever heat the bulbs do produce.

6. The length of the bulbs should be about the same as the length of the aquarium. Obviously, the bulbs should not be longer than the length of the aquarium. If the bulbs that must be used are shorter than the length of the tank, i. e., a six foot tank and four foot bulbs, the freedom of placement allowed by the lack of a rigid fixture allows bulb placement to be staggered so that each end of the tank receives light from the ends of half the bulbs. Figure 17 illustrates a possible arrangement of four fluorescent bulbs over a large marine aquarium.

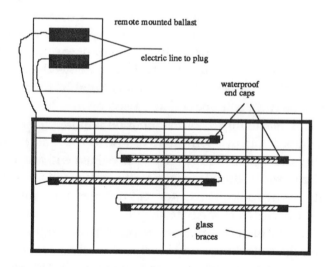

Figure 17. Diagram for placement of four fluorscent bulbs setup over a large aquarium.

Spectrum

There are two considerations, equally important, when the spectral quality of light in the marine aquarium is decided. The first is the spectral quality that is best for life in the aquarium and the second is the spectral quality that is best for human observation. The visible spectrum for normal human sight ranges from violet at 400 nm to red at 700 nm, but the eye sees "best and brightest" in the green - yellow range of 500 to 600 nm. Colors appear most "normal" when light is rich with wave lengths in this range. Thus, the cool white fluorescent bulb, designed to provide efficient light for human use, produces most of its radiant energy in this wave length range. Photosynthesis in plants, however, including algaes and coral symbionts, makes best use of other wave lengths. The absorption of light by chlorophyll has strong peaks in the ranges of 400 to 450 and 600 to 650 nm. Another important point is that blue/green light in the 400 to 550 nm range is dominant at depths where many corals occur in nature. The "best" lighting for a marine aquarium would be sunlight since it contains a relatively equal amount of all wave lengths and certainly has the intensity to provide as much light in all wave lengths as would be necessary for all purposes. Figure 18 illustrates the spectral distribution of 10 types of artificial lights that are frequently used over marine aquarium systems.

Natural sunlight, of course, is the standard. The Color Rendering Index (CRI) of sunlight is 100. The higher the CRI of a bulb, the more all colors appear natural to the human eye. To get natural sunlight, some aquarists have installed plastic skylights in the roof of their homes over the aquarium. These tanks are usually very large, 3000 gallons or more, to warrant such an exceptional installation. Supplemental lighting is also used for night and cloudy day illumination. The inside location of the tank and separation of the direct sunlight by the plastic skylight provides enough temperature control to keep the tank cool enough in the summer and a heater keeps the tank water warm enough in the winter. (Another way to use sunlight for a marine aquarium is to mount a sunlight collector on the roof

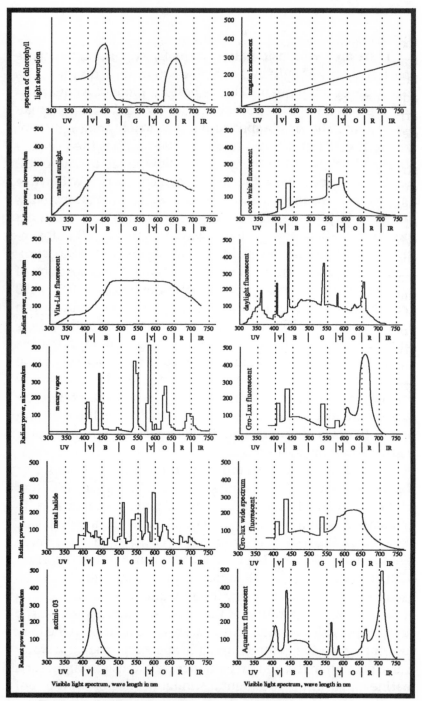

Figure 18. Spectral distribution of various light sources and
the absorption spectra of chlorophyll.

that automatically tracks the sun, collects the light, and then transmits the light with plastic tubes down to a fixture over the tank where the ends of the tubes release the sunlight into the aquarium. Cloudy days and nights present a problem with this arrangement, however, and since this technology is still under development, it is probably better to use artificial light.)

The spectral mix that works for all general purposes—a strong blue peak, 425 nm for corals and photosynthesis; adequate green/yellow, 575 nm for viewing; and an orange/red peak, 650 nm for photosynthesis—is best obtained by a variety of bulbs, although many marine laboratories use only cool white bulbs for their microalgae cultures. Full spectrum bulbs such as the Vita-Lite® and Chroma 50®, or bulbs developed for marine aquarium use, provide some of all of the above including enough of the orange/red range. The spectral distribution of most full spectrum bulbs are generally similar to the spectral graph presented for Vita-Lite® in Figure 18. A cool white bulb gives more of the range needed for viewing and an Actinic 03 bulb provides the intense blue range that seems to help coral growth and survival.

On a four bulb setup, my recommendation would be two full spectrum bulbs, one cool white, and one Actinic 03, and even this bulb set may not produce enough light for some tanks and some organisms. Actinic bulbs were developed for various industrial and medical purposes and produce a high output in a narrow, blue wave length range. The spectral range of the Actinic 03 bulb peaks at about 425 nm and spreads only from about 375 to 475 nm. Despite the "blue glow" of the light, there is no germicidal UV component (in the area of 256 nm) in the light and it can be viewed in complete safety. In fact, the term "actinic" refers to the property of radiation that produces chemical effects and it is used in treatment of some human ailments. These bulbs seem to be a good supplement to full spectrum lighting in the marine aquarium, but should not be used as the only light source, unless the aim is to reproduce conditions on the deep reef. Of the actinic bulbs available, only the 03 Actinic bulb is suitable for an aquarium.

You may have very different ideas on lighting, however, or wish to experiment with various combinations of light sources. The spectrum produced by a number of bulbs is given for general reference, and along with the other data presented in this chapter, should provide most of the information you need for decisions on lighting.

Intensity

The basic question is: how many bulbs of what type should be placed over a particular aquarium to produce the amount of light the tank should receive? First of all, the aquarist has to decide on the spectral quality (type of bulbs) and the total surface lux over the tank. If uncertainty and concern for expense plague this decision, go with about 10,000 to 12,000 lux of full spectrum lighting and make changes based on future experience. The major problem with fluorescent lighting over a reef tank is that the intensity is often too low for many corals and algaes. For this reason the extra high intensity of metal halide and mercury vapor lighting is often preferred over large reef type systems. Note, however, that many large reef systems do very well on just fluorescent lighting if enough bulbs are installed over the tank.

Now, if we assume that a standard four foot, 40 watt fluorescent bulb of any particular type puts out roughly 2500 lumens (a reasonable estimate for full spectrum bulbs) and multiply the lumens by 10.76 to convert to lux, we get 26,900 lux from one standard bulb! Wow, does this mean that one bulb will do a whole tank? Unfortunately, it doesn't work that way. That 2500 lumens is the total output of the entire bulb, outward in every direction, right at the surface of the bulb. Our concern is in the amount of light that enters the surface of the aquarium and the amount that reaches a target organism, not the amount that leaves the bulb.

There are many factors that diminish the light between the bulb and an anemone. These include the distance between the bulb and the anemone, the type of reflector and its distance from the bulb, the total surface area of the aquarium, the characteristics of the water such as color and amount of surface disturbance, the depth of the water, shape of the tank, and the general light absorption characteristics of the entire aquarium environment. The only way you can be absolutely sure of the amount of light at any point above or in a particular aquarium is to measure it at that point with a light meter or luxmeter.

There is a way, however, to develop a working estimate of the number of bulbs required over a tank of a specific size. Even though the patterns of light distribution and light absorption over various aquariums may differ greatly, the formula presented by Spotte (1979) can be used to develop an estimate of the total wattage required to produce a specific amount of Lux over an aquarium of a specific size.

$$\text{watts} = \frac{\text{(lux) (area of tank in square meters)}}{\text{(bulb efficacy) (utilization factor)}}$$

or

$$W = \frac{LA}{EU}$$

L is the total lux desired over the surface of the tank.
A is the total surface area of the tank in square meters.
E is the efficacy of the bulb in lumens per watt.
U is a the utilization factor, a constant (0.5) that represents the light from the bulb that actually strikes the surface of the water.

As an example, let's say we want 15,000 lux over the surface of a 75 to 80 gallon tank that measures 48 inches in length, 20 inches in width and 20 inches in depth. In this case depth doesn't matter since we only need total surface area. The surface area has to be in square meters, however, and we have inches. We can convert to meters in the linear measure by multiplying 48 and 20 by 0.025 to convert inches to meters (1.5 and .5 meters), and then multiply these figures to get the surface area in square meters; or we can get the square inches first (960 square inches) and then divide by the number of square inches in a square meter, 1,550. Either way the surface area of the tank comes out at 0.6 square meters. The efficacy of the bulb can be found in the data table on bulbs or the lumen output divided by the wattage of the bulb will also give this value. If all cool white bulbs were desired, the efficacy would be 79; if all daylight bulbs were desired, the efficacy would be 65. A 1 to 1 ratio of cool white and daylight would give an efficacy value of 72. All Vita-Lites® would give an efficacy value of 60. For the example, we'll use a 3 to 1 ratio of Vita-Light® to cool white, an efficacy value of 65. The utilization factor is the constant, 0.5.

The formula now has all the proper values:

$$W = \frac{(15{,}000)\,(0.6)}{(65)\,(0.5)}$$

$$W = \frac{9{,}000}{32.5}$$

$$W = 277$$

So we have a requirement of 277 watts, which is 7, four foot long, 40 watt bulbs. And at a 3 to 1 ratio of Vita-Light® to cool white bulbs, this is 5.25 Vita-Light® to 1.75 cool white bulbs. (Cutting these bulbs into fractions is difficult because it's hard to keep the vapor in the bulb once it's cut). So in this case we have a choice of going to 8 bulbs (6 and 2), staying at 7 bulbs (5 and 2 or 6 and 1), or dropping to combinations of 6 or 5 bulbs if we feel that perhaps we don't need quite as much light as 7 bulbs will produce. If only 10,000 lux is required (185 watts), we can get by with 4.6 bulbs, and for this size tank, 4 bulbs would probably be enough if good reflectors are used above the bulbs. The decision usually comes down to using either 4 or 6 fluorescent bulbs above the tank, and with a reef tank system, 6 bulbs (240 watts) is *usually* the better choice. This provides more intensity and a greater choice in spectral mix, especially for deep tanks. This is very adequate for macro algae growth, but note that some aquarists use up to 12 fluorescent bulbs (4 actinic and 6 daylight) over reef tank setups (almost 500 watts)

to get the intense, blue supplemented, full spectrum light that
they feel is best for many corals.

Table 7. Technical data on light bulbs

Bulb type	Watts	initial lumens	initial efficacy	Color temp°K	Hours of life	CRI	Length inches
Incandescent							
60 Incan	60	870	14.5	3000	1000	99	N/A
100 Incan	100	1750	17.5	3000	750	99	N/A
200 Incan	200	4010	20.0	3000	750	99	N/A
1000 Incan	1000	23740	23.7	3000	1000	99	N/A
Fluorescent							
cool white	40	3150	78.8	4150	20000	62	48
warm white	40	3200	80.0	3000	20000	52	48
daylight	40	2600	65.0	6250	20000	75	48
Cool white HO	60	4300	62.0	4160	20000	62	48
Vita-Lite® FS	40	2400	60.0	5500	20000	91	48
Chrona 50® FS	40	2210	55.3	5000	20000	90	48
Chrona 75® FS	40	2000	50.0	7500	20000	92	48
Colortone 50® FS	40	2200	55.0	5000	20000	92	48
Verilux® FS	40	2168	54.2	6200	20000	93	48
SP30	40	3325	83.1	3000	15000	70	48
SP35	40	3325	83.1	3500	15000	73	48
SP41	40	3265	81.6	4100	15000	70	48
Green	40	4350	108.8	6975	20000	-	48
Cool green	40	2850	71.3	6450	20000	68	48
Sealux®	40	1600	40.0	5326	20000	G	48
Aquarilux®	40	880	22.0	10500	20000	F	48
Actinic 03	40	——	——	——	——		48
Plant light	40	850	21.3	6750	20000	2	48
Plant WS	40	1950	48.8	3050	20000	90	48
Cool white	75	6300	84.0	4150	12000	62	60
Warm white	75	6500	86.7	3000	12000	52	60
Daylight	75	5450	72.7	6250	12000	75	60
Cool white	110	9200	83.6	4150	12000	62	96
Warm white	110	9200	83.6	3050	12000	52	96
Daylight	110	7800	71.0	6250	12000	75	96
Daylight	215	13300	61.8	6250	12000	75	—

Table 7. Continued

Bulb type	Watts	Initial lumens	Initial efficacy	Color temp°K	Hours of life	CRI	Length inches
High Intensity Discharge							
Mercury vapor							
Clear	400	21000	52.5	N/A	24000	G	N/A
Deluxe white	400	22500	56.3	N/A	24000	G	N/A
Warm white	400	19500	48.8	N/A	24000	G	N/A
Clear	1000	57000	57.0	N/A	24000	G	N/A
Deluxe white	1000	63000	63.0	N/A	24000	G	N/A
Warm white	1000	58000	58.0	N/A	24000	G	N/A
Metal halide							
Clear E-23 1/2	175	16600	94.9	N/A	10000	E	N/A
Diffuse E-23 1/2	175	15750	90.0	N/A	10000	E	N/A
Phosphor E-28	175	14000	80.0	N/A	10000	E	N/A
Clear E-28	250	20500	82.0	N/A	10000	E	N/A
Phosphor E-28	250	20500	82.0	N/A	10000	E	N/A
Clear E-37	400	36000	90.0	N/A	20000	E	N/A
Phosphor E-37	400	36000	90.0	N/A	20000	E	N/A
Clear BT-56	1000	110000	111.0	N/A	12000	E	N/A
Phosphor BT-56	1000	105000	105.0	N/A	12000	E	N/A

Color temperature of metal halide bulbs varies 4300 to 5500 °K.

CRI: F - Fair, G - Good, E - Excellent, 90 - 100 - Excellent

Sources: Weast (1987), Lundegaard (1985), Osborne (1983)

Another option is to install the higher wattage, High Output (HO) bulbs, and produce about the same light with half the bulbs; although getting the proper spectral quality may require a mix of standard and high output bulbs. This formula and the data on bulb types in Table 7 will help you decide the lighting for your particular aquarium. Note that the formula can not be applied to mercury-vapor and metal halide lights.

Metal Halide Lighting

The difference between the "super" setup and the florescent light hood is the use of metal halide (Multi-Vapor) lamps and/or the less expensive mercury vapor bulbs. These lamps produce a great deal of light with an excellent spectral range, but they also produce a lot of heat. They must be positioned some distance above the tank, and this requires that the tank top be open to the lights. The tank can have a glass or plastic cover to reduce evaporation and contain salt spray, but this will reduce the spectrum and alter the effect of the high intensity lighting. Such a cover will also increase maintenance since both surfaces will have to be cleaned regularly. A partial cover or shield that extends a few inches inward around the top of the tank gives protection from water splashes and can support various additional lights, reflectors, shelves, filters, etc. The higher the high intensity lamps are above the tank, the less light enters the tank. The lamps must be high enough, however, so that they will not be affected by water from the tank. Depending on tank size and water movement, this may be 18 inches to 36 inches. Closer is dangerous and further away is ineffective. Metal halide lighting is very intense and the inclusion of a dawn/dusk cycle reduces the shock of immediate strong light and immediate dark. An Actinic 03 florescent bulb that comes on 30 minutes before the metal halide lights and extends 30 minutes after the main lights go out provides a more natural, gradual light cycle and adds a strong blue light element to the daily lighting of the tank. The addition of the blue Actinic 03 is not very noticable to the human eye while the metal halide lights are on, but many corals seem to benefit from this light.

A high intensity lighting system can be composed of only mercury vapor bulbs, only metal halide lamps, a mix of the two, or any of these in combination with certain florescent bulbs. Since the cost of the high intensity lamps is high, a combination with florescent bulbs may be the answer for some aquarists. Mercury vapor bulbs are widely used by European aquarists. The color rendering is good and the spectrum is broad with peaks in the right places, a bit high in the yellow range, however. They are less expensive, but produce less light than the metal halide lamps. The color rendering of metal halide light is excellent and the lumen output is very high.

Sodium vapor lamps should be avoided since the spectrum they produce is not suitable for a marine aquarium.

One very interesting effect obtained by metal halide light over a reef tank is the play of shadows across the reef structures caused by the light passing through the ripples on the surface. This rippling of shadows on the reef is just as one observes while snorkeling over a shallow coral reef on a calm sunlit day. Metal halide lights also produce a lot of ultraviolet light, and this can cause problems if the lamp does not have an ultraviolet screen or filter. Corals may become "burned" if UV light is too intense in the tank and a high, unfiltered UV component is also harmful to the human eye. If an aquarist decides to install metal halide lighting over a reef system, it is best to go with a lighting system that has been designed and manufactured expressly for aquarium installation.

Temperature

Most coral reef organisms can survive a temperature range of 65 to 90°F (18 to 32°C). When the extremes of this range occur in nature, which they do once in a while, coral reef life does little more than hang on to life and hope for a change. (Assuming that corals can hope, of course.) The acceptable temperature range for most marine aquariums systems is 75 to 82°F, (24 to 28°C) and optimum temperature, especially for reef systems, is about 78°F (25.6°C), but variation within the acceptable range seldom has any noticeable effect on aquarium life. Chapter 2 has more general information on temperature.

All marine aquariums, especially those with heating and cooling systems, should have a thermometer that is easily seen when feeding or observing the display. If a heater sticks or a cooling system quits or runs on and on, it can only be discovered by touching the tank or the water if a thermometer is not easily seen. A floating thermometer that has to be retrieved by reaching way to a corner under the cover or one that has to be removed from a box and held in the tank is better than none

at all, but not by much. There are many aquarium ther-
mometers on the market that can be positioned on the outside
or inside of the tank where they can be easily seen. This type of
thermometer is a very inexpensive investment that can save the
tank by giving the aquarist an early warning if something goes
wrong.

Heating

Few systems require cooling in these days of air conditioning, but heating is almost always a requirement except in tropical areas. Heat, incidently, is distributed by conduction,
transmission of heat through a solid material; convection, circular movement of heated air or liquid; and radiation, outward
dispersal of radiant energy. Water retains heat very well, thus
aquariums are slow to warm up and slow to lose excess heat.
This is also why a relatively small heat source can maintain the
proper temperature range in an aquarium, especially if the
water surface is protected from exposure to cool air currents.
Heat enters a marine aquarium system by radiant energy from
the tank lighting, heat generated by pumping, and from exposure to air containing room heat. Heat leaves the aquarium
to the room by radiation and, primarily, convection with air
currents. A trickle filter that efficiently degasses the aquarium
water also increases evaporation and cools the water. Submersible and, to a much lesser extent, air cooled water pumps also
contribute heat that is distributed by water convection. If an
aquarium system is constantly too warm, look for a submersible water pump that is contributing too much heat to the
system. It may be necessary to change to an air cooled pump, a
smaller submersible, or add a water cooling device.

Most aquarium heaters operate on the same basic system.
An electric current moves through a coil or length of high
resistance wire and creates heat that is transferred by conduction to the water in the system. Heat is distributed throughout
the marine aquarium system by convection from water movement. A thermostat, usually within the heater, senses the
temperature of the water and turns the heater on when

temperature drops and off when temperature rises. Water temperature usually has to rise or fall two or three degrees before the thermostat is turned on or off.

A thin, bimetallic coil or strip composed of two metals bonded together side by side, such as copper and zinc, controls the thermostat. The two metals expand and contract at different rates with temperature changes, and the strip of metal then bends one way when temperature declines and the other way when temperature rises. An electrical contact at the end of the strip closes when the bimetallic strip bends toward cool temperatures and this turns on the heater. When temperatures rise, the strip bends the other way, the contacts open, and the heater is turned off. If the thermostat is adjustable, and most aquarium heater thermostats are, the position or pressure on the bimetallic strip can be changed by turning a knob so that the temperature range where contacts close and open can be adjusted. Most heaters also have a small neon light that is on when the heater is active. This gives the aquarist information on the operation of the heater. If the light never comes on, the heater is either not needed, set too low, or may be broken with an open circuit. If the light is always on, the heater may be set too high, have a broken coil so that it does not heat even though the light is on, or may have the contact points stuck together so that it is always on. If the light does not go on and off, the heater must be checked to see if a there is problem.

The standard printed circuit board heater is enclosed in a glass tube and attaches to the top edge of the tank. The thermostat and heating coils extend beneath the surface of the water. The top of the tube has the temperature adjustment knob and is sealed against spray and splash of water. This type of heater is not submersible and the top must always be kept above water level. The glass tube around the heater coil does not overheat and break because the water surrounding it keeps it cool. One of the mistakes an aquarist may make once is to fail to unplug the heater during a water change. If the water level falls to, or below, the level of the heating coils, and the heater turns itself on, the glass tube may overheat and crack or break. If the aquarist is very unlucky, the tube cracks only slightly and then fills with water as the tank is refilled. This can be an electrifying experience for a hapless marine aquarist since salt water can carry a large charge.

Also, always be sure that the cord from any electrical device used in or around an aquarium loops below the plug level of the electric outlet. This will allow any salt water that may run down the cord to drip off and not enter the electric outlet. Be sure that a heater of this type is made for salt water use. The glass tube should be thick and the seals at the top strong and secure. The most common problems with this type of heater is sticking of the points and breakage of the heating element wire. Both of these malfunctions can be repaired, although the cost of heaters is low enough that replacement is often a better option than repair. Dewey (1986) has several articles on the repair and modification of aquarium heaters.

Totally submersible heaters are also now available and these are excellent for marine use if they are of high quality construction. They can remain totally submersed in a horizontal or vertical orientation, and are not subject to unwitting exposure during a water change. They can also be placed in the filter box sump of trickle type filters and not be present in the tank itself. Always use an accurate thermometer in the tank to set the thermostat on the heater, especially if the heater is in a location remote from the tank. The tight seal limits entry into this type of heater for repair. These standard types of aquarium heaters are available in sizes of 25 to 300 watts. Other types of heaters and thermostats are also available, usually at substantial cost, for very large systems or specialized, custom reef systems.

If the heater is too small for the tank, it will remain on far too much and may even remain on continuously during times of low room temperature, and possibly even allow the temperature of the system to drop to dangerously low levels. If the heater is too large for the system, it will heat the water quickly to the upper temperature setting and then allow the temperature to fall to the cut-on point of the thermostat, producing a "yo-yo" temperature effect in the tank. The greatest danger with a heater that is too large is that it can quickly overheat and "cook" an aquarium if the contact points in the thermostat should stick and fail to open.

In most instances, 2 watts per gallon should be all a system needs to keep it in the proper temperature range. An increase to 4 or 5 watts per gallon may be desired if the system is installed in a cool situation and/or if the surface of the tank is open to the room. Obviously a tank in a 65 to 70 °F environment is going to require a larger capacity heater than the same tank in a 75 to 80 °F environment. Also note that a trickle filter increases the rate of evaporation and heat loss in the system, and such a system may require increased heating capacity.

Cooling

Most marine aquarium systems do not need to be cooled. There are times, however, when particular systems do require some cooling, and there are some systems that need constant cooling because of a unique environment or special purpose. Water chillers specially designed for saltwater use are available for marine aquarium systems and also as part of systems developed to hold live American lobsters in retail seafood outlets. These units contain a compressor and operate on the principle that a liquid absorbs heat when it becomes vapor and gives off heat when compressed to a liquid. The vapor is first compressed to high pressure, pumped to a condenser where it becomes a liquid at lower temperature, and is then directed to the evaporator where it boils under lower pressure and absorbs heat from the water (or insulated container) that is to be cooled. These units are controlled by thermostats and can maintain the waters of marine systems at any point below room temperature that is desired. These units are expensive but are very effective in maintaining a cold water aquarium.

A less efficient, but similar and less expensive unit can be made from a small refrigerator or freezer by drilling holes into the cooling box and running non toxic hose or tubing into the box, laying extensive coils of the tubing within the cooling box, and then running the tube back to the system. Water pumped through the coils inside the cool box will lose heat at a rate controlled by the temperature of the box, the number of coils, and the amount of water flow through the tubing. The temperature of the system can be controlled by the amount of flow, but if the box is kept below the freezing point of full salinity saltwater, about minus 2°C (about 28.5°F), then the hose will freeze if the water flow stops or is too slow. Automatic temperature control of the system with this type of cooler is best obtained with a thermostatically controlled heater also operating within the system.

There may be times when some limited cooling is required on a temporary basis. One way to achieve temporary cooling, without changing or adding water, is to freeze fresh water in sealed plastic bottles and place the frozen bottles in the filter sump or aquarium in the afternoon of an extremely hot day. Leave an air space in the bottles to allow for expansion of the ice and use clean fresh water that will not affect the aquarium system if the bottles should happen to leak. Be sure to monitor temperature so that the system does not become too cold, too quickly.

Trickle filters, whether used on reef systems or on traditional, mostly fish tanks, efficiently remove heat from the water because water loses heat during evaporation. This heat loss occurs even if the room is warmer than the system because it is part of the energy exchange that occurs when a substance changes from one state to another, solid to liquid, liquid to gas, etc. Heat loss occurs during the phase change in water from liquid to gas and this is termed the *latent heat of vaporization*. Also if the air is cooler than the tank water, there is an active transfer of heat from the water to the air during the mixing of air and water. Heat enters the water in the system through radiation from the warmer air. It is possible for the heat loss of vaporization and the heat gained from warm air to balance each other. In any event, an aquarist with a reef system should always be aware of the temperature of the system and be prepared to adjust temperatures if necessary.

Filtration Theory

There are three main types of filtration: **biological, mechanical,** and **chemical**. They all function by flowing water through or over the substrate of a filter media. The interface, the surface between the solution and a gas or a solid, is the site where filtration actually occurs. The greater the available surface area, internal and external, the greater the filtration potential of the media.

Biological filtration utilizes living organisms to remove or transform toxic compounds generated within the system. Colonies of nitrifying bacteria, living on a substrate, transform (oxidize) toxic metabolic waste, ammonia and nitrite, into the relatively nontoxic nutrient, nitrate, a process termed **nitrification**. Heterotrophic bacteria break down (decay) complex proteins and other organic compounds containing nitrogen into ammonia, a process termed **mineralization**. Algal growth cultured for removal of nitrate and other nutrients is also a form of biological filtration. **Mechanical filtration** catches and holds large and small particles from water flows for removal or *in situ* decay. The physical size of the pores or matrix structure of the filter media determine the maximum size of the particles that are removed from the solution. **Chemical filtration** removes dissolved molecules from the water and adsorbs or absorbs them onto or into the structure of the filter media. Note that protein foam skimming, an efficient type of chemical filtration, uses tiny bubbles of air with or without ozone as the filter substrate for many organic molecules. Another type of chemical filtration adds or removes dissolved gases from the water through a pressurized reactor. Substrates used as filter media may perform one or more of these filtration functions depending on the type of media and design of the system. **Sterilization** of water may be considered a fourth type of filtration since it removes unwanted life forms from the system. The basic working theory for various types of filtration is presented in this section and the specific applications of different media and filter designs is included in the following sections.

The condition of marine aquarium systems can be determined and monitored by the use of test kits that enable the aquarist to determine pH, and levels of ammonia, nitrite, nitrate, copper and other important chemical parameters. It is very important to realize that these test kits contain dangerous chemicals and are not toys. They should not be turned over to young aquarists without careful supervision and exercise of due caution.

Biological Filtration — Theory and Testing
Since the 60's, biological filtration has been the subject of numerous magazine articles and has been covered extensively in almost every book that mentions marine aquarium systems. It is a complex biological process that is essential to the operation of aquatic culture systems and sewage processing plants. This process should be understood, at least in broad outline, by every marine aquarist. Briefly, and as simply as possible, let me explain the essence of biological filtration.

Fish, invertebrates, and decay of organic matter create nitrogen rich waste that is primarily in the form of ammonia, a chemical compound that is toxic to aquatic life. Billions of aerobic (requiring oxygen) bacteria living on a substrate that is exposed to this water use ammonia for energy and transform it to nitrite during this process. Nitrite is also toxic, but billions of another species of bacteria, also living on the same substrate, use nitrite for energy and transform it into the relatively non-toxic chemical compound, nitrate, a basic plant nutrient. Nitrate accumulates in the aquarium system until it is removed by water change, by plants growing in the system water, or by a denitrifyer. A denitrifyer is a type of biological filter that uses anaerobic (without oxygen) bacteria to break apart nitrate and release the excess nitrogen as free nitrogen gas. Although these few sentences describe the essence of biological filtration there is a bit more to it.

Chemical compounds called proteins make up most of the structure of all plant and animal cells. Plants and animals are constantly creating and destroying cells, and the proteins that compose them, as part of their use of energy (metabolism) during life. The composition of protein molecules includes a great deal of nitrogen, hydrogen, carbon, and oxygen. When protein molecules break down, either due to metabolic processes in the living organism or through the activity of heterotrophic decay bacteria, nitrogen and hydrogen are linked together to form ammonia (NH_3). Carbon and oxygen are linked as carbon dioxide (CO_2). Living animals release the nitrogen of metabolic waste in the form of urea, uric acid, or, in the case of many aquatic animals, directly as ammonia. Decay bacteria (many species of heterotrophic bacteria) use any available organic compounds—urea, proteins, amino acids, fats, and carbohydrates—as energy sources to fuel their own existence. As they remove the energy tied up in the chemical bonds of these organics, they break them down into simpler and simpler compounds until they are finally just simple inorganic minerals. This process is termed **mineralization**. Thus ammonia, the toxic waste product of the metabolic processes of animals and a major end product of mineralization, is liberated in large quantity into aquatic culture systems.

Ammonia is present in aquatic culture water in two forms, as free ammonia (NH_3) and in the ionized state, ammonium (NH_4+). The free ammonia molecule is polar with balanced positive and negative charges. An extra hydrogen atom attached to the free ammonia molecule (composed of one nitrogen and three hydrogen atoms) creates the positively charged ammonium ion. The term ammonia generally refers to total ammonia, the sum of both states. The presence of free ammonia in culture water apparently prevents animals from excreting their own waste ammonia and this retained ammonia is very toxic. Free ammonia can also cross tissue membranes, however, and it is possible that high levels of ammonia in the system water can invade tissues and increase the toxic effect of ammonia. Ammonium ions do not cross membranes as easily as free ammonia, but the charged ions can "burn" delicate animal membranes, cause physical damage, and greatly increase stress on animals exposed to high ammonia levels. Al-

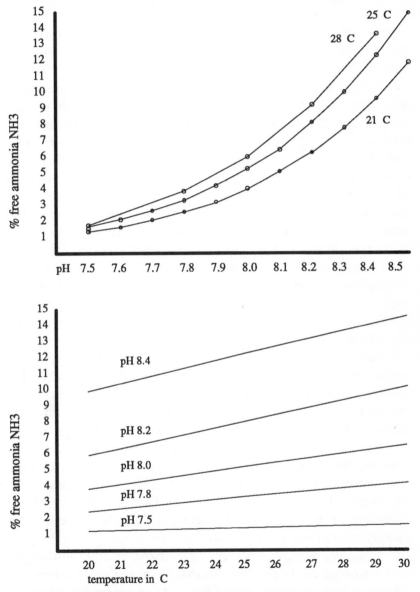

Figure 19. Percent free ammonia (NH3) in seawater at various temperatures and pH.

though both forms are toxic to animals, free ammonia (NH_3) is considered to be much more toxic. The presence of excess ammonia seems to interfere with the ability of hemoglobin in blood cells to carry oxygen, and this has a debilitating and eventually lethal effect on fish.

Fortunately, the less toxic ammonium ion is more abundant in aquatic solutions than the more toxic free ammonia. Free ammonia and ionized ammonium form an equilibrium reaction in water, which means that ammonia bounces back and forth between the free ammonia state and the ammonium ion state at a constant, steady rate. This equilibrium results in a stable balance between the amount of free ammonia and ammonium present in the solution. The reaction rate is affected by temperature and pH of the solution. The equilibrium shifts away from ionized ammonium as temperature and pH rise and the percentage of free ammonia increases. Figure 19 illustrates the relative percentages of free ammonia present in sea water at various temperatures and pH. Note that the toxicity of ammonia increases as temperature and pH increase because there is more free ammonia present. Thus, a marine aquarium system operating at a pH of 8.0 and 77°F is more protected from ammonia toxicity than a system operated at a pH of 8.3 and a temperature of 82°F. Only about 5.0 per cent of the total ammonia is the most toxic free ammonia in the former system while the latter system has about 11.5 percent of total ammonia as toxic free ammonia. Note that all ammonia is eventually removed from a solution even if the filtration method removes only the charged ammonium ion. As ammonium is removed, the balance between free ammonia and ammonium begins to shift, free ammonia is transformed into ammonium and is then also removed from the solution.

Ammonia test. Ammonia is measured as milligrams per liter, same as parts per million (mg/l or ppm), of ammonia nitrogen. It used to be very difficult to measure ammonia in seawater. Tests were complex and toxic. Detection of ammonia was based on use of Nessler's reagent, which is very toxic and quickly forms an insoluble precipitate in salt water. With

Nessler's reagent, the amount of ammonia is determined by the intensity of a yellow color. Technology has moved us rapidly ahead, however, and now test kits that measure total ammonia by the salicylate to hypochlorite method, a green to blue reaction, are readily available. There is even a hydrophobic sensor strip available that measures only free ammonia on a continuous basis. All one needs to do is look at it. It will measure total ammonia at a pH of 11, the point where all ammonia is in the free ammonia state. Note that when testing for ammonia, whatever the method, it is important to be aware of whether the test reports only free ammonia or total ammonia.

With an efficient biological filter, however, there need never be much ammonia in any state in a mature marine aquarium system. There is energy in the chemical bonds of nitrogen and hydrogen in the ammonia molecule, and there are bacteria, chemoautotrophs, that can utilize this energy. Nitrifying bacteria in the genus *Nitrosomonas* are ellipsoidal or rod shaped bacteria that make their living by oxidizing ammonia into nitrite (NO_2). This provides the energy that allows the bacteria to utilize other compounds as well. Other genera that do the same thing are *Nitrosospira*, *Nitrosococcus*, and *Nitrosolobus*. These chemoautotrophic bacteria tear apart molecules of ammonia, utilize the energy in the chemical bonds, and release the waste nitrogen along with two atoms of oxygen as a molecule of nitrite (NO_2). They need a substrate to live on and a source of ammonia and oxygen in a damp or aquatic environment to grow and form colonies.

We aren't out of the woods yet, however, because nitrite is also toxic to aquatic organisms. In the case of fish, nitrite oxidizes hemoglobin to methemoglobin, which cannot carry oxygen. High levels of nitrite, more than 5 to 10 ppm, can cause mortality in some species of fish and some invertebrates. The presence of high levels of ammonia and nitrite cause newly set up marine aquariums to become variably toxic to fish and invertebrates, the infamous "new tank syndrome". A separate order of chemoautotrophic nitrifying bacteria, the Nitrobacteriales, including the genera *Nitrobacter, Nitrospira, Nitrocystis,* and *Nitrococcus,* comes to the rescue of the beleaguered marine aquarist at this point. These bacteria gain energy through the oxidative process of tacking another oxygen atom onto the nitrite molecule (NO_2) and changing it into nitrate (NO_3). To exist, these bacteria need a substrate to live on and a source of nitrite and oxygen in a damp or aquatic environment. The growth of colonies of *Nitrobacter* are inhibited by the presence of high levels of ammonia. They can not grow vigorously until nitrite is present and even when *Nitrosomonas* begins to produce nitrite, *Nitrobacter* colonies can't get off the starting block until ammonia levels are quite low. This is why such high levels of nitrite appear and persist for so long during the establishment of new systems. Nitrifying bacteria of both groups are present in soils, freshwater, and marine waters throughout the world.

Nitrite test. Testing for nitrite is very important since the precipitous drop in nitrite level is the signal that the filter is conditioned well enough to support most marine life. Nitrite is measured as milligrams per liter (mg/l or ppm) of nitrite-nitrogen. The test is also, fortunately, very easy and accurate. One can run very successful marine systems using only the nitrite test to determine when the filter is conditioned and occasionally to check on the function of the biological filter. Ammonia and nitrate testing, however, provide very valuable additional information and better control of the aquarium system. The nitrite test uses the reagents sulfanilamide and a dye, N-(1-naphthyl)-ethylenediamine. This test produces a red color with an intensity dependent on the amount of nitrite present in the sample.

Nitrate is not subject to further bacterial oxidation and tends to accumulate in marine aquarium systems. It is perhaps 1000 times less toxic to fish than nitrite and can be allowed to accumulate to some extent in marine aquarium systems, especially systems devoted to fish keeping. The effects of high nitrate levels on invertebrates is varied and speculative, but general observations indicate that moderate nitrate levels seem to inhibit the well being and development of many invertebrates. Invertebrates also seem less able to acclimate to rapid changes in nitrate concentration. As a general rule, invertebrates should not be moved from a system with very high or very low nitrate concentration to a system with the opposite condition. Also, water changes aimed at lowering high nitrate levels in an invertebrate systems should be accomplished in several steps over a period of several days to a week rather than all at once.

A tank devoted to invertebrates should be maintained at low, less than 10 to 15 ppm, levels of nitrate for best results. The traditional method of lowering nitrate levels is to regularly change a certain percentage of system water. Ten percent per month is usually recommended. Even smaller amounts, three to four percent, can be exchanged per week if desired. This uses a bit more water but reduces water change stress on the creatures in the tank. This method of nitrate control has the added advantage of replacing some trace elements and removing other detrimental compounds as well as nitrate. Since nitrate is utilized as a nutrient by plants, it can also be diminished by active algal growth.

Nitrate test. Nitrate is measured as milligrams per liter (mg/l or ppm) of nitrate-nitrogen. The concentration of the nitrate ion is obtained by multiplying by 4.4. A test kit with a very low range measures nitrate ion concentration. In most test kits, hydrazine or brucine reduces nitrate, and a color intensity reaction measures the amount of nitrate present in the sample. If nitrate is reduced to nitrite as the end product, then the amount of nitrite is first determined and subtracted from the final nitrate determination.

Denitrification

Biological denitrification is a relatively new method of controlling nitrate accumulation in hobbyist's marine systems. Denitrifying bacteria are found in all waters all over the world and most can function in the presence or absence of oxygen. Depending on the species or mix of species, they have the ability to feed on organic compounds (mostly carbohydrates) and respire anaerobically (in the absence of oxygen) through the mechanism of reducing nitrate to a variety of other compounds including nitrite, ammonia, nitrous oxide, and molecular nitrogen. These bacteria, *Micrococcus, Pseudomonas, Denitrobacillas, Bacillus*, and numerous others are found in small populations in all marine systems. The genus *Thiobacillus* (eight species) utilizes reduced sulfur compounds such as sulfide, thiosulfate, and bisulfite as food, and under anaerobic conditions, respires by reducing nitrate and liberating nitrogen from nitrate as nitrogen gas. These bacteria can be used to remove nitrate from marine systems when the proper food in the proper amount is provided under anaerobic conditions. It is the kind of food that is offered that determines the type of bacteria that colonize the filter media. Denitrification can also occur in the oxygenated environments of the system, but this natural process can seldom cope with the normal accumulations of nitrate unless an anaerobic site is provided. See the section on denitrifyers for more information on denitrification.

Establishing Biological Filtration

There are many designs, structures, and types of media that facilitate biological filtration and many of these are discussed in the section on the structure of biological filters. The following comments, however, pertain to all biological filters.

The essence of biological filtration is to bring together, in a continuous process, water containing waste nitrogen in the forms of ammonia and nitrite, ample oxygen, and a media that provides ample substrate for growth of colonies of nitrifying bacteria. The nitrifying bacteria form colonies over all suitable external and internal surface areas of the media. Nitrifying bacteria are in the size range of 0.5 to 2.0 microns, although the colonies are considerably larger. A filter media with pores in the 5 to 50 micron range operates most efficiently since the pores are able to harbor colonies of nitrifying bacteria without quickly clogging with organic material, thus reducing sites for nitrification. A biological filter may also do other things—gas exchange, mechanical or chemical filtration, for example—but it is how well it performs the above function on a long term, continuing basis that determines the efficiency of a particular biological filter design.

Once these three criteria are met, the following colonization sequence usually takes place. Colonies of *Nitrosomonas* and *Nitrobacter* are separate organisms with independent, but similar environmental requirements. For their energy supply, the former requires ammonia and the latter requires nitrite. Colonies of *Nitrosomonas* can not become established on the filter substrate until a source of ammonia is present. And since *Nitrobacter* depends on the waste product of *Nitrosomonas*, it can not grow until *Nitrosomonas* colonies have become established and are actively producing nitrite from ammonia. Populations of heterotrophic bacteria that break nitrogenous organics down to ammonia do not become established until sufficient organic material is present in the system. Strong light seems to inhibit the activity of nitrifying bacteria. Biological filters kept under conditions of low light or darkness function better. Figure 20 illustrates the most probable sequence of bacterial colonization and chemical fluctuation in a newly established marine aquarium system.

The carrying capacity of a biological filter is measured as the total weight per specific volume of water of all the animals that can live in a marine aquarium system without creating excess ammonia or nitrite within the system. This includes fish and invertebrates, of course, and also all the heterotrophic bacteria and the tiny worms, copepods, and other microscopic organisms in the tank and filters. A balance is soon established between the ammonia produced from animal excretion and mineralization of organic matter, and the nitrifying activity of filter bacteria populations. Expansion or reduction of the biological load is followed by increase or decrease in filter bacteria populations. The total potential carrying capacity of the system—as defined by water volume, gas exchange

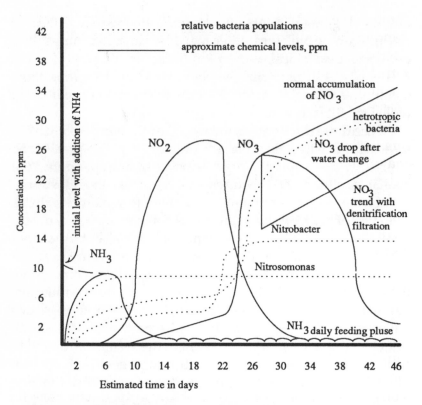

Figure 20 Probable sequence of chemical fluctuation and bacterial colonization in new biological filters.

capacity, active surface area of biological filtration, flow rates through filters, and aeration and water currents in the tank—should always be considerably greater than the actual biological load. This allows for some expansion of the biological load and assures high water quality and decreased need for water change within the capabilities of the filter system.

About six percent of the food added to marine systems shows up as nitrogenous waste within a few hours. Populations of nitrifying bacteria expand or diminish as the waste nitrogen in the system fluctuates. This balance is not a razor edge; an extra fish or two, an extra feeding, or a small dead fish tucked down behind a rock will not send ammonia levels through the roof. Populations of nitrifying bacteria expand to handle the additional load and then decline if the load decreases. There may be a detectable rise in ammonia and nitrite after such an addition, which quickly diminishes when the filter is free of detritus and well populated with nitrifying bacteria.

Trickle filters usually stay clean and give the nitrifyers ample oxygen and substrate. Old undergravel filters, however, may become clogged with detritus and so heavy with heterotrophic bacteria that colonies of nitrifying bacteria are few and occupy little substrate. A system in this condition will not recover quickly from the daily pulses of ammonia due to feeding, the balance of the system tilts toward filter overload, and fish and invertebrates show signs of stress.

The carrying capacity of the biological filter of a marine system can be calculated with some accuracy and the filter preconditioned to support a specific bio load of animals. The aquarist must know the number, species, and size (biomass) of the animals that will occupy the system, their protein nitrogen utilization rate, the amount of food that will be fed, and the amount of nitrogen contained in the food. A hobbyist or professional aquarist that wants to go through the calculations for precise preconditioning of a biological filter for a specific biological load is advised to consult Siddall (1974) and Spotte (1979).

There are two considerations in getting a biological filter up and running. The first is the source of the nitrifying bacteria and the second is the initial source of energy (ammonia and/or nitrite) for the nitrifying bacteria. The two procedures, seeding and feeding new bacterial colonies, are an integrated process; although the aquarist has specific choices on each procedure. The effects of one upon the other can be great or small, depending on many variables that are impossible to predict. There have been a number of laboratory studies and product tests on establishment and maintenance of nitrifying bacteria. The variables are so great, however, that only speculation is possible about what may happen in the particular systems of individual hobbyists. Note that no matter the method of initial seeding and feeding, the nitrifying capacity of the filter soon adjusts to the level of constant ammonia production by the biological load within the system. Some establishment methods allow a greater initial biological load than others. Moe (1982) presents additional comments on establishing a biological filter and a day by day chart on conditioning and maintenance of an undergravel biological filter. In general, this is also applicable to trickle filters.

Seeding nitrifying bacteria

There are four major sources of nitrifying bacteria: environment, commercial preparations, active filter beds, and garden soil.

The environment. The first source is air, water, filter substrates, dust, fish, invertebrates, algae, rocks, hands, hoses, and, in general, anything that is not sterilized that comes in contact with the system. Active and dormant states of nitrifying bacteria, and many other bacteria, are present everywhere. A marine system set up with a source of inorganic or organic ammonia will eventually cycle through the establishment of *Nitrosomonas, Nitrobacter*, and heterotrophic bacteria with no action on the part of the aquarist except patience. The filter may cycle more slowly or more rapidly than bacteria seeded filters, depending on the idiosyncrasy of the particular system. The typical response, however, is a relatively slow initiation of the nitrogen cycle. The only advantage to this method is the elimination of the possibility of introducing parasites or disease causing bacteria along with any active bacterial seed.

Commercial preprations. The second source is commercial preparations of active or dormant nitrifying bacteria. Several preparations of nitrifying bacteria are available that claim to aid the establishment of nitrifying bacteria in marine systems. Some also provide a first food for the filter bacteria as part of the preparation. Although the function of the biological filter is dependent on developing active colonies of *Nitrosomonas* and *Nitrobacter* on the substrate of the filter media, and this will inevitably happen if a source of ammonia is present, inoculating the system with large numbers (very large numbers) of the right kind of bacteria will usually shorten the process.

Commercial preparations of nitrifying bacteria will **not** provide an instant mature or "run in" filter. When everything is right, however—the preparation is not to old and hasn't been subjected to too much heat or cold, and the water contains no chloramine, chlorine or other bactericidal compound—then use of these preparations according to instructions will aid filter establishment. These preparations of nitrifying bacteria come in a sealed powered or liquid form. Most are designed to seed the system with a large charge of active nitrifying bacteria that quickly find a substrate and get down to the business of producing bacterial colonies. A recently released type of dormant bacterial preparation new on the market claims to contain ten different species of mutated hybrid bacteria, including forms that will perform denitrification at low oxygen levels. Repeated applications of the this preparation is required, however, to maintain the dominance of these hybrid bacteria strains in the system.

Active filter beds. Transfer of active filter media from an established biological filter is the third source. Obviously, the amount and condition of filter media transplanted to the new tank is very important. If taken from a long established filter that has seldom been cleaned, the filter media may be heavy with heterotrophic bacteria and hold few colonies of nitrifying bacteria. Media from a clean filter that has been supporting a high biological load will contain many young active colonies of nitrifying bacteria. Bacteria mostly reproduce by fission (division of one cell into two). Under good conditions, one cell can divide every thirty minutes. This means that once large numbers of bacteria have colonized the filter, the populations of bacteria required to handle the ammonia/nitrite load can be attained very quickly. This is why very high levels of nitrite can fall to zero within a day or two once the filter is colonized.

A cupful of active media from a good tank will put large numbers of the right kind of bacteria into the new filter, but will not provide the new system with an instant nitrifying capacity. It will take at least three to four weeks before the new filter is colonized and becomes functional. Alright, then if we put three cups of filter media into the new system, it will only take one week, right? Wrong! The new media does not act like an established filter, the bacteria are jumbled up, many are dislodged from the media (especially gravel media), and the effect of three or four cups instead of one cup does not appreciably alter the establishment sequence of the filter.

Now, if half a filter bed or more is carefully transferred to a new tank, then this is a different situation. There will be a loss of nitrifying ability because of the move, but the transferred filter media, not the new filter media, will be able to support a reduced biological load. For best results, the temperature and pH of the new tank should be the same as the tank providing the filter seed. Bower and Turner (1981) determined through laboratory analysis that seeding new filters with media from an established filter is the most effective method of inoculating new filters. The "critical mass" of media transfer seemed to be about ten percent. When ten percent or more of the filter bed of a new tank is made up of media from a conditioned tank, conditioning of the new filter bed is accomplished in only a few days rather than a few weeks. Evidently the population mass of bacteria that are transferred is great enough to rapidly establish active new colonies of nitrifying bacteria. Even air dried media from a conditioned tank will speed the run-in process in a new tank. The danger in this method, of course, is the transfer of disease organisms with the inoculum of filter seed.

Garden soil. Garden soil extract is the fourth source. If no other source of nitrifying bacteria is available and there seems to be some difficulty in getting the filter established, an extract of garden soil may be helpful. It is important to use only *moist* soil that has not been treated with pesticides or fertilizers. At most, a cup of this soil is mixed with a gallon of seawater and allowed to settle. A few cups of the soil treated water is then added to the tank. Wilkens (1973) suggests this procedure as a way of providing nutrients for algal growth. It will also provide a seed of nitrifying and heterotrophic bacteria.

Feeding nitrifying bacteria

There are three major methods of feeding new colonies of nitrifying bacteria: organic, inorganic, and reverse inorganic.

The organic method. This is the traditional method that was used even before the biology of biological filters were understood. A few hardy fish and/or invertebrates are placed into the tank and given the task of producing the initial ammonia required to start the sequence of filter establishment. The animals that are chosen for this task must be hardy and expendable, killifish and crabs for example. Under most situations, they will live through the cycling of the filter and can then be passed on to another system. *It is important to note that the filter will be conditioned to support about the same biological load after conditioning that it carried during establishment of the filter.* If five relatively small fish were used to run in a 70 gallon system, adding 20 fish and a few invertebrates after nitrite levels drop will cause ammonia and nitrite levels to immediately rise and stay high until the bacteria colonies expand sufficiently to handle the increased load.

This can be expensive to an impatient aquarist that can't wait to add a large number of $50.00 fish to a newly run in tank. Also, with this method, heterotrophic bacteria that compete with nitrifying bacteria for substrate space are stimulated to develop immediately along with the nitrifyers. A variation of this method is to introduce a few dead shrimp or other dead organic material. Ammonia production is delayed until heterotrophic decay bacteria have mineralized the organics, however, and although it will work, I don't think it is the best way of establishing nitrifying bacteria. The initial nitrifying potential of the filter, especially undergravel filters, is diminished by these methods. One advantage, however, is that nitrate production is held to the minimum and the need for water change after filter establishment is also minimal. This method of filter establishment is quite adequate for relatively small systems that will carry relatively small, stable biological loads.

The direct inorganic method. This method was developed after the importance of an initial ammonia source was understood. The essence of this method of filter establishment is to provide the nitrifying bacteria with a large dose of inorganic ammonia. Siddall (1973, 1974) developed this method of establishing colonies of nitrifying bacteria and was able to achieve 2.5 to 3 times the normal nitrifying capacity of biological filters under laboratory conditions. This increase is achieved because growth of the nitrifying bacteria colonies is not limited by ammonia and subsequent nitrite availability. Also, because of the absence of organics, heterotrophic bacteria are not competing for substrate surface.

Siddall's method for small systems is to add 12 grams of ammonium chloride for each 20 gallons of system water and inoculate the tank with 2 or 3 cups of filter media from an active, healthy filter. A commercial preparation of nitrifying bacteria can also be used. When ammonia levels drop below the detectable range, nitrites should be sky high. This is the time to add another inoculum of filter media or nitrifying bacteria culture. This is done to add a viable culture of *Nitrobacter* in case the high levels of ammonia have debilitated the nitrite oxidizers that were in the first inoculum. When nitrite levels drop, the result will be a heavy duty load of nitrifying bacteria on the filter media and an excessive amount of nitrate in the water. Unless a denitrifyer is able to remove this nitrate load in a very short time, all or most of the water in the system must be changed to remove the nitrate. If the aquarist goes through all this and then adds only a few fish, the effort is wasted. If the bacteria do not continuously receive the same levels of ammonia and nitrite, the populations die back to levels commensurate with the steady production of ammonia.

This method establishes a good, high capacity filter for a highly populated commercial system or a reef type system with an immediate and heavy load of live rock and marine organisms, but for the average small tank, it's like renting a truck to return a library book. Cutting the ammonia charge down from 45 ppm to 5 to 10 ppm (1.5 to 3 grams of ammonium chloride) gives the average system a strong nitrifying base for the biological filter that is established without competition from heterotrophic bacteria, and results in more manageable initial nitrate levels.

The reverse inorganic method. This method was suggested in an article by Morin (1983), and although I have not tried it, it makes sense. The concept is to initially feed the inoculated bacteria with nitrite to first establish colonies of *Nitrobacter* and then to feed ammonia to secondarily establish the ammonia eaters, the *Nitrosomonas*. Even though *Nitrobacter* are inhibited by high levels of ammonia, the colonies are already established and will survive well enough through development of the *Nitrosomonas* colonies to be able to pick up the ball on nitrite oxidization and prevent or decrease the long time lag caused by ammonia inhibition on colonization of *Nitrobacter*. Addition of 5 grams of sodium nitrite per 20 gallons at the time of bacterial inoculation will start the *Nitrobacter*. Add about 2 grams of ammonium chloride when nitrite levels begin to drop and then monitor ammonia and nitrite levels until both are near zero. One detrimental result of this method might be higher levels of nitrate when the filter establishment is complete.

Mechanical Filtration

Aquarium system water contains many undissolved particles. Some are very small, a few microns or less, consisting of bacteria and bits of organic and inorganic molecules clumped together. Diatomaceous earth filters capture very small particles in the range of a few microns. Most mechanical filters in marine systems, however, capture particles larger than 50 to 100 microns. A mechanical filter captures smaller and smaller particles as it clogs with organic and inorganic particles, but water flows diminish as resistance increases. Larger particles tend to settle to the bottom in aquariums, especially when there is minimal turbulence and water circulation. Organic particles enter the biological cycles of the system as soon as they settle. A mechanical filter catches and holds particles by physically trapping the particle within the filter (straining or sieving), or by binding the particle to the filter through a chemical or biological process. The composition, grain, pore, or fiber size, and rate of water flow determine the efficiency of the mechanical filter and the size of the smallest particles that are captured. Filters that capture very small particles can quickly clog and need to be cleaned frequently to maintain functional water flows. Coarse filters remove fewer particles but clog more slowly.

An efficient mechanical filter performs a valuable function by capturing organic particles that would otherwise decay and add to the waste nitrogen and dissolved organic compounds in the system water. To perform this function, however, the filter must be frequently cleaned and the particles removed from the system. Now if the mechanical filter is not cleaned frequently and the particles are allowed to accumulate and decay, the filter still acts as a mechanical filter, but it also becomes a biological filter with mineralizing and nitrifying functions. Undergravel filters are designed to perform both functions, thus they are not the most efficient kind of biological or mechanical filter, although they do perform these functions adequately in most situations.

A strictly mechanical filter is usually a foam or fiber pad or a floss layer or plug. These can be very effective if cleaned and replaced regularly. However, if they become clogged and water begins to pass over or around the media rather than through it, then they no longer function as a mechanical filter and become dangerous sites of possible anaerobic decay. Large mechanical filters such as sand filters for swimming pools or for large culture systems are cleaned by reversing the water flow (back flushing), and sending the back flush water to waste. The media for small filters—floss, foam, sand—can be rinsed clean or just replaced. Undergravel filters also function as mechanical filters and must be cleaned regularly to preserve both biological and mechanical filter functions. Moe (1982) contains instructions on cleaning undergravel filter beds.

Chemical Filtration

Chemical filtration removes molecules of dissolved compounds from simple or complex solutions, including the very complex aqueous solution of marine aquarium system water. The important point is that while mechanical filtration removes undissolved particles, chemical filtration removes dissolved substances, molecule by molecule. In a way, however, chemical filtration is actually mechanical filtration on a molecular basis. Many molecules have particular characteristics of size or chemistry that allow us to design a filter media that can remove them from the solution. There are three processes—absorption, ion-exchange, and adsorption—that make up chemical filtration. Figure 21 illustrates how non-charged, polar, charged, and hydrophilic molecules interact at the interface surface of gas and solid filter media.

All three processes are usually at work to some degree in all chemical filter media, although specific types of media are designed to use one of these processes on a primary basis. Activated carbon is most effective in removing nonpolar molecules, and protein foam skimming is most effective in removal of polar molecules. In fact, many chemical filter media, carbons and resins, are now designed to be very specific in the types of molecules that they remove from solutions. Except for absorption (molecular sieving), chemical filtration is basically a surface effect. The total surface area of the media is the sum of all the internal and external surfaces, but the internal surface area far, far exceeds the external surface.

The target molecule is brought very close to the media surface and it is then chemically attracted or even bonded to the surface. For this process to work, the media must have a huge, vast, incomprehensibly great, and very big surface area, and the surfaces must be very, very, close together so that the

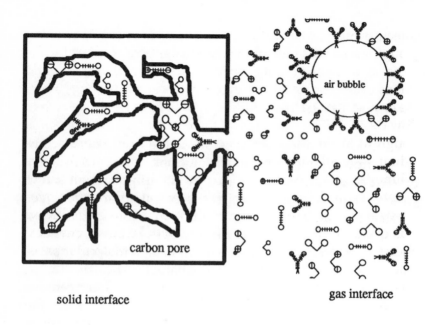

solid interface   gas interface

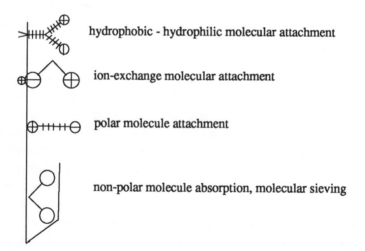

hydrophobic - hydrophilic molecular attachment

ion-exchange molecular attachment

polar molecule attachment

non-polar molecule absorption, molecular sieving

Figure 21. The molecular processes of chemical filtration. Various molecules attach to surface substrates by absorption, adsorption, and ion-exchange.

molecules must brush extremely close to a surface as they move through the media. This is accomplished by structuring the media as a small granule, fiber, or sphere with billions and billions of tiny pores and channels extending through the particle or fiber. The particle of filter media has to be big enough to allow development of extensive internal surface area yet small enough to allow water good access to all internal areas. The optimum particle size for this effect has a diameter of about one millimeter. This size allows utilization of almost 90 percent of the internal surface area before exhaustion, while larger particle sizes may be able to fill only 50 percent of the internal area. Thus chemical filter media are in the form of small granules, spheres, or fibers and are used in filters usually shaped as tubes or boxes so that water can flow efficiently through the media. Water flowing over or around a bag of chemical filter media is not nearly as effective as a water flow forced through the media. Chemical filtration works at the molecular level and it works the same way in large and small systems.

Absorption
     The term absorption usually brings to mind a sponge soaking up water, and a particle of carbon filter media functions much the same. At the molecular level, however, the term molecular sieving is more accurate. This process removes molecules on the basis of size. Water molecules are very small, polar but uncharged, and can travel easily through very tiny pores, tunnels, and crevices in the filter media without getting trapped in the structure of the media. The water carries many other molecules with it into the media, and if the pores are the right size, large organic molecules become physically trapped within the structure of the media. Thus absorption, or molecular sieving, is the physical collection of molecules that are just the right size to be trapped within the structure of the media.
     A good molecular sieve particle has many pores and channels that wind inward, vary in direction, and diminish in size. Over time, the media can fill up with these molecules and when

this happens, the efficiency of the media to remove a particular size molecule declines sharply. The trapped molecules are not held within the media by any chemical attraction and are free to leave if they can find their way out of the maze of channels and pores. In filled (exhausted) media, these molecules do move in and out of the media structure. Although very important, molecular sieving is the least effective of the chemical filtration processes. It sort of just happens in media that are designed for ion-exchange or adsorption.

Ion-exchange

This process uses the charge on an ionized molecule to bond the molecule to an oppositely charged surface. A polar molecule has both positive and negative charges that are balanced within the molecule. A polar molecule will orient in an electrical field, positive pole toward negative charge and negative pole toward positive charge, but will not migrate toward either charge. A charged or ionized molecule, however, has an extra positive or negative charge that is not internally balanced. A positively charged molecule, a cation, will migrate toward the negative pole in a electrical field and a negatively charged molecule, an anion, will migrate toward the positive pole. When an ionized (charged) molecule touches a surface with the opposite charge, a chemical bond (an ion exchange) is established between surface and molecule and the charged molecule becomes firmly attached to the surface. The charged surface usually gives up a sodium ion in exchange for the ion it accepts. In effect, the molecule becomes bonded to the surface and is removed from the solution.

This is how zeolite clays remove the positively charged ammonium molecules from freshwater. However, there are so many positively charged cations in seawater, such as sodium, that zeolite is essentially nonfunctional in removing ammonium from salt water. Ion exchange systems are of limited use in marine systems because of the large variety of cations and anions in salt water. Interionic competition presents the greatest limitation to use of ion exchange systems, but particle size and organic fouling of the exchange sites also limit effectiveness. Ion exchange resins are manufactured as little plastic beads with specific, internal pore sizes. They have specific surface charge characteristics (strong or weak—cation or anion exchange) and specific impurities. The impurities affect the ion-exchange characteristics of the resin. Different types have been developed to remove particular ionized molecules from a wide range of solutions in various industrial processes. Some of these ion exchange resins find use in marine and freshwater aquarium systems.

Adsorption

A molecule that has been adsorbed is physically attached to the filter media. Complex, organic, polar molecules with balanced internal charges, including polar molecules with hydrophilic and hydrophobic ends (mostly proteins) are the best candidates for an adsorption process. Solid surface adsorption, which takes place in activated carbon and some resins, occurs when a polar molecule drifts close enough to a polar surface to be attracted and then attached to it. The molecule is held to the surface by a weak or strong charge and is effectively removed from solution. A permanent bond is created if the attractive charge is strong. Weak attractive charges (*van der Waals* forces) create a physical adsorption that can be reversed (desorption). Some organic molecules, for example, are released from a particular surface when the pH of the solution changes. The molecules must first enter a pore of the filter media particle and then attach to a site on the vast inner surface. The media does not release an ion in exchange for a charged molecule as does an ion-exchange media.

Adsorption can also take place on a water/gas interface as well as on a water/solid interface. Many organic molecules (dissolved organic carbon, DOC) are polar on one end ($-OH$, $-COOH$, $=NH$, $-NH_2$, $-CN$, $=PO_4$, etc.) and that end is attracted to water, a polar solution. This is termed the "water loving" or hydrophilic end. The other end of the molecule is the "water hating" or hydrophobic end. These surface active molecules (surfactants) are attracted to a water/gas surface. The hydrophobic end tends to leave the water while the hydrophilic end tends to remain in the water. The shiny, greasy surface of old aquarium water is the result of the accumulation of these molecules at the water surface. Organic molecules adsorbed onto the surface of a bubble of air create a sort of "skin" around the bubble and allow it to temporarily retain its form when it leaves the water. These bubbles form a foam when active and a scum when they collapse. Generating and removing this foam before it can reenter the culture system is the principle behind protein foam skimmer devices.

Reverse osmosis

Osmosis is the selective movement of molecules in a aqueous solution through a semipermeable membrane. A semipermeable membrane allows some molecules to move freely back and forth through the membrane while denying passage to other molecules. Molecules of certain sizes, shapes and charges can not pass through membranes with certain characteristics. Most biological membranes, cell walls for example, are semipermeable, thus cells can retain some molecules (certain nutrients) and freely pass other molecules (CO_2, O_2, and water). Semipermeable membranes can be made that allow water molecules to pass back and forth, but prevent passage of larger molecules of organic and inorganic compounds, including salts.

Now if we have two containers of water separated by a semipermeable membrane that excludes salts, water molecules can move between the two containers, but the salts must remain in their original container. If both containers hold only freshwater or the *same* concentrations of salts, then the system is stable. Water molecules move back and forth and the salt molecules stay on their own side of the membrane. We create an **osmotic pressure**, however, if there is an uneven concentration of salts on opposite sides of the membrane. If one side has freshwater and the other an equal volume of saltwater, there are more water molecules on the side that has no salts because the salt molecules also take up space. Water flows through the semipermeable membrane from the freshwater side toward the salt side to balance this unequal distribution of water. The water level rises in the salty container and falls in the fresh-water container and an osmotic pressure, negative on the fresh side and positive on the salt side, is the result. This is fine if we want to dilute salt water with pure freshwater, but what if we want to get rid of the salts completely and create freshwater from salt water. In this case we have to persuade the water molecules to move through the semipermeable membrane *against normal osmotic pressure* and accumulate on the fresh water side. The way to do this is to physically increase the pressure of the water on the salty side of the membrane beyond the osmotic pressure and cause the water molecules to reverse their normal flow and go through the membrane away from the salt concentration. When this is done, pure water without any salt or other large molecules accumulates on the low pres-sure side of the membrane and salt concentrations increase on the salty side. This procedure is called reverse osmosis.

Reverse osmosis can be valuable to marine aquarists under certain conditions. It is important in some marine reef systems to use water that is clear of any nutrients—especially nitrogen containing compounds, organic phosphates and salicic acid—to prevent excess algae growth. Tap water in some locations contains considerable nutrients and reverse osmosis can be used to prepare the initial water for the system and to process the water that is used to make up for evaporation loss. In certain locations, under certain conditions, use of nutrient free make up water greatly improves the ecology of the captive reef system. Some marine reef aquarists pass the tap water used to make up evaporative water loss through first a reverse osmosis filter and then a de-ionization resin filter to remove all organic and inorganic contaminatents. Although the average reef sys-tem aquarist propably does not need to go to such lengths to prepare their freshwater, water problems in certain areas may require use of bottled water or special processing to eliminate recurrent problems with algal and diatom growth. Reverse osmosis is a filtration technique used only to prepare the fresh water used to make up artificial seawater and not as a filter for continuous use.

Reactors — gas and substrate

A "reactor" is basically a separate trickle or tube filter that operates independently of the main filter unit and is designed to accomplish a specific function. Water is drawn from the tank or some point in the main filter system, processed in the reactor, and returned to the tank or to the main filter system.

The function of a **gas reactor** is to add a gas to the water more efficiently than is possible by bubbling or by conventional trickle filters. Under normal atmospheric pressure, water can contain only a specific amount of any particular gas: oxygen, ozone, nitrogen, carbon dioxide, etc. For example, if the water has less dissolved oxygen than it can hold, oxygen enters the water from the atmosphere until the water is "saturated" with oxygen, and then oxygen molecules enter and leave the water at the same rate. If the water has more oxygen than it can hold it is said to be "super saturated" with oxygen, and excess oxygen leaves the water and goes into the atmosphere. This exchange takes place through the surface or "interface" between the water and the air.

Get a glass of hypothetical tap water and place it on the table. Chances are that the water has a little more or less oxygen and carbon dioxide than it can hold according to the atmospheric conditions around the table. Over time, maybe overnight, oxygen and carbon dioxide in the water in the glass will equilibrate with the air, the gases will leave or enter the water through the surface, and the concentration of various gases in the water become "balanced" with the atmosphere. Now pour the water out of the glass onto the table, (It's OK, it's just hypothetical water. Tell your mother I said it wouldn't hurt anything.) Now the water that was in the glass has a lot of surface area. In fact, the thin film of water on the table is mostly surface area. Gases in the air and water can go back and forth very quickly because most of the water is very near the air. The gases are balanced with the atmosphere in seconds rather than hours. This is the same thing that happens when water is trickled in a thin film over a substrate in a typical trickle filter. The vast amount of surface area allows oxygen and carbon dioxide to enter and leave the water very quickly, and through this rapid gas exchange, the amount of oxygen and carbon dioxide in the water is balanced with the atmosphere. Usually, oxygen enters the water and carbon dioxide leaves.

Things like temperature, pressure, and salinity affect how much oxygen—and other gases—water can hold. Warm, saltwater, for example, as we mentioned in Chapter 1, holds considerably less oxygen than cold, freshwater. Under certain conditions, an aquarist may wish to dissolve more oxygen, ozone or carbon dioxide into the water than it can normally hold, or in other words, to supersaturate the water with a particular gas. Supersaturation with oxygen and/or ozone improves the redox potential of the system, and supersaturation with carbon dioxide aids growth of algae and reduces pH when strong algal photosynthesis drives pH upward during daylight hours. We can't conveniently change temperature or salinity, but we can easily construct a trickle filter in a pressurized container—a "gas reactor". It operates under higher than normal air pressure and forces the water to accept more dissolved gas than it would at normal atmospheric pressure. The "extra" gas is quickly accepted by the water when it is trickling in a thin film over the filter substrate within the pressurized container. The gas remains in the water for a relatively long time after it is collected and replaced in the tank where there is limited surface area for gas exchange. Now we're not talking about a lot of gas, not nearly as much as the carbon dioxide that bubbles out of solution when a bottle of soda water is opened. We're adding just enough to get a few more parts per million of oxygen or carbon dioxide, which is enough to make important changes in the chemistry of the system.

A gas reactor is transparent tube, or narrow box, filled with a trickle filter substrate and sealed on the top and bottom. Length is important, and it may be 1 to 3 feet high and 4 to 8 inches in diameter. An air valve allows pumped air to enter the top of the container. A hose fitting allows water to enter the top of the container, and a rotating spray bar or drip plate distributes water over the top of the filter media. The water discharge tube extends from the bottom of the container upwards and out the top.

In a typical oxygen reactor, Figure 22, water enters the container at the top, sprays over the filter media, fills the container, and then flows out the discharge tube. Water has now filled the container and is flowing through it as it would flow through a tube filter. Air from a good air pump that can operate under a strong back pressure is now applied at the top of the container through the air valve. Air (mostly nitrogen and oxygen) now fills the top of the reactor and water trickles over the filter media in an environment that is under a pressure of 1 to 3 psi, about 0.1 to 0.2 bar. The water level in the reactor—and the air pressure above the water level—is controlled by the air pressure introduced into the reactor and the amount of water flow through the reactor. If the pressure in the reactor is too great, air will push all the water out of the bottom of the reactor and will then bubble out the water discharge tube. If the pressure in the reactor is too low, water will slowly fill the reactor and begin to flow back into the air lines. A pressurized gas reactor has to be carefully monitored. Run the air pump at a stable, usually maximum,

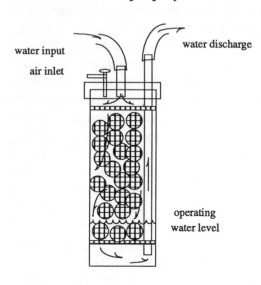

water input
air inlet
water discharge
operating
water level

Figure 22. Structure of a simple oxygen reactor.

pressure and adjust the water flow so that the water level is about two inches above the bottom of the reactor. Watch it closely to be sure that air and water pressure are stable and the water level remains at this point.

Air moves through the system by being dissolved and carried out in the water or by controlling the air flow in and out with valves if the air pump is strong enough. The water that leaves the reactor is lightly supersaturated with nitrogen and oxygen. There is not enough supersaturation with nitrogen to cause the bends in fish or to create tiny air bubbles, but the oxygen from ordinary air (20%) is also supersaturated in the water, and this raises the oxygen content enough to improve the redox potential and assure that the oxygen content of the system water always remains high. Pure oxygen can also be added to the water with a reactor, but this is a more complex system, and good results with pure oxygen have not been reported. Ozone and carbon dioxide are also added to the water with similar systems. An ozone reactor increases redox potential much quicker and much more strongly than an oxygen reactor. Oxidation resistant fittings must be used with ozone. Carbon dioxide reactors are usually smaller than oxygen reactors and are operated with a source of compressed carbon dioxide, a CO_2 cylinder. Burleson (1989) and Thiel (1989) contain good discussions on construction and operation of gas reactors.

The function of a **substrate reactor** is to efficiently bring the system water into contact with a particular substrate such as activated carbon, resins, and sources of calcium carbonate. Most substrate reactors are simply tube filters as there is little need for a pressurized, trickle filter atmosphere. A pressurized gas reactor must be mounted vertically, but a substrate reactor can be mounted horizontally. A prefilter on the substrate reactor, or pulling the water into the reactor after it has been through a prefilter, helps to reduce detritus accumulation in the filter.

Substrates and Filter Media

Technically, the substrate in an aquarium system is the surfaces of all the structures, including the glass walls, that are within the tank and the filter system. Traditionally, the term substrate is usually applied only to the media that make up the surface layer of the undergravel filter or tank bottom. Rock and coral formations within any type of tank, however, are also substrate as is the filter media in any internal or external filters. Bacteria, and some plants and animals, are able to colonize the internal and external surfaces and pores of all substrates, and by controlling the type and amount of available substrate, we are able to control, in large measure, what happens within the aquarium system. The substrates in marine systems serve two important functions, filtration and display.

Filter substrates provide the surface area for biological, chemical, or mechanical filtration. Display substrates provide the surfaces for attachment of algaes and invertebrates and serve as background for the inhabitants of the tank.

Media Surface Area

In all closed systems, the most important function of the filter substrate is to serve as the media for biological filtration. All substrates support nitrifying bacteria, but the substrates that are designed to support large colonies of these bacteria within a flow of aerated system water, function as the biological filter media. Although there are many criteria for judging the value and efficiency of biological filter media, and many varied opinions on what constitutes a good biological filter media, one basic consideration is the amount of surface area available for colonies of nitrifying bacteria. The amount of surface area required for good biological filtration is in the range of 2 to 5 square feet (ft^2) (0.19 to 0.46 m^2) per gallon of water, depending on the biological load in the system. Note that the best media for a particular purpose is not necessarily the media with the greatest surface area since there are many other factors to consider for each system design, for example: flow rates, channeled water flows, and gas exchange. If biological filtration is the primary purpose of the filter, then amount of surface area is of considerable importance. However, if gas exchange—venting ammonia, gaining oxygen, and losing excess carbon dioxide—is the main consideration, then void space in the media, rapid flow rates, and filter aeration are more important. See the sections on types of filter media for more information.

The total available surface area for most media, especially gravels, can not be reported with any real accuracy because of great variations in particle size and, when present, internal pore size. The biologically active surface area of media used in a trickle filter varies with the shape and volume of the filter, method of water dispersal into the filter, characteristics of water flow through the filter, structure and surface characteristics of the filter media, accumulation and distribution of organic matter in the filter, and rate of water flow through the filter. These factors greatly affect the amount of surface area in constant contact with water flow and the growth of bacterial colonies on the available surface. Good water dispersal through a filter with a low surface area media may provide a greater biologically active surface area than a restricted or channeled water flow through a high surface area media. Given these qualifications, Table 8 should provide at least a little perspective on surface area of various biological and chemical media.

The function, structure, and design of undergravel, trickle, wet/dry, and rapid flow tube filters are discussed in the next section. Here we are just concerned with the composition, handling, and nature of the substrates used in traditional and reef type marine aquarium systems. There are a few very well known substances that are widely used as media for undergravel and biological filters. There are also a number of other types of media that can be used quite successfully in biological filters and as tank substrates. Some of these are discussed to broaden the possibilities for marine aquarists with an experimental bent. There are three general categories of substrate/filter media: natural, artificial, and chemically active.

Table 8. Total surface area estimates for various types of filter media substrates.

Filter Media	Estimate of Total Surface Area (TSA)
Biological Media	
gravel bed one in^3	= about 25 in^2 (0.016 m^2) TSA
gravel bed 10" x 10" x 1"	= about 250 in^2, 1.7 ft^2 (0.16 m^2) Great variability in TSA of gravels
ceramic structures one in^3	= about 14 in^2, 0.1 ft^2 (90 cm^2, 0.009 m^2) Great variability in TSA depending on particle size, surface roughness, microscopic pore configuration, and structural configuration. Small, hollow ceramic cylinders about 1 cm in diameter and length provide about 22.5 ft^2 (2.1 m^2) TSA per gallon volume (surface pore structure not considered).
plastic structures* one in^3	= 5 to 18 in^2 TSA, max 0.13 ft^2 (0.01 m^2) TSA for plastic structures varies greatly depending on size, shape, surface and openness of structure.
porous polymer sheet structures** one in^2 x $\frac{1}{16}$ in thick	= 43 in^2, 0.3 ft.^{2} (0.028 m^2) TSA.
porous polymer sheet structures** 10" x 10" x $\frac{1}{16}$	= 4,300 in^2, 30 ft^2 (2.8 m^2) TSA.
porous diatomaceous earth beads** one in^3	= 510 in^2, 3.54 ft^2 (0.328 m^2) TSA.
Chemical Media	
activated carbon one cc (about one half gram)	= about 5,400 ft^2 (500 m^2) TSA. (Note that carbon has a great range of TSA.)
zeolite one cc	= about 324 ft^2 (30 m^2) TSA. (Pores are too small for biological filtration.)
macroporous ion-exchange resins one cc	= 270 to 5400 ft^2 (25 to 500 m^2) TSA.
polymeric resins one cc	= 3,240 to 5,400 ft^2 (300 to 500 m^2) TSA.

*Bioball® claims a TSA of 23 ft^2 (2.1 m^2)in a gallon volume containing 55 Bioballs® or 14.3 in^2 (0.009 m^2) surface area per in^3. One Bioball® has a TSA of 0.4 ft^2 (60 in^2, 0.04 m^2).

*BioBlocks™, a cubic two inch square structure, reports a TSA of about 1.0 ft^2 (144 in^2) per block equaling 18.0 in^2 (0.01 m^2) TSA per in^3. A gallon volume contains about 29 BioBlocks™ with a TSA of 28.8 ft^2 (2.6 m^2) per gallon. (Note that the manufacturer claims that microscopic surface irregularities increase the TSA of BioBlocks™ from the approximate smooth surface estimate of 0.8 ft^2 per block to the reported 1.0 ft^2 TSA per block.)

*Bio-Pak®, an open ball shaped structure about 30 mm diameter, reports a TSA of about 6 in^2 (38.7 cm^2) per ball. These structures pack together and the distributor claims 260 balls per gallon volume, a TSA of 10.8 ft^2 (1 m^2) per gallon. (Note that the distributor claims that ridges and microscopic irregularities increase the TSA of Bio-Pak® from the approximate smooth surface estimae of 5 in^2 per ball to the reported 6 in^2 per ball.)

*Norton Bio Ring™ (Number 13) is an open structure cylinder one inch diameter by one inch long with an apparent TSA of about 6.3 in^2 (0.004 m^3) per in^3. A gallon volume of Bio Rings™, maximum 231, would have about 10.1 ft^2 TSA.

**Matrix II™ claims 2 m^2 (21.6 ft^2) TSA available for bacterial colonies per each 72 in^2 porous polymer sheet.

**Matrix™ claims 2 m^2 (21.6 ft^2) TSA available for bacterial colonies per each 100 ml volume of DE beads. A one gallon volume contains about 818 ft^2 (76 m^2) TSA.

Bioballs® are a product of Dupula USA.

BioBlocks™ are a product of Dynasty Marine, Inc.

Bio-Pak® is a product of Import Associates, Inc.

Norton Bio Rings™ are a product of Norton Company

Matrix™ and Matrix II™ are a product of SeaChem Laboratories.

(specific products are mentioned only as examples, no endorsement is given or implied.)

Note: m^2 - square meter, cm^2 - square centimeter, ft^2 - square foot, in^2 - square inch, cm^3 - cubic centimeter, in^3 - cubic inch, ft^3 - cubic foot.

1 m^2 = 10.8 ft^2 = 1,555.2 in^2 = 10,000 cm^2 ; 1 cm^2 = 0.155 in.^{2} ; ft^2 = 144 in^2 ; 1 in^2 = 6.45 cm^2 ; 1 cc = 0.061 in^3 ; 1 gal. = 231 in^3 ; 1 ft^3 = 7.5 gal.

Natural Substrates

Silica sand

With good reason, the media most recommended for un-dergravel biological filters for the past two decades has almost always been some type of calcareous gravel. Before this, silica sand was the media of choice for biological filters. In fact, in the earlier books, Simkatis (1958) and Straughan (1964), the typical undergravel, biological filter was termed the sub-sand filter. Even though silica sand has no buffering capacity, it does have some advantages. It is cheap, the small grains offer a great deal of surface area for nitrifying bacteria, it functions as an effective mechanical filter, and it works very well in marine aquaria. I have used silica sand or a combination of crushed coral or oyster shell and silica sand in almost every closed system tank I have set up with excellent, predictable results.

There are some disadvantages to this media, however. Even the coarsest sand is a bit too fine and detritus and organics tend to cake the sand grains together and restrict or channel water flow. Silica sand has no pores or crevices and colonies of nitrify-ing bacteria can only occupy the external surfaces of the sand grains. The small, fine sand grains are also difficult to retain in the proper place in the aquarium. Fish and invertebrates often move the sand about, piling it up in one area and digging it out down to the filter plate in another. Two thin layers separated by plastic window screen can minimize this problem. The sand also tends to drift under the filter plate where sand piles can restrict water flow and accumulate organics. Frequent cleaning and stirring of the filter bed is required for optimum operation.

Silica and other sands are usually heavy with dust and dirt and need a lot of washing before they are clean enough to use in an aquarium. A good source of silica sand is the bags of sand sold for sand blasting. The coarsest grade, 6-20, is preferable. This means that the sand was graded to fall through a grid of 6 wires per inch, but be retained on a grid of 20 wires per inch. Thus the particles are between 1/6th and 1/20 of an inch. Sand of indeterminate composition can be collected from beaches and other areas, but this is generally too fine and contains too many unknown contaminants. In tanks that have external biological filters and do not utilize undergravel (or sub-sand) filters, sand, perhaps a bit finer than the coarsest grade sand blast sand, is often used to cover the tank bottom in a thin layer. Since water does not flow though this bottom cover it must be only a few millimeters thick to avoid trapping organics in anaerobic decomposition. When used in this manner it does require occasional stirring to release organics and redistribute it evenly over the bottom. A medium fine sand should also be used to anchor certain green algaes such as *Penicillus capitatus*, *Udotea flabellum*, and even the sea grasses *Thalassia testudinum* and *Halophila engelmannii*.

Coral sand

Coral sand is composed of calcareous compounds rather than silica and is lighter and softer than silica. It does not make good media for a biological filter since it tends to pack and cake and restrict water flow. It can be used as a thin bottom cover or as a substrate for some macro algaes.

Dolomite

Dolomite is a common calcareous mineral, usually found as rock formations, and is composed of calcium magnesium carbonate, $CaMg(CO_3)_2$. It is formed from the action of ground water on deposits of limestone and is quarried for many industrial and agricultural uses such as the manufacture of magnesium, animal feed supplements, fertilizers, and building material. Crushed dolomite is readily available and can be purchased especially packaged for use in marine aquarium systems. The crushed dolomite is graded to many sizes for many uses, but the 6-16 dolomite, a particle size of 2 to 4 mm, works best in marine systems for both undergravel and wet/dry trickle filters. Sharp cornered, rough angular grains of any gravel-like media work best because they resist compaction and retain the spacing between grains that allows continuous water flow. Like all gravels for aquarium systems, dolomite must be well washed before placing it in the system. Dolomite rock may carry toxic impurities such as lead, arsenic, aluminum, and mercury. These impurities might create a problem if the aquarist powdered or dissolved the dolomite in the system in an attempt at pH control. These compounds, however, are bound within the chemical structure of the gravel particles. Thus the chance of developing toxic concentrations of heavy metals within the system from surface dissolution of the dolomite grains is slight.

Dolomite is also popular because of its supposed buffering capability. All calcareous materials will dissolve in acid water, release carbonate minerals, and cause the pH of the water to rise. In simple theory, using calcareous gravel in a marine aquarium system buffers the water and prevents or delays the decline of pH due to the accumulation of organic acids. In actuality, it's not this simple. In the first place, marine systems should be maintained at a pH of 8.2, although some systems may occasionally drop down to 7.8. Calcareous gravel material will help maintain pH up to about 7.5, maybe up to 7.8, but are not particularly effective buffers of the marine carbonate system at pH levels above 7.5 (see the section on pH in Chapter 1).

Some of the reasons for this are that magnesium in solution tends to crystalize as magnesium calcite over the surface of the particle and this reduces the limited solubility of calcium carbonate at the higher pH. Free phosphate ions also form crystals of apatite (calcium phosphate) in the surface of the calcareous media and contribute to the reduction of surface solubility. Dissolved organic compounds, particularly organic phosphate compounds, also coat the particles, reduce ionic exchange sites, and further limit solubility. Thus the limited initial capability of calcareous gravels to maintain a suitable pH for a marine system diminishes over time because of the decrease in surface availability to ion exchange. Cleaning a third of the gravel bed each month to remove detritus and grinding the gravel grains against each other will aid the buffer capacity by removing some organics and exposing new gravel surfaces to water flow. Disturbing only a third of the bed each time leaves the nitrifying capacity of the majority of the bed fully functional. Even with cleaning, however, some gravel should be exchanged every few months to provide new surfaces if the limited buffering of calcareous media is desired.

Dolomite is the least soluble of the calcareous gravels used for marine filter media and should not be chosen on the basis of buffering capability. It works fine, however, as an inert particle for attachment of nitrifying bacteria and as the media for a mechanical filter.

Crushed coral

Crushed coral is fossil coral rock that has been quarried, crushed and graded. An aquarist can obtain it in various sizes but #3 is generally best for marine systems. It usually carries a lot of dust and should be rinsed well. It is one of the most soluble of the calcareous filter media because it has a high amount of magnesian calcite. This is the most soluble form of carbonate mineral in seawater followed by aragonite, low magnesian calcite, pure calcite, and dolomite. Crushed coral provides a greater buffering capacity than dolomite, but will not maintain a system above 7.8 indefinitely. The grains are highly irregular and very porous and form a good substrate for nitrifying bacteria. Note, however, that the relatively high solubility of crushed coral also releases minerals other than carbonates into the water and this *may* cause problems in some systems by creating an ionic imbalance. Crushed coral rock, however, is a good source of calcium for reef systems. Note that it is not necessary to use calcareous gravel to maintain a sucessful marine aquarium system and that some aquarists eschew the use of any calcareous media.

Pea rock

Pea rock is a form of coral rock that is graded to a relatively large particle size, 4 to 8 mm. It makes a good substrate for undergravel and wet/dry filters since the large particle size prevents clogging or compaction of the filter media and the irregular surface provides a large surface area for colonies of nitrifying bacteria.

Shell hash, shell bottom, coral bottom

There are a variety of non uniform, calcareous filter medias available that go by various names. These are generally natural mixes of gravel, broken shells, coral bits, and coarse sand. They be sorted into particles of all the same size or mixed in a wide range of particle sizes. One can also gather this type of material from many beaches. As long as there is a variety of shapes and sizes to avoid compaction, and the average size of the particles is not too large or too small, this material works very well in marine systems. Depending on the origin of the material, contamination by persistent chemicals and bits of metals should be considered and checked. Rinsing and sieving is of particular importance. Buffering of the system to pH levels above 7.5 is no better or worse then other calcareous media.

Oyster shell

Crushed oyster shell is available at farm supply, feed stores, and some aquarium shops and can be used as marine filter media. It is the most effective media for maintenance of high pH. It is a very dusty media and requires a good bit of washing. In fact, it is just not possible to remove all the calcareous dust from this media. Have patience, however, for it will settle out and the water will become clear after a few hours. The shell dust may settle on the inner aquarium glass and this must be wiped off before the tank will appear clear.

Contamination by metal bits and other odds and ends is a real possibility, so the media must be carefully examined before use, especially if it is obtained at feed or farm supply stores. Oyster shell obtained as an aquarium media at a tropical fish store has been screened and sorted, and this is the preferred source. Oyster shell is more friable and breaks up more easily than other media and may retain a limited buffering capacity, pH 7.8, for a longer time than other media. The flat, soft particles of shell may tend to compact over time and restrict water flow.

River gravel

Small size river gravel, 4 to 8 mm, can also be used as a substrate and/or as a filter media. It is inert and will not even pretend to aid buffering in the system. It is not porous and has a relatively large particle size, and so has limited surface area for colonies of nitrifying bacteria. It does allow water to percolate freely through it, however, and will not cake up or accumulate detritus as readily as smaller particle sized media. The only reason one may choose river or Chattahoochee gravel over a calcareous gravel would be to achieve a particular effect within the tank. It does work as a tank substrate or a limited biological filter media, it is just less efficient than other types of biological media. It is heavier than calcareous gravels and is more difficult for fish and invertebrates to push around.

Calcareous algae hash

The calcareous algae, *Halimeda opuntia*, grows in vast profusion in shallow, protected canals and bays in the Florida Keys. Calcite is incorporated into the structure of the algae and when it dies and dries, the algae becomes a grey, lightweight calcareous matrix. Although the calcareous remains of this algae has been used successfully as a filter media, it may break down over long term use. It may be useful, however, as a buffer in marine systems. To my knowledge, little experimentation has been done with this media.

Wood

No, no, I'm not suggesting the use of wood chips in a biological filter, in fact, I don't really recommend the use of wood in a marine aquarium. Wood, however, is a very common substrate in the marine environment. A number of boring animals, *Teredo* shipworms (actually a mollusk) for example, have evolved to depend on wood as a substrate for attachment and even possibly nutrition. There are various displays and experiments that include the use of wood in an aquarium. Although it floats for quite some time, most wood eventually becomes waterlogged and sinks, and in the form of sunken driftwood or pilings, can be a fascinating aquarium display. Wood is organic and does decay in water over time. As wood decays it releases dyes and other organics, and this speeds the accumulation of organic products in the system water. Wood should not be a permanent part of a marine system unless the aquarist is willing to perform the additional maintenance and water changes that may be necessary.

Terrestrial rock

Rocks of many types can add interest and variety to marine systems, and as long as they are nontoxic, inert, and do not decompose in the tank, there is no reason why they can not be used. Any rock that is a candidate for a marine aquariums should be carefully cleaned and carefully examined for soft areas, metallic discolorations and possible contaminants. Rocks and shells with small openings into large internal cavities should not be used, however, because large restricted cavities can create a volume of stagnant, anaerobic water. Rocks placed in marine aquarium systems soon develop populations of marine bacteria of all types and become colonized by many types of invertebrate growth as well.

Sedimentary rocks such as limestone and sandstone may be hard and tightly bound or loose and crumbly. Avoid loose, crumbly rocks as they may decompose in the aquarium. It's a good idea to place a questionable rock in a bucket of seawater for a week or so and see what happens to the surface and structure of the rock, and to the seawater in the bucket, before adding it to the display. Igneous rocks are formed from volcanic activity and may be hard and massive like granite and obsidian (a natural glass) or soft and friable like mica and some olivines. Lava and pumice are types of igneous rock and, because of the highly porous nature of pumice, it is frequently used in marine systems as functional decorative rock (live rock) or as a filter media.

Even zeolite is a form of igneous rock. The name means "boiling stone" as it tends to bubble extensively and give off water when heated. Metamorphic rocks are formed from sedimentary and igneous rock that has been subjected to great heat and pressure deep under the earth. These rocks, such as gneiss, marble, and quartzite, make good decorative rocks because they are hard surfaced, attractive, and non reactive in a marine environment. There are now a wide variety of beautiful terrestrial rocks that are collected, sized, and sculpted especially for use in marine and freshwater aquariums. Of course, avoid rocks containing metallic ores like iron and copper.

Live rock

In the past a mother at the beach might have said to her young son, "Oh yuck! Joey, Put that rock down. It's full of bugs and worms." That same mother may now say, "Oh great, Joey. You found a live rock. Uncle Mike will pay you $50.00 for it!" Times change, and live rock is changing the face of at least part of the marine aquarium hobby. Interest in reef tanks is booming, and marine aquarium systems are getting a whole new look. Marine aquarists are developing a new appreciation for invertebrates and the physical and biological structure of the marine environment; and live rock is the substrate on which this is built. Live rock can be one of the neatest and most interesting things that one can put in an marine aquarium or one of the most costly disasters a marine aquarist can suffer. Let me give you my opinions on this.

First of all, live rock is **not** alive. Secondly, there is nothing magic about live rock! Live rock is simply a calcareous or other porous rock taken from the waters of a tropical or subtropical area and transported to a marine aquarium system with some or most of the natural microscopic and macroscopic life forms still viable. Important considerations and categorizations for live rock are methods of collection and treatment, composition, structure, and the microscopic and macroscopic life forms still alive on the rock. The best live rock is hard and porous. Calcareous rock formed from hard coral rock is perhaps the best. Limestone may be a bit crumbly, but hard limestone is also suitable. Porous volcanic rock, some types of pumice, can also be used.

Rock that has particular invertebrates or algae attached are often named for the organism. Bubble and leather coral, mushroom coral, colonial anemones, and *Caulerpa, Halimeda* and *Hypnea* and *Bryopsis* algae are organisms frequently sold attached to live rock. Pink and red coralline algae often coat the rock, and tiny growths of filamentous algae such as *Cladophora, Chaetomorpha, Enteromorpha, Boodleopsis* and *Derbesia* are hidden deep in crevices and pores. They bloom in growth when good conditions are established and may even become a problem if nurtient levels in the system are too high. Live rock is collected for the marine aquarium trade along the west coast of Florida (including primarily the Florida Keys), the Sea of Cortez, Hawaii, and a few other coastal areas.

Collection of live rock does not harm the environment as long as it is done responsibly. Reef formations and live coral should not be broken up to produce rock pieces, and all rock should not be removed from localized, specific areas. Terrestrial rocks of particular size and composition that are well adapted to marine reef aquariums may also be placed in particular areas and later havested by collectors, a practice that is now beginning in the Florida Keys and perhaps other areas as well. Some restrictions and management may be necessary in heavily havested locations, but rock is very abundant in nature and there will always be a way to provide active live rock for marine aquarists.

Collection and treatment. Road and bridge construction in tropical areas and the natural erosion process around coral and limestone reefs create many chunks of various types of limestone and coral rock in the baseball to football size range. In the marine environment, these rocks are colonized by microscopic and macroscopic marine life of all types. Collectors have different handling techniques depending on equipment, environment, and their own work habits; but generally, they select the individual rocks based on current orders, the type of life attached, and the size and composition that experience has taught them are most suitable. Rocks with particularly desireable species of anemones and algae are usually given special treatment. The rocks are picked up from the bottom and placed on the boat, usually in old milk crates or other containers. Water is usually splashed over the rocks during the time on the boat to keep them from drying out and a cover may be placed over them for shade.

Most of the small motile invertebrates such as crustaceans and echinoderms leave the rock during this period and are flushed off the boat. Some of these small invertebrates are undesirable in reef systems. The post larval and juvenile stage of the mantis shrimp, *Squilla*, for example, is common in the deep holes and crevices of the rocks and grows up to be an efficient predator of other invertebrates and small fish. Small stone crabs also ride along with live rock and can develop into problems in reef systems. Some collectors may keep all (or at least the rocks with special algal or invertebrate attachments) in a tank of aerated water. The rocks are then transported to a wholesaler the day of collection or on the next day. Depending on facilities, the wholesaler may keep the rocks in a tank of aerated water, stacked under a constant or occasional spray of salt water, or just stacked up until shipment time. The rocks are shipped "dry", which means damp, but without water. The wholesaler generally places the rocks in a tank of aerated, filtered water upon arrival. Rocks with special invertebrate or algal growths are, or should be, kept in water except during actual shipment, and some organisms should even be shipped under water.

At some point during the early collection and shipment process, the collector or wholesaler may put the rock through a process known as "seeding" or "grooming". Seeded live rock has been through two processes. First it has been carefully cleaned of all macroscopic (large enough to see with the naked eye) growths of invertebrates and algae. Brushes and picks may be used to clean the rock. Some growths may be left if they are interesting to the aquarist. The cleaned rock still contains a great deal of dead and decomposing organic matter in the pores and crevices. A nose test usually gives one a rough idea of how much and how dead.

The next step is removal of the dead organic material and replacement and/or expansion of the microscopic life that helps establish the natural balance of a marine aquarium system. This second part is the "curing" or bacterial stabilization of the rock and is accomplished by placing it in a well established, stable marine system. Heterotrophic bacteria then mineralize the dead organic matter and this is followed by colonization of populations of beneficial organisms throughout the rock. These include nitrifying bacteria, denitrifying bacteria, heterotrophic bacteria, various protozoans, some blue-green and other single celled and filamentous algae, various lower animals such as flat worms, round worms, and rotifers, which the aquarist seldom sees, and larval forms and cysts and spores of various macroalgae and invertebrates.

This second part of the process, stabilization, takes some time and may begin in the tanks of the wholesaler and retailer, but it is completed in the tank of the aquarist. All live rock, whether seeded or not, goes through a stabilization or curing process in a marine system. Blackburn (1988) has written a good article from the aquarist's perspective on collection and treatment of live rock, and Sprung (1989) adds valuable insights to use of live rock in marine systems.

When the aquarist gets it, every live rock has a particular ratio of living organisms to dead organic matter. The more living organisms and the less dead organic matter, the better the live rock is for the aquarium system. Dead organic matter brought into the system with the rock must be mineralized by heterotrophic bacteria and oxidized by nitrifying bacteria, and this results in increased nitrate levels that have to be handled by the system or by water change. Live organisms, if they survive, grow and reproduce and aid the function of the system. The ratio of living to dead material depends on the amount of dead organic matter in the rock when it was collected, how the process of collection and transportation affected life on and in the rock (this includes time out of water, exposure to heat and cold, and degree of desiccation), and whether or not, and how carefully, the rock was cleaned. All these considerations affect how well and how soon the rock will perform as part of the stable biological balance of the tank, and whether it will contribute algal growths and larval forms of invertebrates to the tank inhabitants.

This next paragraph is very important to any aquarist that is planning to set up a reef type marine aquarium system. Placing 50 pounds of fully seeded, that is cleaned and completely stabilized, live rock in a marine system is the equivalent of transplanting a fully functional biological filter into a new system. *Placing unseeded rock, that is uncleaned rock that has not developed a population of nitrifying bacteria and that has a high concentration of dead organic matter, into a new marine system is the equivalent of putting several pounds of dead fish and shrimp in a system with an unprepared and unconditioned biological filter.* In the case of the former, the system is functional and is ready to receive fish and invertebrates. In the latter case, however, extensive decay occurs; fish and invertebrates die; ammonia, nitrite, and eventually nitrate levels shoot to the sky; and in most instances, the rock is useless as live rock, and the aquarist has created an organic disaster. There is now little alive on or in the rock that is worthwhile. If the rock is completely anaerobic, the best thing to do is to remove the rock, rinse it well, soak it in a chlorine bleach solution for a day or two to remove the decayed organic material, rinse it again, and soak it again in water with a dechlorinater (sodium thiosulfate) added to it. After another rinse it can then be replaced in the system and will eventually develop populations of the proper bacteria and microorganisms.

This brings up another very important point. The major difference between a "live" coral rock and a "dead" coral rock is a few months in the sea or a few months in an aquarium system. It is important to use rocks that have been colonized by bacteria and invertebrates in the sea, but it is not necessary that every rock in the tank comes from the bed of the ocean. In fact, some marine specimen collectors are seeding favorable areas with the right size and type of rock and then returning and harvesting the live rock three to six months later. Porous rocks of terrestrial origin provides sites for colonization and development of bacteria and invertebrates within the system that were originally introduced from rock colonized in the sea. The main trade off is development time of the tank's reef against initial expense of live rock. Of course, the more live rock, the greater the kind and quantity of marine life that is introduced to the tank. The reef in a system set up with only 10 percent "live rock" will take longer to develop than a reef in a system set up with 50 or 75 or 100 percent live rock; but within a few months, or perhaps a year or so, the low percentage live rock system will catch up with the totally transplanted live rock reef system. These are options that the reef tank aquarist should know and consider.

Another very important point is that the fundamental process of biological filtration is exactly the same in a reef tank system as it is in a traditional marine aquarium system.

Putting live rock into a system does not change the conditioning sequence of biological filtration. Nitrifying bacteria are present on and in the rock, but the rock can not take the place of a properly designed biological filter. Denitrification bacteria are also present in the deep crevices and pores of the rock, but assuming that the tank contains a fair number of animals, the denitrification capacity of the bacteria in the rock will not take the place of active algal growth and a properly designed and functioning denitrification filter device. Depending on the condition of the live rock, it either enhances biological filtration or increases the need for it. In either situation, it is very important to have a fully functional, completely conditioned biological filter in operation before placing any valuable marine life, including live rock, into the system. This will go a long way toward preventing a biological and financial disaster.

Artificial Substrates

Fibers.

Polyester fiberfill is very useful product for aquarists. It is inert and nontoxic, soft and compactable, and inexpensive. Water flows freely through it but the tiny fibers catch and hold particles of very small size. It can be formed to fit any size filter from a thin layer under the gravel of a biological filter to a tiny plastic corner filter, to mat layer over a trickle filter. It finds its best use in small external filters or in a mechanical filter compartment in reef tank filters. The degree of mechanical filtration can be somewhat controlled by the density of the pack in the filter. A loose pack allows greater water flow and a dense pack provides finer filtration. Depending on water flow, fiber fill clogs with organic matter in a few days or weeks and must be cleaned or replaced. It is usually best to discard fiberfill loaded with organics, but it can be rinsed and sprayed clean and used again. It tends to mat and twist after a few cleanings, however. Never wash it with soap or other chemical cleanser. It makes an excellent disposable mechanical filter media, but clogs too easily to make a good biological filter. The fiberfill purchased at aquarium shops is designed for use in aquariums and has been exposed to no preservatives or chemical treatments.

Glass wool or spun glass fiber was the precursor of polyester fiberfill. It is rare to find glass wool packaged for aquarium use today. It had most of the features of the fiber fill, but was hard, brittle, and dangerous. The tiny glass fibers broke easily and could enter the aquarium environment as well as the fingers and hands of unwary aquarists. It is a good mechanical filter media when it remains in place and is perhaps a little less easily clogged than fiber fill, however its use is not recommended.

Filter pads

Filter pads composed of fiber layers are in common use. Many auxiliary filters are designed to use pads that function as mechanical filters and also often contain a chemical media such as activated carbon. These pads separate areas of the filter, and water is forced to travel through the pads on its journey through the filter. These pads are generally quite effective; however, the surface area is small relative to the water flow through the pads, and they do clog eventually. The media is also quite thin, and chemical filtration does not last long. It is important to always be aware of the condition of the pads and replace them before water begins to flow over or around the pad. Filtration through such pads is most efficient when water must flow through a number of pads in sequence. Frequent replacement is the key to keeping filter pad filters in full operation.

Media mat material composed of double layer spirals (DLS) is widely used in trickle filters. The loosely woven, fairly ridged mat of synthetic fibers (nylon and/or polyethylene) is often used as an upright coil in trickle filters, a cut-to-size pad for partitions in box filters, surface pads under spray bars and drip plates, and can be used as discs in bio nitro wheel filters. Much of this type of material is made for industrial uses other than filter media, so it is very important to be sure that it is not treated with any toxic coating. DLS material specially prepared for aquarium filtration is now available from many sources.

Polyurethane foam, blocks, and pads

Polyurethane foam, mattress and chair cushion material (make sure it is not chemically treated), can also be used as a mechanical and/or biological filter. A slab of one half or one inch thickness can be placed on top of an undergravel filter plate in place of the gravel, and it will function quite well, especially for slow water flows. This material is dense and functions well as a mechanical filter, but rapid flows are quickly restricted. A foam bottom is not the most aesthetically pleasing media for a display tank, but it may serve well in auxiliary or commercial tanks. Cutting the bottom pad about a half inch too big fits it tightly in the tank and assures that all the water goes through and not around the pad. Making up the pad in three pieces allows cleaning of one third of the filter each month without disturbing the biological filtering capacity of two thirds of the filter.

After a year or so, a foam pad begins to break down and must be replaced. Also some fish and invertebrates (triggerfish and crabs) can tear up the soft foam if it is not in a separate compartment or protected by a perforated plastic plate. A simple, but effective, portable biological filter can also be made from this foam by wrapping and tying a short section of foam around a perforated pipe, or by inserting a perforated pipe into a 3" by 3", by 10" long foam block and air lifting water through the foam (see Figure 23). Foam blocks can also be used as denitrifyers in marine aquarium systems. See the section on denitrifyer design and operation.

Ceramic structures

Nitrifying bacteria can colonize natural filter media and perform quite well, but efficiency can be improved by designing and manufacturing media from nontoxic ceramic (and plastic) materials for specific applications. These artificial media are designed to provide the optimum ratio of surface area and oxygenated water flow under various conditions. Ceramic biological filter media are usually in the shape of small beads or tubes with unglazed surfaces. The small, open shape of the short tubes allows ample mixing of air and water or diffuse, rapid flow-through of oxygenated water when submerged. The unglazed surface provides pores that greatly increase the surface area available for bacterial colonization. This type of biological filter media is considerably more expensive than calcareous gravel, but it is also a considerably more efficient biological filter media.

Plastic structures

Inert plastics such as polyethylene, polyurethane, and nylon can be formed into structures that make excellent filter media for a variety of filter designs. For trickle filters, the emphasis is on achieving the maximum surface area with the greatest possible mix of air and water, free water flows, and the least possible capture and clogging of organic matter. An open ball, cube, or cylinder structure with many internal supports allows the greatest mix of air and water, but the limited non-porous surface area requires a relatively large amount of filter media to provide sufficient surface area for biological filtration. Aeration of the water and opportunity for gas exchange with the atmosphere is excellent, however. A roll of ridged, open weave plastic mat material (DLS) provides more surface area and greater potential nitrifying capability, but does not have as much gas exchange capability as ball and cube structures, and has a greater tendency to clog with detritus. Cubes, balls, and mats can be used as submerged media rather than trickle-through media, but the restricted surface area, compared to small, particle size, porous media, greatly limits their efficiency in submerged applications. Any open, non toxic plastic structure such as hair curlers, broken up egg crate light diffuser, and even plastic shotgun shell cases can be used in trickle filter applications with variable results. Wide use is also made of plastic structures designed for aeration of sewage and other industrial uses with somewhat better results.

The most expensive plastic structures are those designed specifically for marine reef tank trickle filter applications. Some of these structures emphasize void space, rapid water movement, and gas exchange characteristics over the expanse of surface area available for biological filtration. These designs tend to be very open in structure, some no more than narrow rings with spokes, and while they provide excellent gas exchange, surface area for biological filtration is limited. An auxiliary biological filter may well be necessary under moderate biological loads when this style plastic trickle flow media is used. Other designs emphasize maximum surface area for biological filtration at the expense of the open void space that facilitates gas exchange. These designs tend to be compact with many internal structures to provide maximum surface area. Such dense structures have a greater biological filtration capacity than open structures. Gas exchange is improved if considerable air is injected into the bottom of the filter container when dense, close structured media is used.

Open, large void structures vent off more ammonia before it is oxidized to nitrate, and slow, but do not prevent, accumulation of nitrate. Open structures also allow high flow rates without water back up. Dense, high surface area structures blow off some ammonia and quickly oxidize any that remains. Water evaporation is high with both design types and the water level in the system must be monitored frequently. See the Table 8 for more information on the surface area of various media.

Ball, cube, and cylinder structures are most useful in trickle filters since they are more functional in producing aeration (gas exchange) than other media. They do provide sites for colonies of nitrifying bacteria, but are limited in the extent of available surface area. There is enough surface area in about 2.5 cubic feet of these larger open structures, however, to provide for the nitrifying needs of most normally loaded marine aquarium systems in the 100 gallon capacity range.

Micro pore media

Porous plastic sheets and diatomaceous earth beads can provide excellent biological filtering capacity in submerged and trickle filters if pore size is in the proper range, below 50 microns. Water flow should be directed over and not through the micropore sheets, but through the container that holds the micropore beads. The small pores in this type of media provide a vast surface area for colonies of nitrifying bacteria, but the pores and surfaces of the media can become clogged with algae, detritus, and heterotrophic bacterial growth. Prefiltering water before it enters the micropore media container, and keeping the filter media away from light, will help prevent clogging. If organic clogging of pores occurs, the surface area available for colonies of nitrifying bacteria rapidly decreases. Occasional cleaning by soaking in bleach, rinsing well, and then using a dechlorinator may be required to reopen the pores of the plastic media. The compacted diatomaceous earth beads may break up with this treatment. Don't do the entire filter at the same time, however, or all the nitrifying bacteria will be lost. Relatively small beads and particles, or small tube media, are best for submerged filters, and porous sheets or fiber mats do well in trickle filters.

Chemical Filter Media

Activated carbon

This is the most common and most cost effective media used for chemical filtration in marine aquarium systems. Activated carbon is a black granular material that gives off a black dust and looks a lot like the stuff at the bottom of the fireplace. This is also a description of "aquarium charcoal" and coal particles. Activated carbon adsorbs the nonpolar, hydrophobic organic molecules from the system water and acts as a molecular sieve (absorption) for other organic molecules. It is highly effective in removing the organic molecules that create color and odor in aquarium water and also very effective in removing toxic organic compounds and heavy metals. Charcoal and coal bits do sort of the same thing but have very limited capacity compared to activated carbon, and their use is not recommended.

Activated carbon is manufactured by carbonizing bituminous coal (the best source), nut shells, wood, or animal bone in the absence of air at about 900 °C. The result is a char that is then activated by heating it once again to 800 to 900 °C in the presence of a gas such as steam, air, or carbon dioxide. This hot gas treatment removes remaining hydrocarbons and creates the highly porous internal and external surfaces of the carbon granules. Particle size, type of gas, activation temperatures, and, in some instances, inorganic salts of zinc, copper, phosphate, silicate, and sulphate added before activation, provide the carbon with specific adsorption characteristics. Acid and alkaline rinses may also be used to create various adsorption characteristics.

The adsorption characteristics of different carbons may vary greatly. A carbon that is effective in removing chlorine may have limited capacity for removing organic compounds. The adsorption capacity of acid washed carbons is somewhat reduced, but acid washed carbons have fewer metallic and carbonate contaminants that may cause problems in marine systems. The only way to determine the suitability and efficiency of a specific activated carbon in a marine aquarium application is through rather sophisticated testing of how much and how fast different compounds are removed from salt water. The only carbon testing most aquarists can do is to determine how effective the carbon is at removing the yellow color that develops in aquarium water.

There are only about five manufacturers of activated carbon in the U.S., but these manufacturers produce many grades of activated carbon designed for many purposes. Purchase of an activated carbon designed for water purification may not provide the very best grade of carbon for a marine system, but it will probably be adequate. However, purchase of a carbon packaged for aquarium use by a quality manufacturer of aquarium products should provide a carbon that has been tested and selected for its superior performance in this particular application. It may also be the most economical grade of black stuff that they could get a hold of that week. Fortunately, reputable suppliers do take pride in producing the best product possible, and a good company will produce a consistently high quality carbon that has been tested to perform well in marine aquarium systems. It helps, however, to know something about what the characteristics of the product should be like.

There are seven considerations for aquarists to ponder on the effectiveness of activated carbon and these are also, to a great extent, applicable to ion-exchange and polymeric adsorbents.

- 1. *The activity of the carbon and the nature of the compounds that will be removed, the adsorbates.* This is beyond the expertise of most aquarists. All media sold for water purification is not activated carbon, and all activated carbon is not the same, and except for a few easily observed physical characteristics, the aquarist can't determine the best quality for aquarium application. The best bet for the average aquarist is to buy a brand packed by a reputable company and recommended by a good retail dealer. Even this does not absolutely guarantee the right carbon for the job, but absolute guarantees are hard to find in this life.

- 2. *Contact time.* Contact time is the period of time that the water containing the adsorbate is in contact with the carbon. Slow water flow through a large quantity of carbon gives a long contact time. Rapid flow though a small quantity of carbon produces a short contact time. Contact time is of greatest importance when the water passes through the carbon only once—a single pass, flow-through system. If the carbon doesn't catch it on the first pass, there is no second chance so the water can not move through the carbon too fast. In a recirculating system, however, the same water is constantly picking up organic compounds from the tank and is repeatedly passing through the carbon. The situation then becomes more complex. There has to be enough carbon to keep up with the production of organics in the system, and the water has to flow though the carbon rapidly enough to recirculate most of the water through the carbon in a relatively short period, a few hours. Although the speed of the water flow through the carbon is important in a closed system, of more importance to the life and effectiveness of the carbon filtration is the amount of carbon and the efficiency of the flow through the carbon container. The optimum quantity of carbon and speed of flow will differ with system size and biological load, and some experimentation may be necessary to find the best combination for each system.

- *3. Concentrations of the adsorbates.* The rapidity of the uptake of an adsorbate at different concentrations depends on the nature of the carbon and the nature of the adsorbate. Generally, small molecules are adsorbed more rapidly and more completely than large molecules, particularly large molecules with complex branching chains. The rate of adsorption at a particular contact time increases with concentration, but removal at low concentrations is generally more efficient.

- *4. Particle size of the carbon.* As mentioned in the theory section, the most efficient particle size—a compromise between optimum water penetration, flow rate, and maximum internal surface area—is a particle with a diameter of about one millimeter, roughly the size of a pinhead.

- *5. Pore size and volume.* A particle of carbon or resin has a vast number of microscopic pores and channels of various sizes that create the matrix of the particle. A particle may have fewer large pores or more numerous smaller pores, and pore size determines some of the adsorptive characteristics of the media. Pore volume is the important measure, however, and it refers to the volume of the open space within the particle. A carbon with a high pore volume is more fragile, more efficient, lighter in weight, and has a greater total surface area then an equal amount of carbon with a low pore volume. Pore volume (PV), is expressed as milliliters per cubic centimeter (ml/cc). The amount of carbon may also be expressed in grams, a measure of weight (ml/g). The volume of one gram of activated carbon would be a little greater than one cubic centimeter of the same carbon. Morin (1983) suggests that a pore volume of 0.45 to 0.60 ml/cc is best for aquarium carbon. The function and pore size of activated carbon is also compared by its adsorption capacity for certain compounds of different sized molecules: iodine, molasses, phenol, and carbon tetrachloride. Larger pores take up more of the larger molecules of molasses (a high molasses number) and smaller pores are more efficient for the smaller molecules of iodine (a high iodine number).

- *6. Total surface area (TSA)*. Surface area refers to the total extent of surface, mostly the internal surface of the pores, found in a certain volume of activated carbon. Total surface area is measured as square meters of surface area per cubic centimeter of carbon (m^2/cc). This is a measure of the capacity of the carbon. How much of this surface area is available to molecules of various sizes and chemical characteristics, the efficiency of the carbon, is dependent on pore volume and the chemical nature of the surface. Morin (1983) suggests that the best carbons for aquarium use have a total surface area of 450 to 550 m^2/cc and a TSA/PV of 700 to 1000.

- *7. Organic and bacterial coating of the particles*. Activated carbon for marine aquarium systems is used in a solution rich in many types of organic compounds and many species of bacteria. Like all particles in such an environment, it soon acquires a coating of organic compounds and bacterial colonies. These coatings fill pores, confound ionic exchange, change chemical characteristics of adsorbates and surfaces, and diminish the effectiveness of activated carbon and resin filtration. Frequent changing of the filter media is the best way to maintain the efficiency of chemical filtration.

Most aquarists have a few basic questions concerning activated carbon, such as: What are the characteristics of a good activated carbon for marine aquarium use? How much carbon does my system require? Should activated carbon be used constantly? When is the carbon exhausted? How do I know when to replace it? Can activated carbon be regenerated by washing or heating?

Characteristics of a good activated carbon. The granules of a good activated carbon are about a pinhead, 1 mm in diameter, and after washing off the dust, the granules are hard, but crushable, and have a dull surface. Soft crumbly granules are characteristic of ordinary charcoal, and a shiny surface is characteristic of coal bits. Good activated charcoal is highly porous, hydrophobic, and air filled. These characteristics cause it to float when first added to water and to emit a hissing sound as water enters the granules. Carbon that sinks quickly with no hissing sound is not the best for marine aquarium systems. A good carbon is light; it has a lot of volume for its weight, which is an indicator of a high total surface area. A good carbon for marine aquarium use has a variety of pore sizes since it is required to adsorb a wide variety of molecules. A pore volume of around 0.5 ml/cc and a total surface areas of about 500 m^2/cc is recommended.

How much carbon should be used?

The optimum amount of carbon will vary from system to system. Systems with high biological loads, no protein foam skimming, no trickle filter, and little algal growth will benefit from more extensive carbon filtration than more balanced, well filtered systems. An efficient water flow through the carbon will also reduce the amount of carbon required for effective surface contact. Thiel (1988) recommends using 34 ounces of activated carbon for each 50 gallons of water for reef type, marine aquarium systems and changing the carbon every 26 days. This is a considerably greater amount, with more frequent change, than most marine aquarists follow, but it will certainly result in effective carbon filtration. One may wish to keep this in mind as the upper optimum limit and experiment with lesser amounts and less frequent changes until the best strategy for a particular system is developed. Under typical conditions, most activated carbon retains the capability for removing organic dyes from marine systems for at least six months.

Should activated carbon be used constantly?

Activated carbon can be used in large amounts and changed frequently, and the tank water will always be clean and crystal clear. Under these conditions, careful observation and attention must be paid to the invertebrates in the tank to be sure that they show no signs of stress or trace element deficiencies. Careful attention should also be paid to the chemical parameters of the system to make sure that everything stays in the proper range. Activated carbon can also be used in moderate amounts, 10 grams per 50 gallons, and changed when the water yellows a bit, perhaps every 3 to 6 months if this schedule suits the purpose of the system and the aquarist's schedule. Intermittent use, once a week or once a month, also works if the aquarist finds that invertebrates do very well under this type of schedule. Be sure to prevent development of anaerobic conditions in carbon filters that are not in use, especially old carbon that has accumulated an organic load. The big danger with constant carbon filtration is that the need for water change may be masked by the clear water, and nitrate levels may climb to 100 ppm and beyond before the aquarist is aware of the distress of the invertebrates.

When is the carbon exhausted and replacement required?

Because of the various types of carbon available to the aquarist and the wide range of molecules that carbon removes, most aquarists have few clues as to what their carbon is actually doing, and to what extent it is doing it. Water clarity and healthy invertebrates is what the aquarist expects from carbon filtration, however, and both of these can be observed. Marine system water quickly picks up an off yellow color from biological activity, and activated carbon is very effective at removing these organic colors. Sometimes it is hard to determine if the water has a slight yellow color, so a simple color comparison test strip can be made and used to monitor the effectiveness of carbon filtration. A pure white strip of plastic, a strip cut from an old white bleach bottle works well, or a clean, pure white tile make a good base for the test strip. The plastic strip or tile must be absolutely white or the test is not effective. Use a light lemon yellow permanent or highlighting marker, a light yellow crayon will also do, and color half the strip making sure that a sharp line divides the white and yellow sections. Suspend the strip a foot or so into the tank and look at it from a distance of a few feet in front of the tank. If the white and yellow sides of the strip are hard to distinguish, the water has a yellow tinge and the carbon should be replaced.

Can activated carbon be regenerated?

To completely regenerate the adsorption characteristics of activated carbon it would have to go through the activation process again, high heat and steam or gas exposure, to drive out the adsorbed organics and clear the pores. This is not practical. An aquarist can wash and rinse the carbon in clear water and even heat it on a pan in the oven, which will clean some surfaces and a few pores of organic matter. Carbon so treated is not regenerated, although some surface organics are removed and this exposes some additional pore space. A little additional use of the carbon may be achieved, but the effort is not really worthwhile. Unless the carbon has been in use for a very short time, it is far better to replace it with new activated carbon.

Ion-exchange resins

The use of ion-exchange resins and polymeric adsorbents in marine systems is still controversial. These synthetic, chemically active filtrants were originally developed for use in ion poor, fresh waters. Turner and Bower (1983) reported on laboratory experimentation with two commercially available, resin based filtrants in artificial seawater and concluded that they were not as effective as activated carbon. The editor of Freshwater And Marine Aquarium Magazine (Editor, 1983), however, took strong issue with their results because of their methods and because the work was not conducted with the rich ionic and organic soup of an established marine life support system. Several companies package mixes of ion-exchange resins and preparations of polymeric adsorbents.

Ion exchange resins are manufactured in the form of tiny beads about a millimeter in diameter and they exchange either anions (negatively charged ions) or cations (positively charged ions) with an aqueous solution. The microporous resins have very tiny pores and are designed to deionize water for domestic use. They are not at all effective in marine systems, but can be used to deionize fresh water before adding synthetic sea salts. The macroporous resins have larger pores and greater surface area than microporous resins, more in the range of activated carbon, and, on a subjective basis, seem to be helpful to marine systems. Microporous resin beads are shiny and translucent. Macroporous resin beads are dull and opaque. Cation exchange resins are usually gray, brown to dark brown, and anion exchange resins are usually off white, beige to tan. Macroporous anion and cation resins can be either strong or weak exchangers.

In marine systems, strong exchangers are quickly flooded with ions of sodium, calcium, magnesium, sulphate, and chloride and are soon noneffective. Weak exchangers, however, retain a capacity to remove some organic acids and heavy metals. This aids pH control and improves water quality. Weak anion exchangers have a great capacity for removing copper and heavy metals and turn a dark blue to back when exhausted. Resins that remove organics turn from yellow to deep brown when exhausted. These resins can be repeatedly regenerated. Ion exchange resins are regenerated by soaking for 24 hours in pure laundry bleach. The resin is then rinsed, soaked in water treated with a dechlorinator for about eight hours, and then rinsed again. A third soaking for four hours in a marine buffer solution completes the regeneration process. Return of the original color to the resin beads indicates restoration of the activity of the resin. Various mixes of activated carbon and/or ion-exchange resins are available as proprietary products from several companies. The precise mix of carbon types and weak and/or strong, anion and/or cation resins are guarded secrets. Given the complexities of the use of these resins in marine systems, the effectiveness and value of these products must be determined by the individual aquarist.

Ion-exchange minerals

The natural ion-exchangers, kaolins and zeolites and other types of active clays, are of very limited use to marine aquarists. These mineral clays adsorb ammonia from fresh water and are useful to freshwater aquarists and cat keepers (kitty litter). Marine aquarists may use them in initial treatment of freshwater before dissolution of synthetic sea salts. Their capacity is limited, and it is primarily their economy in large quantities that makes use of natural ion-exchangers worthwhile for certain applications. Zeolite can be used as a substrate for undergravel filters. It quickly becomes inert in a marine aquarium and functions as a nonreactive, non calcereous substrate for biological and mechanical filtration.

Polymeric adsorbents

Polymeric adsorbents operate much the same as activated carbon. They are made from styrene or acrylic polymers and have controlled pore sizes and controlled, uncharged surface characteristics for adsorption of polar molecules. They are white to tan in color with a dull surface and are in the form of small beads or fibers. Polymeric filter media function primarily as molecular sieves and hydrophilic molecular adsorbents rather than ion-exchangers. They generally have a less efficient porous structure but more efficient surface adsorbent characteristics than carbon. Organic acids and organic and inorganic nitrogen compounds are generally removed more efficiently by polymeric adsorbents than by carbon. The combination of carbon and polymeric adsorbents and/or ion-exchange resins as filter media in a marine system seems to provide some synergistic chemical filtration effect that benefits fish and invertebrates, but this effect is difficult to quantify. Many marine aquarists feel that use of these carbon/resin or just resin products greatly enhances the life supporting capability of their marine systems.

Filter System Structures

Biological Filters

The typical biological filter brings together three things:

- oxygen
- water containing waste nitrogen compounds
- a substrate that supports colonies of nitrifying bacteria

The efficiency of a biological filter depends on how well it performs this task on a long term basis. Because of the nature of the beast, however, a biological filter always does more than just biological filtration. Depending on the design, construction, and type of filter media, it does other things as well, such as mechanical filtration, mineralization, gas exchange (aeration), and chemical filtration; and can even act as a substrate for algaes and invertebrates. These secondary functions often work to gradually diminish the populations and function of the nitrifying bacteria, thus most biological filters require some type of maintenance.

The major factors that limit function and efficiency of biological filters are lack of oxygen, diminished or channeled water flows, excessively rapid water flow, restricted substrate area for colonies of nitrifying bacteria, accumulation of detritus and competitive heterotrophic bacteria, the presence of light which inhibits growth of nitrifying bacteria and encourages algae growth, and large variations in availability of nitrogenous waste (ammonia). Efficiency of biological filtration is improved by increasing the area available for colonies of nitrifying bacteria, providing uniform optimum oxygenation of the filter media, providing a media surface that encourages growth of nitrifying bacteria and limits detritus accumulation and competition from heterotrophic bacteria, providing optimum water flow through the filter (adjusted for the size of the system), even distribution of water and oxygen over all areas of the filter media, keeping the filter in a dark area, and maintaining a relatively constant supply of nitrogenous waste. There are many trade offs and compromises inherent in designing biological filter systems. The "perfect" filter system for one application may be very inefficient and inappropriate for a system of different design and purpose. Biological filters continue to be improved through changes in design and filter media, and there is plenty of room for an enterprising and resourceful aquarist to develop new, economical, and more effective systems for biological filtration. Although there are many variations on each theme that alter efficiency and function in different ways, there are three basic categories of biological filters in common use.

Slow Flow Filters. These are filters that have a very slow water flow through a broad, thin, layer of filter media. Dissolved oxygen rapidly diminishes as the water flows slowly through the filter media, but this is offset by the extensive surface area and the thin stratum of filter media. The advantages are the ease and economy of powering slow, gentle flows (air lifts), and the disadvantages are the rapid loss of oxygen as water moves slowly through the media, accumulation of detritus, and fouling from deposition of organics and competitive bacterial populations. Undergravel filters that cover the entire tank bottom are the typical filters in this category.

Rapid Flow Filters. These are filters that depend on a relatively rapid flow of water through a thick layer, or numerous thin layers, of filter media. Rapid water flows though the contained media maintain high oxygen levels from beginning to end of the media layer, but the amount of media is restricted by the shape and volume of the container. The advantages are control of the media, control of the water flow, decreased fouling by detritus and heterotrophic bacteria, and the addition of biological filtration to a compact, multifunction filter system. The disadvantages are the power required for rapid flows, a need for a relatively large particle size to allow unrestricted water flow, and limitations on size and amount of media. Examples are the wet section of wet/dry filters, box and tube type filters, and some types of powered, auxiliary container filters.

Trickle Filters. These are filters that mix air and water by trickling water evenly over a substrate and collecting the flow in a sump beneath the substrate. There are many ways to construct a trickle filter and many types of filter media of varying unit size and design that can be used in a trickle filter. The choice of design and media greatly affect the function of the filter. The major design limitation is the use of gravity to pull the water through the filter. Generally, however, the advantages of a trickle filter are the high oxygenation of the substrate and nitrifying bacteria, lack of detritus accumulation, an efficient secondary function of gas exchange, and relatively low required maintenance. The disadvantages are a relatively high rate of water evaporation, a possible tendency for channeling of water flows, and limited substrate for bacteria depending on design and type of filter media. Trickle filters are most commonly a part of the filtration system on reef type marine aquariums. They may be stand alone units or function as the "dry" section of a wet/dry filter system.

The function and basic design of common biological filters in the above categories are discussed below.

Slow Flow Filters

Most slow flow filters are inexpensive, undergravel or other filters internal to the aquarium and powered by air lifts.

Undergravel filters

This is the traditional, basic biological filter design for marine systems. It consists of a flat, highly perforated plate that extends over the entire bottom area of the tank and is supported about a half inch to an inch above the bottom. The filter media is placed on the filter plate and retained above the plate, although water can easily flow through the media to the space under the filter plate. There are two to six uplift tubes that extend through the filter media and the filter plate. The tubes are open to the space under the filter plate. Water is drawn up through these tubes by either the action of an air lift in the tubes or the use of a small pump (powerhead) on the top of the uplift tube. Thus water is drawn from the tank, through the filter media layered on the tank bottom, and then returned to the surface of the tank. Be sure that water is drawn up all the air lift tubes at about the same rate. If one or more air lift tubes are not functioning, some portion of the water will flow down the nonfunctioning tube and up the active tube, bypassing the undergravel filter. Figure 16 illustrates the structure and function of the typical undergravel filter. Undergravel filters that have been especially designed and manufactured for marine systems are widely available. They work well if properly set up and maintained. The high demand for oxygen (BOD) and accumulation of detritus and organics within and under the filter bed are the major drawbacks. If the aquarist is handy, an undergravel filter can be made from commonly available plastic materials. Moe (1982) describes the construction of a quick and easy undergravel filter. The craftsman, however, may wish to make a sturdy, well designed, well constructed filter, and in this situation, the article on undergravel filter construction by Dewey (1986) is recommended.

The selection of a filter media for the undergravel filter is a very important decision. A fine grain filter media such as coarse silica sand provides extensive surface area for bacterial colonies and good mechanical filtration, but it requires frequent cleaning and stirring to keep it functioning well. This is a good choice if no supplemental mechanical filtration is used. Sand also has a tendency to make its way through the filter plate, form drifts between the tank bottom and the filter plate, and obstruct water flows under the plate. Use of sand requires very fine holes or slits in the filter plate and perhaps even a piece of plastic window screen fitted over the filter plate under the sand media may be necessary. A larger particle size gravel, such as dolomite, oyster shell, and crushed coral, provides a more porous filter bed that is less likely to form cakes and channel water flow, but additional mechanical filtration is then recommended. See the previous section on substrates for more information on filter media for undergravel filters. Light on the upper surface of the undergravel filter encourages algae growth and such growth often binds small grains together, further reducing and channeling water flows.

Use of coarse media for undergravel filters enhances efficiency of biological filtration by reducing accumulation of detritus within the filter bed, but the trade off is the increased accumulation of detritus in the space between the filter plate and the tank bottom. This detritus is difficult to remove without pulling up the entire filter bed and filter plate, not a fun job. Some control can be achieved by setting up a strong power head pump to push water down the up lift tube at one end of the tank, capping off all the tubes except for the one at the other end of the tank, and pushing water and detritus through the under space and up the far tube. A fine mesh net may help catch the detritus as it leaves the open tube top. Depending on the structure of the filter, it may also be possible to extend a length of small tubing down one of the air lift tubes to the under space and siphon out some detrital accumulations. This is one of those "do as necessary" jobs and probably would not have to be done more often than once every 8 months to a year, depending, of course, on the bio load in the system.

An undergravel filter is not necessary for a reef type system with an extensive, external biological filter. However, in some instances an undergravel filter may be an aid in that siphoning and cleaning the bottom is not required as frequently with an undergravel filter as in bare bottomed tanks, especially in tanks that contain many fish. Algae and invertebrate tanks do not accumulate as much benthic organic material, and a bare bottom is not necessarily a high maintenance feature. Also, if only a trickle filter is used in the external system, an undergravel filter increases the biological filtration potential of the system. Some invertebrates and algaes may also do better with a deeper substrate, and an undergravel filter allows use of a thick substrate without the need for frequent stirring to prevent organic accumulation and anaerobic decay. Note that an undergravel filter does not need to cover the entire bottom of the tank. It is much better, of course, in traditional systems that rely on the undergravel filter for biological filtration, for the filter to cover the entire bottom. But for systems that have external biological filtration, it is quite possible for the aquarist to set up only one section of the tank with an undergravel filter for a particular type of display or culture experiment.

Reverse flow undergravel filters

As the name implies, these are undergravel filters that operate in reverse of the traditional filter. Water from the tank is forced down the "uplift" tubes, or otherwise injected under the filter bed, to flow upward through the filter media. There are advantages to this design *provided that the water is evenly distributed to all areas under the filter plate.* As with typical undergravel filters, it is very important to keep the filter bed clean to prevent channeling most of the water through a small, restricted area of the bed.

Because of slow water flow through the filter media, the activity of heterotrophic and nitrifying bacteria quickly use much of the oxygen in water that moves slowly through the media. Thus the thin surface layer of the media is the most active part of the biological filter. When oxygenated water is pushed under the filter plate, the under surface of the filter becomes the most biologically active surface. However, even though water is moving upward through the filter bed, there is active circulation of aerated water around the interior of the tank and over the filter bed. Thus the upper surface of the filter bed is also exposed to relatively high oxygen levels. This means that both the upper and lower surface of the filter bed are exposed to oxygenated water, and the nitrification capability of the filter bed is enhanced. The under surface of the filter bed is also shielded from light, and this eliminates site competition from algae and the inhibiting effects of light on nitrifying bacteria on the most active filter surface.

Whether or not the system really benefits from this enhancement of function is up to the aquarist to decide. Since water is

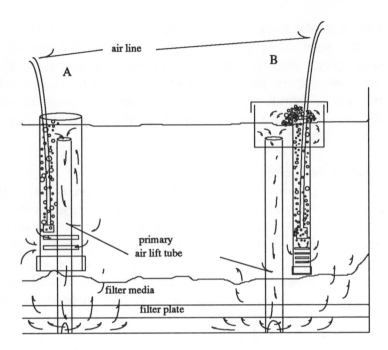

A. This is a 2" or 3" PVC pipe with 1" hole in the bottom cap fitted over the 1" air lift tube. The air release in the outer pipe draws water up the cover pipe and it flows down the standing pipe to the area under the gravel bed.

B. A small covered plastic box has two holes that fit over the standing pipe and an air lift tube. Air release in the air lift tube brings water into the box and then down the standing pipe to under the gravel filter bed.

Figure 23. Two possible modifications of standard air lift tubes to convert undergravel filters to reverse flow.

drawn from the tank and pushed under the filter plate, it is easy to accumulate organic particles and detritus under the filter plate. It may be necessary to "back flush" the under space, as mentioned above, more frequently with a reverse flow filter than with a top flow, undergravel filter. Two possibilities for modification of typical uplift tubes into a reverse flow operation are illustrated in Figure 23. It is also possible to mount a powerhead on the uplift tube so that the water is picked up from the tank and directed down the tube to create a powered reverse flow undergravel filter. There are some units designed for powered reverse flow now commercially available. Remember that in the case of reverse flow filters, what goes down must come up, so be sure to cap off or mount power heads on all up lift tubes so the water moves through the filter bed and does not return to the tank through an open air lift tube.

Foam block filters

Small, portable, inexpensive, air lift powered, slow flow filters can be made from sheets and blocks of polyurethane foam. Figure 24 illustrates two possible designs for this type of filter. Such filters can be easily cleaned, without totally destroying populations of nitrifying bacteria, by rinsing and squeezing the foam in a bucket of salt water. Although foam block biological filters are not usually appropriate for display tanks, they

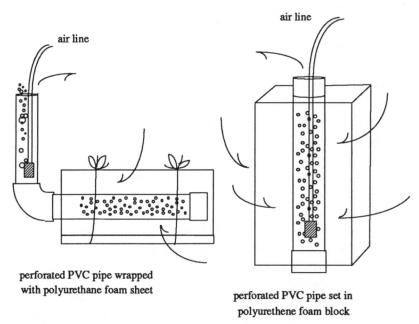

perforated PVC pipe wrapped
with polyurethane foam sheet

perforated PVC pipe set in
polyurethene foam block

Figure 24. Polyurethane foam air lift filters made from preforated PVC pipe and sheet or block foam.

find good use in holding tanks, quarantine tanks, and some commercial situations. If it is desired to transfer a foam block filter for the purpose of establishing a biological filter in a new tank, it is best not to squeeze or compress the foam when it is removed from the tank. Just allow the water to gently flow from the foam while holding the filter above the old tank. Wrap the active filter in a damp towel or newspaper to keep it from drying out during transport to the new tank. Do not keep it sealed up in a plastic bag for many hours or days as lack of oxygen will kill the colonies of nitrifying bacteria. Keep the filter damp with salt water if is kept out of a marine tank for some time.

Small, plastic box corner filters are in the same general catagory as foam block filters. They are powered by air lifts and contain a media of floss and/or activated carbon. Although small box filters are usually found only in small freshwater tanks, a mini salt water aquarium may also use such a filter.

Rapid flow filters

The most common use of rapid flow filter configurations is to house mechanical or chemical filter media, but biological filtration can also be accomplished in this type of filter. The most common type of rapid flow filter is the external box filter that hangs on the back of the tank and is operated by a small pump and siphon system. Container or cartridge filters that fit under the tank and operate under pump pressure are also common rapid flow filters. The primary purpose of these types of filters, discussed below, is almost always mechanical or chemical rather than biological filtration. It is important, whenever possible, to keep rapid flow filters in dark areas. Darkness reduces or eliminates algal growth on and in the filter, and this reduces mechanical clogging and site competition for the nitrifying bacteria.

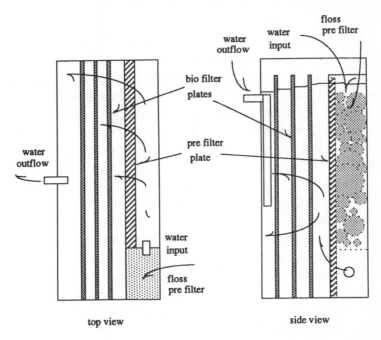

Figure 25. Configuration of one design for a biological filter composed of flow-through porous plates.

Partitioned box biofilters

A partitioned box filter consists of a box of various dimensions that contains several independent, thin, strong and rigid layers of a bio-mesh, fiber, or matrix type material. The top of the box is open or lightly covered so that the individual media partitions may be removed for cleaning or replacement as needed. The size of these media partitions or layers may vary from 3" by 6" to 10" by 10" to 18" by 18" depending on the size of the system and number of partitions. Water flows may be 200 to 500 gph or greater, also depending on the volume of the system. Large commercial or research systems, of course, are contained in boxes that may be 3' wide by 3' deep and 15' long with ten or more removable filter partitions and strong water flows. An air release between filter media partitions in these large installations may improve the efficiency of biological filtration.

The filter box can be made of glass, but acrylic plastic is easier to work and is much lighter. The box is usually hung on the back or side of the aquarium but may be installed underneath (with proper plumbing) or even inside the tank. Many configurations of this type of filter are possible, see Figure 25, but the basic principle is the same. Water enters the box and meets the first partition, usually a relatively dense fiber layer that acts as a mechanical filter. The density of this first partition can be controlled to provide whatever degree of mechanical filtration is required. A pre filtration partition of high density requires more frequent cleaning of this first layer, but provides more protection from fouling for the following bio filtration partitions. The partitions that provide biological filtration are made of a material that allows water to flow freely through, yet still provides exceptional surface area for colonies of nitrifying bacteria. The material is formed from a dense mat of tiny fibers and/or a porous material with extensive internal surface area of the right size for bacterial growth (Double Layer Spiral mat material should work well).

After passing through the first mechanical sieve, the water passes through all remaining 2 to 10 bio filtration partitions rapidly enough to maintain a proper oxygen level. The bio filtration partitions can be sequentially cleaned, three or four a month, to maintain proper water flows yet preserve constant biological filtration. This type of biological filtration can also be adapted to the wet portion of a wet/dry filter unit. The advantages of a partitioned box filter are extensive surface area in a small space and ease of cleaning the media. The disadvantages are the need for fairly rapid water flows and the potential for rapid clogging of the media. There are a few commercially available filters of this design for small marine systems now available.

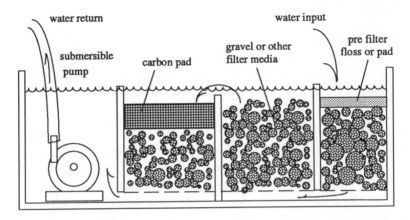

Figure 26. A "wet" media box filter with under-over water flow including a pre filter and activiated carbon pad.

Media box biofilter

A media box filter contains a biological filter media, usually granules or massed fibers, and is constructed to channel water flows through the entire mass of the media. Channeling is usually accomplished by a series of over/under partitions that break the media up into narrow, vertical, flow through sections as illustrated in Figure 26. This configuration insures that water flows through all the media and not just along the surface or bottom of the packed media. Water flows must be rapid enough to maintain adequate oxygen concentrations in the last as well as the first compartment. These filters are usually the "wet" stage of wet/dry filter units. The advantages of this type of media filter are that the flow is channeled through all the media avoiding dead areas, and if coarse granules are used, clogging is seldom a problem. The disadvantages are the need for strong water flows and difficulty in cleaning the media. A good mechanical prefilter is recommended to reduce detritus formation in the filter box. Coarse calcareous gravel can be used as a filter media, but better water flow is achieved with a a more open media. Detritus tends to accumulate on the bottom of the compartments and the filter must be emptied and cleaned occasionally.

Tube biofilter

The tube filter contains biological filter media in a relatively long, narrow channel. Water is pushed or drawn relatively rapidly through the tube, and this maintains high oxygen levels throughout the length of the media. The potential for biological filtration is good if the filter media has the substrate to support high populations of nitrifying bacteria and the structure to prevent channeling of water flow. Coarse gravel or small artificial structures function well in this type of filter. Tube filters can be mounted vertically or horizontally and

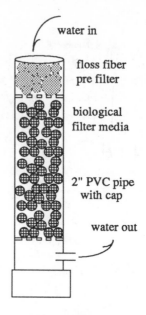

Figure 27. Simple PVC pipe tube filter with biological filter media.

can function as a trickle filter, submerged flow, or combination of both as illustrated in Figure 27. Compound filters that include surface skimming, mechanical filtration, biological filtration, protein foam skimming, and chemical filtration can be constructed on a tube filter concept, as mentioned in Chapter 5.

The advantages of this type of filter are space saving, portability between tanks, internal or external tank use, and non-clogging, rapid flow capability. The disadvantages are limited filter media volume (requiring light weight, high surface area media) and necessity for rapid flows. This general design is often used as a corner filter in reef type installations (mostly as a mechanical prefilter in this application) and in homemade and specialized commercial systems. A tube filter, when used with a chemical or mineral media is also termed a substrate reactor.

Trickle Filters and Wet/dry Systems

Comments on trickle filters usually fall into two groups. "Trickle filters are the newest, greatest thing to happen to marine aquarium systems since the all glass tank!"—or— "Trickle filters ain't nothin new. They've been around for years!"

Actually, there is truth in both statements. The use of trickle filters has provided the home aquarist with an efficient, low maintenance form of biological filtration and, just as important, a method of achieving optimum water/atmosphere gas exchange. Trickle filters have been used for many years by commercial operations and advanced hobbyists (I built and used trickle filters for multitank rearing systems back in 1973), and de Graaf (1973) also described two trickle or "dry" filter designs for small marine systems. It is only recently, however, in the mid 80's, that trickle filters have come into wide use, and along with other innovations such as intense, full spectrum lighting, denitrifyers, and protein foam skimming, have exploded the horizons of the average hobbyist.

A trickle filter provides a media substrate through which water and air mix as the water flows downward to be collected in a sump tank below the trickle filter. Water trickles over the exposed filter media, and biological filtration and gas exchange occur as the water moves in thin flows over the extensive media surface. An open media with low surface area and large void space favors gas exchange, while a dense media with a high surface area favors biological filtration. The design of the filter, including media selection, can favor either gas exchange or biological filtration. Both are required, and the best small, general purpose system is one that provides ample open air/water mixing along with efficient biological filtration. This strong aeration also serves to increase the redox potential of the system water. A trickle filter can also be configured as a tall, vertical tube filled with a very open structured media. Water flows downward through the media against a vigorous upward air flow. This configuration of a trickle filter is very effective in removing dissolved gases, including ammonia, and is termed an "ammonia tower".

Trickle filters are the "dry" portion of wet/dry filter systems and provide efficient gas exchange while the "wet" portion provides biological filtration and/or other auxiliary filtration. The trickle filter and the wet filter section contained in the sump tank, which may or may not contain a "wet" biological filter, are always considered as part of the same system since they logically fit together, although they perform different, and separable, functions. The dry, trickle section of the filter can also provide biological filtration and a trickle filter with sufficient surface area can decrease or eliminate the need for a separate section with wet biological filter media.

It is important to be aware of, and wherever possible to design against, one of the few disadvantages of this type of filter. Trickle filters of all types speed evaporation of water from the system and produce a high humidity in the cabinet where they are enclosed. The high humidity, with accompanying salt molecules, speeds corrosion of pumps and other equipment. High evaporation rates are enhanced by an air conditioned environment, and increased evaporation also causes additional heat loss from the water in the system. A heater may be necessary for a trickle filtered system where it was not necessary for the same size system with a traditional undergravel filter in the same location. The high evaporation rate can increase salinity of an untended system and even decrease the volume in the sump tank to the point that the pump runs dry and burns out if it is not protected by a low water cut off switch.

There are as many ways to build a trickle filter as there are ways for water to run downhill. A bucket with holes in the bottom and filled with gravel is a trickle filter, as is a huge aeration tower at a sewage treatment plant. Trickle filters for the hobbyist, however, generally fall into two categories—a tower filter or a tray filter—although there are other possibilities such as the box or "deep tray" type trickle filter and the "bio nitro filter wheel". It is important to note that many systems run quite well with trickle filtration that favors gas exchange at the expense of biological filtration—an open media, tower trickle filter. The reverse is also true; systems that favor biological filtration at the expense of gas exchange—tray type trickle filters—also function very well. Each type of system has its own maintenance requirements. Although trickle filters are usually part of a compound filter system with a water collection sump tank, they can be built as stand alone units that have some of the characteristics of both tower and tray units.

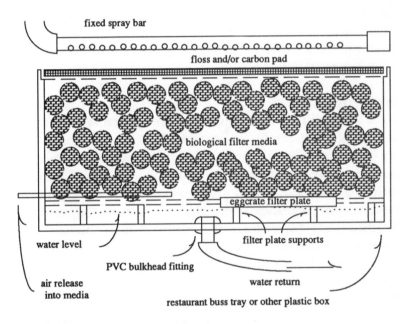

Figure 28. Greco's buss tray trickle filter.

Box and deep tray trickle filters

Greco (1988) describes the construction and function of a trickle filter made from a plastic 36" by 15" by 20" restaurant buss tray, Figure 28. A hole is cut in the bottom of the tray and a PVC bulkhead fitting is installed for the piping that carries the water to a pump and then back to the tank. The filter media —a plastic ball or other light weight media—is held an inch or so off the bottom by a second bottom of plastic eggcrate. The filter media fills the tray, and a porous plate on top of the filter media acts as a drip plate to distribute the water evenly over the filter media. Water is introduced to the filter by a fixed spray bar that extends along the top of the filter. Polyester fiber-fill can be spread over the top of the drip plate to act as an easily changed mechanical filter and to reduce splash from the spray bar. Air from a small vibrator pump can be released at one or two points inside the filter media to improve gas exchange inside the filter. Simple in design and inexpensive in construction, this type of trickle filter is a good example of the type of unit a handy aquarist can easily build to greatly improve biological filtration for a small reef type or a traditional marine aquarium system.

Tower trickle filters

A tower trickle filter is usually part of the type of system illustrated in Figure 29. The rectangular tower measures about 15" by 15" by 20" high (size varies greatly with the volume of the total system) and usually contains a loose, rigid filter media such as a vertical coiled, double layer spiral (DLS) plastic fiber mat, porous plates, or open plastic structures. Open plastic structures or DLS mat are the most common media used in tower trickle filters. The entire tower system and sump tank can be built of glass or acrylic plastic. Glass is less expensive, but heavier, breakable and less easy to drill and cut. The volume of media required depends on the water volume of the system and the surface area of the media intended for the system. The recommended surface area available for colonies of nitrifying bacteria for each gallon of system water is 3 to 5 square feet. A system with a very heavy biological load might require 5 to 6 square feet of active surface area, but most systems operate quite well on 3 to 4 square feet.

The total available surface area of most manufactured, commercially available biological filter media, by volume or by weight, is usually printed on the product label or is available on product information sheets or from the company. The basic choice on plastic structure media is one with low surface area, high void space for maximum gas exchange, or high surface area, low void space for maximum biological filtration. Some units try to provide both void space and adequate surface area for biological filtration. Additional information on surface areas of typical filter media can be found in the previous section on substrates.

It is necessary to break up the water flow as it enters the tower to prevent rapid water flow through only small sections of the filter media (channeling). Therefore, water is introduced at the top of the tower through a spray bar, drip plate, or rotating spray bar. A spray bar extends over the top of the tower and releases water through small holes over the top of the media. The resulting spray constantly hits the media in the same places and, as a result, water drips through the filter media in the same pattern over the same media all the time. If all the media is not equally exposed to the water flow, the efficiency of the filter is lowered. Small, very numerous holes and a wide spray pattern improve the efficiency of water introduction by a fixed spray bar.

One of the primary functions of the tower type trickle filter is the exchange of gasses between air and water. Since the tower trickle filter design does not expose filter media to the open air, it is very helpful to provide an air flow at the bottom of the tower just above the water level. The air moves upward through the filter media, mixes with the downward flow of water, and maintains high oxygen levels throughout the filter. A vibrator pump that produces 200 to 400 cubic inches per minute is all that is necessary. Note that 200 to 400 cubic inches per minute is roughly equivalent to 200 to 400 liters per hour. The volume of one liter is equal to 61.024 cubic inches.

A drip plate perforated with numerous small holes fits snugly into the top of the tower. Water spreads out evenly over the plate, runs equally through all the holes, and drips evenly through the filter media. The plate must be level to avoid a heavier flow-through on one side. The holes must be few and small enough to prevent most of the water from flowing through at one point on the plate, yet large and numerous

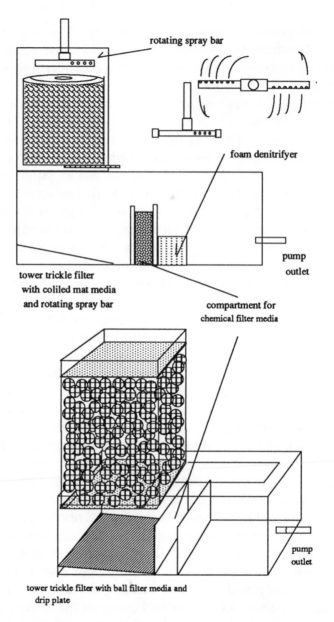

rotating spray bar

foam denitrifyer

pump
outlet

tower trickle filter
with coliled mat media
and rotating spray bar

compartment for
chemical filter media

pump
outlet

tower trickle filter with ball filter media and
drip plate

Figure 29. Tower type trickle filters. DLS (double layer spiral) mat
material or any type of open plastic or ceramic, non toxic material may used
to fill the tower chamber.

enough to prevent clogging and allow a free flow. An overflow provision should be included so that if the holes do clog, the water will bypass the drip plate and run into the sump without spilling out of the system.

Even with a drip or spray pattern there is a tendency for water to flow through the media in a constant pattern creating some constantly wet and some constantly dry areas in the media. The rotating spray bar, see Figure 29, is powered by the energy of the water flow (every action has an equal and opposite reaction) and constantly revolves, spreading water evenly over the surface of the media. The moving spray usually provides as even a distribution of water over the surface as it is practically possible to obtain. However, if the holes are too large and flows too few, or if the rotating bar freezes in one position, water distribution is far worse than that from a fixed spray bar and/or drip plate. It is important to be sure that the rotating spray bar that one buys, or builds, rotates on a nylon or teflon bearing to reduce the possibility of sticking in one position.

Once the water enters the sump tank, many options are possible. A "wet" biological filter section may be included in the sump tank, partitions for mechanical and chemical filtration and/or a denitrifying foam block, a protein foam skimmer, heater, and, of course, a float switch and pump must also be included. The float switch is a safety feature that turns the pump off if the water level falls too low. Water levels in this type of system may fall if evaporated water is not replaced, if a leak has occurred and water is lost, or if a restriction to water flow (clogged overflow or prefilter) develops in the system and the pump moves water out of the sump faster than it can flow into the sump. In these situations, the float switch turns the pump off and protects it from running dry and burning out. Another important item is a check valve in the water line that runs up to the tank, especially if the pump outlet is some distance under the surface of the tank. If the pump does give out for some reason (power outage or breakdown), and if the outlet is under the surface, the water line then becomes a siphon and water flows back out of the tank, fills the sump, and then overflows onto the antique, oriental rug that just set you back $50,000.00. Not a happy prospect, and well worth the installation of a float switch and check valve. Note that if the pump outlet is beneath the surface level in the tank, a small hole in the pump line (to provide a small water spray to disturb and aerate the water surface) will allow air into the line and break a siphon if the pump should fail.

There are numerous models and designs of the basic tower system built by many companies and now commercially available. An aquarist/craftsman may wish to build a unit of his own custom design or follow the specific instructions given by Thiel (1988).

Tray trickle filters

The shallow tray structure of this type of trickle filter is designed for small particle size filter media. Tray type trickle filters typically use a calcareous gravel as a biological filter media, but other small particle size media that allow a rapid flow-through of water are also acceptable. The filter media is contained in three to five relatively large, shallow trays with an open mesh bottom placed in vertical tiers with a few inches of space between the trays. Water is introduced over the surface of the upper tray and trickles down through each tray to a collector plate under the bottom tray that directs the flow into one end of a sump tank located beneath the tray array. A long spray bar usually brings the water to the top filter tray. This type of filter arrangement usually also includes a wet, partitioned biological filter in the sump tank. Figure 30 illustrates a typical tray type trickle filter. Smit (1986) describes the general structure and function of this style trickle filter and Belorusky (1988) describes in detail the materials and methods for construction of a filter of this design.

Many of the comments mentioned above for the tower type trickle filter also apply to the tray type filter. Use of shell or coral gravel provides whatever buffering capacity a calcareous media may add to the system and provides extensive surface

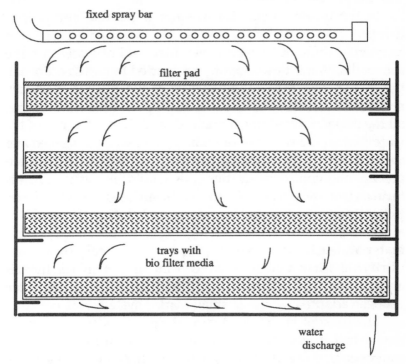

Figure 30. A tray type trickle filter. This is the configuration of the "dry" section of many wet-dry systems.

area for biological filtration. The drip from tray to tray exposes the water to air, and the surface area of the numerous trays also provides exposure to air. A counter current of air should be provided to enhance air/water gas exchange if the trays are enclosed. Tray trickle filters include extensive surface area for biological filtration, but are not as efficient in gas exchange as tower trickle filters. Use of an open media improves gas exchage characteristics and including a drip plate over each tray inproves water distribution over the media and reduces channeling of water through the media.

The bio nitro filter wheel

In the typical trickle filter, water is poured, sprayed, or dripped over a stationary media. This works well, but it is frequently difficult to get an even dispersal of water through the media. Water flows are often restricted to small sections of the media, and then the efficiency of the filter is markedly reduced. Now if the media could be dipped in the water so that all the surfaces would be immersed, and then lifted out of the water so that the water would mix with air while it drained and trickled evenly through the media, and the cycle repeated quickly and continuously, then this would be a very efficient form of biological trickle filtration. *All* surfaces would be intermittently exposed to water and air, and the media would be repeatedly flushed to prevent clogging by accumulated organic material. Such systems—bio nitro filter wheels (biological nitrifying filter wheels)—have been in use in freshwater aquaculture applications for some time, although they have not yet been adapted for use in small marine systems.

The concept is simple. A disc of rigid filter media is positioned half in and half out of the water with the axis at the water surface. The disc slowly turns and the media is alternately immersed and exposed. Water drains through the media in the upper portion of the disc and the media is submerged again as the disc turns. The number of discs that make up the filter wheel is variable. The more discs, of course, and the more surface area in the media of the disc, the greater the nitrifying potential of the filter wheel. Since aeration of the filter media does not depend on water flowing through many layers, numerous discs of porous or fibrous filter material can be closely mounted on one axle. The edges of the discs can be alternately tied together to increase structural rigidity and water/air distribution during the drip cycle. Alternatively, a coil of open weave, filter mat material could be wrapped around the axle to provide a compact mass of whatever thickness of filter media is desired.

A very compact trickle filter can be constructed from this basic design. A great deal of filter media is concentrated in a

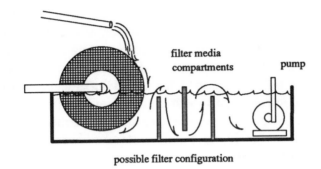

possible filter configuration

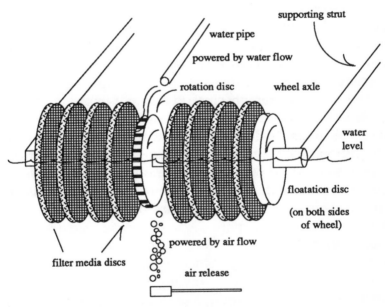

Figure 31. Elements of the Bio Nitro Filter Wheel.

small, shallow tank or tray since half the filter media is always out of the water. Figure 31 illustrates one possible construction scheme of a small bio nitro filter wheel for a marine aquarium system. Rotation of the wheel is accomplished by a directed flow of water or air over a series of cups or paddles attached to a rotation disc mounted in the center or at the end of the wheel.

The speed of rotation can be controlled by the velocity and/or volume of the air or water flow or by a friction check on the rotating axle. The filter wheel can be braced in place by supports mounted on the side of the filter tank or floated on the surface by a hollow, buoyant axle or by constructing the two end discs of styrofoam or other buoyant material. The bio nitro filter wheel can be used under a trickle tower filter to provide additional biological filtration to complement the strong gas exchange function of the trickle tower, or it can be used at one end of an over/under media box filter to provide trickle filtration in a small, compressed area. If so desired, a bio nitro filter wheel could also be used at the surface of the display tank, but like all biological filters, it will operate best away from light. A small bio nitro filter wheel could also be totally immersed in the tank and the rotation of the wheel would keep the filter discs exposed to aerated water, but the advantages of trickle filtration would be lost.

The bio nitro filter wheel could also be adapted to enhance the buffering effect of calcareous gravels. A hollow wheel half filled with oyster shell or crushed coral would turn continuously and tumble the gravel grains against each other. The surfaces of the grains would then remain free of chemical and organic surface contaminants and maximum solubility of the calcium carbonate would automatically be retained.

Algae Filters

A biological filter uses living organisms to chemically modify or remove compounds from the water in an aquatic system. The term biological filter usually refers to the activity of nitrifying bacteria, but in the broad sense, filters that use bacteria to denitrify water (reduce nitrate) or algaes to assimilate nitrate are also biological filters. Strong growths of algae remove nutrients from, and add oxygen to, closed system water and, in effect, "scrub" the water clean. Thus a device that provides lush algae growth in a closed system is often called an "algae scrubber". Reef type systems that are designed and

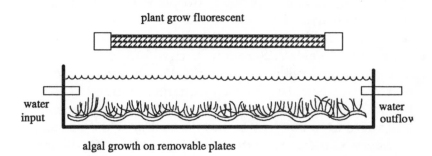

plant grow fluorescent

water input

water outflow

algal growth on removable plates

Figure 32. Structure of an algae tray filter.

maintained to grow macro algaes do not need an external algae filter, but some systems that are designed to maintain a high load of fish and invertebrates that consume algae will benefit from an external or internal algae filter.

An algae filter requires an intense source of light (refer to the section on algae in Chapter 3), a substrate, and water containing plant nutrients. An algae filter is most effective when nitrate is the limiting nutrient for algal growth. When other nutrients, such as phosphorus or iron, are limited, the algae stop growing and nitrate will continue to accumulate. Keeping other nutrients in adequate supply allows the algae to utilize all excess nitrate for growth, thus low nitrate levels are maintained in the system. The typical algae filter (Figure 32) consists of a shallow solid bottom tray with a water inlet on one end and an outlet on the other. Removable plates of a rough surfaced media such as unglazed tile, acrylic plastic, or even field stone, cover the bottom of the tray. One to two inches of water flows over this media. Full spectrum or plant growth spectrum fluorescent lights are placed a few inches above the tray. The lights should not remain on continuously as this is not good for the algae. They need time to respire as well as to photosynthesize. A light period of 12 to 16 hours per day will produce good results.

Green algae, usually the hair algae, *Enteromorpha*, is encouraged to grow in great proliferation attached to these plates. The plates are removed and cleaned of algae as required. Some algae should remain attached to the plates to serve as seed for the next growth. The collected algae can be discarded or recycled by feeding it to the fish and/or invertebrates in the main tank. An algae filter is an effective, efficient, and natural method of controlling the accumulation of nitrate and other plant nutrients in large marine aquarium systems. The algae filter can be located at any point in the external filter array, or as a separate unit, but may be best located after the mechanical prefilter and before the external biological filter. The biological filter should be shielded from the light that powers the algae filter to prevent algal growth on the biological filter media and preserve the activity of the nitrifying bacteria.

Algae can also be grown in a compartment in the main tank if desired. There are a number of ways to do this. Narrow plates, perhaps 12" long and 4" to 6" wide, can be suspended with nylon monofilament line a few inches below the surface at the back of the tank. The narrow water space between the plates and the surface will prevent grazing by fish and the proximity to the light encourages algal growth. A water flow directed over the plates also helps algal growth. When sufficient algal growth has occurred, the plates may be turned over to allow fish to graze on the under surface while the upper surface gains another growth of algae. The algae may also be scraped off and discarded if algae grazing fish are not present. Another possibility is to establish a "fish free" compartment at one end of the tank with a perforated plastic tank divider. Providing the light is sufficiently intense, algae will grow on the protected substrate. Removal of the divider and placing it on the other side of the tank will allow the fish to feed on the now accessible algae growths and induce algal growth on the other newly protected side of the tank.

A large, efficient algae filter may increase the pH of the system water above acceptable levels. High temperatures and high levels of plant nutrients stimulate the active photosynthesis that pushes up the pH. If this situation occurs, harvesting the algae, limiting the hours of light the algae receives, or regulated addition of carbon dioxide controls the rise in pH.

Denitrifying Filters

Not so long ago, frequent water changes and algae growth were the only ways an aquarist could relieve nitrate accumulation in marine systems. Recently, however, several methods of bacterial denitrification have become available to marine aquarists. Denitrifying filters do not totally eliminate the need for water changes in most systems, but by controlling nitrate accumulation they greatly reduce the volume of exchange and extend the period between water changes. Denitrification is the opposite of nitrification. A typical biological filter uses nitrifying bacteria in an oxygen rich (aerobic) environment to oxidize ammonia first to nitrite and then to nitrate. A denitrifying filter uses chemoheterotrophic bacteria (bacteria that eat a variety of chemicals) in an oxygen poor (anaerobic) environment to reduce nitrate first to nitrite, then to nitrous oxide and finally to nitrogen gas. The nitrogen gas is vented from the filter and is eliminated from the system.

The bacteria are able to respire in the absence of oxygen by using nitrate as the terminal electron acceptor. They also require organic compounds for growth and energy. The bacteria that operate a denitrifying filter also live under aerobic conditions and are part of the heterotrophic bacteria population found in all systems. It is not necessary to provide a seed of specialized bacteria for these filters. A well designed and carefully operated denitrifying filter can maintain nitrate levels in the 0.0 to 10.0 ppm range in large and small marine and freshwater systems.

Batch denitrification. An aquarist can use either a "batch" method or "through-flow" method of bacterial denitrification. The batch method consists of isolating a relatively small volume of system water under still and stagnant anaerobic or very low oxygen conditions for 24 to 48 hours. The isolation chamber contains a surface substrate of plastic matting or gravel for bacterial growth. It may be connected with pipes and valves to the system so that it can be filled from and emptied back to the main system with a pumped or gravity fed flow, or it can be entirely separate and filled and emptied just by physical bailing, although this would not be very efficient. The denitrification chamber is cycled and fed every day or two for systems with heavy biological loads that produce a lot of nitrate. Batch denitrifiers for systems with light biological loads that produce little nitrate may be run with a few days between cycles. It takes three to five weeks for the proper levels of bacteria to develop in the chamber so some activity (water and light feeding) should be continuously maintained to keep bacterial populations active. The denitrification chamber can not be emptied and left dry between uses or the bacterial colonies will not remain active.

The organic food for a batch denitrifyer may be a ten to twenty percent lactose or glucose solution or even just alcohol—methanol or ethanol (a little high test vodka). The amount of "food" given to the chamber depends on the volume of the chamber, the amount of nitrate to be reduced, and the treatment time. One or two ounces of the food solution per 10 gallons of chamber water is reasonable starting point. The amount of feed can be increased if all the nitrate is not reduced in a day or two, or decreased if reduction seems to be going too fast and hydrogen sulphide and/or black slime is produced.

The volume of a batch denitrification chamber is variable, but somewhere around five to ten percent of the system volume is probably most workable. A ten gallon aquarium for a 75 to 125 gallon system makes a good chamber. The chamber need not be sealed since little oxygen exchange takes place through the still surface layer of a stagnant tank, but a tight cover with a small vent hole is a good idea. Nitrate and nitrite should be tested when the chamber is filled and then tested a day or two later to make sure that all the nitrate, and any nitrite that may be formed from incomplete reduction, is completely gone before cycling the water back to the system. High initial nitrate levels will require higher feeding levels and perhaps more treatment time than an established batch routine for an old system. Testing nitrate and nitrite is very important initially to make sure that the proper bacterial populations have developed in the denitrification chamber and feeding levels and cycling time is right, but once the routine is proven, testing can be done every five to ten cycles to make sure the denitrification system is working properly.

A batch denitrifyer is not as efficient as a through-flow system and it does require more routine care and maintenance from the aquarist, but it does have a few advantages. It is easy and inexpensive to set up and operate. There is also less chance of a malfunction affecting the entire system because the output of the filter is not added back to the system until the aquarist has evaluated the condition of the water. If necessary, a batch denitrifyer can be located remote from the system and water transported back and forth, but only a masochistic aquarist would favor such an arrangement. A batch denitrification system will work well, but once control of a through-flow system is mastered, its ease and automatic operation is usually much preferred.

Flow-through denitrification. A flow-through denitrifying filter consists of an air and water tight box or series of boxes, valves that precisely control a slow flow of water into and out of the filter, a one way valve to allow escape of nitrogen gas, an internal substrate for bacterial colonies, and a provision for supplying the bacteria with a simple carbohydrate food source. Water is supplied from a constant pressure source, valved from either a pump pressured line or a simple gravity flow through system. The bacteria "food" is supplied as a commercial preparation in a slow release package or as a frequently added liquid, or can be made up from a lactose or glucose powder. Generally, a 10 percent lactose solution is prepared and refrigerated and one ounce of this solution is fed to the filter every one to two weeks. The frequency of feeding depends on the size of the filter and the rate of nitrate production in the system. If at all possible, the lactose solution should be added to the filter without allowing air to enter the filter. A drip feed of the lactose is better than adding the solution all at one time and a hospital I/V bag can be adapted for this task. Figure 33 illustrates the structure of a typical denitrifying filter.

There are three controlling factors in the long term operation of a denitrifying filter:

- The rate of production of nitrate in the system.

- The flow rate of water through the filter.

- The amount of organic food available to the bacteria.

The short term factor is the growth of the populations of denitrifying bacteria. As with other biological filters, it takes several weeks for the proper bacterial populations to become established. Rate of nitrate production is a function of the biological load and the size of the system, and although under the "control" of the aquarist, nitrate production is not directly manipulated by the aquarist. The aquarist can control the size of the denitrifying filter, the rate of water flow through the filter, and the amount of food the bacteria receive. There is usually an initial amount of nitrate in the system when a denitrifying filter is first started, and food and flow levels are adjusted for this initial "unlimited" level. When nitrate drops to production rate levels, water flow and feeding rates must be readjusted to balance nitrate production rates. It is the adjustment between flow rate and food consumption that makes the filter function most efficiently at nitrate reduction.

The normal water flow rate through a denitrifying filter is somewhere between 10 and 50 milliliters per minute. Water entering the system is near saturation with oxygen and this oxygen must be consumed by the bacteria at the front of the filter before nitrate reduction can begin. If water flows through the filter too rapidly, too much oxygen is introduced, the process of denitrification is not completed, and nitrite is discharged from the system. Thus the filter discharge should always be directed to the biological filter so that if nitrite is discharged, it is oxidized back to nitrate before it can return to the display tank. The discharge from the filter should be tested periodically, and if nitrite is detected, the flow should be restricted. Not enough organic food may also cause nitrite to be discharged, so if flow rates are relatively slow, an increase in

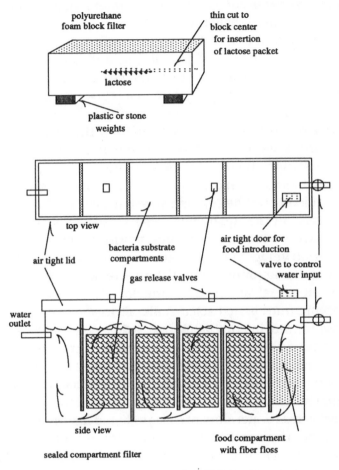

Figure 33. Elements of two types of denitrifying filters.

the amount of organic food may increase bacterial activity and nitrate reduction. If too much food is present or if flow rates are too slow, then the bacteria begin to reduce sulfates and hydrogen sulfide is produced.

This gas smells like rotten eggs and is detectable at very low levels. Interestingly, one good whiff of hydrogen sulfide reduces the ability to continue to detect it by smell. If you get one whiff of hydrogen sulfide and then can't detect it again, leave the area of the filter for an hour or so and then try again.

Smelling hydrogen sulfide around the filter indicates that food levels are too high and/or flow rates are too low. Operation of a denitrifying filter is a bit tricky and experience is needed to achieve the right balance of organic food and flow rates to meet the needs of a particular system. The patient aquarist will be rewarded, however, with a system that is always almost nitrate free. Three references on the theory and operation of denitrifying filters are Blok (1986), Greco (1987) and Ewing (1987).

It is also possible to reduce nitrate with a very simple, but far less efficient method. Some aquarists place a block of polyurethane foam, about 3 or 4 inches square and 8 to 12 inches long, in the filter system where water can flow around, but not through, the foam block. The absence of water flow in the interior of the block creates anaerobic conditions and fosters the development of denitrifying bacteria in the center of the block. These bacteria populations reduce nitrate as water slowly percolates through the foam block.

Aerobic, nitrifying bacteria inhabit the oxygenated areas near the surface of the block and oxidize any incompletely reduced nitrate (in the form of nitrite) that may be released from the center of the block. This type of passive denitrifying filter, although less efficient, needs no feeding or flow rate adjustment. The efficiency of the block may be greatly enhanced by inserting a slow release packet of lactose solution in the center of the block. How much lactose in how big a block, and how often the packet is replaced, however, is a subject for experimentation.

This type of passive denitrification can also be done with a slow flow through or over a sediment pack, such as a mud-silt area used to grow seagrass, but control of the anaerobic activity in such an area is difficult. The Smithsonian Reef flows water through a separate system with such a sediment-grass area, and this adds to the biological balance of the system. A reef system aquarist, however, will get better results with proper operation of a proven, commercially manufactured denitrifying filter.

Auxiliary Filters

It is difficult to define auxiliary filters, especially in these times when so much new development is taking place in filtration of marine systems. The broad definition I favor is any device, internal or external to the tank, that augments the basic biological and mechanical filtration of an undergravel filter in a traditional marine aquarium system. These filters now range from small, submersed box type, bubble up filters to large compound filters that are mounted remote from the tank. I remember back to the 50's when the only common auxiliary filters available were small plastic boxes containing filter floss that hung on the back of the tank. Water was siphoned from the tank into the filter box and the filtered water was returned to the tank with a flow of air bubbles that made an air lift out of the return tube, Figure 34. Soon pump powered external box filters became available and then powered canister filters of many designs and purposes, and now small, elaborate compound "reef" filters that hang on the back of the tank, or are installed beneath the tank, are available as auxiliary filters.

Internal or submerged auxiliary filters are useful, but are rarely placed in major marine display tanks. The most common internal filter is a small box filter containing fiber floss and carbon or other chemical media. The box is placed in a corner of the aquarium and is operated by an air lift that draws water through the slotted lid, down through the media and then up the central air lift tube. Common in small freshwater tanks, it can also provide inexpensive chemical filtration for a small marine system and can be hidden out of sight behind a rock or coral structure.

Protein foam skimmers can also be designed as internal auxiliary filters. Internal filters save external space and expense and eliminate complex plumbing and potential leakage. Internal, submerged filters can be quite elaborate and can constitute an entire filter system for a 20 to 50 gallon marine aquarium. I recently designed and built an inexpensive internal filter system that provides surface skimming, mechanical filtration, biological filtration, protein foam skimming, and chemical filtration in one relatively small air or powerhead driven unit. The filter system was constructed from materials available at hardware and kitchen supply stores. Although it works well, it is not the most beautiful structure to place in a display aquarium. Since this type of unit is the basis for a particular type of system, it is described in Chapter 5.

One thing most external auxiliary filters have in common is a siphon apparatus that pulls water over the side of the tank and into the filter. The best external filter systems use a drain hole drilled in the tank bottom or side, but this is big deal modification and over the side siphon tubes are much more widely used. Although most newly designed external filters use a direct pump line on the siphon tube, some systems do not. Siphon tubes often develop air pockets and flow restrictions, and when the siphon breaks, the filter runs dry and pumps can be damaged. Installation of a siphon retaining cup on the inside of the filter box (Figure 34) insures that the siphon tube always has a restriction free, water-to-water connection and minimizes the exasperating loss of water in the siphon tube. The upper edge of the retaining cup is positioned a little below the water level in the tank. Water flows through the siphon tube into the water retaining cup and then overflows into the body of the filter box. The siphon tube remains full no matter how fast or how slow water flows through the filter or how low the tank water level falls.

Of course, tiny air bubbles can still be captured by the flow into the siphon tubes and will eventually build up an air pocket at the top of the tube. A high quality aquarium air valve or a one way air valve placed in the top of the siphon can be used to remove air from the inside of the siphon. The air can be removed by pulling it out with the venturii attachment of a powerhead pump or just lungpower. As long as the valve is airtight, air will not enter the siphon through the valve and any accumulation of air in the siphon can be easily removed. It is up to the aquarist, however, to frequently check the stataus of the siphon and remove any accumulated air. A similar siphon

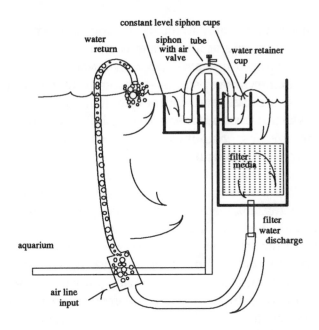

Figure 34. A constant flow, constant level filter box with antique "bubble up" water return tube.

retaining cup placed just below the water level in the tank allows the siphon intake to act as a surface skimmer and still keeps the constant water to water connection on each end of the siphon tube.

I once made a complete filter box, like the one illustrated in Figure 34, out of cardboard. Oh, a question in the back of the room? You there with the glasses. Cardboard isn't waterproof you say, the unit will quickly dissolve into a flacid mess? Well, I must have neglected to mention that after construction I gave the cardboard three coats of fiberglass resin, which transformed the easy-to-work-with cardboard and tape contraption into a firm, waterproof, rigid structure. The cardboard construction, fiberglass resin trick works well for small, unusually shaped containers with many tubes and compartments. Check for leaks carefully and use an epoxy putty to patch any holes before the final coat of fiberglass resin. There are now so many excellent auxiliary filters and filter systems commercially available at reasonable prices, however, that unless one is on a super tight budget or delights in construction and experimentation, it is not necessary to build small filter systems. There are three primary types of external auxiliary filters: the very common, basic, hanging box unit; the pump powered canister unit; and the "reef" type compound unit.

Hanging box filters

There are many, many modifications of this old standby design available today. They all draw water from the aquarium, put it through one or more compartments containing particulate and chemical filter media, and then return the water to the aquarium. A traditional marine aquarium system of 20 to 75 gallons can be operated very successfully with the help of a good external box, power filter. Today, all such units are pump powered. The pump is mounted on the top or on the bottom of the filter box. The impeller of the pump is usually powered by an electromagnetic field and is separated from the motor coil by a waterproof barrier.

Modern units no longer use the old fashioned, fiberfill-carbon-fiberfill sandwiches, layers that were messy and time consuming to clean and repack, but they did do the job. Simple pads of mechanical and particulate filter media slip into the filter and can be replaced quickly and easily. Of course, the expense of filter pads is greater than that of floss and carbon layers, but the ease of operation makes them worthwhile. Chemical filter media is now also placed in flow through bags that makes replacement easy. Incidently, sections of old nylon panty hose make good bags for chemical filter media if one wants to mix and pack these media. Mechanical filter media, whether pad or pack, eventually becomes clogged, and water flow is restricted or blocked. The filter is no longer functional when this happens, and the media must be cleaned or replaced. It is important to be aware of the condition of this media and replace it when necessary.

The flow rate of these filters varies with size and application. The smaller ones pump 100 to 200 gallons per hour, and the larger ones push around 600 gph. Most external box filters have a bypass feature that allows water to go over, around, or back into the tank if the media is clogged. This is an important feature, for with pump powered filter boxes, if water can not return to the aquarium when the media is clogged, it has to go somewhere, and this is usually the floor. Note that a filter with bypassed media may not be spilling on the floor, but it is also not filtering the water. Make it a point to check the operation of these filters at least once a week to be sure that the filter media is working properly.

Canister filters

A canister filter is a sealed unit, usually with its own pump, that is mounted under or away from the display tank. Water is drawn from the tank and pumped under pressure through the filter media in the canister and is then returned to the tank. Canister filters usually function as mechanical and/or chemical filters, but some units also include biological filter media. Because of high flow rates and limited internal volume for biological filter media, it is wise not to depend on canister filters alone for biological filtration. They can not substitute for trickle and undergravel filters, but they do provide an exceptional additional filtration capacity to all types of systems. Because they operate under pressure in a sealed container, this filter design can accommodate high water flow rates. Depending on size and purpose, flow rates vary from 100 to 1000 gph.

The flow from canister filters is strong and can provide good water circulation in the aquarium if properly directed. Some units also include a surface water extractor, or surface skimmer, that draws water from the surface of the tank into the filter. Although this does not remove the organic molecules attached to the gas/water interface (surfactants) from the system, as does a protein foam skimmer, it does remove them from the surface and improves system gas exchange.

Some canister filters are designed only for mechanical filtration and may use a disposable cartridge with a pleated surface area of 10 to 30 square feet or may be designed for use with diatomaceous earth. A diatom filter uses the very fine, hard powder of diatomaceous earth to build a coat on a porous fabric and provides extremely fine mechanical filtration, removing particles down to a few microns in size. Diatom filters polish the water in a marine system to great clarity but they must be flushed and regenerated frequently. Mechanical filters that use pad or pleated sheet media must be checked frequently to make sure that the flow rate through the filter is strong and that the media has not clogged with organics.

Multi media canister filters are designed to contain various combinations of mechanical, chemical, and biological filter media. The flow from canister filters, especially those with mechanical filter media cartridges, diminishes as the filter pores clog, and it is important to monitor the operation of these filters and clean and replace mechanical filter media when flow rates markedly decrease. An accurate measure of flow rate from these filters can be obtained using the data in Table 6.

Canister filters are sealed units that accumulate organics. When the water flow is stopped, oxygen no longer enters the unit and the bacteria that are present go into anaerobic respiration. A clogged canister that is switched off until "I can find the time to clean it" can build up a heavy growth of black slime and a potent load of hydrogen sulfide. Be sure never to start up such a neglected filter and flush its contents back into the system. Hydrogen sulfide accumulated from the anaerobic decay of organics trapped in the filter may be strong enough to stress or kill organisms in the aquarium. Power losses do not usually cause problems unless the power is out for 10 hours or more. Correctly sized to the system and properly operated, canister filters are an excellent auxiliary to large and small traditional marine aquariums. They provide strong, positive mechanical and chemical filtration for any type of system. The handy aquarist can build a canister filter, but it is not an easy task. Vecellio (1987) describes in detail the construction of a homemade canister filter.

Compound or "reef" auxiliary filters

The popularity of large trickle and compound filters for reef structure systems has stimulated development of small compound filters that function as auxiliary systems for traditional marine aquariums. These small units provide some of the advantages of large compound filters and are often designed to hang on the rear of the tank and draw water from the tank by a siphon system. If such a system totally replaces the undergravel biological filter, it is then no longer an auxiliary filter, but should be considered and judged on its merits as a complete filter system. Some of these small, compound external filter systems can easily function as a complete filter unit for tanks under 50 to 75 gallons. These systems usually include most or some of the following features: a surface skimming feature, a "dry" or trickle filtration capacity (which greatly improves gas exchange in small aquariums), a mechanical filter chamber for a pad or pack, a protein foam skimmer, a denitrifying filter, a chamber for chemical or calcareous buffer media, and a pump that provides a strong, guided water flow, or spray, back to the tank.

These small units require a constant water level in the tank. If water lost to evaporation is not frequently replaced, the lip of the surface skimmer cup (unless its a floating cup) extends above the water level and water flow into the system is restricted or lost. Some of these units are well designed and well constructed and some are not. The cost of these compound filters is considerably more than a hanging box filter and should provide considerably better filtration. The most important new features to look for in the filters that are designed for marine use is a good system for mixing air and water and a good protein skimming function. Providing that the tank receives proper lighting, a good compound auxiliary filter can greatly expand the life support capacity of the system.

Protein Foam Skimmers

The first time I saw a protein foam skimmer at work was in the fall of 1969. We were visiting the National Fisheries Center and Aquarium in Washington, D.C. and Craig Phillips was giving us the tour. He pointed to a bulbous contraption sprouting tubes and pipes, a pump powered, venturi driven, protein skimmer, and said something like, "This baby can pull out 90 percent of the protein that goes into a tank". To illustrate his point he hooked up the skimmer to a 100 gallon marine display tank. The skimmer whizzed and burped and not much happened. He then took a cup of fresh shrimp that just came from a blender and poured it into the tank. After a few minutes the whizzing and burping turned into fizzing and frothing and the collection cup soon filled with a skuzzy brown pasty liquid, almost a full cup. I left with the impression that protein foam skimmers really work.

Adsorptive foam separation or foam fractionation has been used since at least the 1890's to separate various surface active compounds from aqueous solutions, and the principle has been applied to marine aquarium and marine culture systems since at least the mid 1960's. Far more than just protein is removed by efficient foam separation, and this is a more accurate term for the process than protein foam skimming. Protein skimming, however, is the commonly used aquarist's term for the process. Although European aquarists have been familiar with protein skimmers for many years, Wilkens (1973), it is a relatively new form of auxiliary filtration to most American aquarists.

On the surface, protein foam skimming is deceptively simple. Foam is created by mixing air and salt water together, the finer the mix, the smaller the bubbles, and the better the process works. Proteins and other organic compounds in the water coat the bubbles as they rise and make a relatively stable foam. This foam is then captured and removed before it can reenter the system. Proteins and other organics are removed before they are mineralized into nitrogen compounds and other toxins, and this is very beneficial to the health and maintenance of the system. *Note that of all the various filtration capabilities available to the marine aquarist, only protein foam skimming completely removes most organics from the system before they break down.* It is reported, Lundegaard (1985), that protein foam skimming prevents tank "wipe outs" (the toxic tank syndrome) from accumulations of unknown toxins. These internally generated toxins can kill all susceptible fish and invertebrates within the space of a few hours, usually overnight. Use of ozone and activiated carbon filtration along with protein foam skimming provides good protection against this syndrome.

A disadvantage to protein foam skimming, however, is that some beneficial organic and inorganic trace elements are also removed; so systems with efficient protein foam skimmers must be monitored for loss of these elements. The skimming process does not work well in freshwater because pH is close to neutral, and this reduces the electrical interaction between organic molecules and water, which decreases foam formation. Also, the lower density of freshwater reduces the formation and stability of tiny air bubbles. Skimming will work in brackish water with as low as 5 ppt salt.

The operation of a protein foam skimmer also effectively aerates the system water and increases redox potential almost as well as a trickle filter, which is an excellent reason for adding a skimmer to a system that does not have trickle filtration. Although this is all the casual aquarist needs to understand about protein foam skimming, this simple description conceals some complicated organic and inorganic chemistry and complex physical design and engineering considerations.

A word of caution. A protein foam skimmer can be very beneficial to a marine system, but it does not fit within the *modus operandi* of every aquarist. It is not a static piece of equipment. It has to be cleaned, adjusted, and cared for on a daily or weekly basis, or else it is useless. If you are the type of aquarist that services a tank once every month or two and doesn't have time for frequent observation and adjustment, it is best to stick with just trickle filtration and a chemical media filter. A neglected, non-functioning protein foam skimmer is a total waste of money and effort—kind of like keeping a radio with a broken speaker turned on just because you like to see the little red light.

Theory

Proteins and other organics get into marine aquarium systems through feeding, excretion, and organic decay. Through the intricate process of biological filtration, these organic substances eventually become nitrates, dyes, acids, and basic nutrients that accumulate in the system water. Foam separation removes complex organic substances before they are transformed by the processes of biological filtration. As illustrated in Figure 21, many complex organic molecules have a "water loving" (hydrophilic) end and a "water hating" (hydrophobic) end. Such molecules quickly orient themselves at a gas\water interface with the hydrophobic end extending into the gas and the hydrophilic end extending into the water. (See the previous section on adsorption theory.) Because these compounds are so attracted to the water surface, they are called surface active agents or **surfactants**. They form an "organic skin" about an air bubble and give the surface of the bubble the stability to maintain its form after it leaves the water.

The stabilized bubbles form a temporary foam above the water surface. This foam, termed the foamate, contains water soluble proteins, amino acids, some organic dyes, fatty acids, fats, carbohydrates, enzymes, detergents, many inorganic compounds, metal ions (particularly copper and zinc) that are tied up in sulphide compounds, iodine, phosphorus, tiny cells of algae, protozoa, and bacteria, and tiny buoyant particles of organic detritus.

When the foam is first formed, the water content is high and it is quite "wet". As the foam breaks down, the water drains downward carrying dissolved and particulate matter. If the foam contains a lot of protein, however, the upper bubbles reform into a "dry" foam that contains less water and more organics. This dry protein foam "floats" on the wet water foam, accumulates organics from the watery foam beneath it, and is pushed up into the collection cup of a protein skimmer. An optimally adjusted and maintained protein skimmer collects all the dry protein foam and only a small amount of the wet water foam. If there is little protein or other organic colloids present in the water, dry foam does not form, and the optimally adjusted protein skimmer collects little material. A protein skimmer operated at this adjustment point collects most of the excess protein and organics, but since foam collection does not include much of the constant production of wet foam, loss of trace elements is minimal.

The basic factors that enhance the operation of a protein foam skimmer are: small bubble size (0.5 to 1.0 mm), adequate contact time between the bubbles and the water, optimum air flow rate, low temperature (foam breaks down faster at high temperatures), high pH (efficiency is increased at high pH, 8.2 is much better than 7.8), high protein concentrations, and use of ozone with the air in the contact chamber. Other factors such as liquid viscosity, surface tension, air injection rate, air release system, liquid chamber size and shape, foam chamber size and shape, foam stability, foam drainage, and liquid flow rates become important when the purpose, economics, design, and construction of the separation device is considered.

For marine aquarium systems, there are three important factors that the aquarist can control:

- bubble size

- air flow rate

- contact time

If bubbles are too small, they loose buoyancy, will not properly rise in the skimmer, and tend to diffuse throughout the tank. If bubbles are too big, they rise too rapidly in the contact chamber, and the total bubble surface area available to collect surface active compounds is relatively small. Spotte (1979) recommends a bubble size of 0.8 mm.

The rate of air flow into the device determines the ratio of air to water that exists within the contact chamber. Assuming ideal bubble size, an air flow rate that is too slow restricts the total available bubble surface area for the volume of water present in the chamber, and foam formation is slow and limited. Foams may break down before they enter the collection cup. Too great a flow of air creates excessive turbulence and a very wet, unstable foam that drains excessively, breaks down quickly, and reduces the efficiency of the skimmer. Again according to Spotte (1979), the recommended air to water ratio is provided by an air flow of $1.8\,cm\,sec^{-1}\,cm^{-2}$ of contact column cross-sectional area. Every system is different, however, and even if it were easy to adjust bubble size and precisely measure air flow rates, each aquarist would still have to carefully adjust air flow rates to a skimmer for optimum operation in each particular system. The air bubble/water contact time can be increased by long (tall) contact tubes and by flowing the air bubbles and the water in opposite directions, a counter current contact tube. Note that the more rapidly the water flows through the skimmer, the shorter the contact time. Water flow rates through the skimmer must be adjusted for the operation of each particular system

It is important to understand the operational theory of protein foam skimmers, but in actual practice the marine aquarist must depend on observation, experimentation, and experience to achieve optimum operation of a commercial or homemade skimmer device.

Design and construction

There are many, many ways to bubble water and collect foam, and as American marine aquarists become more aware of the value of protein foam skimming, more commercial skimmers of various designs are becoming available. I am sure we will see widespread use and development of many innovative designs of protein skimmers in the years ahead. The easiest way to acquire a well designed protein foam skimmer that suits the design and function of the system is to purchase one produced by a reputable manufacturer of aquarium products.

Although there are many styles and design variations to choose from, there are three basic types of protein foam skimmers: cocurrent, countercurrent, and venturi. It is not difficult to build a homemade skimmer, and I will also provide some ideas on this alternative. The drawings that illustrate the function of various types of skimmers are based on designs for homemade models rather than commercial models. The principles of operation are the same, but the possibilities for the aquarist are greater. Note, however, that although homemade skimmers are much less expensive than commercial models, they seldom equal the efficiency and operational ease of well designed, manufactured units.

Placement

The first, most fundamental consideration in design and/or selection of a skimmer is whether it will be placed within the tank or external to the tank. Internal, submerged skimmers work well and are relatively inexpensive to buy and easy to build. Skimmers that operate in a large trickle filter system are essentially modifications of external type skimmer units. The disadvantages of internal skimmers are that they are usually visible in the display tank, maintenance of proper adjustment and replacement of the air diffuser is often difficult, and proper operation depends on a constant, fixed water level in the display tank. A drop in water level due to evaporation may prevent the foam from rising into the collection cup, and an increase in water level may fill the collection cup with too much wet foam.

External skimmers are usually stand alone units that are pump powered and venturi driven, although a few counter current models with air valves or air diffusers are available. They are complex, expensive, and very efficient. Water flows to internal and external skimmers may be powered by either pump or air lift, and air flows may be introduced by an air release diffuser, valve, or venturi. Water flows to a protein foam skimmer should come directly from the display tank as passage through a mechanical or biological filter alters the compounds that the skimmer removes most effectively.

Cocurrent skimmers

These are the simplest skimmers. Efficiency and cost are low, and operation is easy. They are always placed internally and are most suitable for small tanks, 30 gallons or less. Figure 35 illustrates the construction of a simple cocurrent skimmer. This is a homemade unit that is constructed of 1½" or 2" thin wall PVC pipe, a couple of rounded PVC caps, a standard PVC coupling, a wooden or fine bubble air diffuser block, some air line, and a plastic kitchen funnel.

One air release powers the unit. Small air bubbles flow rapidly upward within the contact tube and draw water into the tube from holes near the bottom. Fine air bubbles mix with water and create and upward flow; water escapes from holes placed well below the water line; and the air bubbles move upward continuing to interact with water and forming foam in the tube above the water level. As the foam drains and moves upward, it pushes through the inverted funnel leading to the collection cup. The foamate collects in the cup as the foam breaks down and either drains to a scuzz bottle below the tank or is periodically cleaned from the collection cup.

The advantages of this design are that the air and water mix is prolonged by the enclosed upper end of the contact tube, and air spilling from the exhaust holes is an indication of too great an air flow. An aquarist can experiment with length of the contact tube above and below water level and the size and placement of water introduction and exhaust holes. Note that commercial units of cocurrent and counter current design are constructed of clear acrylic plastic rather than opaque PVC, and it is much easier to see how the skimmer is working and adjust it properly. Although PVC pipe is inexpensive and easy to work with, homemade skimmers can be constructed from various types of transparent tubes.

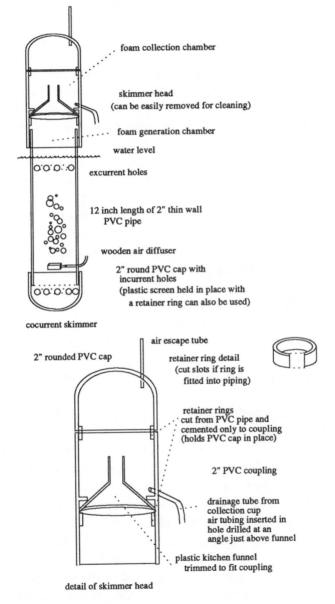

foam collection chamber

skimmer head
(can be easily removed for cleaning)

foam generation chamber

water level

excurrent holes

12 inch length of 2" thin wall
PVC pipe

wooden air diffuser

2" round PVC cap with
incurrent holes
(plastic screen held in place with
a retainer ring can also be used)

cocurrent skimmer

2" rounded PVC cap

air escape tube

retainer ring detail
(cut slots if ring is
fitted into piping)

retainer rings
cut from PVC pipe and
cemented only to coupling
(holds PVC cap in place)

2" PVC coupling

drainage tube from
collection cup
air tubing inserted in
hole drilled at an
angle just above funnel

plastic kitchen funnel
trimmed to fit coupling

detail of skimmer head

Figure 35. A homemade cocurrent skimmer made from PVC pipe, fittings, and a plastic funnel.

Counter current skimmers

Basically, a counter current skimmer consists of a contact tube, a foam development chamber, and a collection cup. They can be designed for operation within the aquarium or as stand alone, external units. There are two air control valves. These valves should be made of high quality plastic and be capable of very fine control of air flow. Screw type valves give finer control over air flow than lever type valves. One valve controls the air that enters the diffuser at the bottom of the tube and then flows upward in small bubbles to the foam development chamber at the top of the tube. Water is introduced near the top of the tube and flows gently downward against the upward air flow. Water is drawn out of the contact tube near the bottom by a separate air lift, controlled by the second air valve. This small air lift controls the rate of water flow through the skimmer.

The unit should also have a bracket adjustment that allows positioning the skimmer at a range of water surface levels. If it doesn't have such an adjustment feature, the water level of the display tank may have to be adjusted to the level where the skimmer operates most efficiently. A number of commercial designs are available. Greco (1987) and Giovanetti (1988) discusses some of the commercial types currently available and their operation.

Figure 36 illustrates construction of a simple internal counter current skimmer made from 2" PVC pipe, a plastic kitchen funnel, and air valves and tubing. This skimmer, and others, can be made from PVC pipe narrower than 2" diameter, but efficiency declines at diameters less than 1½", probably mainly because the foam development chamber also decreases in size when smaller diameter pipe is used. Size of the foam development chamber in skimmers constructed of PVC pipe can be adjusted by using rings of pipe and coupler to extend and/or shorten the length of the pipe above the water level in the tube. There are many ways to configure this skimmer depending on the materials available and the construction skills of the aquarist. Figure 35 can serve as an idea bank and guide.

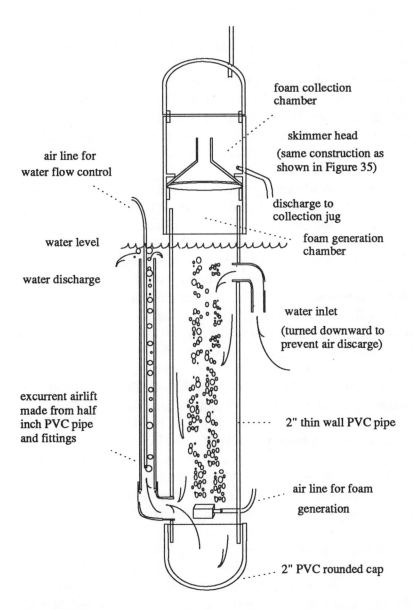

foam collection
chamber

skimmer head
(same construction as
shown in Figure 35)

air line for
water flow control

discharge to
collection jug

water level

foam generation
chamber

water discharge

water inlet

(turned downward to
prevent air discarge)

excurrent airlift
made from half
inch PVC pipe
and fittings

2" thin wall PVC pipe

air line for foam

generation

2" PVC rounded cap

Figure 36. An internal counter current skimmer constructed from PVC
pipe and fittings.

One of the features easy to include in homemade skimmers is a drain tube from the bottom of the collection cup down to a gallon jug located beneath the aquarium. This simple feature eliminates the daily chore of emptying the cup and guards against a sudden over production of foam that overflows the cup back into the tank, or worse, all over the floor. Internal skimmers made from PVC pipe should not be glued together, except for the retainer ring that holds the plastic funnel in place in the skimmer head, since the skimmer must be taken apart for cleaning and replacement of the air diffuser.

There are advantages to an external, stand alone, counter current protein foam skimmer. The unit is no longer a funny fixture in a beautiful natural marine display, and the length of the contact tube is no longer limited to the depth of the tank. A 3 foot high skimmer is a very effective foam fractionater for a home system. The longer the contact tube, the longer the contact time between air bubble and water, the more surface active agents the bubble can acquire, the less air is needed and the efficiency of the skimmer is increased. Water tight construction and a pumped, or gravity fed, slow flow through the contact tube is required, of course. The contact tube can now be of larger diameter, 3" or 4", and only one air lift is required since water flow through the unit can be directly controlled. Units that operate in the shallow sump tank of trickle filters are very similar to stand alone units. Figure 36 also illustrates a possible design for an external counter current protein skimmer made from PVC pipe. Wilkens (1973), Delbeek (1986), and Thiel (1988) all discuss construction and operation of external, stand alone, counter current protein skimmer units.

Venturi driven skimmers

A venturi, as mentioned earlier in Chapter 4, Figure 15, is a device that draws air into water flowing through a pipe or tube. Air and water are combined into a mixture of fine bubbles and water, which is then ejected into the foam generation chamber of the skimmer. This type of skimmer is very efficient because of the long contact time between bubbles and water, produc-

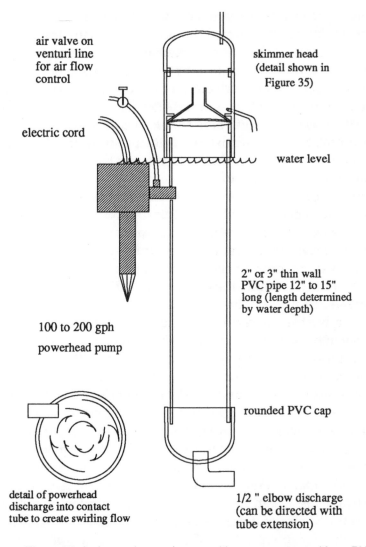

air valve on
venturi line
for air flow
control

skimmer head
(detail shown in
Figure 35)

electric cord

water level

2" or 3" thin wall
PVC pipe 12" to 15"
long (length determined
by water depth)

100 to 200 gph

powerhead pump

rounded PVC cap

detail of powerhead
discharge into contact
tube to create swirling flow

1/2 " elbow discharge
(can be directed with
tube extension)

Figure 37. An internal venturi power skimmer constructed from PVC pipe
and a powerhead pump.

tion of uniformly sized bubbles, strong continuous foaming
activity, and relatively rapid water flow through the unit. Venturi driven units can be either internal or external, although
stand alone, external units are most common. These large

capacity, highly efficient skimmers are best used on commercial tank installations and large home systems that carry high biological loads of fish. Some internal venturi driven units powered by powerhead pumps are now commercially available. A PVC pipe venturi driven skimmer designed for internal tank operation can be constructed by the handy hobbyist. Greco (1988) describes the construction of such a skimmer and the construction of a similar one is described in Figure 37.

Operation and maintenance

As mentioned previously, operation and maintenance of a protein foam skimmer requires attention and adjustment based on experience. The cocurrent type is easiest to operate. The primary control after initial installation is the amount of air released at the bottom of the contact tube. The rate of water flow through the skimmer also has to be adjusted on counter current models.

Two adjustments accomplished during installation of cocurrent and counter current internal skimmers are the placement of the skimmer relative to the water level in the tank and the height (size) of the foam generation chamber. These are usually already fixed or indicated in commercially manufactured units, although the height of the foam generation chamber is often adjustable. Note that these two factors are interrelated. When the position of the contact tube on the tank is secured in a fixed position, the size of the foam generation chamber depends on the water level in the tank. If tank water level drops, the water level in the foam generation chamber also drops, the size of the chamber increases, and the foam has to climb higher to enter the collection cup. If the tank water level rises, the chamber size decreases, and foam can enter the collection cup more easily. A tall collection chamber favors collection of a smaller amount of dry foam, while a short collection chamber favors greater collection of wet foam. The length of the foam generation chamber depends on the extension of the contact tube above the tank water level. The optimum size of the foam generation chamber varies with conditions, but for many small skimmers, 1 inch above water level is too short and 3 inches is too long. Once the position of the skimmer is adjusted, the tank water level should always be kept within a few millimeters of the set level.

Air bubble size is controlled by selection of the air diffuser, which is usually a small block of limewood, silver birch, basswood, or other finely porous material. After initial set up and adjustment, air flow into the unit is the primary consideration. In almost all installations, it is wise to have a separate air pump dedicated solely to the operation of the skimmer. This insures a supply of constant, high pressure air to the fine pored air diffuser, and also allows use of an ozonizer with the skimmer. Be sure to use an air drier if an ozonizer is installed. It is important to keep the air diffuser in good condition by replacement and/or cleaning. See the previous section on air release diffusers and air driers.

Once the skimmer is installed, open the air valve to the wood air diffuser all the way and adjust the valve that controls the water flow through counter current skimmers so that only a small, but constant water flow is produced. Air flow is more important for control of foam production than water flow through the skimmer. Production of too much wet foam indicates that too much air is entering the tube, while no foam production indicates either no dissolved protein, too little air flow, or air bubbles that are too large. Excessive production of wet foam is common in systems with new water and clean skimmers. The gradual build up of fatty deposits on the sides of the foam generation chamber will limit the formation of wet foam. If too much foam is produced, a little vegetable oil spread very thinly on the inside walls of the foam generation chamber will decrease foam production; however this is not generally recommended. In fact, daily, weekly, or monthly cleaning of the upper skimmer parts with stiff brushes is the typical recommended maintenance. Since operation of skimmers is so attuned to the individual system, the aquarist must determine the best cleaning schedule depending on condition and operation of the particular system.

Venturi or power skimmers are controlled by the amount of air and water that enter the skimmer. Water flow into the skimmer can not be greater than the output of the pump and is regulated by a valve on the input line. Air may be pumped into the air input line or drawn passively into it through a one way air valve. Either way, the amount of air taken into the skimmer is controlled by an air valve on the venturi line. If too much wet foam is deposited in the collection cup, the contact tube can be extended further above the tank water level for units placed inside the tank. This increases the height of the foam generation chamber and allows the foam to lose more water before entering the foam collection chamber. Water flow and /or air flow can also be decreased to reduce foam generation in both internal and external units.

The most effective control in external, pump powered units is decrease of water flow. Once the proper balance of air and water is obtained, only changes in output from the pump or restrictions in the air and water lines or valves will alter adjustments. Venturi driven power skimmers are much more efficient than bubble flow designs, and water travels rapidly through them. Water flow through the skimmer should be between 1 to 2 times the total volume of the system each hour. The aquarist will soon determine through operational experience what settings are best for the size and condition of the particular system.

As the system water is depleted of dissolved protein and other organics, foam production markedly decreases. A weekly dose of protein causes the skimmer to again produce foam. This cleanses the system of accumulated toxins, heavy metals, and other "tag alongs" captured by the foam generation. Organic colloids, produced by some aquarium supply manufacturers to coat and reduce stress on fish, often work well to stimulate foam generation. Strong algal growth in a system is said to produce colloids that also stimulate low levels of continuous foam generation.

A little dried albumin added to the system also stimulates foam production. Be careful not to add so much that an over production of foam is created. New acquisitions and chemical additions may also cause increased foaming. I can say from experience that adding new live rock to a system with a skimmer is one way of creating the foam monster that ate the garage. Incidently, skimmers do not have to be operated all the time. It's a good idea to suspend operation of the skimmer for a day or so after adding trace elements or adjusting pH, and a couple of hours after feeding any suspended invertebrate food. Depending on the system, an aquarist may wish to run the skimmer only a few days a week, especially if it is adjusted to continuously produce a lot of foam. A skimmer that continuously produces a lot of wet foam is also likely to reduce the trace elements required for strong algal growth.

Water Sterilization

The purpose of sterilizing the water in marine aquarium systems is to kill bad bacteria and other mean microorganisms. Water sterilization sounds like a good idea, and it is, but there are important considerations. First of all, the health of the system depends on the activity of certain "good" bacteria and microorganisms, and it is important that sterilization is not so effective that it destroys populations of beneficial organisms. This means that the actual environment populated by fish, invertebrates, and filtration bacteria can never be completely "sterilized". *Thus populations of detrimental microorganisms can be controlled to a great extent by ozonation or UV irradiation, but these agents can not always be relied upon to completely eliminate them.*

Secondly, sterilization utilizes technologies—ozone generation and germicidal UV light—that are potentially dangerous to humans. These technologies must be understood and applied by the aquarist with care and respect for their inherent danger. Water sterilization is not all that these techniques accomplish. Many organic compounds are oxidized and the redox potential of the system is increased, and this is very beneficial to organisms in the system. Although the effects are similar, ozonation and UV irradiation are not simply two methods of achieving the same result. While they both sterilize water in a contact chamber, the effects of UV are primarily limited to water sterilization, while ozonation has broad range chemical effects as well. Lastly, although use of a sterilization system can be very helpful in controlling disease and improving redox potential, it is not essential for successful maintenance of simple or complex marine aquarium systems.

Ozone

A molecule of the bluish gas ozone (O_3) is composed of three atoms of oxygen held together in an unstable bond. The presence of ozone can easily be detected at very low levels by its odor. Its presence in air down to 0.02 ppm can be detected by most people. The sharp, "fresh" smell associated with electrical discharge, lighting, and sparks is ozone. It always reminds me of electric trains. Two atoms of oxygen (O_2) form a relatively stable molecule, and oxygen in this form is the oxygen gas that composes twenty percent of the atmosphere. The three oxygen atoms in an ozone molecule are not "happy" together, and one of them is very quick to break off the relationship. This loosely bound single oxygen atom will interact with most of the inorganic and organic molecules it contacts, thus ozone is a powerful oxidant. The oxidizing power of pure ozone is almost twice that of chlorine. It "burns" delicate membranes and kills bacteria and viruses. It strips the cilia from protozoa and small multicellular organisms and usually kills them too. It has to actually enter the cell, however, before it is lethal to the microorganism. Once inside, ozone destroys the nuclear chemistry of the cell.

Ozone clarifies water by oxidizing dissolved organics, small organic particles, and also reduces bacteria populations. It greatly helps wound repair in aquatic animals because of the effective reduction of water borne bacteria. It does not significantly increase the amount of dissolved oxygen in the water but it does increase redox potential. Ozone changes some complex organics into more surface active compounds, which increases the organic content of the foam. Protein foam skimmers

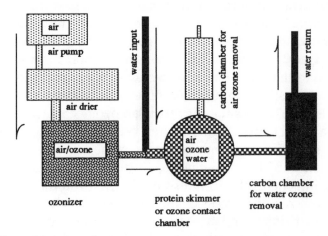

Figure 38. Layout for an ozone water treatment system.

produce a more stable foam when ozone is added to the air released in the skimmer, increasing the efficiency of operation.

On the negative side, however, ozone reacts with chloride and bromide ions, and hypochlorite and hypobromite may be formed. These residual oxidants are persistent and can extend oxidative effects into areas where oxidizers can damage delicate organisms, particularly fish and invertebrate gill tissue, larval forms, and various beneficial microorganisms. Use of ozone as water treatment in marine hatcheries can be dangerous, especially to larvae, and must be very carefully controlled. Ozone also reacts with calcium in the water and may deplete levels of this important element in the system. Note that moderately high levels of ozone may also kill some macro algaes. Ozone can also oxidize and change the characteristics of chemical and antibiotic treatments; so *always* turn off the ozonizer for a few hours to a day before treating the system with any medication.

A faint smell of ozone in the filter cabinet or under the tank hood is normal. Too much ozone, however, to the point that it can be smelled throughout the room most of the time is not good for humans. It can cause headaches, nausea, and irritation of eyes and other delicate tissues. Rubber items are especially susceptible to deterioration from ozone, and plastic doesn't fair much better. Don't store rubber or plastic items near the ozone generator or the air flow from it. Avoid rubber washers or O rings in equipment where ozonated water flows, or be prepared to change them often. Excessive use of ozone shortens the life of plastic skimmers and other plastic items in the system. It is wise to pass the flow from an ozone contact chamber through an activated carbon filter before returning it to the display tank. This will remove excess ozone and other oxidants from the water. The air discharged from the protein skimmer or ozone contact chamber can also be directed through a carbon chamber to remove excess ozone from the air release if necessary. (Note that passing **dry** ozonated air through **dry** activated carbon may create a fire hazard.) The components of a system set up for ozone injection is illustrated in Figure 38.

According to Stopka (1975), six out of ten aquarists in western Europe used ozone in their systems in the 1970's. Some European aquarists depend completely on the oxidizing action of ozone and removal of protein foam to control organic accumulation in the system. This requires precise control and careful observation, and constant testing of the system. Few American aquarists use ozone, although with careful application it is a very beneficial addition to the typical filtration of standard systems and also greatly improves the environment of reef systems.

Ozone can be generated for aquarium use by ultra violet light irradiation between 100 to 200 nm (1000 to 2000 Å) or electric discharge. UV irradiation is the less efficient method. A UV bulb emitting radiation at 195 nm (1950 Å) is contained in a chamber, and dry air is passed through the chamber. The activity of the UV light on oxygen passing through the chamber breaks up O_2 molecules. Some of these single oxygen atoms attach to O_2 molecules and form ozone, O_3. O_3 production is measured as milligrams of ozone produced each hour (mg/hr). O_3 generators of this type produce less than 10 mg/hr. This is adequate for a small system where the intent is just to improve protein foam skimming and enhance the redox potential.

Most modern ozonizers use the silent electric discharge method of ozone production. Air or oxygen is passed between two electrodes that are separated by an insulator. The discharge gap between the electrodes is very small and contains the insulator. An alternating electric current is applied to the electrodes. A charge of electrons is accumulated and released by the insulator during each electrical cycle. A cloud of electrons (the corona) on the insulator produces ozone in the oxygenated air that passes through the unit. Production of ozone is dependent on the structure and design of the ozonator, regulation of the charge on the electrodes, the amount of oxygen and humidity in the air, and the rate of air flow. It is important to pass the air through an air drying chamber before passing it through the ozonizer. This will not only allow the ozonizer to operate near maximum efficiency, but will also reduce fluctuations in ozone production caused by variations in room humidity. The rate of ozone production can be controlled by a dial on the unit that regulates the electric charge. This control is very important for it allows the aquarist to adjust the ozone output for the specific conditions of air and water in each individual system.

Use of a gas reactor will greatly improve the efficiency of mixing any gas—oxygen, ozone, or carbon dioxide—with the system water. A reactor mixes the gas and system water under low pressure, 2 to 3 psi, over a high void space trickle filter media. The slight pressure and extensive interface between gas and liquid quickly saturates the gas into the liquid (see the section on gas reactors). When the water leaves the reactor, it has a higher content of dissolved gas than would be possible with the same exposure at normal atmospheric pressure. A reactor provides much greater control over the ozone and/or carbon dioxide input into an advanced reef system. Burleson (1989) and Thiel (1988, 1989) describe the structure and operation of oxygen and ozone reactors.

Salt water inside an ozonizer is bad news! Whenever possible, mount the ozonizer above the water level of the tank. If it has to be located below the tank, be sure to use a one way check valve to prevent water from siphoning back into the ozonizer if the air pump fails. (Be sure the check valve doesn't have a rubber seal; silicone is safer with ozone.) The maximum amount of ozone produced by small units designed for home use ranges from 25 to 250 mg/hr. Most systems under 100 gallons can get by very well with a unit capable of 50 mg/hr, but some systems with a heavy biological load or more than 100 gallons may need an ozonator rated at 100 mg/hr.

The amount of ozone a system requires increases with the total gallons of water in the system and varies with the condition of the water, the type of filtration on the system, and, most important, the concentration of dissolved organics (DOC). Systems with old water and/or heavy biological loads use more ozone than systems with new water and little dissolved organics. Ozone use is also greater after feeding or if ozone is used part time, such as only during the night hours. The amount of ozone the system requires decreases as ozone removes accumulated organic compounds. As ozone strips the water of dissolved organics, less ozone is used for DOC destruction and more free ozone is present in the system water. It is important to cut back on ozone output a few days after initial installation of an ozonizer on an old system.

Residual ozone in marine system water should not be more than 0.5 ppm for fish treatment and less on a continuous basis. Residual levels 0.01 to 0.3 ppm are said to prevent growth of virus and bacteria but do not affect most invertebrates. Since such low levels have a great bactericidal effect, it is important not to add so much ozone that biological filtration is affected. Ammonia and nitrite levels should remain at or near zero. Because of chemical interactions and creation of other oxidants, accurate measurement of ozone levels in salt water is difficult and beyond the capacity of most hobbyists. Ozone level in small marine systems is best controlled by adjusting the production of ozone according to the dial (rheostat) on the ozonizer.

It is possible, however, to get a working estimate of the presence of ozone in the water with an orthotolidine (OTO) swimming pool or aquarium test kit for chlorine. Five or six drops of OTO in about 10 cc of water will produce a yellow color if ozone is present. One can follow the instructions for chlorine determination that come with an OTO chlorine test kit or set a standard volume of test water and number of OTO drops that is followed at every test. As in chlorine determination, the more intense the yellow color, the more ozone is present. Anything more than a very light yellow tinge produced in water from the display tank is cause to reduce the ozone input. Total absence of any yellow color is an indication that ozone output can be increased. Frequent testing along with observation for any distress of the animals in the system will give one a "feel" for evaluating the results of the OTO test.

Redox potential is also a good guide to ozone use. Use of ozone increases redox potential, and constant use can elevate a low redox potential of 200 mv to high levels of 300 to 325 mv. It is possible to raise the redox potential to uncomfortable levels, above 400 mv, with continuous use of excess ozone. If redox potential is measured, it is possible to maintain it at about 300 to 350 mv with careful ozone regulation. Commercial automatic control units are now available that continuously monitor redox potential and adjust ozone input to maintain redox potential at a specific level. It is important to regulate ozone output depending on the condition of the system water; thus each aquarist has to determine the proper amount of ozone to use according to the size and condition of the system. There are some basic guidelines, however.

The range of recommended ozone production varies from 0.1 to 1.0 mg/hr/gal (0.03 to 0.26 mg/l/hr) depending on system condition and biological load. For a 75 gallon system this is 7.5 to 75 mg/hr—a rather broad range. Systems with old water should be started on a constant rate of about 0.8 to 1.0 mg/gal/hr (0.21 to 0.26 mg/l/hr) and cut back within a few days or a week to 0.5 mg/gal/hr (0.13 mg/l/hr). If the system contains a high biological load of mostly fish, 0.5 mg/gal/hr may be the best continuous rate of ozone production. This can be increased to 0.8 or 1.0 mg/gal/hr for a couple of hours after feeding or if the ozonizer is only turned on during night hours. If few fish and many invertebrates are maintained in the system, then lower concentrations of ozone are desirable. Levels of ozone production as low as 0.05 mg/gal/hr (0.013 mg/l/hr) can maintain good water quality in small, well filtered systems.

Generally, ozone production of 0.5 to 1.0 mg/gal/hr is adequate for systems in the 40 to 75 gallon range. Because of the persistence of ozone and ozone generated oxidants in system water, the trend is for large volume systems to require a little less ozone on a per gallon basis than small systems. Remember, each system is different, and ozonation requires the attention and regulation of the aquarist to find the optimum level of ozone production for each individual system. Some good references to use of ozone in marine systems are Blogoslawski and Rice (1975), Spotte (1979), Greco (1987), Giovanetti (1988), and Thiel (1988, 1989).

Ultra Violet irradiation
Ultra violet light between the wave lengths of 190 and 300 nm (1900 to 3000 Å) produces energy that kills bacteria, viruses, fungi, and small protozoans. The most effective wave lengths are in the 2500 to 2600 Å range. Germicidal UV bulbs are designed to produce most of their energy at wave lengths of 2537 Å. UV light kills these organisms by interrupting the genetic chemistry (DNA) of the cell or by creating oxidants and other toxins in the water in and around the cell. **Never, never look directly at a lighted germicidal bulb!** Don't even look indirectly at a bulb that is in operation. The same wave lengths that kill microorganisms can damage the delicate tissues of the human eye. Always unplug the unit before doing any cleaning, bulb changing, or any other fooling around with the unit. Make sure the unit is off before doing any water changes. The bulb will heat up if it is in operation in air instead of water. If it is submerged in water while it is still hot after or during operation in air, it may break and cause the tank to become electrically charged.

In water, the effect of UV light is almost entirely restricted to the contained area around the germicidal bulb, however some of the oxidants produced may have a positive effect on the redox potential of the water, which improves the entire environment of the system. Unlike ozone treatment, there is little potential for destruction of any microorganisms in the system that do not pass through the UV unit. Use of a UV unit is thus "safer" and less complex than ozone application. Because of this, however, UV is less effective in control of parasites and bacteria in the display tank then proper use of ozone.

A very effective use of a UV sterilizer is in the water return line of multi tank, compound system. The UV unit sterilizes the water after it leaves the filters, but before it returns to the holding tanks. This acts as a sterile barrier between the tanks and allows use of a large common biological filter while preventing the spread of bacteria and parasites between tanks. On small, single tank systems, UV kills bacteria and most parasites that pass through the unit and creates some oxidants in the water. Depending on the individual system and the size and condition of the UV unit, benefits to the system vary from none to very helpful. Less so than ozone, UV will help control, but will not remove, all harmful bacteria and parasites from a marine aquarium system. Depending on the amount of residual oxidents, the effects of ozone can extend beyond the ozonator, but the effects of UV irradiation are mostly confined to within the UV unit.

The most efficient placement of a UV unit in a single tank system is as a separate filter unit. Water moves from the tank, through the unit, and back to the tank. This provides maximum removal of harmful bacteria and parasites from display tank water, but not maximum water sterilization. Other external filters remove some harmful microorganisms, and also add some beneficial, but not essential, filter bacteria to the display tank water. Placing the UV unit at the end of the filter line just before water returns to the tank provides maximum sterilization, including killing harmful microorganisms that travelled through mechanical and biological filters and any filter bacteria shed from the filter media during water passage. This is the best placement for an in line UV unit, but greatest destruction of harmful microorganisms is achieved in single tank systems by separate UV water treatment.

The "kill" efficiency of a UV unit depends upon many factors, including the following list.

- The available energy (wattage) of the bulb.

- Age of the bulb.

- The species and individual characteristics (age and size) of the microorganism.

- Temperature of the bulb and system.

- Distance between the bulb and the target organism.

- Duration and intensity of exposure, determined by the flow rate of water through the unit. Clarity and turbidity (color and particles) in the water reduce intensity.

- Presence of slime and other biological or mineral deposits on the bulb surface.

These factors and the following considerations are very important in the design, construction, operation, and maintenance of UV units.

Bactericidal UV waves can not penetrate ordinary glass. Quartz glass allows passage of the greatest percentage of UV rays.

UV rays can only penetrate a maximum of about 2 inches (5 cm) of water and penetration through freshwater is greater than through saltwater. Dyes and particles in the water absorb and scatter UV irradiation and reduce efficiency. A thin flow of water close to the bulb provides the greatest exposure to UV irradiation. The flow should not be more than one inch (2.5 cm) thick to insure complete irradiation.

Turbulent water flow through the UV unit is better than a smooth laminar flow, because all portions of the flow are exposed to some areas of maximum irradiation.

The efficiency of a UV lamp declines with age due to degradation of the electrodes, caused mostly by switching on and off, and the gradual darkening of the inner glass of the bulb, which reduces the energy output. The effective life of the bulb in a UV unit is a little more than 6 months (5000 hours), so if the bulb is not replaced after about 6 months of use, the unit is ineffective.

Biological slime builds up on quartz or bulb surfaces exposed to water and greatly reduces the efficiency of the unit. Surfaces exposed to water, or bulbs that accumulate salt and other mineral deposits, must be wiped clean every few days to a week to maintain maximum efficiency.

The efficiency of operation of a UV bulb is best at about 106 °F (40 °C). Efficiency declines as temperature drops, and it is only about 50% at temperatures around 72 °F (21 °C). Thus bulbs that operate at higher temperatures (suspended and jacketed bulbs) are more effective than bulbs that operate at the temperature of the system water. Low pressure, high intensity bulbs are the type of UV lamp usually used in aquatic sterilization units.

The energy production of a UV sterilizer is measured as the number of microwatts delivered each second for each square centimeter of contact area (uw/sec/cm^2). Microwatts are determined by the output of the bulb; exposure time in seconds is determined by flow rate, and square centimeters by the internal area of the tube or other contact area. Spotte (1979) suggests that 35,000 uw sec cm^2 is the minimum irradiation level for disinfection of aquarium water. This will destroy most viruses, bacteria, fungi, and small protozoans. The free swimming stage of the parasite *Amyloodinium* is probably destroyed at this level of irradiation, but *Cryptocaryon* may require levels well above 100,000 uw sec cm^2.

UV units designed for small marine aquarium systems use bulbs of 4 to 30 watts. For most small aquarium installations, a maximum flow rate of 25 to 30 gallons per hour per watt through small UV units should provide adequate sterilization of system water. This is a maximum flow rate of 120 gph through a unit with a 4 watt bulb. A slower flow rate, 20 gph/watt, will produce a better kill if bulb efficiency has declined and/or disease problems exist. Note that the more rapidly water flows through the UV unit, the more rapid the turn over of tank water through the unit and the greater the kill of microorganisms each day. However, the more rapid the flow, the less exposure time for the microorganism to UV irradiation. If the flow is too fast, the efficiency of the kill declines. Thus the aquarist must take into account all the factors that effect efficiency of UV irradiation on a particular system and use judgement to adjust the flow rate through the system for best results.

Flow rate in gph can be easily determined by holding a two cup (16 oz) measuring cup under the outflow of the filter and recording the number of seconds it takes to fill the cup. Refer to Table 6 under Water Movement to convert the number of seconds to fill the cup into the flow rate in gallons per hour. This table also provides gallons per minute and liters per hour. This method and table can be used to measure the flow from any filter between 10 and 450 gph.

There are three basic types of UV sterilization units for small marine aquarium systems:

- suspended

- submerged

- jacketed

Suspended bulb units. This is the old fashioned way. Suspended units are easy and inexpensive to make; the bulbs operate at a high temperature, the units are relatively easy to clean, and can be built to handle a large system. Unfortunately, this type of unit is also messy, maintenance intensive, and space consuming. Its best application is probably in a small, tight budget hatchery or commercial holding facility. The unit consists of a vented lid that usually contains the bulbs with the

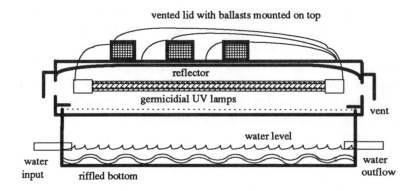

Figure 39. A suspended bulb UV irradiation unit.

ballasts mounted on top (remote location of the ballasts is far better); a reflector above the bulbs; two to six, 30 watt germicidal UV bulbs (large units may have 14 bulbs); a water tight tray with bottom riffles or baffles that tumble and thin out water flow to about 5 mm at the top of each riffle; and an inlet and outlet. The lid containing the bulbs fits tightly on or overlaps the tray, and UV light does not leave the box. The reflectors increase the efficiency of the unit by redirecting light from the top of the bulbs downward into the water. The bulbs are suspended about two to six inches above the water. The closer the bulbs are to the water, the more effective the germicidal action, but they are also more susceptible to salt deposits. Of course, the electrical contacts on the ends of the bulbs must be protected from salt spray and salt creep. One advantage to this type of UV unit is that the bulbs are easy to clean and replace. The unit need only be turned off, the lid lifted, and bulbs wiped clean. Figure 39 illustrates the structure of a typical suspended bulb unit.

Submerged bulb units. Most small, inexpensive aquarium UV units are of this type of construction. The bulb is contained within a PVC tube and a water tight seal around the bulb allows water to flow between the bulb and the inner wall of the tube. The entire circumference of the bulb is equally exposed to water flow, which provides maximum exposure of bulb output and eliminates the need for reflectors. The unit may be designed for horizontal mounting to operate as part of a filter system or may be designed to operate hanging on the tank in a vertical orientation with out-flow from the unit going directly into the tank. The units are designed to allow cleaning and bulb changing. The operating temperature of the bulb is that of the water in the system, so the efficiency of the bulb is only 50 to 75 percent. Figure 40 illustrates the structure of this type of unit.

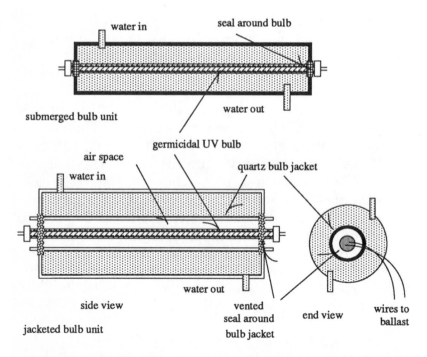

Figure 40. Configuration of submerged bulb and jacketed bulb UV irradiation units.

The system is designed to operate with water around the bulb. Never drain the water from the unit while the bulb is turned on. Even more important, do not turn the bulb on and then fill the unit with the water. The cold water coming in contact with the hot bulb may cause the bulb to crack or break. Some units may have a built in cleaning wand, a ring that can be moved the length of the bulb and wipes it clean without having to remove the bulb from the unit for cleaning. However, this feature is more commonly found in jacketed units.

Jacketed bulb units. This type of UV unit incorporates some of the best features of both of the above described systems. A quartz glass tube (jacket) is sealed within a PVC tube, and the germicidal UV bulb is inserted within the quartz tube. Water enters one end of the chamber between the quartz jacket and the PVC water tube and exits at the opposite end. The bulb is not exposed to water and can operate at its most efficient temperature, and the entire circumference of the bulb is also used in direct irradiation of the water. Changing the bulb is simply a matter of slipping the old bulb out of the quartz jacket and inserting a new bulb. Some units may contain several quartz jacketed bulbs in the same containment chamber. Jacketed units contain pressurized water flow and can be used at any point in the filter line. Flow adjustment can be made with valves. Special considerations for gravity flows through trays and banks of lights are not needed. These types of units are efficient, compact, and easy to maintain and clean.

The major disadvantage to this type of unit is that biological slime can build up on the water side of the quartz jacket and greatly reduce the efficiency of the bulb. This is easy to remedy, however, with a cleaning wand ring for each quartz jacket. A soft narrow neoprene ring or other material resistant to ultra violet irradiation is fitted snugly over the quartz jacket and fitted with a waterproof linkage to a control knob outside the unit. Running the ring over the length of the jacket every day or two keeps the biological deposit problem under control. This same type of wiper can be incorporated in the structure of a submerged bulb unit, but it makes changing the bulb a bit more difficult. Most modern, large commercial units are jacketed bulb units and incorporate an intensity meter and flow rate meter. Knowledge of flow rate and intensity are important to regulate irradiation dosage in large units. Spotte (1979) should be consulted when contemplating installation and use of large, commercial UV units. Figure 40 also illustrates the general structural features of this type of UV sterilizer.

Chapter 5

Marine Aquarium Systems

Purchasing Equipment

Marine aquarium systems are made up from equipment described in Chapter 4. Few systems are sold complete as "turn key" installations, and even with a complete unit, many aquarists soon begin to modify the system. The aquarist usually enjoys the responsibility of planning the system and evaluating and selecting the equipment that will make up a particular marine aquarium installation. Purpose, design, and financial investment are the three major considerations when a marine system is planned. Systems vary from mini aquariums for desk tops at a cost of $40.00 or less to high tech, reef installations with a cost of $3,000.00 or more. Traditional type systems can be economically made up from a used 20 gallon tank and inexpensive accessory equipment, or can be a 100 gallon display tank with an elaborate external filtration system. There is great flexibility in design and structure of systems to suit almost any purpose and pocketbook.

As you know, there are five ways to obtain marine aquarium equipment (six if you count gifts): construction, purchase of used equipment, retail shop, discount store, and mail order house. All have pros and cons. Whatever the method of purchase, it helps to have some idea of the type of system you want before making the decision to purchase.

One of the great things about the marine aquarium hobby is that with a little imagination and engineering and construction talent, one can make almost everything that is needed in the way of tanks and filters. Equipment construction, however, requires time, materials, tools, and talent. Building systems is really an enhancement of the hobby into the realms of engineering and fabrication. What is saved financially is usually expended in time and effort, but great satisfaction can be derived from building a marine aquarium system from raw materials.

Buying used equipment is usually the most inexpensive way to get a system up and running. Newspaper advertisements and aquarium societies are good places to check for used equipment. Of course, *"caveat emptor"* (let the buyer beware) is the watch word. Good aquarium equipment is quite reliable these days, but still, fill the tank and run the pump before loading a bargain into the car. If repairs are needed, one should know about it before purchase.

Agreed, unless there is a special sale or a general discount policy, a small retail store will get top price for a specific item. They have to at least come close to the standard retail price to stay in business. Although there may be a few dingy, dark, and dreadful aquarium stores around, most retail shops are clean and bright, have polite and knowledgeable personnel, handle modern equipment and know how to set it up and use it, and consider your success as an aquarist to be more important than a quick sale of unnecessary equipment. When you find a store like this, and there are many of them, the value gained from such a dealer is worth far more than a few dollars saved at discount.

The aquarium business is unique and retail shops offer much more than reasonable prices and good equipment. Presenting a wide selection of healthy livestock requires a great deal more time and effort than stocking goods, dusting shelves, and ringing up sales. A good retailer selects strong healthy fish and invertebrates, expertly cares for them before sale, spends hours with customers, and, all too often, absorbs the financial losses from weak and dying livestock. The retailer's service of providing good livestock is the foundation of the hobby. Mail order houses and department stores cannot provide the time, expense, and talent that is required to offer the hobbyist a wide selection of healthy livestock. It's your money, spend it wisely, but a good aquarium shop deserves your business.

A discount and/or department store usually, but not always, gives a better price than a small retail shop. However, personal service and knowledgeable sales people are not strong points in most large stores. Again, if you know exactly what you want, the store has the item in stock, and price is the most important consideration—a discount store is the place to go.

Buying from mail order houses is usually the least expensive way to get new equipment, but not always. Discount and retail stores may often be competitive with mail order prices when shipping and handling costs and store sales and discounts are taken into consideration. Also, purchasing equipment that is not the right quality or will not perform the intended task can be a waste of money. It's nice to be able to see, hold, and evaluate the item before purchase, especially if one is not familiar with the specific item. Some mail order houses offer telephone support after the sale, but telephone advice has limitations and long distance calls are costly. However, if you know exactly what you want, know the price differential, don't mind the wait for delivery, don't need to consult with knowledgeable sales people, have confidence in a particular mail order house—and if getting the best price is more important than personal service—then mail order is the way to go.

Types of Systems

Suddenly, a typical marine aquarium is no longer the ultimate challenge for an aquarist. Many new kinds of systems are now possible, and this section may spark ideas on how to create and explore new aquatic horizons. Some aquarists maintain systems that are very strict in purpose and design, culturing only algaes, only fish of a particular type, or only specific invertebrates. Most systems, however, are more multipurpose and contain a variety of organisms defined primarily by the limits of compatibility. Most marine aquarists maintain one or two traditional system tanks and are perhaps thinking of creating a reef type system as well. There are also other types of systems that can be fun to set up and maintain. The systems mentioned below should provide a few interesting alternatives that can send an aquarist off into a little different aquatic world. So, with the emphasis on invertebrate tanks, we will examine the structure and function of various types of systems and look at some of the possibilities at different levels of complexity and expense. Look to Chapter 4 for descriptions and discussions on specific types of equipment mentioned in each category.

There are many types of marine aquariums. We generally categorize aquariums based on how many gallons of water they hold, what kind of life we keep in them, and, to a greater extent these days, by the type of filter system. Although there are many classifications that can be constructed for marine systems, there are only a few broad, general categories.

The "traditional" system is the basic marine aquarium that has been the standard of the hobby for the last 25 years. In its typical configuration, the traditional marine aquarium is perhaps 40 to 50 gallons, has an undergravel biological filter and outside power filter, is lighted by one or two fluorescent bulbs, contains about 12 fish and a few invertebrates from all oceans and many habitats, and needs a good cleaning. It's interesting, educational, and fun to keep.

The "invertebrate" tank is another generalized, broad category of marine display. An invertebrate tank is restricted to invertebrates, and although a few small fish also gratefully inhabit such tanks, invertebrates are the stars of the show. Size and filtration vary greatly and the denizens of the tank may come from all oceans and all habitats.

A new category of marine tank that is gaining in popularity is the "miniature reef" or "reef" tank. This type of marine aquarium is characterized by intense lighting, an elaborate external filter system, and the introduction of "living rock". These are rocks taken up from the ocean bottom with all manner of life attached, and when transplanted to the aquarium, all the corals and crabs, and algaes and anemones, continue their natural lives in full view of the aquarist. The essence of the miniature reef system is the maintenance and growth of living corals and marine algaes—previously the impossible dream of marine aquarists. In this sense, these aquariums are the ultimate expression of the natural marine aquarium. Most miniature reef systems are large and expensive, but it is possible to use the concepts developed for these systems to create smaller, less expensive displays. We shall see some remarkable developments in the reef system category in future years.

Also of interest is the miniature category, perhaps best termed the "mini aquarium". These are actually tiny aquarium systems, less than 10 gallons, perhaps as small as one gallon. They are designed to fit on a desk top and are a miniature display of aquatic life, fresh or salt water. These tanks have at least a biological filter, and some may even have a more complex filtering system. These tiny systems can be very fascinating and educational, but care must be exercised to select the proper types and numbers of animals and plants so as not to overload the system, and not to include organisms that can not adapt to such small areas.

Of course, in actual practice the elements of all the various categories of marine systems are shuffled and jumbled according to the desires, theories, and budgets of individual aquarists. The following specific information on various types of marine aquarium systems can aid aquarists in deciding what size and type of system they might wish to set up as a first or second tank and what additional filtration may be needed or helpful on an existing system. The discussions of the various systems vary in depth and substance, but I have tried to follow a general format. The elements of the format are description and purpose, organization and variety of the elements of the system, operation of the system, and organisms common to the type of system.

Elaborate, efficient marine aquarium systems tend to separate filtration functions into individual components so that each type of filtration—biological, mechanical, chemical, gas exchange, etc.—is performed by a specific unit and can be evaluated, adjusted, and maintained without much conflict with another component. Simple marine aquarium systems tend to combine filtration functions and sacrifice efficiency and control for simplicity and economy. One type of system is not necessarily better than another as long as it fulfills the purpose of the aquarist. Consistently high water quality with minimal maintenance is achieved by complex filter systems *as long as the aquarist understands what each part of the filter does and knows how to make it function properly.* On the other hand, simple systems work very well for most fish and many invertebrates if the aquarist understands and performs the required scheduled maintenance.

Whatever the system, every aquarist will benefit from keeping a log book on system changes, treatments, and scheduled maintenance. Dated entries on amounts of water changes, filter cleaning and other maintenance, medications, new additions, test results, and significant changes in the system or inhabitants are important to record. Moe (1982) contains a sample log sheet in the back that may be of help and Thiel (1989) has a discussion on keeping records on reef tank systems. A fascinating history of the display tank, especially reef systems, can be kept by taking a picture of the tank every month. Some changes are so gradual that a photographic record is the only way an aquarist can really be aware of the extent of changes and developments in the tank.

Mini (desk top) aquariums

The mini aquarium is usually a freshwater tank, but can very well be a marine display. It may be as small as one gallon, but they are usually in the 2 to 5 gallon range. Mini aquariums are complete systems, including filtration and lighting, that compose a small unit that fits on a desktop, counter, or end table. They are an attractive point of interest in an office, a kitchen, a bedroom, or in the line of sight of one sitting in a dentist's chair. They can be homemade, but there are many commercial units available. Most are of standard aquarium design, but some are built to serve as lamps or look like gas pumps, gumball machines, or some other whimsical design. In simplest form, a mini aquarium consists of the tank, an undergravel filter plate and air lift, a small vibrator air pump (or at least a place for one), and a tank cover with a light.

Aquarium filtration, with exception of mechanical particle filtration, takes place at the molecular level, and there is no reason why most filtration methods can not be designed to operate in miniature. The same processes that maintain large systems work the same way in small systems. The main difference is that it is so much easier to overload small systems with fish and invertebrates. Trickle filters, gas exchange, carbon filters, and other systems that aid marine systems can be developed for miniature applications. However, because of the small volume of these aquariums, routine maintenance takes only minutes a day, and water change is a very simple operation. Ten minutes on a Friday afternoon, two gallon jugs (one empty and one full with a new salt water mix), and a small bore siphon is all that's needed for a water change. Two or three gallon aquariums need a change of only a couple of quarts. Fill the empty jug by siphoning water from the tank. Then place the siphon in the jug of new water and lift this jug above the level of the tank to slowly refill the tank with the clean water. (Water changes can be done on Monday morning, but the International Registry of Aquarium Water Change prefers Friday or Saturday.)

A two to five gallon marine system can be operated very well with only an undergravel filter, a small air driven filter with fiber floss and activated carbon, a 10 to 20 percent water change every two weeks or so, replacement of evaporated water as necessary, a cleaning wand or a set of those little fuzz coated magnets to keep the glass or plastic free of algae (get soft fuzz on the wands or magnets so a plastic tank doesn't get scratched), and plenty of light. The type of light that comes with these small tanks is usually the bare minimum needed for marine organisms, so place the tank by a window where it will get natural light. Also, a daily wipe around the cover with a soft, damp cloth or paper towel will prevent development of salt deposits outside the cover. If there is no provision for a fiber floss / carbon filter outside the tank, a small box filter can be purchased or made that will fit inside the tank, possibly disguised as a rock; or a layer of floss and carbon (or a carbon containing filter pad) can be included in the center of the undergravel filter.

Marine tanks need more aeration than freshwater tanks so be sure that the air pump puts out a good volume of air. A second air release in the tank that does nothing but move the water around is also a good idea. Small volumes of water gain and lose temperature quickly so consider what happens to the temperature in the area of the tank. It can become too cool if placed in front of the air conditioning duct or too hot if the sun hits it directly for several hours. The light above the tank is usually an incandescent bulb, which produces a lot of heat and may even overheat the tank. It may be possible to replace the incandescent bulb with a small fluorescent bulb. Ventilation around the bulb may be increased with additional holes or, if possible, by supporting the light a little above the hood. Check the temperature frequently in a newly established mini aquarium until the temperature patterns of the particular set up are known.

A small heater may be necessary for mini aquariums in constantly cool environmental conditions. A miniature marine system, however, may be more stable and easier to care for if operated at the lower acceptable temperature ranges, 72 to 76 °F (22 to 25 °C). Algae will grow more slowly, fish will not require as much food, the tank will not accumulate waste compounds as rapidly, and fish and invertebrates will not grow as much or as fast as at higher temperatures. Activity levels of the animals, however, will be lower. Depending on the individual system, it will be necessary to remove the animals and clean the undergravel filter every 6 to 12 months. A "mini marine" is a little more work than a freshwater mini, but not much, and definitely more interesting.

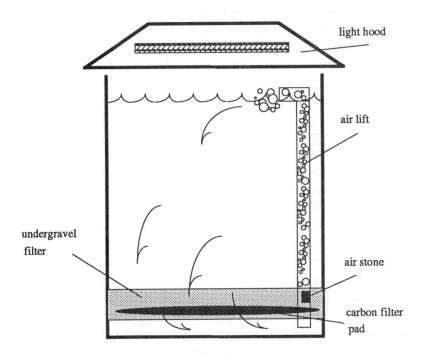

Figure 41. Structure of a mini marine system.

The key to keeping marine organisms in a mini tank is to be lean and selective. The fewer animals, the better. A pair of small clownfish and a small anemone is a beautiful display. If light permits, a little green algae is very good for the tank and the display. However, the more algae, the more required maintenance. A pair of cleaner shrimp under a cave rock and single small angelfish is also a neat display. The personalities of many fascinating small fish such as gobies, blennies, dragonetts, and damsels are almost lost in large tanks. These fish can be really appreciated and even achieve "pet" status in small tanks. There are an infinite number of possibilities as long as the aquarist can conquer the dreaded "just one more fish" syndrome. The structure of a typical mini marine setup is illustrated in Figure 41. The idea for mini marine tanks has been around for some time, but has only recently captured the imagination of aquarists. Birdsill (1985) and Tommasini (1988) are two articles that discuss mini aquariums in depth.

Traditional marine systems

The essential feature of a traditional marine aquarium is the undergravel filter system. The tank may be small (10 to 30 gallons) or large (75 to 125 gallons); lighting intense or subdued; and external filtration simple, elaborate, or absent; but the base of the system is the biological filtration supplied by the undergravel filter. Once the aquarist knows about establishing the bacterial fauna in the filter, there is little problem in getting the tank to support marine life. Despite drawbacks in ease of maintenance and gas exchange, this economical and functional method of setting up a marine system will probably be the heart of the hobby for some time to come. Even if a hobbyist has an elaborate reef tank set up in the living room, chances are that another tank or two set up in the traditional method will be found in the bedroom, bathroom, or garage. Many books, including Moe (1982), have been written on maintaining marine aquaria so I'll refer you to these books for basic setup and operation of traditional systems.

All types of auxiliary, external and internal filters can be used to augment the basic undergravel system. Generally, small tanks do well with only a hanging box filter with activated carbon and perhaps a small protein foam skimmer to support the undergravel filter. Large tanks are helped more by the addition of powered canister filters and powered protein skimmers with a little ozone added if biological loads are high. Increased lighting and increased aeration are also a big help to most traditional setups. A trickle filter is also a good addition. These filters are just as effective, if not more so, on marine fish tanks as on reef systems. Large tanks with considerable biological loads are most helped by effective protein foam skimming since this provides additional aeration to the system water and removes organic compounds before they are mineralized to ammonia. Activated carbon filtration is also very helpful be-

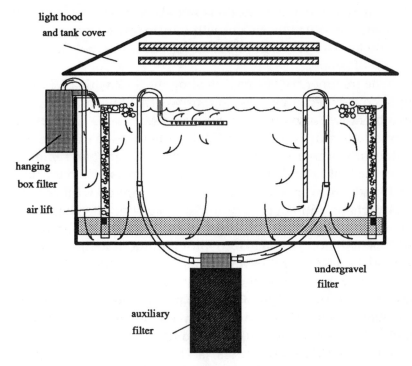

Figure 42. Structure of a traditional marine aquarium system.

cause it removes the organics that discolor water, including yellow dyes, and gives the aquarium a crystal clear appearance. Figure 42 illustrates the typical configuration of a traditional marine aquarium system. With proper lighting and regular routine maintenance, including water changes, a vast array of marine organisms can be well kept in such a setup.

Traditional systems can contain either fish or invertebrates or both. If both fish and invertebrates are kept in the same tank, the aquarist should be prepared for conflict. It helps to make a determination as to whether the fish or the invertebrates are the main purpose of the tank. Sooner or later most marine aquarists that keep fish encounter the dinoflagellate parasite *Amyloodinium (oodinium)* in their fish tank. Despite elaborate filtration systems, this tiny parasite can reproduce in the tank and infect the fish. Many, if not most, of the fish in the tank will eventually die if this parasite is not eliminated. Occasionally, the parasite seems to die out without treatment, especially in reef tanks with low fish populations, but this is not the usual course of events.

The treatment of choice is treating the tank with a 1.5 to 3.0 ppm copper level for three to four weeks. Unfortunately, this treatment will also kill most invertebrates. The aquarist with a mixed tank may have to sacrifice invertebrates to treat the fish in the tank or sacrifice fish that cannot be caught and removed from the tank. Another cure is to remove the fish from the tank and place them in a separate tank for treatment with copper, and perhaps antibiotics if secondary bacterial infections have developed. Then keep the infected tank with its invertebrates free of fish for six weeks to provide enough time for the parasites, which require fish to complete their life cycle, to die out. Fish and invertebrates can be kept together if great care is taken to be sure that the fish are parasite free before they are placed in the tank. Keeping the fish in a separate, parasite free and/or copper treated tank for a month or more before placing them in with invertebrates is the best way of keeping *Amyloodinium* out of a main tank. Sometimes fish and invertebrates eat each other. It happens in the best of tanks. Some butterfly fish nibble on anemones and some shrimps and crabs eat small fish. Parrot fish scrape corals and tangs eat algae. Marine aquarists that keep mixed tanks soon learn which fish and invertebrates are compatible in their particular systems. Always watch new introductions carefully to make sure that they do not destroy a valued tank mate.

Natural marine systems

In the strictest sense, a "natural" system marine tank has no mechanical or undergravel filtration system and relies only on an air stone or two to move water about the tank. It was often thought that the balance of a successful natural tank depended only on the interaction of plants, invertebrates, and fish. Biological filtration (the activity of nitrifying bacteria) takes place in such a system, of course, but the nitrifying bacteria are

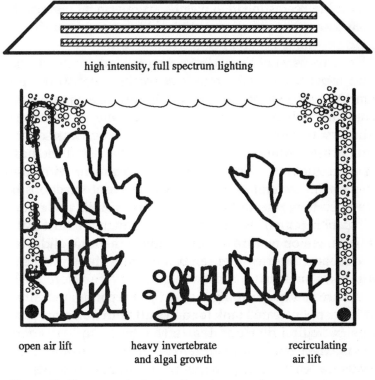

high intensity, full spectrum lighting

open air lift   heavy invertebrate   recirculating
                         and algal growth   air lift

Figure 43. Elements of a "natural" marine aquarium system.

limited to surface substrates present within the tank. Without the activity of these limited populations of nitrifying bacteria, a natural system marine tank could not exist. Very low fish populations, intense natural or full spectrum lighting, and strong invertebrate and algal growth make the system work by decreasing the demand for nitrifying activity. Many marine algaes are able to take up nitrogen directly in the form of ammonia, and this also helps reduce accumulation of toxic waste compounds. The "biological balance" is narrow, however, and the failure rate of such setups is high. An algal die back or the unseen death of a large organism can quickly tip the balance toward disaster.

Some aquarists in tropical areas with coral reefs nearby may find it interesting to experiment with such systems. Baker (1983) describes a successful natural tank setup in an 80 gallon aquarium on the island of Guam near a coral reef environment. Water changes were 12 percent per month and many species of corals, algaes, and fish were successfully kept. Some public aquariums also experiment with natural systems and are successful in maintaining large balanced tanks. The larger the natural system tank, the greater the chance of success, because large water volumes and increased variety and biomass of algae are stabilizing factors. Modern reef tanks with masses of live rock and extensive algal growth are very similar to these natural systems, but they have the added stability of extensive biological filtration and strong gas exchange. The natural system balances on a narrow curb, while a reef tank glides along on a broad highway. Figure 43 illustrates the structure of a natural system tank.

A natural aquarium may also have a different definition. This type of "natural" tank is equipped with at least an undergravel biological filter and is an effort by the aquarist to maintain marine life, including plants, that is an accurate representation of a particular natural marine environment. The specific marine ecosystem that usually attracts the aquarist is an Atlantic or Pacific coral reef; but it's equally interesting to work with local marine environments such as estuaries, tidal flats, mud bottoms, algae flats, and temperate zone, rocky bottoms. In my opinion, it is appropriate to use whatever filtration is necessary to maintain this type of a natural aquarium. The important thing is to be as faithful as possible to the particular environment that is being created.

Compound internal filtration

It is quite possible to run a modest (20 to 50 gallon) marine system without an undergravel filter, but on a more stable basis than is afforded by the "natural" system. This can be accomplished with a "compound internal filter". These filter systems are not particularly popular because they take up some tank area, however small, and because the filter is present in the tank display area. There are some advantages, however. Such filter units are portable and can be moved from one tank to another without disruption of the biological filter, thus they can make a newly set up marine tank function instantly with a mature biological filter. In this capacity, they are useful as a starter filter for a traditional setup and can be removed in a couple of months after the undergravel filter is fully run in. They can also be transported to remote locations and provide run in, fully functional filters in bare tanks at temporary collecting sites.

Since the filter is totally within the tank, there is no possibility of leakage due to malfunction of an external filter system. The internal placement also allows for a compact installation of the tank and eliminates salt build up on filters and tubes. They allow complete, inexpensive filtration on a number of secondary tanks for an active hobbyist; a number of quarantine tanks, for example. If the aesthetics of the tank do not permit the filter to be in sight, it can be hidden by an artificial or natural structure within the tank. The filter system can be run entirely on an air pump or with a small powerhead water pump. Various types of chemical and biological filter media can be used in such filters.

As far as I know there are no commercial units of an internal compound filter available, other than a few expensive, built in custom reef tank systems. While researching filtration for this book, I developed a small, compound internal filter that performs the following functions: surface skimming, mechanical filtration, biological filtration, water aeration, water circulation, protein foam skimming, and chemical filtration. Water sterilization can also be effected if ozone is used with the protein foam skimmer. The unit can be built entirely of PVC pipe, a few pieces of acrylic plastic, and a plastic kitchen funnel. Figure 44 illustrates one design of this type of filter for small tanks. The height of the filter may vary from 10 to 20 inches or so depending on the height of the water column in the tank. It can be built in various sizes to service systems from 20 to 50

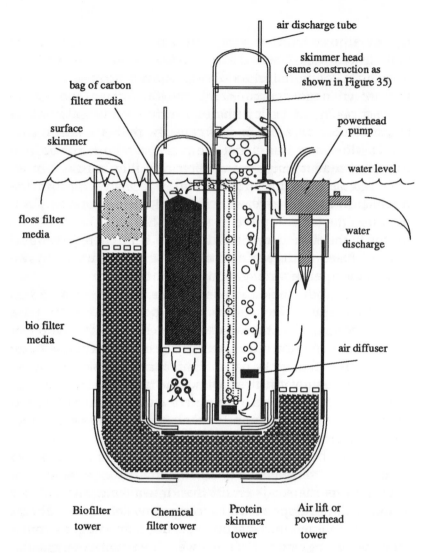

Figure 44. A design for a compound internal filter made from 2" thin wall PVC pipe and fittings.

gallons, 75 to 150 gallons, or even larger for commercial holding or rearing tanks. PVC pipe in the 1½ to 2 inch diameter range works well for typical marine aquaria in the 30 to 75 gallon range. Three to four or even six inch diameter pipe can be used on large tanks.

My "tower filter" design includes four towers. The two outer towers are connected in a U shape unit and the two inner towers are connected in an upside down U shaped unit. The first tower in the mechanical/biological filter is the *Surface skimmer biofilter tower*. It includes a surface skimmer, an easily changed mechanical filter, and a biological filter media chamber. This tower is connected to the *air lift tower* with a horizontal bottom tube that also contains biological filter media. The *air lift, or powerhead, tower* pulls water rapidly through the mechanical and biological filter, aerates the water, and jets it back into the tank. A protein skimmer head can be placed on the top of the air lift tower if an air lift rather than a powerhead pump is used to draw water through the filter unit. This increases the total skimming capacity of the filter.

The skimmer/chemical filter unit fits inside the two towers of the mechanical/biological unit. This provides a compact, unified design. Note, however, that each of these two tower units function independently and can be used separately. Water is drawn into the upper part of the *protein foam skimmer tower* through a downward directed external tube. The downward bend prevents discharge of air from the water intake tube, and pulling water directly from the tank removes organics before they pass through the biological filter. There are two air diffusers at the bottom of the skimmer tower. One provides the small bubbles to create the foam and power the skimmer. The other powers the small air lift that draws water through the skimmer. Both are controlled by independent air valves. The air lift can be internal in the skimmer unit or, for better skimmer function, can be external to the tower. The bottom of the skimmer tower is capped. The skimmer air lift deposits the small water flow into the top of the *chemical filter tower*, which is capped to prevent spray and overflow. The water flows downward through activated carbon or other chemical filter media and then back into the tank through holes in the bottom of the tower. The chemical filter receives water after passage through the skimmer, so if ozone is used in the skimmer, the chemical filter media reduces the amount of ozone that is released to the tank.

The fiber floss in the mechanical filter and the filter media in the chemical filter chamber can be changed without removing the filter from the tank by simply lifting the floss or the bag containing the chemical media from the towers and replacing it. Cleaning the biological media (when necessary) and replacing the air diffusers requires removal of the filter from the tank. The PVC caps and pipes are not glued together, so the entire unit can be easily dismantled and reassembled. Use of thin walled, schedule 80 PVC pipe makes for a light, easily worked filter assembly. We plan to prepare a booklet with detailed construction and operation instructions for this filter. You can write to Green Turtle Publications for more information.

Reef systems

The creation of a living reef system at the Smithsonian Institution in Washington, D.C. in the late 70's and the subsequent publication of European techniques and successes in keeping coral reef invertebrates fired the imagination and activity of American marine aquarists. Many aquarists saw what was possible and said, "Hey, I can do that."—and the hobby took on a new dimension. The dust has not yet settled. There are many types and sizes of "reef systems" with many possible filter configurations. The term reef system now has a very broad definition, and systems of many sizes and configurations are termed reef systems. As George Smit (the father of marine reef systems in the U.S.) said at the recent Marine Aquarium Conference of North America in Toronto, Canada, "Reef tanks can be high-tech, low-tech or no-tech—they all work." Even the simplest, basic reef type system allows an aquarist to keep fish and/or invertebrates with greater succss than any traditional marine aquarium setup. A knowlegable aquarist with a high-tech system, however, does a lot less "guess work" than those with low-tech or no-tech systems.

The three features most common to reef systems are full spectrum, high intensity lighting; some type of a wet/dry trickle filter; and a strong movement of water through and around the reef structures in the tank. Also, to be a true reef system, the display should contain rock reef with some live rock, and the primary cultured organisms should be live corals, other reef animals, and abundant algaes. A reef tank is based on a filter system that provides superior life support for all marine aquarium displays, but it is not a true "reef tank" unless the main purpose of the system is to maintain a coral reef community that is as close to nature as possible. A reef system need not be based on a spectacular 100 to 300 gallon display tank, although such a system is the current epitome of a marine aquarium. Reef type systems can be built around tanks as small as 10 gallons, and can be just as spectacular, in their own small way, as large reef systems.

Lighting is of critical importance in a reef system. *More than any other feature, high intensity, full spectrum lighting is the cornerstone of the system.* Reef tanks can be operated on either fluorescent or metal halide lighting, or a combination of both. As long as the light is close to the surface of the tank, small shallow systems can operate on less intense light than large, deep systems. For corals, wide shallow tanks are preferred over tall narrow tanks because the organisms are closer to the light, and relative bottom area is greater. Refer to the section on lighting in Chapters 3 and 4 for specific information on reef system lighting.

Water that leaves the tank should come from an overflow at the surface. This skims off organic compounds that accumulate at the surface, and removal of "old" surface water enhances gas exchange. Most reef system tanks have a hole drilled in the bottom at a back corner and have an overflow compartment built into the tank by sealing in two narrow glass walls around the hole from the bottom to almost the top of the tank. Placing fiberfill floss, or other mechanical filter media, into this compartment also serves as a particle filter and removes large particles before the water enters the filter system below the tank. This particle filter should be cleaned often and have an overflow provision so that water always flows freely from the tank despite the condition of the prefilter. The water then flows into a trickle filter beneath the tank.

Water is collected in a sump tank under the trickle filter and is then pumped back into the display tank. Water movement about the tank and through the reef is very important. The return flow from the filter should be utilized to provide maximum circulation about the tank, and separate powerhead pumps can be used to provide strong flows and even surge patterns in particular areas of large tanks. Although a bit beyond the usual home reef setup, it is possible to create a strong surge pattern in a reef tank with a container set above the tank that slowly fills and then tips to empty a large quantity of water, mixed with some air, all at once into the tank. A large bucket with a flapper valve in the bottom (like a toilet tank valve) could also produce this effect. Such a containment and release system produces a regular strong surge into one particular area of the reef.

There are various auxiliary filter units that may be utilized after the trickle filter. These additional filters enhance the ability of the system to maintain high water quality over time. A well adjusted denitrifying filter can maintain nitrate at levels below 1.0 ppm, an important consideration in keeping live corals. A good protein skimmer removes dissolved organic compounds and keeps organic acids and toxins at very low levels, which is very important to fish and invertebrate maintenance. A protein skimmer is most effective if water is taken directly from the display tank and returned above the trickle filter. If ozone is used in the protein foam skimmer, however, the outflow of the skimmer should be passed through activated carbon and returned to the sump tank without biological filtration to *protect nitrifying bacteria from ozone residuals*. Use of activated carbon and/or resins reduces organic dyes and other organic compounds and enhances water quality and clarity. Ozonation and ultra violet filtration also enhance the life support capability of the system *when used correctly*. An algae filter, or algae "scrubber" as such a filter is termed, is a natural way of removing excess nutrients and adding oxygen to the system

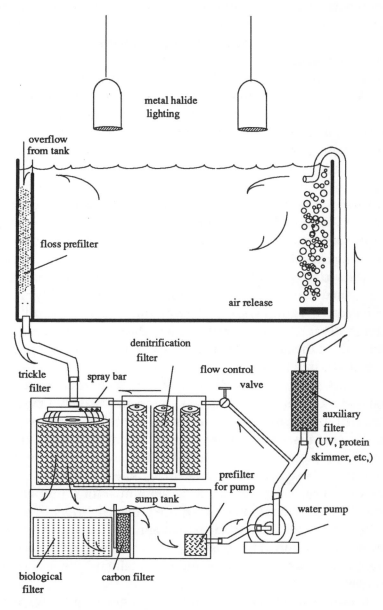

Figure 45. General structure of a marine reef tank aquarium system.

water. Use of any or all of these auxiliary devices depends on the design of the system and the philosophy and purpose of the aquarist. Figure 45 illustrates the basic structure of one possible reef tank system.

There are many possible trickle filter configurations. I would prefer a tower type unit with a plastic ball or cube media for optimum gas exchange, followed by a tray or media box filter filled with a calcareous gravel. One may wish to use a very coarse silica gravel or plastic bead media instead of a calcareous gravel and supplement calcium with a buffer preparation in some reef system setups. Water return to the tank would be part surface spray and part directed flow into the reef. This configuration provides good gas exchange with ample surface area for biological filtration and some calcareous buffering capacity. Note that there is plenty of room for various opinions on the "best" design for trickle filtration and the "best" media for these filters. Beautiful reef tank displays have been created with a wide variety of simple and sophisticated filter systems. Given a proven system, the care, understanding, and skill of the aquarist is more important than design variations in the filter.

As one might surmise, the operation of a large, complex, reef system aquarium is not a task to assume casually. One may read that reef systems are "maintenance free", and although it may be true that there is less "routine" maintenance associated with a reef system, it is also true that the level of "operational knowledge" (experience and technical know how) that is required to keep all parts of the system operating properly is considerably higher than that required for a traditional system. Thiel (1988, 1989) directs his books entirely toward the structure and operation of reef systems. They are good references for any aquarist who wishes to build or maintain a reef system aquarium.

Routine maintenance on a reef system should be done weekly. The tasks that are required are cleaning the viewing glass of algae growth, cleaning the fluorescent bulbs and tank top surfaces of salt deposits, cleaning the filter assemblies of salt deposits, cleaning protein foam skimmers (this is a daily task unless there is an automatic drain on the collection cup), and inspection and adjustment of the entire system for malfunction of skimmers, spray bars, denitrifying filters, and pumps. *Perhaps the most critical weekly maintenance task is replacement of evaporated water.* If evaporated water is not replaced, salinity rises, which is not good for the organisms in the tank; but more important, the pump may suck up air, or run dry and burn out, or just shut off if the sump has a cut off float switch (which it should have). As long as everything is in good operating condition, this is all that needs be done on the mechanical and water systems for many months. It is very wise to get the highest possible quality pumps, fittings, and valves; for it is often the failure of the simplest unit that causes the greatest headaches.

There is also a biological system, however, and this must be planted and tended just as a garden is tended. The base of reef systems is a reef composed of calcareous rock. Most, or some, of this rock must come from the sea as "live rock". Chapter 4 has a section on live rock and the reader is directed back to this section for information on collection and treatment of live rock. Algae in the genus *Caulerpa* is also an important part of most reef systems. Besides being attractive and part of the natural reef environment, *Caulerpa* grows abundantly without much site competition to corals, can easily be harvested to control growth, and provides the system with an "algae scrubber" that helps maintain a high water quality.

A vigorous growth of *Caulerpa* inhibits growth of hair algae, *Entromorpha*, that can quickly overtake a tank, crowd out other algae, and kill corals. Development of strong growths of the calcareous agae in the genus *Halimeda* are preferred by many marine reef aquarists over *Caulerpa* growths because this alage is more natural to the reef, and while it enhances water quality as well as *Caulerpa*, it does not "take over" the tank as *Caulerpa* often does. *Halimeda* requires sufficient calcium in the water at all times, 3.5 meq./l minimum, up to 6.4 meq./l (18dKH), which is also good for the corals.

The presence of extensive growths of hair algae indicates that nutrients may be too high and redox potential too low. A few easily removed, algae eating invertebrates (sea urchins and herbivorous mollusks for example) may be introduced to try to control hair algae growth in some systems. Phosphate levels may also be too high. Sometimes too much phosphate enters a reef system if the tap water used to make up for evaporation loss is high in organic phosphate. If this is the case, use of distilled, bottled water will limit introduction of excess phosphate. If necessary, passing the freshwater through a reverse osmosis filter and then treating it with de-ionizing resins will usually assure that the water used to make up the saltwater is free of nutrient compounds. Removal of detritus will also remove phosphate that is being cycled within the system. It is important to establish a good growth of *Caulerpa* or *Halimeda* before introducing much in the way of corals and other animals. Unless there is extensive auxiliary filtration, *Caulerpa* and/or other algaes "set" the water quality in the system at the point where corals can best survive. Adding much in the way of animals before the *Caulerpa* is established encourages hair algae growth and makes establishment of a good coral reef tank more difficult.

Many reef tank systems are well balanced between animal and plant life and need little feeding. The energy of light is used by the plants, including *zooxanthellae*, to produce the food energy consumed by the animals. In well established reef systems, there are many benthic copepods and other small marine animals that produce planktonic forms that provide some food for plankton feeders and recycle nutrients in the tank. Even infrequent feeding of tank inhabitants may not be necessary and may only introduce excess nutrients. Some corals and other filter feeders, however, may be benefited by occasional feeding of phytoplankton and zooplankton, depending on the individual system. Such supplemental feeding may make successful husbandry of a particular species possible. It is possible to culture plankton in fairly large amounts, as discussed later in this chapter, for feeding to reef systems.

For maximum utilization of plankton, feeding should be done at night a couple of hours after the lights have been turned off. The filters should be turned off but air lifts and/or small pumps should circulate water vigorously about the tank. Pour the plankton (microalgae, rotifers, new hatch brine shrimp) into the tank and wait an hour or two before resuming filtration. Other foods such as powdered plankton substitutes and very small amounts of finely blended shrimp may also be fed this way. See Chapter 6. Addition of vitamin supplements and organic nutrients can also be fed at this time since the activity of filtration will not immediately diminish the concentrations. Calcium supplements are important to reef systems with corals and especially calcareous algaes such as *Halimeda*. Fish and large invertebrates requiring occasional feeding of larger particle food or live adult brine shrimp can be fed sparingly during the day hours.

Sometimes it is obvious that a particular specimen of coral is suffering from a bacterial infection. The coral produces mucus, and a white film of bacteria begins to form around the edge or in spots on the coral colony. This is a good indication that water quality is not adequate and that the system may require a partial water change. There may also be a need for greater water movement over and around the coral colony. In some instances, it may be helpful to remove the coral piece from the tank and give it a bath of several hours in a well aerated, antibiotic solution. Such treatment will kill any bacteria, good and bad, that may be on and in the live rock the coral is attached to, but it may save the coral colony. Chloramphenicol, neomycin, and streptomycin are antibiotics that may help. Specific antibiotics, dosages, and duration of treatment are all guesswork at this point. One might try half the recommended dosage for typical aquarium treatment and evaluate the results. The risk of destroying the specimen through such treatment is high, so consider carefully before treatment. If corals and other sessile invertebrates do not survive in a particular system, the chances are that the environmental conditions in the tank are not adequate for survival. The aquarist's efforts may be better spent on improvement of the system rather than treatment of the already stressed organisms.

Suppose that an aquarist makes a investment of time and money in a reef system and things don't work out well. Eight to ten months down the road one finds that *Caulerpa* or *Halimeda* will not grow, the hair algae monster has taken over the tank and is eyeing the living room, and the words HELP ME appear written in reverse on the inside, algae covered sides of the tank. Mats of dense green *Derbesia* and blue-green algaes give off bubbles of oxygen during the day and may even float up to the surface.

What to do? There are several options. First of all clean the thing up. Turn off the filter systems during the cleaning. Take out the rocks one by one and scrub them in a bucket of salt water. Do this very carefully if they still have coral or other growths that should be preserved. Keep the rocks immersed in salt water if possible or at least covered by a towel wet with salt water to keep the bacterial colonies alive. Clean all the sides and bottom of the tank and siphon out the detritus and detached hair algae. Then rebuild the reef in the tank and wipe everything clean. A partial water change is now a good idea to reduce nutrients in the water and replace trace elements. Now there are two possibilities. One, find a good source of *Caulerpa* or *Halimeda* and try again to establish a good growth of macro algae instead of hair algae. Review the lighting on the system and the function of any auxiliary filtration devices. Consider installation of a denitrifying filter and protein foam skimmer if this equipment is not already on the system. *Do not feed the animals in the system*, or at least feed as little as possible while the *Caulerpa* is getting established.

A reef system is representative of a natural environment where free nutrients are always at low levels and nutrients are economically recycled. *It is important not to overfeed reef systems*. It is possible that the fresh water used to make up the salt mix and replace evaporation loss contains too much organic phosphate and this, along with other nutrients, is stimulating excess algal growth. Use of rain water or a reverse osmosis system to remove nutrients from make up water may greatly reduce excess fouling algal growth. It is also possible that use of calcareous gravels may enhance the availability of phosphate to algae growth, thus removal of carbonate gravel from the filters may be helpful. Detritus often acts as a nutrient "bank" and it is helpful to frequently remove accumulations of detritus from the system.

The second possibility is to accept the unwanted algae growth and maintain a modified reef system where coral and sessile invertebrate growth is limited and more emphasis is placed on fish and larger invertebrates. Tangs and angelfish, and some hermit crabs, sea urchins, and molluscs feed on algaes and are not compatible with lush growths of green algae and the "undersea garden" that is the ultimate reef system; but in those circumstances where the aquarist settles on a more traditional marine display, algae eating fish and invertebrates can control algal growth. Be sure to pass fish through a good quarantine system before adding them to a reef system. Otherwise difficult problems with the parasite *Amyloodinium (oodinium)* may occur. See the previous section on traditional systems for more information on parasite control and treatment. Also Moe (1982) has a section on control of this parasite.

Some fish are very compatible with reef systems and add color, movement, and an ecological "completeness" to a reef system. Fish that are small as adults, brightly colored, active in daylight hours, and have broad feeding habits are best. Small clownfish, most gobies, cardinalfish, royal grammas, hawkfish, and blue and green damsels are examples of fish that do well in reef systems. The spectacular mandarin fish seldom do well in typical marine aquariums because they require the tiny organisms that abound in detritus accumulations. Old reef tank systems are wonderful places for fish such as these. Avoid the temptation to have more than a just a few fish in reef tank system. The dartfish, in particular the firefish (*Nemateleotris magnifica*), make a magnificent addition to a reef tank. These small, brilliantly colored fish, plankton feeders in nature, swim in the currents just above the reef formations and add much interest and excitement to the reef display.

The garden analogy is very pertinent to reef systems. In a garden, we plant things and watch them grow. In a reef system tank, we plant things and watch them grow. Some organisms, algaes and colonial invertebrates in particular, will flourish, grow, and reproduce in well kept reef systems. Others may not reproduce, but will live long and look natural and healthy. As with a garden, part of the satisfaction of a reef system is planting a "seed" and watching it develop. It is not necessary to fill a reef system with every possible type of invertebrate on the market and then watch the ecological battle for survival and the decline of water quality. *Go slowly*, establish the algae first, select corals and other invertebrates carefully, read all you can about each invertebrate you acquire and watch it closely as it acclimates to the system. Avoid large, spectacular, algae eating fish (or make the decision not to strive for a coral/algae based reef system). It may take a year or more, but the patient aquarist that establishes a reef tank will be well rewarded with a technical and aesthetic achievement that few can equal.

Multi tank systems

It is quite possible to run more than one tank on a single filter system. Large trickle filters are very effective and have the capacity to run more than one tank. A true reef tank system, however, should have its own dedicated filter system, since other tanks can contribute nutrients that will probably degrade the water quality of the reef tank system. There may be instances, however, where an advanced hobbyist does wish to run more than one tank on a single large filter system. There are many ways to set up a multi tank array from a single filter system. Each installation demands its own modifications depending on the skills and requirements of the aquarists.

The advantages of multi tank systems are that only one filter need be installed; and this can provide better, more constant water quality for several tanks than that provided by several small, single tank filters. Maintenance may also be lighter on a single, well designed filter system. Multi tank systems can be simple, consisting of little more than a sump tank, trickle and/or biological filter, pump and piping. At the other extreme they can be complex, computer controlled, aquatic environmental systems. There are several important design features that should be incorporated in any multi tank system.

- There should never be more "free" water in the system than the sump tank can hold. In other words, the sump tank of the system must have the capacity to hold all the water that drains from any pipes and tanks if the pump dies. The sump tank is always lower than any other tank so gravity returns can always be used. A system that uses two pumps, one to deliver water and one to return water, seldom works because it is most difficult to keep the flows exactly balanced.

- Drains clog and siphons break, so overflow outlets from tanks and filters back to the sump tank should be provided if at all possible. Otherwise, great care is required to protect outlets from clogs and to frequently inspect siphons for air accumulation.

- An ultra violet sterilizer should be installed in the system before the water returns to the culture tanks to prevent distribution of parasites and disease.

- In most installations, valves that control the flow to each tank are very handy. With valves, flows to individual tanks can be regulated and one tank can receive a greater flow or all tanks can receive an equal flow. In addition, the flow to one tank can be easily stopped for treatment or cleaning without disruption of filtration to the other tanks.

- Regardless of the amount of water flow, each tank in the system should have an individual air release. The air pump should also be on a separate electrical circuit from the water pump. If the water pump burns out, or if the circuit that powers the water pump breaks, then the air release in each tank will keep the animals alive until the water system can be repaired.

The sump tank is the heart of a multi tank system. Although systems can be designed without a sump tank, totally pressurized, multi tank systems without a sump tank have little reserve capacity for evaporation and no aeration capability. Filtration augmentation such as protein foam skimming and denitrification can operate directly from the sump tank and process water for the entire system. Water outlets from individual tanks are best designed as overflow standpipes from a hole drilled in the bottom or side of the tank. Secondarily, a constant flow siphon (Figure 34), with a water retainer cup on both sides of the siphon, can be used. Clear siphon tubes are preferred, so that air accumulations or clogs can be easily observed. Three possible system designs are presented here in broad outline just to provide ideas on types of multi tank systems. Figure 46 illustrates the basic design of the three systems.

1. A simple, multi tank system for remotely located tanks. Tanks on a single central filter unit need not be located side by side, although that is the most efficient placement. As long as enough pumps and piping are used, tanks can be located in different rooms and run off the same central filter unit. Make sure that the drain pipes are at least twice the diameter of the water delivery pipes. There are not too many situations where remote location of tanks is practical. (Of course, one could set up the filter unit in the spare bath tub and run the pipes tastefully along the edge of the walls. Build little wooden ramps where the pipes go across hallways. No problem!)

In this design, two pumps are utilized. One supplies the tanks with filtered water from the sump tank, through a UV filter and then to the tanks. Water is returned by gravity from the tanks to the sump tank. A smaller separate pump circulates

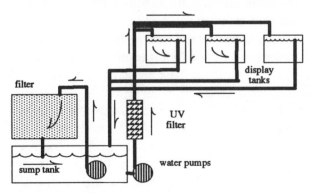

1. Two pump, remote multi tank system.

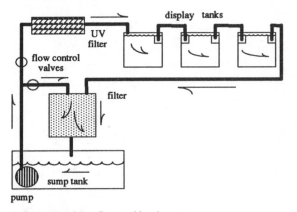

2. One pump, siphon flow, multi tank system.

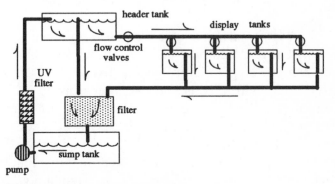

3. Large, multi tank system with header tank.

Figure 46. Examples of multi tank system designs.

water from the sump tank through the trickle and biological filters and then back to the sump.

2. *A simple, multi tank system for tanks set side by side.* The most common small, multi tank setup is for a bank of tanks in a single room, usually a basement or fish room. This design works well for a small number of tanks and can operate on a single pump. (A back up pump that can be quickly installed is a very good thing to have.) Water drains from the culture or display tanks through the trickle and biological filters and down into the sump tank. The pump pulls water from the sump and distributes it through a UV filter to the display tanks. Exposure to UV radiation benefits the system, but does not create a sterile barrier between tanks when tanks flow into each other in series. A valved shunt allows diversion of a controlled amount of water from the pumped line to flow back into the filter without going to the tanks. This allows control of the amount of flow to the tanks without putting much back pressure on the pump, and also gains maximum filtration with all the water that can be moved. Tanks can be individually supplied with water and have individual drains, the best arrangement, or, as illustrated, water can move from tank to tank by siphon flow. If siphons or a direct flow system is used to move water from tank to tank, then the last tank in the system gets the lowest quality water. If algae is grown in this last tank, however, this tank then functions as an algae filter for the entire system.

3. *A large, single pump, tank system.* In some situations, an aquarist or small commercial operation may wish to set up an inexpensive single pump system that services a number of large tanks with a constant water pressure to each tank and continuous, strong system filtration. There are many possible designs, but the one I favor includes a header tank that provides gravity flow to the tanks and gravity flow through the filters and plenty of overflow protection. (Note that the flow to each tank in a gravity pressured flow system is always constant regardless of changes in flow rates to other tanks. In a system operated by water pressure from a water pump, shutting down

one tank proportionally increases the flow to other tanks and increasing the flow to one tank decreases the flow to other tanks.)

The water is pumped from an oversize sump tank into a large holding tank above the filter and above the level of the display tanks. The flow provided is about 20 percent greater than that required by all the tanks in the system. An overflow standpipe in the header tank directs the overflow back to the filter. The delivery pipe to the display tanks leaves the bottom of the header tank and provides a constant pressure, gravity flow to all holding tanks. Each tank has its own valve control-led inlet and a large valve can be installed on the delivery line as it leaves the header tank so that the flow to all the tanks can be shut off without changing the settings on the individual tank valves. A UV filter in the line to the tanks assures a sterile barrier between the tanks as long as each tank drains in-dividually. The return from the tank goes back to the filter. The capacity of the sump tank must include the volume of the header tank so that all free flowing water can be collected by the sump tank. Measured water changes can be easily ac-complished by shutting off the pump, collecting all free water in the sump tank, and then removing and adding the volume desired. Protein skimming, denitrification, and other auxiliary filtration can be pulled off the pump line going to the header tank and then returned to the sump through the trickle filter.

Commercial systems

Commercial systems for the marine aquarium industry vary from two or three small, separate tanks set up in retail shop to a wholesalers's warehouse filled with rows and rows of large tanks, tiny compartments, big vats, and huge filter sys-tems with sump tanks the size of swimming pools. Many retail shops operate on four or five single marine tank setups just like the ones they recommend to their customers. Shops with large marine sections, however, usually install a central filtration system. This can be a complete system designed especially for a retail store—a custom installation by firms that specialize in building store systems—or an installation built by the retailer.

Most commercial installations are now based on some type of trickle and biological filtration, and use at least two separate systems, one for fish and one for invertebrates. A third system is often used to quarantine new fish for a week or two before placing them in sale tanks. The systems used by collectors and small wholesalers are usually also centrally filtered. Most small wholesalers that fabricate their own systems use a number of smaller systems rather than one or two large systems. (That old platitude about eggs and baskets seems appropriate at this point.) At any rate, the information elsewhere in this book will be helpful to small commercial operations in evaluating commercial systems now on the market or in designing a custom system.

Deep water systems

Zonation is an important concept in marine ecology. Reef animals and plants favor certain areas on the reef and are best adapted to the particular conditions that exist in those areas. Stony corals, strong as concrete and massive in form, live in the buttress zone where light intensity is high and wave surge is ceaseless and often violent. The reef flats are more protected and many more species of corals and algaes can grow where light is less, but wave surge is calmer. As depth increases, the species of organisms change and/or adapt to low levels of mostly blue light and an absence of wave surge, although oceanic currents may be strong in many areas. Stony corals that grow as massive bolders in the surf zone, become thin, flattened plates in deep water. Water temperature is also more constant and cooler at depths 50 to 100 feet below the surface of tropical seas. Most modern reef tank systems are based on the relatively shallow, brightly lighted reef flat environment. Organisms that favor the buttress zone on the reef crest or the quiet deep reef may survive for a while in the typical reef tank, but they are not primarily adapted to the environment created in such a tank.

It is possible to maintain a marine tank that is reasonably faithful to the conditions of the deep reef, over 80 feet, and contains mostly organisms that normally live in these deeper areas. Of course, it is not feasible to create the water pressure that exists in these depths, but other conditions of light, temperature, water quality, and water movement can be established. Lighting should be of low intensity and heavy on the blue side of the spectrum. Actinic 03 bulbs may be used or a blue sleeve placed over a full spectrum bulb may be adequate. One of each of these may be the best lighting arrangement. A sheet of blue acetate plastic may alternatively be placed over the top of the tank. To be true to the light conditions on the deep reef, room light should be prevented from entering the tank from the sides and back. Water temperature should be in the range of 65 to 70 °F, although it should be possible to keep most of the deep water organisms in the 70 to 75 °F range. Water movement, as in other reef systems, should be constant and reasonably strong throughout the tank. Typical reef system filtration that provides for good gas exchange, removal of organics, and biological filtration is also required.

There are a number of fish and invertebrates on the market that are either taken at these depths or have a depth range that extends down to a 100 feet (30 meters) or more. It may be possible to obtain live rock, invertebrates, and algaes from a collector that makes a deep dive specifically for that collection. Many interesting organisms may develop from live rock taken at depths and maintained in a simulated deep reef tank. A retailer or wholesaler may be able to contract for such a collection and make arrangements for a specific shipment. Otherwise, some research is in order to identify the specific organisms that one would want to include in such a tank. The Cuban hogfish (*Bodianus pulchellus*), blue chromis (*Chromis cyanea*), pygmy angelfish (*Centropyge argi*), and blackcap or purple gramma (*Gramma melacara*) are examples of deepwater Caribbean fishes that are frequently encountered on the marine tropical market.

Low light levels in deep reef tanks will not allow many shallow water invertebrates to survive. The red finger sponge, *Haliclona rubens*, and many other sponges occur on the deep reef and may be easier to keep in a "deep" tank than a typical reef tank system. The soft Pacific tree corals, *Dendronephthya*, are good specimens for a deep reef tank. Many gorgonians also live at depths and may do well in deep reef systems. Small crustaceans are also good candidates for deep tanks. Experimental work on deep reef tanks would be a fascinating project for many advanced aquarists.

Night systems

A coral reef does not quietly slumber away the night time hours. If anything, more activity takes place around and on the reef during the night. Great swarms of zooplankton migrate from the depths to shallow waters after nightfall, and most filter feeders come alive after dark to capture their share of plankton protein. Basket stars and feather stars unfurl and cast their nets upward into the currents. Coral polyps embedded in their soft or stony matrix also stretch out and reach their tentacles into the sea. The octopus leaves its lair and flows over the sea bottom searching for mollusks and crabs. Lobsters, hidden by day in the furthest crevices of the reef, wander the rocks and nearby grass flats. Reef fish court and spawn as the sun sets and then move out to feed around reef rubble and grass flat. Cardinalfish and copper sweepers leave their dark caves and feed on the large zooplankters that swarm through the reef. To see the reef in day is to see less than half the story.

With a little modification, an invertebrate or reef tank can become an enchanting display of nighttime activity on the reef. Most feeding of plankton or plankton substitutes should be done at night, for that is when most filter feeders feed most actively. The tank can be observed with a small flashlight a couple of hours after the lights switch off. Many interesting animals may be seen that the aquarist many not even know are in the tank, and old friends may exhibit new and unusual behavior patterns. There are better methods of creating a night system than wielding a small flashlight, however.

The tank can be illuminated with a dull, red light that will allow full observation when one's eyes become dark adapted. The animals in the tank do not recognize the red light as day and readily begin their nighttime activity in full view of the aquarist. A red incandescent light can be mounted over the tank and turned on as the tank lights go off or, even better, a red, transparent plastic sleeve can be placed over a two or four foot cool white fluorescent bulb. This red light may be operated by a second timer that turns the red light on a few minutes before the regular tank lights go off and keeps it on for a few hours in late evening. Plankton feeding and night observation can then be done in late evening.

A reef system can be developed to favor nighttime activity by purposeful selection of night active animals. Of course, the system must have proper daytime illumination to remain healthy, but red light illumination can occupy a greater portion of the evening on systems designed to display nighttime activity. A twist on the nighttime system is to use a black light bulb. Many species of coral exhibit biofluorescense when lit by a black light (long wave ultraviolet). Anemones and coral polyps glow with soft blue and violet fluorescence. Certainly not a natural effect, but one that is beautiful and very interesting. Long wave ultraviolet is also said to have a beneficial effect on fish and invertebrates.

Cold water systems

The flora and fauna of temperate cold water environments, with one exception, are not commonly maintained in aquaria. Public aquariums usually have one or two displays given to the rocky temperate environment, but only the rare hobbyist keeps a cold water aquarium. The technology is not that difficult, many supermarkets and seafood markets keep American lobsters (the exception mentioned above), and the animals of cold water rocky reefs are often spectacular in form and color; but even so, few aquarists are moved to keep a 100 gallons of

50 °F water in their living rooms. Such systems can be kept, but special chiller units must be incorporated in the system to maintain the proper temperatures. Cold water aquarists will also probably have to do their own collecting for few cold water fish and invertebrates are found in aquarium shops. If one is interested in maintaining a cold water aquarium, a visit to a number of public aquariums is recommended. The professional aquarists at these institutions, if you catch them at the right time, will probably be happy to instruct you in the fine points of keeping cold water marine systems.

Larval rearing systems

The actual, physical system for rearing larvae of marine fish and invertebrates is very simple: a full spectrum light, a bare tank, and an air stone. It is the support systems—spawning tanks and procedures, water handling, and planktonic food generation—that are time consuming and difficult to master. As discussed in Chapter 3, the earliest life stages, the larval forms, of almost all tropical marine organisms are tiny creatures of the plankton. There are innumerable kinds of creatures in the plankton, including myriad forms and shapes of marine larvae. When animals in a reef tank reproduce, these larvae are present in the reef tank. Marine animals usually spawn at night, and about the only way most aquarists can find eggs and larvae that are released in the tank is to observe the water at night with a flashlight. Shine the light through one end of the tank and observe the cone of light closely through the front glass for tiny moving specks. Many larval forms are attracted to light (positive phototropism) and can be concentrated in a corner of the tank with a small light. They can then be dipped from the tank with a glass or jar. Although there are many kinds and variations of kinds of marine planktonic larvae, it is possible to get some idea of what is spawning by examining the shape and form of the larvae with a microscope or hand lens.

Most of the basic types of marine larvae are illustrated in Figure 47 and labeled with the types of animals that produce that kind of larvae. Comparison of the larvae found in the tank with the types of larvae illustrated may help identify which animals are spawning. There are great variations in form and structure of larvae produced by animals in the same class. The veliger larvae of various snails and bivalves, for example, can be very different with a single valved or bivalved form, but to the practiced eye the general veliger form is easily discerned. Examination of tiny larvae is difficult and the drawings are very limited, but they may help determine if the larvae are from corals, crustaceans, mollusks, echinoderms, or fish. If only eggs are observed, the early larval stages can be obtained if the eggs are held in a clean glass of seawater for a day or two until hatching occurs. Later larval stages can also be obtained by allowing the larvae to continue development in the glass for several days. Only early larval forms are illustrated, so be aware that great change in larval form usually occurs as they develop through different stages toward metamorphism into juveniles. A microscope is required to identify the specific type of larvae, but a high powered hand lens, 10 or 12 X, may allow rough identification of some larvae. Place the larvae in a drop of water on a black background and use the hand lens with a strong light source.

Marine larvae require high water quality, proper lighting and background, gentle to moderate water movement, freedom from bacterial growths, and high concentrations of the right kind of tiny, live, planktonic organisms for food. The specific requirements of some larvae are relatively easy to provide, and the requirements of other species are very difficult to provide. No aquatic systems are static, but tropical larval rearing systems are probably the most dynamic of all marine systems. The larvae grow fast and require frequent and critical food changes. Abundant food must be added often, and organics accumulate rapidly, which, along with high tropical temperatures, stimulates rapid bacterial growth. Add to this the fact that any filtration or water change filters out the planktonic food as well as the larvae themselves, and some of the difficulties in working with marine larvae become more clearly understood.

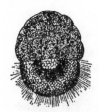

Early sponge larvae
(amphiblastula)

Planula larvae
corals, anemones

Medusae
planktonic form of
many Cnidaria

Trochophore larvae
short term planktonic
larvae of polychete
worms

Muller's larvae
planktonic larvae of
marine flatworms

Gastropod veliger

Early veliger

Molluskan trochophore larvae
first larval form before the
veliger larval stage

Pelecypoda veliger

Figure 47. Planktonic larval forms of selected taxons of
marine aquarium animals.

Nauplius larvae
The first larval
stage of many
species of
crustaceans

Two types of zoaea,
larvae typical of
crabs and some
shrimp

Brittle star larvae
ophiopluteus

Sea urchin larvae
echinopluteus

Pluteus type larval echinoderms

Starfish larvae
bipinnaria

Echinoderm larvae
There are many
forms and stages of
echinoderm larvae .
Four common types
are illustrated.

Sea cucumber larvae
auricularia

Invertebrate egg

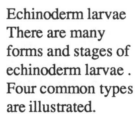

Tunicate larvae
appendicularia

Fish egg,
pelagic

Larval fish, after hatch

Fish egg, before hatch

Figure 47. Planktonic larval forms of selected taxons of
marine aquarium animals.

The detailed process of rearing marine larvae is beyond the scope of this book. Moe (1982) has a chapter on rearing marine fish that may help the aquarist that wants to try rearing marine animals. The support systems that are required are a traditional or reef system setup to contain the adults of the species that is to be spawned and culture systems for microalgaes and zooplankton. The following ten steps present in brief outline one path to follow in rearing a marine animal.

First, learn all you can about the organism that you want to rear. Go to a marine science library, if possible, and look in the scientific journals for papers that will be helpful. There is a great deal of information on commercial species so if you are interested in a crustacean, look for papers on shrimp, crabs, and lobsters. If a mollusk is your quarry, look for papers on oysters, scallops, abalone, and clams. There are many papers on fish, of course, including pompano, flounder, sea bass, red-fish, and many others.

Second, set up a marine system that will best care for the juveniles and adults of that species.

Third, maintain the adults and strive to provide the specific conditions of environment and feeding that will condition them for spawning and stimulate reproductive activity. Temperature, lighting, photoperiod, cover, and diet are all important. Learn about the natural environment and the conditions that prevail when the animals spawn. If they spawn in late spring, then that tells you something about temperatures and photoperiods leading up to the time of spawning.

Fourth, observe the animals very closely, analyze their behavior, and adjust diet and environment in ways that you feel may induce them to spawn. Watch the behavior closely at night for this is when most marine animals spawn. Watch the water column near the surface at night, shine a flashlight through the tank from end to end and look within the light beam for the presence of larval organisms

Fifth, when larvae are observed in the breeding tank, carefully remove them and transfer them to a separate larval rearing tank. A 20 gallon tank works well as a rearing tank for a hobbyist, for it is not too large to work with and still large enough to provide some environmental stability for the larvae. A single, two foot, full spectrum fluorescent bulb placed about 4 to 6 inches from the top of the tank will provide enough light.

Sixth, set the air stone to provide a gentle turn of the water and observe the larvae closely for at least several hours. Most marine larvae hatched from planktonic eggs carry a yolk that provides 24 to 48 hours of sustenance before feeding must commence. Depending on the larvae, they will require either phytoplankton cells, cultured ciliates, cultured rotifers, marine plankton (including copepod napulii, larval oysters, tintinnids, etc.), brine shrimp napulii, or even a combination of these, as a food source. Only experimentation and careful, continuous observation will tell you what food in what concentration is required to bring that species through the larval stage. Determining the initial concentration of food organisms that the larvae require is one of the most difficult tasks in culture of a new organism. Too many food organisms may degrade water quality below the survival point for a delicate larvae, and too few may not provide enough feeding opportunities to allow for larval survival. Phytoplankton feeders generally require more food organisms per milliliter than those that feed on zooplankton.

Phytoplankton in the rearing tank generally does no harm and usually improves the water quality as long as the bloom does not crash. It also keeps the rotifers and/or copepods well fed while they are waiting for a hungry zooea or fish larvae. Some zooplankton feeding species may do well on one rotifer per ml in the culture tank and others may require up to 20 per ml. Generally, 5 to 10 rotifers per ml is a good starting level for most larvae. There are about 25 to 50 rotifers in a teaspoon of rearing tank water. When the larvae are ready to take new hatch brine shrimp, it is time to stop feeding the tank (maintaining a population of food organisms) and to begin feeding the larvae (adding only enough food organisms to feed the larvae). Feeding levels are now determined by the number and kind of larvae and the size of the rearing tank.

Seventh, keep the bottom of the rearing tank as clean as possible with a small bore siphon. It's a good idea to examine the detrital material removed by the siphon with a microscope or hand lens to make sure that any settled larval/juvenile stages were not removed by the siphon. Replace the water lost to siphoning with clean new water.

Eighth, examine the larvae under a microscope from time to time, at least once a day, to see if they are feeding, on what they are feeding, and if they are growing.

Ninth, be prepared to change the food to a larger food organism, or perhaps even to a tiny particle of high quality flake food, if the larvae appear to be able to take a different food.

Tenth, be aware that some species of invertebrates require the presence of certain algae before they can metamorphose from the larval to juvenile stage. Add some rocks and algae from the spawning tank to the larval tank after 12 to 15 days if the larvae have grown well, but appear not to be able to progress past a certain point of development. This may add just the right algal environment to stimulate metamorphosis from the larval to the juvenile stage.

Of course, there is a lot more to rearing marine animals then these 10 points—hands on experience is everything in this game—but they may get you started on the right fin, er, foot.

Microalgae rearing systems

Phytoplankton is at the base of the marine food chain. It is also at the base of the process of food organism culture in farming of marine animals. An advanced marine aquarist has two reasons for rearing marine microalgae (phytoplankton) and zooplankton: such cultures are essential for rearing most marine larvae, and these planktonic cultures are an important food source for many corals and filter feeders that are found in reef systems. Many corals and other filter feeders that might not otherwise survive will greatly benefit from feedings of live plankton three or four nights each week.

Phytoplankton is usually not directly consumed by the larval animals under culture, but is used to feed the rotifers, brine shrimp, or other zooplankters that are fed directly to the cultured larvae. Note, however, that many larvae (cniderians, annelids, echinoderms) that have never been cultured may feed directly on phytoplankton. It is possible to avoid phytoplankton culture and use other foods such as bakers yeast or specially developed yeast based foods for feeding rotifers, but relying only on yeast produces a rotifer that may not be nutritionally adequate for the larvae under culture. Also, feeding yeast increases organic and bacterial fouling in rotifer cultures. However, phytoplankton cultures are unpredictable creatures and often crash (die out) just when they are needed most. If one does have active rotifer cultures, it is a good idea to have a yeast based rotifer food on hand for supplemental feeding and for emergency use.

Because they provide a wide nutritional base, it is wise to use phytoplankton cultures as the foundation of any experimental rearing programs. Specific species that are easy to culture, available from several sources, and that are nutritious are in the genera *Chlorella, Dunaliella, Isochrysis, Monochrysis,* and *Tetraselmis. Chlorella* is the most commonly cultured micro algae. It is possible, not recommended, but possible, to establish mixed wild algae cultures by fertilizing a container of natural seawater filtered through an 80 to 100 micron filter, and then putting it in culture. Sometimes useable cultures develop, but all too often the major species cultured is a hairy diatom or some other species that plates out on the bottom or is otherwise inadequate for the job.

The main purpose most marine aquarists have for culturing a phytoplankton algae is for use as food for rotifer and brine shrimp cultures. Growing phytoplankton algae is almost always the front end of a culture system designed to produce rotifers and/or brine shrimp; so phytoplankton culture is presented as part of a total plankton culture system. A plankton culture unit can be constructed from common materials available at the supermarket, hardware store, and aquarium shop.

Such a unit is briefly described in the next section. Two references that describe these systems in detail are Sieswerda (1977) and Florida Aqua Farms (1987). Building the unit is easy. The hard part is the dedication and daily maintenance that is required to keep it in production.

Live food culture systems

There are many, many different organisms that can be cultured as live food for fish and other aquatic animals. Worms, flies, ciliates, crickets, oyster larvae, even cockroaches and mosquitos are cultured. Lutz, et. al. (1937) is a compendium of culture techniques for invertebrates and is still a basic reference for general culture techniques. For our purposes, however, the culture of phytoplankton, rotifers, and brine shrimp are of most use in rearing marine animals and in feeding live plankton to reef systems.

Rotifers reared in culture systems are of the species *Brachionus plicatilis*. They have been used in marine culture for about 20 years. They are very small (about 250 microns long and 100 microns wide), about half the size of new hatched brine

Brchionus pilicatilis
cultured rotifer

shrimp. This species is discussed in Chapter 8. In growing, expanding cultures, almost all the rotifers are female. Female rotifers reproduce parthenogenetically during the asexual phase of their life cycle. This means that the eggs produced by a female rotifer during the asexual part of the life cycle are diploid (containing a full chromosome complement), are not created by sexual reproduction, and are genetically identical to the female. They hatch into females, grow to maturity, and begin producing eggs within a day. As long as environmental conditions are favorable (salinity, food, temperature, water quality, light, etc.), female rotifers continue in an asexual cycle and rotifer populations can increase to astronomical numbers. Under unfavorable conditions, a female may produce a haploid egg (a gamete) that contains only half the chromosome complement, a result of nuclear reduction division (meiosis). If not fertilized, the haploid egg hatches directly into a male rotifer, a rare creature, and this male produces haploid sperm instead of eggs. The sperm fertilizes other haploid eggs, and the resulting zygote (now with the full complement of chromosomes and the benefit of the genetic mixing of sexual reproduction) becomes a thick walled, resting egg. The resting eggs wait quietly on the bottom until conditions are again favorable and then hatch out as females to begin the cycle of asexual reproduction and population expansion once again.

This mode of reproduction makes rotifers an ideal food organism for cultivators of marine animals; for if the rotifers can be kept in the asexual cycle by balancing feeding and harvest, then millions and millions of female rotifers can be continuously produced from a relatively small culture volume. The environmental requirements for rotifers are fairly broad. Temperatures should be between 70 to 85 °F (21 to 29 °C). Cool temperatures create stable cultures, but cause slow growth. Reproduction and growth are greatly increased by warm temperatures, but cultures are not as stable and may "crash" more quickly and more often. Cultures kept at 77 to 82 °F (25 to 28 °C) seem to do best. pH should be kept about 8.0, but can vary from 7.5 to 8.5. A light intensity of 4000 to 5000 lumens (two 40 watt fluorescent bulbs) and a photoperiod of 14 to 16 hours of light is fine for rotifer and phytoplankton cultures.

The real value of rotifers to marine culturists depends on what the rotifers eat. Think of a rotifer as a tiny little grocery bag. If you fill the bag with candy and cake, the little fish or shrimp will not grow big and strong. But if you fill the bag with quality carbohydrates, proteins, vitamins and minerals, the little fish and shrimp will grow fast and be strong and healthy. A starved rotifer is an empty bag and has little food value for a marine larvae. Rotifers should always be fed before they themselves are fed to other marine creatures. This why it is important to feed the rotifers good algal cultures and enriched yeast based foods or other rotifer food supplements. Enriched food supplements made especially for rotifers are available in small quantities for hobbyists.

Rotifers can be grown in batch or continuous culture. Batch culture consists of building an algal bloom in a container, inoculating the culture with rotifers, waiting until rotifer populations reach a high density, and then harvesting the rotifers from the culture all at once or for as long as possible. After the culture is completely harvested, or organics accumulate and rotifer populations decline, the container is cleaned and another algae culture begun.

A continuous culture system maintains relatively small containers with rotifer populations that are fed and harvested regularly. Water change is usually accomplished as a part of the harvest process. The culture vessels still need to be cleaned and restarted fairly often, especially if yeast is used, but cultures are maintained for many days by the balance of feeding algae and harvesting rotifers. Continuous culture seems to work best for aquarists that have fluctuating demands for rotifers. The system can be maintained at low levels during periods of low demand and scaled up when spawns occur and rotifer demand is high.

Figure 48 illustrates the elements of a basic, integrated aquarist's continuous culture system. There are many ways that a phytoplankton/rotifer culture system can be set up, but there are several important, basic considerations that need to be considered in any home culture system design.

- Spills, salt creep, and spray are inherent in these small culture systems. If the system is set up in a closet or other area with finished walls and floors, be sure to protect the walls and the floors with plastic sheeting.

- The system is powered by light so it helps to use aluminum foil, shiny side out, to reflect light from the walls back to the cultures.

- One of the major difficulties in operation of these small culture systems (large ones also) is the contamination of the algae cultures with rotifers. If the rotifers get into the algae cultures, they consume all the algae the aquarist has under culture and all food cultures crash. The aquarist then has to resort to yeast based rotifer food while the algae systems are being sterilized and restarted. Positive physical and operational barriers should be erected between the algae and rotifer cultures to prevent back contamination of algae cultures with rotifers. Use a separate set of siphons, containers, cups, spoons, etc. for algae and rotifer work.

- Use separate air pumps for the algae and rotifer cultures. This will minimize contamination possibilities and assure that failure of one air pump will not destroy all cultures.

- Keep newly made up salt water, stored for use in algae culture, covered and physically removed from any possible rotifer or blue-green algae contamination.

The culture system setup. There are three separate units to this system: algae culture, rotifer culture, and waste water containment (which can also be used to grow out brine shrimp). This type of system can be set up in a straight line on a bench with the algae culture bottles on one end and the rotifer culture separated by a spray barrier on the other end. It can also be set up in three vertical levels with the algae culture bottle on top, rotifer culture in the middle and waste water storage on the bottom. The three tier system allows use of siphons to move water downward and is a more efficient use of space. This is the system diagramed in Figure 48.

The upper tier is for algae culture. A four foot, fluorescent light fixture placed about 6 inches behind the cultures provides the necessary light. Cool white bulbs are adequate, but better results may be had with one plant grow bulb and one full spectrum bulb. There are 7 to 10 individual algae cultures in

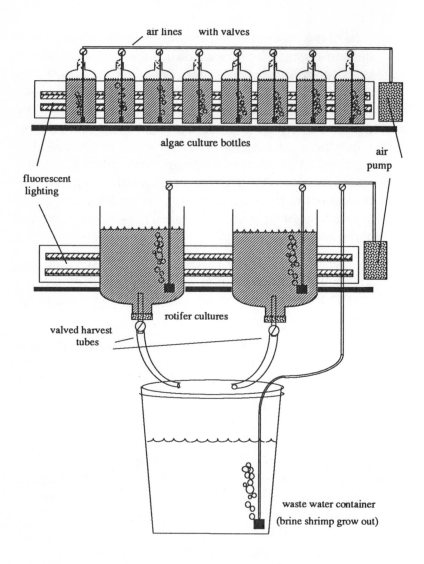

Figure 48. A small, two shelf microalgae and rotifer culture system.

various stages of bloom development in front of this light. The algae containers can be made from clear glass gallon jugs, clear plastic soda bottles, strong plastic bags, or other transparent containers. Algae culture containers must be cleaned before each use, so there is a definite advantage to using a container that can be disposed of after one or a few uses. (Rinse and scrub the containers as well as possible *without* use of soap or detergent, final rinse with hot, hot water.) If strong, clear plastic bags are used, a device to hold the bags in place must be constructed. The mouth of the bag can be held tightly around a short section of PVC pipe to create a small, rigid opening. Plastic soda bottles also work well and can be disposed of when they become difficult to clean. A section of rigid air tubing, with or without an air stone at the end, extends down into the algae culture container to provide water circulation and gas exchange to the algae culture. A plug of clean floss in the mouth of the container allows air flow from the container and limits contamination and escape of spray and foam. A small air pump powers all the air lifts in the algae culture section and can also provide aeration to a container of clean saltwater stored for future use. A dedicated siphon (one that really loves its work and is used only for the algae cultures) is used to move dense culture from the algae containers down to the rotifer cultures on the shelf below.

Generally, two rotifer cultures are required. One culture produces while the other is being cleaned or is developing a culture. Also, continuous harvest of one culture during a time of heavy demand may reduce the rotifer population to a point where recovery is very slow. There should be a population of at least 50 rotifers per ml after harvest to insure rapid regrowth of the population. The rotifer culture containers should be transparent to provide light for algal growth and to allow examination of the state of the culture. The size of the containers depend on the projected demand for rotifers. They can be 5, 10, or 20 gallon aquaria, inverted cut off plastic 5 gallon water jugs, or even small plastic food containers. Algae is introduced from the cultures above with a siphon, and rotifers are removed by harvest with a fine mesh net directly from the cultures or by siphoning the culture into to a concentrating net in the waste water container below. A single small air pump provides aeration to the rotifer cultures (two air stones may be needed in a wide, shallow container) and to the container of waste water below. A fluorescent light fixture behind the rotifer cultures provides light.

A fairly large container, a tough 20 gallon plastic garbage can, for example, can be used to contain used rotifer culture water before disposal. This enriched water may also be used to grow out brine shrimp for fish and reef tank use. There should be enough light in the culture area so that a separate light over the container is not needed. Some light is needed if brine shrimp are grown in this container. The container is partially or completely emptied as necessary.

Operation of the culture system. Starter cultures of algae and rotifers can be obtained from various sources. The biology or marine science department of a nearby university *may* have cultures and be willing to provide a seed culture. A large aquarium shop may have cultures or know of a hobbyist that will share. There are a number of commercial sources. Florida Aqua Farms provides algae cultures, resting rotifer eggs, and culture equipment to hobbyists. Other biological supply firms and firms that supply marine algaes to hobbyists may also provide various micro algae cultures.

The algae cultures must be started first, of course. They are started in sequence, one each day. The first culture started is ready for harvest after 7 to 10 days. It is fed to the rotifer culture and the container cleaned and restarted as a new culture. One culture is harvested and restarted each day to keep the algae culture system in continuous production. If several days go by without harvest and renewal, the culture continuity may be broken if old cultures bloom out and crash, and there may be a gap of a few days in the production of algae.

Algae culture water should be prepared with a good grade of artificial sea salt. In most instances, tap water is fine for the make up of the algae culture water, but if difficulties in getting algae cultures to bloom are encountered, try using bottled water and see if that makes a difference. The salinity of the seawater mix should be somewhere between 20 to 30 ppt (1.015 to 1.022 SG). Although the exact salinity is not important, it is important to use the same salinity for all the cultures every time. The saltwater for the algal cultures can be made up and stored in a large container or made up in the algae culture container two to four hours before starting the culture. Adding about two tablespoons per quart produces a salinity of about 25 ppt. Making up the salt solution directly in the algae culture vessel eliminates saltwater storage and the possibility of contamination of the stored water. Algae cultures can be started from cells plated onto disks or in liquid samples. If plated cultures are used, gently rub the disks in the culture water to release plated cells into the water.

Algae cultures require fertilization to come to a dense bloom at every start up. Nitrogen and phosphorous need to be supplied, and the B vitamin complex, particularly B12, thiamine and biotin are also important since most microalgaes can not synthesize these vitamins, and they are not available as trace elements in salt mixes. Other required trace elements such as iron, copper, zinc, magnesium, cobalt, vanadium, calcium and molybdenum are variably present in sea salt mixes. Commercial preparations with exactly the right mix of nutrients and vitamins for microalgae culture are available from several companies. If a commercial preparation specifically designed for microalgae is not available, an aquarist can experiment with one of the many soluble, complete plant foods available for house plants and vegetables. An eighth to a half teaspoon of one of these preparations per gallon may allow the algae to bloom in the culture container. A drop or two of a B vitamin complex may also help.

Experimentation on the part of the aquarist is required to determine the amount of a specific combination fertilizer required for the best algal growth. Extract from garden soil, as described in Chapter 4, may also be used to stimulate growth of algae cultures, but who knows what strange compounds might be in such extracts. Each algae container is filled with the same volume of new saltwater, fertilized, and inoculated with algae from a dense, vigorous culture at each start up. Each day the oldest culture is harvested and a new culture started. The harvested culture is fed to the rotifer cultures. An ounce or two of the harvested culture (or of a younger culture if the older one is turning a little yellowish) is used to start the new culture.

Microalgae cultures can become contaminated with blue-green algae, ciliates, rotifers, and bacteria. If this occurs, and dense algae cultures are difficult or impossible to develop, the best course of action is to clean and sterilize all culture equipment with bleach and begin again with a new inoculum of a pure algae culture.

The two rotifer cultures are run as needed. It is important to have an active culture of rotifers at all times to avoid complete loss of the culture. It is sometimes wise to set up a small third rotifer culture in a old algae culture (removed from the algae shelf). If only one rotifer culture is active, there is a possibility that it may crash (suddenly die out). If a rotifer culture suddenly crashes and no live rotifers can be found to start a new culture, placing detritus from the bottom of the old culture into a new culture *may* save resting eggs and start rotifer populations once again. Feed and harvest rotifers daily to maintain vigorous population growth. Overharvesting and underharvesting are both detrimental to the maintenance of the culture.

Brine shrimp are a very important live food source for marine aquarists. They are often available as live, grown adults in small portions from aquarium shops. It is expensive to purchase them in this form, but live brine shrimp are greedily enjoyed by most freshwater and marine aquarium fish. The other alternative is to rear them yourself. Brine shrimp cysts (eggs) can also be purchased and then hatched by the aquarist. The cysts hatch out about 24 hours after placing them in seawater. Newly hatched larval brine shrimp (napulii) have a rich yolk sac and are an excellent food for large larvae and many filter feeders. The yolk is soon used up in growth of the brine shrimp, and if brine shrimp in larval or adult stages are held long without food, their food value to other animals sharply decreases. Moe (1982) and Florida Aqua Farms (1987) have detailed sections on hatching and growth of brine shrimp.

Brine shrimp cysts can be hatched in gallon jars, plastic soda bottles, and specially designed hatcheries. They should have moderate light, full salinity saltwater, temperatures in the high 70's °F, and continuous strong aeration. After hatching, remove aeration and allow the empty egg cases to float to the top and the unhatched eggs to sink to the bottom. The hatched

napulii are attracted to light and will accumulate at some point in the hatchery where light is brightest. They can be siphoned from that point into a fine mesh net for transfer to a rearing container or to be fed to other organisms. Avoid including any hatched or unhatched eggs with the harvested nauplii. Some of the hatched brine shrimp can be reared in the waste water can under the rotifer

Brine shrimp napulii

tanks. They will feed well on waste algae and can also be fed lightly on yeast or other powered preparations. They can be netted from the can and fed to larger fish when they gain the proper size.

It is important to avoid including the unhatched cysts or the empty shells of the hatched cysts with the napulii that are to be fed to larval fish. The hard protein cyst walls are not digestible and can plug small intestinal passages and kill larval fish. Professional marine culturists now remove the hard protein walls from brine shrimp cysts before hatching and feeding the napulii. This process, termed "decapsulation", removes the thin brown covering and the thick white wall from around the thin membrane that encloses the orange embryo. The decapsulated cyst is then hatched normally. After hatch, there are no coarse empty shells and all unhatched cysts can still be fed and digested by larvae and filter feeders. Decapsulated brine shrimp cysts are stored in heavy brine after decapsulation and are now available in small quantities to hobbyists. Decapsulation of brine shrimp cysts is a complex process that involves dangerous chemicals and is not something the average aquarist can do in a garage or kitchen.

Briefly, the procedure for **decapsulation of brine shrimp** cysts is as follows. The cysts, 50 to 100 grams, are first hydrated in seawater for one hour, drained, and then placed in a solution of 33 ml of 40 % sodium hydroxide and 600 ml of Clorox® (5.25 % NaOCl). This mixture is stirred continuously to keep all cysts in solution. This mixture heats up and ice should be added to keep the mixture below 40°C. This should be done under a chemical hood or with eye and body protection. Watch the color of the cysts closely. They will turn from brown to white to orange in 10 to 15 minutes. Continue treatment for a few minutes after most of the cysts are bright orange. Not all cysts will decapsulate. Drain and wash the cysts over a fine mesh screen. Immerse the cysts in water and add 5 to 10 ml of 1 % sodium thiosulfate solution to remove all traces of the chlorine bleach. Place the decapsulated cysts in about 700 ml of brine (300 g or one cup of artificial sea salt mix to one liter of water) and aerate for four hours. The decapsulated cysts sink to the bottom and shelled cysts float. Skim off the floating cysts and store the decapsulated cysts in brine water until hatching. Store under refrigeration and hatch as usual in a typical brine shrimp hatchery at normal salinity within a few days. Longer storage times of several weeks can be obtained by storing at -4°C. Cysts from various sources may require modifications of the above technique for best results. Sorgeloos, et. al. (1977) is a good technical reference to brine shrimp decapsulation.

Marsh and estuarine systems
Most marine aquarists will have little interest in creating a marsh or estuarine system, although there are more to such systems than meets the eye. An estuarine system is run at salinities of 5 to 15 ppt and includes the plants and animals found in those broad areas where freshwater mixes with the sea. In nature, the salinities of these areas change with tide and season. It is not necessary to change salinities in an estuarine aquarium system, however, to gain an appreciation of the life in this environment. A traditional or reef type system will allow one to build a community of organisms typical of tropical or

temperate estuarine conditions. The aquarist will also have to collect the organisms for the system, for few aquarium stores carry such creatures. Some freshwater fish such as scats, monos, clown loaches, and mollies are typical brackish, estuarine fish and will fit quite well into such a system.

A marsh system is more rare than a brackish or estuarine system. This type of system requires a section of thick muddy sediment, anaerobic at the bottom, in which marsh grass and other vegetation grows and a section of flowing brackish or fully marine water that circulates through the marsh and a filter system. Fishes and invertebrates that occupy such areas are kept in simulated natural conditions and much of their natural life cycles can be observed.

Tidal systems

Tidal systems are similar to marsh systems in that the object of the system is the area at the edge of the sea. Only public aquariums usually have the expertise and funding to create a good tidal system. Water levels have to be controlled on a simulated tidal basis, rising and falling by the hour. Wave action on the shore is also occasionally simulated. Such an effect can be created with a system of storage tanks and timed valves and pumps. It would be most interesting and different to put something like this together, and I'm sure the aquarist that creates such a system will have the only one on the block.

Future trends

And where do we go from here? I think we will see development in four directions: toward sophisticated small systems, into spectacular large systems, undoubtedly use of computer controls for automated systems, and increased development of a broad support industry of food, livestock, and equipment. Reef systems are near the beginning, not the end, of biological and technical developments in marine aquarium keeping. Small systems will become more and more complex with improved lighting and filtration, and I think we shall see selection and marketing of organisms particularly suited for small, mini systems. Large systems may include open pools and display tanks run off the same large filtration units with larger fish and invertebrates in the pools. Wave generators may be developed that will create even more natural environments for coral growth in large systems. Some wave surge units are already available.

A greater understanding and appreciation of the biology of natural areas will encourage development of more systems that strive to replicate a particular environment. We may see multi tank systems that physically separate environments, a marsh and a reef, in separate tanks, yet have a common filter system. The biological activity of each system complements the other but, as in nature, the environments are separate.

Collection techniques must improve and breeding will become more successful and more widespread. Commercial techniques now restricted to oysters, clams, abalones, shrimp, and fish can be modified and applied to ornamental marine organisms; and specialized new techniques will be developed. I think marine aquarists will have a lot of fun and accomplish a great deal in the next 20 years.

Chapter 6

Foods and Feeding of Marine Invertebrates

Feeding Modes

Feeding most species of marine fish is relatively easy. There are many commercial fish foods available that do a good job, and a few small pieces of frozen shrimp, oysters, and scallops along with algae, lettuce, and spinach complete the basic feeding requirements for most fish. Moe (1982) has a chapter on foods and feeding that covers everything but the most particular and specialized marine fish food requirements. Many invertebrates feed the same way as fish. They pick up a bit of food, kill it, mash it or grind it, stuff it in their gut, digest out whatever nutrition they can, and then get rid of the undigestible waste. This is a familiar feeding pattern, one that most people can relate to very closely. In fact, this feeding pattern is so common that we may not even recognize other types of feeding behavior and may inadvertently starve some invertebrates that have more exotic methods of obtaining nutrients.

Many invertebrates depend as much, or more so, on lighting, water chemistry, and sediments for their nutrition as on particulate foods. For many invertebrates, lighting, water quality, and culture techniques are as nutritionally important as the food that is routinely placed in the tank.

Parasitism is an important feeding mode in nature, although this is not a feeding mode an aquarist strives to pro-

vide. Many marine invertebrates are parasitic on other invertebrates, fish, and even marine mammals. Few marine
aquarists, except for scientists, are interested in keeping
parasites. In fact, the aquarist that speaks of a tank of parasites
is probably not talking about his aquatic interests.

Many internal and external parasites are present in marine
aquariums, and some can become a serious problem to the
organisms in the tank. Parasites feed on their host and may
debilitate and even kill the host in rare instances. In nature, the
parasite and its prey exist in an uneasy balance. Unlike a sym-
botic relationship that provides mutual benefit, only one participant benefits from a host-parasite relationship. If the
parasite is too successful, it may drive its host, and itself, to
extinction. On the other hand, if the host species is too successful in protecting itself from the parasite, the parasite faces extinction. This balance is broken in the artificial environment of
a marine aquarium, and if the parasite can close its life cycle, as
can the dinoflagellate *Amyloodinium*, then the host, captive to
the aquarist and the parasite, suffers extreme infection.

In nature, two or more species can not occupy the same
ecological niche. They can not live in exactly the same
microhabitat and feed on exactly the same foods. Such competition either drives one species to extinction or creates changes in one, both, or all species that are in conflict. Every species
is special in some way, or it can not survive. Ecology and
evolutionary biology are the broad scientific disciplines that
provide an understanding of the relationships between organisms and their environments. The organisms of the sea have
endured hundreds of millions of years of competition and
biological divergence and exhibit a vast array of feeding
strategies.

Many marine animals utilize more than one way to gain
nutritional energy. They may be part filter feeders, scavengers,
and farmers, as are many corals, or may graze, eat sediment,
and absorb dissolved nutrients as well, as do some
echinoderms. To keep these organisms in marine aquarium
systems, we must give them an adequate substitute for their

natural environmental and nutritional requirements. In many situations this is relatively simple—a hiding place and a piece of shrimp for a crab. In other situations it is rather complex—bacterioplankton, strong water flows, and proper light levels for a sponge. Because of great diversity, complexity, and overlap of feeding modes, it is difficult, if not impossible, to organize the feeding modes of marine invertebrates into neat little categories that describes how each group satisfies their nutritional requirements. But, of course, we must try.

Filter feeders
    The term filter feeder refers to the capture and ingestion by a feeding animal of an organism or particle suspended in water. The filter feeder "captures" a flow of water by either creating a current through its body (oysters and sponges) or by extending outward into a current (basket stars and coral polyps); and then feeding on the proper food particles that happen to drift into its net. This broad definition includes the capture of a fish larvae in the outstretched net of a basket star, a copepod speared and entangled in the nematocysts of a coral polyp, a phytoplankter captured in the mucus net on the gills of an oyster, and bacterioplankton drawn into the tiny pores of a sponge and captured and digested by the collar cells that line the internal passages of the sponge. These are all very different feeding modes that utilize very different kinds and sizes of food organisms; yet they are all types of filter feeding since they depend on suspended food particles.
    Filter feeders usually capture plankton within a particular size range. The **macroplankton** is large, over 1 mm, and is taken mostly by "plankton pickers", predators that select individual organisms from the currents. The **microplankton**, 60 to 1000 microns, are mostly zooplankters. **Nanoplankton** is in the range of 5 to 60 microns and is mostly phytoplankton, although a lot of zooplankters also fall into this size range. The **ultraplankton** is below 5 microns and is mostly very small flagellates and bacteria. Most filter feeders are sessile animals and depend on water currents to bring food to their place of

attachment. Scallops, however, have the power to move about. They filter the particle rich water just above the sediments and can move to avoid sedimentation and predators, and to find the best feeding areas. It is important to know the size and kind of food a particular filter feeder requires. The structure of the planktonic community is discussed in Chapter 3.

Predators

A predator is an animal that seeks out and kills a specific food organism and then ingests all or part of it. It may lay in wait or actively seek its prey, but it always selects a specific food organism. This may occur in the blink of an eye, as a mantis shrimp captures a small fish and disappears into the rocks, or in agonizing slow motion as a starfish surrounds a clam and finally opens it after hours of pulling the valves apart. It then inserts its stomach into the clam and digests the animal in its own shell. A predator may have very specific prey organisms, such as the flamingo tongue snail that feeds only on gorgonians, or have broad tastes, such as a spiny lobster that feeds on anything it can catch from mollusks to crustaceans to fish. Obviously, the more catholic the predator (meaning the more prey organisms it will accept), the easier it is to feed.

Most generalized predators readily take various types of prepared particle foods. Many animals, such as clownfish, are planktonic predators and swim in the passing currents selecting particular planktonic organisms that sweep past. Others, such as some crabs, are benthic predators and comb the bottom sediments and growths for small worms and mollusks. The cleaner shrimp are also predators, although their prey is delivered to their doorstep by fish that carry external parasites.

Scavengers

A scavenger feeds on dead or dying organisms or decaying organic matter. There are few absolute scavengers among the organisms that interest most marine aquarists, but many predators are opportunistic scavengers. A shark, a lobster, a tulip snail, and an octopus would not hesitate to feed on a fish head tossed over the side of a boat, but none of them can make a living feeding only as a scavenger. Scavenging is important to deep sea animals that live at depths where light does not power photosynthesis. Although predation is very important in the depths, the only source of new food is dead organisms that fall from above. Animals that feed only on accumulated detritus may be considered scavengers, but utilization of a specialized food source is a more accurate description. Some corals may even be considered scavengers since they feed heavily on the droppings of fish that hover over the reefs during the day.

Other animals, such as hermit crabs, may scavenge when possible on the reef, but rely almost exclusively on their scavenging abilities when in captivity. Their natural foods are almost absent in many systems, and they can not compete with fish and other invertebrates for fresh food particles, so they make their living scrounging the tank for bits of food missed by other, faster creatures.

Grazers

A grazer is an animal that consumes part of a vegetative growth for its own sustenance, usually without destroying the food organism which continues to exist and grow. Grazers and vegetation live in precarious balance throughout nature, each constantly developing special attributes to enhance either consumption or protection from consumption. The existence of each, however, is dependent on the existence of the other. There are many "secondary grazers" in the sea, animals that consume considerable algae along with other food organisms. Adult Atlantic angelfish, for example, fed heavily on sponges and pick up a lot of algae in this rather indiscriminate feeding behavior. In fact, an angelfish seldom eats the entire sponge, which can grow back—so in one sense the angelfish can be said to graze on sponges and parrot fish to graze on corals. Many sea urchins and chitons graze on tiny algae growths on rocks, and many mollusks and some fish feed exclusively on macro algae growths.

Sediment feeders

There's a lot of organic energy in marine sediments. Detritus, bacteria, tiny plants and animals, and organic compounds exist in their own little ecosystem nestled between the grains of sand and silt. Larger animals can use this food source if they eat everything and let their digestive system sort things out. Some fish, like the hogfish, *Lachnolaimus maximus*, are heavy into sediments, but some of the sea urchins and sea cucumbers are the champion sediment feeders. They burrow into the sediments and, like earthworms, eat their way through the sand and silt of the bottom. Some sea urchins do not burrow, but are "deposit feeders" that feed indiscriminately on the surface sediments and pack their gut with the detritus, sand, and shell that forms the upper sediment layer of the bottom. Some animals—round worms, some flatworms, some crustaceans—feed almost exclusively on soft, organic detrital sediments. Other animals such as clams, sea pens, and worms depend on the hard sediments to construct protective burrows or cemented tubes, and feed on particles suspended just above the soft bottom. The grain size and structure of the sediments is very important to these animals, and they live only where the proper sediment structure exists.

Farmers

A "farmer" is an animal that supports and encourages the growth of a separate organism, usually one capable of photosynthesis, that contributes to its own sustenance. This is often considered a symbiotic relationship since the animal offers the plant environmental protection and perhaps CO_2, nitrogen, and trace elements in exchange for food production. Unlike a parasitic relationship, the animal-plant association is usually essential for the survival of both species and the photosynthetic organism may provide all the food necessary for the existence of both. The corals and sponges with their *zooxanthellae* are the most well known "farmers"; although some mollusks such as the giant clam, *Tridacna*, and the lettuce slug, *Tridachia*, also harbor photosynthetic organisms.

Solution feeders

Marine animals live in intimacy with the solution of the sea. In fact, many species use seawater as part of their bodily fluids. Many dissolved compounds in seawater—amino acids, sugars, vitamins, and other organics and inorganics—are taken up with seawater and contribute directly to the nutritional requirements of the animal. Much work has yet to be done on exactly what compounds in what concentrations are required by various animals. The cnidarians (corals), annelids (worms), and echinoderms (starfish and sea urchins) are the popular marine invertebrates that are probably most dependent on dissolved compounds in seawater.

All of these modes of feeding are important to the marine aquarist that maintains invertebrates. Even if the specific requirements of the animals in culture are not known, attempts can be made to provide the basic elements of the general feeding modes of the animals present in the tank. Table 9 provides information on the natural foods of the broad groups of invertebrates that are commonly kept in marine systems. Use this table only as a general guide, for each group has many species and many exceptions to the rule. Additional information on these groups and some comments on more specific feeding behavior are included in Chapter 8.

This information will get one started on an acceptable feeding program for most invertebrates, but note that the natural feeding behavior of many specific species is not known. An aquarist will have to experiment to find acceptable substitutes for natural foods for the particular species under culture. The second section of this chapter provides a summary of the foods and feeding techniques generally available to marine aquarists in all of the major categories of marine invertebrate foods. A really serious marine aquarist/culturist will go to the scientific literature to learn as much as possible about feeding the organisms they wish to culture. The Proceedings of the World Mariculture Society is an excellent place to start and Tamura (1970) and Bardach, et. al. (1972) are good general references to commercial culture of marine organisms.

Table 9. Foods and feeding modes of selected marine Invertebrates.

Organism	Feeding Modes	Natural Foods
Porifera A-2		
sponges	filter feeders, farmers, solution feeders	nanoplankton, ultraplankton, low light levels, vitamins, organics
Cnidaria A-3		
corals, anemones	filter feeders, farmers, solution feeders	microplankton, macroplankton, high light levels, vitamins
Platyhelminthes A-6		
flatworms	predators, scavengers	small benthic organisms, worms, small crustaceans
Ectoprocta A-17		
bryozoans	filter feeders, solution feeders	nanoplankton vitamins, organics ?
Mollusca A-20		
Chitons	grazers	encrusting algaes
Gastropods		
snails, slugs	predators grazers	echinoderms, other mollusks, macro and micro algaes
Pelecypods		
clams	farmers, filter feeders	high light levels, nanoplankton
oysters		
scallops		
Cephalopods		
octopus	predators, scavengers	fish, crustaceans, other mollusks
squid		
nautilus		
Annelida A-24		
bristleworms	predators, scavengers	small benthic animals, detritus
fanworms	filter feeders, solution feeders	micro and nanoplankton, vitamins, organics

Organism	Feeding Modes	Natural Foods
Arthropoda A-28		
horseshoe crabs	predators, scavengers	small clams, worms, other small benthic animals
barnacles	filter feeders	microplankton
mantis shrimps	predators	fish, crustaceans
shrimps, crabs, hermit crabs, lobsters	predators, scavengers, grazers	mollusks, other small marine animals, micro and macroalgae, parasites, detritus (various species, various foods)
Echinodermata A-30		
Feather stars	filter feeders, solution feeders	microplankton, macroplankton, vitamins, organics
Starfish	predators, scavengers, solution feeders	mollusks, small benthic animals, vitamins, organics
Basket stars	filter feeders, solution feeders	macroplankton, vitamins, organics
Brittle stars	predators, scavengers, solution feeders	small benthic animals, vitamins, organics
Sea urchins	sediment feeders, grazers, solution feeders	organics in marine sediments, encrusting algae, macroalgae
Sea cucumbers	filter feeders, sediment feeders, solution feeders	micro and nanoplankton, organics in marine sediments, vitamins, organics
Chordata A-33		
Tunicates	filter feeders	micro and nanoplankton
Fish	predators, scavengers, grazers	all other marine animals, encrusting and macroalgae

Foods and Feeding Techniques

The following section pertains primarily to feeding marine invertebrates. Moe (1982) contains a chapter on foods and feeding for marine fish. As in feeding marine fish, remember that overfeeding is a greater danger than underfeeding. Also, the more variety in foods and feeding, the better—especially when processed foods are the main food base for the system.

Live Foods

Live foods require the most time, trouble, and expense from the aquarist, but they are better for the animals and the system than dead foods. Live foods stimulate the animals to feed, provide close to a complete nutritional package, contribute to less detrital accumulation, tend to remain alive until eaten thus increasing food utilization efficiency, and reduce accumulation of organics. The amount of live food an aquarist can feed depends primarily on how much time the aquarist is willing to spend on the hobby. The expense is not great, but "live food factories" do require extra effort. Most aquarists settle on a mix of some live food and some prepared food, depending on their individual situation. There are many live food possibilities for marine aquarists. Some are tried and true, and some require experimentation to determine what works best in each situation. There are so many variables that any particular live food culture may work in some instances and fail in others.

Planktonic Food Organisms

Marine invertebrates live in an environment that is always rich in plankton. Although this natural environment can not be duplicated in a marine aquarium system, the best substitute is addition of live cultures of planktonic organisms that remain suspended in the water for some time. However, the very filtration system the aquarist depends upon to maintain high water quality quickly removes most suspended particles and/or organisms. Thus filtration in the system should be suspended for one to two hours when feeding live planktonic organisms. Water must be moved strongly about the tank during the feeding time, and air lifts and small powerhead pumps can serve this purpose.

Excess nutrients are introduced into the marine aquarium system with the feeding of cultured live foods, especially in the case of infusoria and phytoplankton when the culture medium is introduced along with the cultured organism. Whenever possible, it is important to separate the cultured organism from the culture medium with nets or sieves and transfer the cultured organism to clean saltwater before feeding. If the nutrient rich culture water is fed along with the nanoplankton and ultraplankton, which is usually necessary, it is helpful to feed sparingly and directly in the vicinity of the target specimen.

The frequency of feeding varies with the system. Once a day is probably the greatest feeding frequency that may be required and once a week the least. Two or three times a week may be a good initial frequency until the aquarist can determine if this is too often or not often enough. Unlike dead particles, live organisms remain suspended until they are eaten or die, so it is not necessary to liberate the food within a particular area of the tank unless a specific target organism is being fed. The planktonic organisms can be poured onto the surface, and they soon diffuse throughout the tank. A baster with a long tube can be used to direct a stream of plankton towards a particular specimen if necessary.

Most filter feeders feed mostly at night. It is important to feed filter feeders when they are expanded in the feeding mode. If daytime filter feeders are present in the tank, a daytime feeding once or twice a week may be in order. Cultured phytoplankton, cultured rotifers, new hatch brine shrimp, and grown out brine shrimp are the most common types of marine plankton fed to reef tanks and larval rearing systems, although there are other possibilities some aquarists may wish to try. A variety of planktonic foods, including the most common, are listed below.

It is possible to freeze planktonic foods at times of abundance, and then thaw and feed them at times of scarcity. Of course, the organisms are also dead when they are thawed, and in many instances, freezing has caused the containing membranes of the tiny organisms to burst. If so, body fluids escape when the organism is thawed, and food value is greatly diminished. Also, a dead organism will not keep itself suspended in the water column, and it quickly settles out on the bottom. Even so, frozen plankton is often far better than blended shrimp or scallop for filter feeding animals. It is even possible to rear some marine tropical fish through the larval stage on frozen rotifers if care is taken not to over feed and to keep the tank bottom clean. If you do wish to freeze planktonic organisms, first concentrate the organisms as much as possible in about half strength seawater. Then freeze the mixture in ice cube trays as quickly as possible. The frozen cubes can be stored in air tight plastic bags and removed, thawed, and fed as required. Feed with the same techniques as dead particulate foods.

Marine infusoria. Freshwater aquarists are well acquainted with infusoria. Hay or dried grass clippings are mixed with a jar of pond water, and in time a rich culture of protozoa, tiny animals, and algae develops. This is then used to feed the fry of freshwater fish. The same sort of thing can be done in the marine world. First, a ten gallon tank, or other suitable container, is filled with seawater or saltwater from an active system. Water from an aged aquarium is best for it already has organics and nitrifying bacteria. A live rock from the system, or the sea shore, is scrubbed in the tank to release algal spores, bacteria, and detritus. Some encrusting algae from a good system can also be added. A little fertilizer and perhaps a few drops of B vitamins, an air stone to keep things gently rolling, a good light for photosynthesis, and who knows what will bloom in the tank. A good marine infusoria culture often develops, and the result is many varied types of plankton that provide food for larval animals and filter feeders. A little live bakers yeast added to the culture often helps it along and gives it a longer life. Microplankton, nanoplankton, and ultraplankton grow, and the variety can feed many different types of filter feeders. The yeast and bacteria can be fed carefully to sponges on an experimental basis. The microplankton in the culture can be harvested by fine mesh net. Phytoplankton and ultraplankton is present in the water that goes through a 35 to 53 micron, plankton net sieve, and microplankton is captured above the sieve.

There is some danger in such a culture, especially when natural seawater or material from wild sea bottoms is used for seed, because it is possible for undesirable planktonic and benthic animals to be introduced to the tank. Once a good culture is developed, it may be possible to harvest the microorganisms in the culture for a couple of weeks before the culture crashes. If the culture is a good one, it can be used to seed the next culture. Sometimes, however, this type of culture does not work and the water gets clear as gin with a layer of dark sticky stuff on the bottom. Then it's time to discard the culture and try again, perhaps with a little less fertilizer and more light. Marine infusorias are not as predictable as their freshwater counterparts.

Freshwater infusoria. Freshwater infusorias can also be created and fed to marine filter feeders. The advantages are that freshwater infusorias are easy and inexpensive to culture, and the organisms can not survive and do not have the potential to cause problems in marine systems. The disadvantages are that the organisms rupture and die when introduced to salt waters and must be carefully fed to particular specimens to be effective as food organisms. It would be interesting to experiment with brackish water infusorias, which may be more stable and productive than marine cultures, yet more adaptable as food for marine organisms.

Phytoplankton culture. Cultured phytoplankton falls into the size range of nanoplankton. Most filter feeders take zooplankters in the microplankton size range, but phytoplankton is important to some sponges, clams, scallops, and other filter feeders and many types of invertebrate larvae. Phytoplankton culture can be easily done by a home aquarist. A typical home phytoplankton culture system is described in Chapter 5.

Rotifer culture. The best way to produce large numbers of small zooplankters in the microplankton range is to raise rotifers, *Brachionus plicatilis*. In width and length, adult rotifers are in the area of 75 to 300 microns. The culture of rotifers is described in Chapter 5. Corals, anemones, feather stars, and many types of fish and invertebrate larvae greatly appreciate fat, well fed rotifers and new hatch brine shrimp.

New hatch brine shrimp. Brine shrimp, *Artemia salina*, hatch out into a nauplii stage that has a large orange yolk. The yolk is rich in oils and nutrients and makes a very good food for filter feeders and marine larvae that prey on larger microplankton. The amount of brine shrimp cultured is easily controlled by the number of cysts (eggs) that are hatched. This element of control, and the high nutritious value of brine shrimp napulii, gives this species great value as a food for cultured marine animals. New hatch brine shrimp are about 400 microns long and quickly increase in size during the 24 hours after hatch. Brine shrimp napulii are an excellent food for most corals and other filter feeders that prefer large zooplankters. It is not good to wait to feed new hatch brine shrimp, for they quickly loose their nutritious yolk and gain rapidly in size. Hatching and rearing brine shrimp is discussed in Chapter 5.

Grown out brine shrimp. Brine shrimp are essentially pelagic animals. They continuously swim in the water column, although they do visit the sides and bottom of rearing containers. They are filter feeders themselves and take small organic particles and nanoplankton from the water. Brine shrimp can be reared on yeast or phytoplankton and will even grow to maturity in just organic rich water. I have heard of some commercial hatcheries that used to rear brine shrimp in large outdoor ponds by tossing in dead sea gulls and road killed possums once in a while. This is not recommended! It does say something for the hardiness of brine shrimp, however. Modern hatcheries that use grown out brine shrimp use foods specially prepared in nutritional content and particle size for brine shrimp and pay attention to the water quality of the cultures. Full grown brine shrimp vary between 5 and 10 mm long and are an excellent live food for plankton pickers and filter feeders that take macroplankton. Basket stars, anemones, and some corals take large brine shrimp. The grow out of brine shrimp is discussed in Chapter 5.

Copepods. Copepods make up perhaps 95% of the plankton and may be the most numerous animals on Earth. They are rich in waxy esters and marine oils and form the nutritional base for many populations of marine animals. However, they are difficult to culture in numbers great enough for routine feeding purposes. Rotifers have a hatch to reproduction cycle of a day or two, which allows development of great numbers in the space of a couple of weeks. Copepods, on the other hand, take almost a month to complete a reproductive cycle. This means that although copepods are not difficult to grow, it is difficult to create and maintain a culture that can produce sufficient copepods to sustain a large population of rapidly growing larvae. Copepod nauplii are in the range of 30 to 80 microns, small microplankton, and make an excellent first food for many larval fish and invertebrates. It is possible to selectively remove the small copepod larvae, the napulii, by straining the culture through a sieve (90 to 130 micron mesh) that will capture the adults and pass the young. The young can then be used for feeding, and the adults returned to culture to continue breeding.

Copepods will probably be a major component of any "marine infusoria" culture that is developed. The harpacticoid copepods are the species most frequently cultured. The adults are benthic and live in bottom muds and sediments, but the larval forms are pelagic and can be collected to feed to other organisms. Copepod cultures can be based on yeast, ground rice bran, phytoplankton, and other foods adequate for the culture of rotifers and brine shrimp. Foods such as finely ground rice bran and yeast must be sparingly fed to avoid pollution of the rearing culture. Lamm (1988) presents an article on home culture of copepods and the scientific literature holds many papers on copepod culture.

Marine protozoa. Undoubtedly, marine ciliates will appear in marine infusorias. They may often completely take over such cultures. In general, they are small and have little food value unless they are fed just before feeding them to other organisms. Marine ciliates in the genus *Euplotes* often contaminate rotifer and phytoplankton cultures and are sometimes fed to larvae and filter feeders along with the specifically cultured organism. The advantages of culturing marine protozoa, ciliates in particular, are their small size and rapid reproductive rate. Certain animals may require or do well on a food organism that is in the range of 20 to 50 microns, the size of many marine protozoa. A number of dinoflagellates, *Gymnodinium* sp., and ciliates are relatively easy to culture and fall within this size range. There are many, many species of marine protozoa, and an enterprising aquarist may well come up with a hardy, nutritious species that is easy to culture and that makes a good food base for filter feeders and marine larvae. Marine bacteria, small phytoplankters, and yeast can support cultures of marine protozoa.

Wild plankton. This is the natural food of filter feeders and planktonic larvae. It occurs in abundance in most marine environments in all sizes and many species and can be captured, sorted, and fed to filter feeders and marine larval forms. Of course the danger of getting species that are undesirable for larval cultures (chaetognaths and medusae) and reef systems (blue-green algae and fish parasites) is considerable. Freezing wild plankton collections preserves some of the desireable nutritional qualities of this food and removes the possibility of introduction of unwanted live organisms. To collect wild plankton one needs a plankton net, a bridge and a current or a boat; and of course, a relatively unpolluted marine environment. Official plankton nets are made from nylon mesh cloth that is carefully manufactured to produce a specific mesh size, and they are usually labeled with the size of the mesh opening in microns—a 53 micron net or a 120 micron net, for example. A variety of mesh sizes are available. A mesh size that is too small, below 35 to 53 microns, will rapidly clog and will not catch a lot of plankton. Mesh sizes that are too large, over 120 microns, will allow too much small plankton to escape thought the net.

Plankton nets are of various sizes; a half meter net has a round mouth with a diameter of a half meter. A jar or other collector is clamped on the tail end of the net; the mouth of the net is tied to a sturdy brass or steel ring to keep it open, and a rope or wire bridle is rigged to this ring to pull the net directly into the current. The net is pulled slowly by boat or held into a current off a bridge or dock. The water filters through the net and the plankton that can not slip through the mesh is captured in the jar. After 15 to 30 minutes depending on the density of the plankton, the net is pulled and the contents of the jar are poured into a couple of gallons of water in a holding container, usually with an air stone at the bottom to keep the plankton suspended and aerated. The resulting collection, two or three tows, is poured through a 1 mm screen (plastic window screen) to remove the large organisms and trash, and the collection can then be sorted further or fed or frozen as it stands. Plankton quickly dies and decays, so it is good to allow it to settle for a five minutes or so and discard the sediment that collects on the bottom. Moe (1982) discusses wild plankton as a food for the larvae of tropical marine fish.

Live baby guppies. Many filter feeders (basket stars, bubble coral, anemones) like large macroplankton organisms, and aside from grown out brine shrimp, this is hard to come by. One source is a population of "trash guppies" kept in a freshwater aquarium. Production of young is regular and abundant in a well kept guppy tank, and the excess young can be fed to these filter feeders. The young guppies live long enough in the saltwater to be alive when captured by the filter feeders. They will also be avidly eaten by any plankton picking fish in the tank, so they are best fed after dark and directed to the specific filter feeder that one wishes to feed.

Spawns within the tank. A reef system tank, one that has the ecological balance and water quality to maintain a variety of filter feeders and algaes, is capable of supporting numerous animals that can spawn regularly within the tank. These may include various worms, copepods, shrimp (small cleaner shrimp that live in pairs are regular spawners), other crustaceans, sea urchins, clownfish and gobies. The larvae produced by these spawns can not escape to the plankton pastures at the surface of the open sea and are quickly consumed by filter feeders and plankton pickers within the tank. Only a very few larvae spawned in nature, perhaps less than one percent, are able to survive, reproduce, and carry on the species. Most larvae quickly enter the bottom levels of the food chain of the community. A good reef tank mirrors the natural environment as much as possible, and encouragement and use of spawns within a reef tank system is an important and very interesting management stratagem in reef tank maintenance. Such spawns not only add to the ecological balance of the system, they provide exceptional opportunities for the aquarist to observe, learn, and even attempt to rear the various larvae that are produced.

Benthic Food Organisms

Live benthic food organisms are more easily replaced by processed dead food particles than are planktonic organisms. Most reef system tanks have few predatory animals and have little requirement for live, benthic food organisms. Other aquarists, however, are more interested in the predatory invertebrates than the sessile filter feeders and farmers, and maintain a more dynamic type of reef tank. Tanks with a large number of predators have more activity, and the ecological balance changes more rapidly. The addition of live benthic food organisms benefits this type of system. Most marine predators that feed primarily on small benthic animals readily adapt to processed or natural food particles offered by the aquarist, and it is possible to maintain a predator based marine system on processed foods. However, it is very beneficial to carnivorous mollusks, crabs, shrimp, lobsters, starfish, brittle stars, and fish to offer them small live or fresh dead prey organisms once in a while. Anemones benefit from live prey such as small amphipods and shrimp, small freshwater fish, brine shrimp, and even worms. Capture and consumption of the active live prey organism stimulates the nerve network of the anemone and results in a better feeding response.

Marine benthic food organisms. It is difficult to provide small, live, marine benthic food organisms if one does not live near the sea. Some amphipods (small shrimp-like crustaceans) can be cultured in separate systems, or even in the main tank, and will provide a live organism food for many small predators. One species of small Atlantic amphipod makes a nest of detrital and algal material and emerges at night to feed on algae. It is easy to culture and may be an excellent food organism for small crabs and other predatory crustaceans. Other amphipods are very common on the beaches among piles of decaying seaweed. These beach hoppers or beach fleas can be easily collected by shaking seaweed over a box or net. Other small marine animals, shrimp and other crustaceans, and small mollusks can be collected in shallow water with nets or seines and held in a separate system for feeding to the main tank over a period of days. Small coquina clams (*Donax*) can often be collected in large numbers on the beaches in the intertidal areas and make excellent food organisms. Oysters and barnacles can be scraped from pilings and also make good food organisms. Many small mollusks live in the sediments of low energy beaches and can be collected by sieving the sediments through a large mesh wire or plastic screen.

Be sure to rinse these "wild caught" foods well with fresh water before placing them in the tank. This will remove excess organic fluids and help (only help) prevent introduction of fish parasites. Unless they are broken up or killed in the collection process, they will survive for a while in the aquarium and be available for the predators as they find them. Interesting new tenants may develop in the tank as a result of feeding natural marine foods. Feed these collected food organisms sparingly, for they add nutrients and organics to the system just as processed foods do, but more quickly since they decay rapidly after death. Protein foam skimmers may be overwhelmed by an introduction of dying marine food organisms. In some instances where many sediment loving marine animals are kept, it may be good to introduce fresh marine sediments to the tank. Sand and silt from a quiet natural bottom area can be introduced to a corner of the tank, carefully, and the response of the tank inhabitants observed. Again, there may be a lot of organic matter in the sediments, so be careful and don't add too much. If you do this, especially adding sediments from a temperate area to a tropical tank environment, be sure to write up the results for a club newsletter or magazine.

Freshwater and terrestrial food organisms. There are many live food organisms that are cultured for feeding to freshwater tanks that can also be fed to marine tanks. Galtsoff (1937) is a good general reference to the culture of hundreds of potential food organisms. Freshwater aquarists are a good source of many of these foods. Annelid, oligochete worms in the genus *Tubifex*, are an important benthic food organism for many fresh water aquarists. They are easy to culture and are readily eaten by freshwater and marine animals. They are nasty critters, however, mud and manure worms by nature, and they must be cleaned inside and out before being fed in marine or freshwater systems. Flushing in cool water for a day and then rinsing the balled worm well will clean them. Commercially prepared *Tubifex* worms are available as freshwater fish food in aquarium shops.

Microworms are also used extensively by freshwater aquarists and can be fed to organisms in marine systems. They are very tiny, and although they are not planktonic organisms, they can be fed in a suspension to filter feeders or fed to small predators. Earthworms can be cleaned and stripped of intestinal contents and fed whole or chopped. Fruit flies, *Drosophila* sp., can be very easily cultured in a screened dish or bottle on mashed banana or other media, and the abundant larvae harvested and fed to marine animals.

These freshwater and terrestrial food organisms are not marine, however, and they are not natural foods of marine animals. The digestive systems of marine animals are not "programed" to utilize all the specific proteins, carbohydrates, and fats that compose these animals. Whenever possible, a marine aquarist should use foods of marine origin when feeding marine animals. Substitutes for marine foods are better than nothing, of course, but feed non marine foods sparingly, and watch for food rejection or other possible problems.

Dead Foods

Few marine aquarists bother with culture or collection of live foods. Those that do are well rewarded by the health and vitality of the animals in their systems, and those that don't can get by very well with good judgement, common sense, and a variety of processed commercial and home prepared foods.

Suspended Particles (plankton substitutes)

Feeding tiny suspended particles to filter feeders (and marine larvae) is as much a matter of technique as it is selection of the food. Dry foods of any particle size have a strong tendency to float when first placed in water. Most reef systems remove water from the tank through an overflow, which continuously skims the surface of the tank and removes surface active compounds and floating particles. Feeding dry food (flake food, freeze dried plankton, floating pellets, etc.) while the pump is in operation results in loss of much of the food into the filter. This increases nutrients in the system without benefit to the invertebrates and fish. Sometimes it is good to scatter dry food on the surface, for this increases the time that it is available to fish by providing a period of surface floatation for fish that can feed from or near the surface. However, if dry food is fed while the overflow is in operation, it is best to first soak the food in cup of water so that when it does enter the tank it will immediately drift downward and not float off into the overflow.

Dead food particles will not stay suspended in the water column as do live food organisms. They float for a variable period of time and then sink as water penetrates the structure of the particle. The settling rate of the food particle depends on the density of the food and the strength and structure of the water currents in the tank. Some particles may be buoyant enough to remain suspended for some time, thus be of maximum benefit to filter feeders. Other food particles may sink quickly and aid only those that feed on the bottom of the tank. If the intent is to feed tiny dead food particles to sessile filter feeders, it is important to get the food, in suspension, in the area of the target specimen, at a time when the animal is in a feeding mode. In most cases, this is after the tank is dark and feeding tentacles are expanded.

Sometimes, in some marine systems where dissolved organic compounds are few and no plankton exists, filter feeders are not stimulated to enter feeding modes and may miss the dead food particles that sink to the bottom before they are ready to feed. There are now "appetite stimulants" on the market that can be added to the tank a hour or so before feeding to stimulate the filter feeder to begin feeding behavior. A little dilute "shellfish milk" (finely blended shrimp or oysters) performs the same function, but may make the protein skimmer work overtime.

The best way to get the food to a particular specimen is to release it into a current that will carry the food particles toward the animal. This can be a problem in large deep tanks. A turkey baster has a short tube and can release a lot of food in one squeeze. This may be fine for some applications—a large volume of food particles put out over a broad general area— but may not provide enough control over volume and placement of food in other situations. A long section of ridged air tubing can come in handy. Draw the food solution up the tube with mouth suction (a small rubber bulb that fits tightly on the tube is even better), place a finger over the end of the tube to prevent the discharge of the food solution, and extend the tube into the tank to the area where the food particles should be released. Remove the finger from the end of the tube and the food solution will slowly diffuse into the tank and wash toward the animal. Moving the tube sightly upward or blowing on the end will speed the release of the particles. Generally, however, the heavier particles move down the tube and are washed toward the target specimen. Since dead food particles settle quickly, it is best to feed slowly and carefully to obtain maximum benefit from the feeding. The long length of narrow air tubing will carry plenty of food particles, but not so much that feeding can not be controlled.

It is important to pay attention to particle size when feeding suspended plankton substitute foods. It is useless to feed very fine dust-like particles to animals that feed on large zooplankters or to wash large grain size particles over animals that take up very small food organisms.

Dry and paste foods. Most commercial preparations are dry or in the form of a paste. Some such as flake foods are in large flakes or particles designed for feeding fish. If the food is dry and hard enough, a mortar and pestle can grind the food into most any particle size. A good quality flake food contains meal from shrimp, fish, squid, and other marine animals as well as algae and other vegetable matter. Liver is usually included as a source of B vitamins. Fat should not exceed 5 to 8 percent and protein should be 35 to 50 percent. Some flake foods are designed for cold water, freshwater fish and contain too much fat and not enough protein. Inexpensive flake foods *may* contain ingredients from sources inappropriate for marine animals. Be sure to check ingredients on labels. Some flake foods are designed to enhance colors in freshwater fish and contain the male hormone methyl testosterone—which brings out male breeding colors in many male and female freshwater fish. Note that this hormone may cause changes in growth, color, and reproductive patterns in marine animals that may not be desired. To feed flake food to filter feeders, it should be ground to the proper size, stirred up in a cup of salt water until it no longer floats, and fed directly to the target specimen.

There are a number of commercial "fry" foods on the market in liquid, paste, or dry form that are manufactured in a tiny, microscopic size particle. These specialized foods are uniform, usually the right particle size for small larvae and nanoplankton filter feeders, composed of good ingredients, and somewhat expensive. Be sure they do not form lumps when fed. Break them up in a small quantity of water before feeding if lumping is a problem. Also be sure that fine dry food does not spread out over the surface in a fine film that is quickly skimmed out of the tank. It is wise to release these expensive specialty foods directly towards the target specimen. The currents will spread enough about the tank for other filter feeders as well. Keep all dry foods in cool dry storage before use.

Raw and wet foods. Most of the foods in this category are prepared by the aquarist for feeding as fine particles to filter feeders, larval stages, and plankton pickers. The base of these foods are raw shrimp, raw squid, raw scallops, marine algaes or other green plant food, crab meat, small amounts of lean beef heart and calf liver, and, sparingly, raw fish. Many types of fish are very oily, and it is not good to add much fish oil to a marine system. These food items, especially raw shrimp, can be feed in many ways. Relatively large particles can be produced by first freezing raw peeled shrimp compressed in a small ball. The frozen ball of shrimp is grated over a bowl with a fine kitchen grater. Graters with tiny cup shaped cusps are preferred over those with just tiny sharp points. The softer the shrimp and the harder the ball is pressed into the grater, the larger the particles. Very fine particles can be produced with a hard frozen shrimp and light pressure on the grater. Only what is needed can be grated and the shrimp returned to the freezer. A particle mix produced in this manner contains a minimum of excess body fluid.

Special mixtures can be prepared by adding shrimp, scallops, oysters, a little liver, some algaes and other ingredients to a little water in a blender. The speed and duration of the blending can provide some control over particle size, but the blending always seem to produce a very tiny particle and a lot of protein liquid. The resulting seafood soup or "milk" can be fed as it comes from the blender, and this is often useful as a feeding stimulant for animals that have not been feeding. The juices penetrate the retracted polyps and stimulate feeding responses. The blended shrimp based mix can be prepared with a lot of water to form a soup-like constancy, or with limited water to form a paste. After preparation, it can be frozen in portions for future use.

The proteins in the shrimp hold the mix together in a solid paste. Upon thawing, a wet mix forms a liquid again. A paste mix can be finely grated while still hard frozen, and a very fine particle mix results. The soupy mix is fed to filter feeders that require very fine particles and the particle mix to filter feeders that require small particles. Particles produced from wet, raw foods are lighter than those produced from hard, dry foods and will generally remain in suspension for a longer time. Fish row is sometimes available at seafood markets or from fishermen and makes a good planktonic food. The yellow or orange female row is best as the tiny eggs are bundles of food energy well packaged in just the right size for many filter feeders. Break the row up in a cup of seawater and the tiny eggs will separate from the ovarian tissues and can then be fed as small particles.

Benthic Food Particles

Benthic food particles are relatively large food particles that drift to the bottom and are taken by predators and scavengers. They can be processed dry flakes and pellets, processed frozen food mixes, or pieces of raw foods prepared by the aquarist. They can be scattered over the tank bottom for opportunistic feeding by any tank inhabitant or fed directly to a specific animal. A feeding wand is often useful for feeding pieces of shrimp or other seafood to anemones and other sessile animals. Fasten a straight pin securely to the end of a length of thin dowel or rigid plastic air tubing with glue or tape. A small piece of shrimp impaled on the pin can be transported directly to an anemone, placed among the tentacles, and moved about to simulate movement of a captured animal. Hide the point of the pin in the food particle so as not to injure the anemone. The anemone responds by grasping the shrimp piece as it would capture a prey organism. The unbarbed pin is easily withdrawn and the shrimp piece is left with the anemone. The shrimp or other food may be rejected by the anemone before or even after ingestion, so watch carefully after feeding and remove any uneaten food whenever possible before it can decay and add unnecessary nutrients to the system.

Dry flakes, pellets, and processed frozen foods

Most commercial foods are processed as flakes, pellets, and frozen mixes or packages of a specific type of marine product such as krill, clams, scallops, or shrimp. The convenience of these processed foods is a major selling point to most marine aquarists. Shrimp from the seafood counter at the local super-market is less expensive than frozen shrimp packaged for the aquarium trade, but it still needs to be cleaned, peeled, and wrapped for the freezer. Frozen food mixes are better buys, however, for they usually contain a great variety of natural marine ingredients that the average aquarist would have difficulty gathering. The selection of commercial foods for marine aquarium systems is large and growing every year. As with all aquarium foods, consider the nature of the animals that will consume the foods and read the label carefully.

Homemade food mixes

Shrimp, scallop, clam, crab, fish, and other seafoods can be cut to the proper sized pieces, rinsed, and offered to predators and scavengers in reef and traditional systems with great success. The added variety and convenience of some commercial foods helps an aquarist to maintain a good system. It is relatively easy to prepare a paste food mix that incorporates the foods an aquarist feels is best for a particular system. All mixes should be very low in fat. A food mix for a system with many herbivores may include a good quantity of vegetable matter such as oatmeal, fresh water algae and plants, spinach, and romaine lettuce held together with shrimp protein or agar. Baby food mixes are often a good source of green vegetable material if marine algae are not available.

A system with more carnivorous animals may require more animal based foods in the mix including the hulls (peeled shells) of shrimp to provide abundant chitin in the diet. Chitin provides needed roughage in the diet of animals that feed mostly on crustaceans. There are also important pigments in the flesh and shells of shrimp and other crustaceans. A little fresh calf liver added to the mix will provide needed A and B vitamins. A few drops of a vitamin mix developed for marine animals or even a liquid vitamin mix designed for infants or pregnant women is a good addition. Egg yolk is also a nutritious addition but be careful of egg white because it binds biotin (B vitamins) and makes it unavailable to the fish. A paste mix for marine fish and invertebrates should be based on marine foods rather than beef products or terrestrial animals. The relative amounts and types of proteins, carbohydrates, fats, vitamins, and trace elements in seafoods better fit the requirements of marine animals than do terrestrial food sources.

Dry fish food can be sparingly added to the mix to provide a broad nutritional base, but avoid, or use sparingly, trout and salmon feeds because they are high in fat, 10 % or more. Because of the sticky consistency of the shrimp protein, a thick paste mix based on shrimp flesh is reasonably stable and resists rapid disintegration after grating or cutting a frozen block into small particles. Agar and gelatin can be used to "set" a mix developed for benthic feeding, and this will help prevent the rapid break-up of pieces of the mix. Moe (1982) contains a recipe for a gelatin based food mix. Agar is a natural algae product and may be better for marine animals than animal protein based gelatin. " Agar agar" can be purchased in oriental food stores and health food stores. Boil the flaked or filamentous agar gently until it is completely dissolved. The more agar dissolved in the water, the harder and firmer the resulting mix. Add the blended ingredients to the agar water before it cools, mix it well until it forms a library paste consistency, place it in a plastic bag (Ziplock® freezer bags provide a good seal), flatten it out, and freeze it in a thin flat sheet. Pieces can be broken off and fed as required and the bag resealed to prevent freezer burn.

Sediments and Detritus

Some echinoderms, primarily sea urchins, take in a great deal of calcareous sediments in feeding. The invertebrates that consume these sediments do much better in tanks that contain a section of fine shell and coral sand at some place on the bottom of the tank. Detritus forms in all tanks, and removal of excess detritus is important for control of phosphorus accumulation. Detritus is also an important food source for many invertebrates. A reef or traditional system that maintains a variety of invertebrates should contain some detritus, but it shouldn't accumulate in dense layers over the tank bottom. Detritus should be removed from filters and open tank bottoms, but a modest accumulation tucked between the rocks is good for systems that maintain a wide variety of small invertebrates.

Algae

Algae are important food sources for many invertebrates. A good reef system has abundant encrusting and macroalgae that serve as a food source for a few algae eating invertebrates. Sea urchins, herbivorous mollusks such as chitons and some gastropods, and many hermit crabs require encrusting and some macroalgae to live well in a marine aquarium system. Encrusting algae grow in almost all marine tanks, but macroalgae need particular conditions of light and water quality. *Caulerpa* is a good macroalgae for fish and invertebrate food and can be grown in a separate system if it can not be grown in the tank with the algae eaters.

It is possible to provide algal substitutes if algae growth is not sufficient for the algae consuming invertebrates present in the tank. Green leafy vegetables such as romaine lettuce and spinach are usually consumed by algae eaters, and a few leaves can be fed every few days. Plants grown in freshwater aquariums can also be used to feed marine fish and invertebrates that require algae. A couple of freshwater tanks with good growths of the soft, floating crystalwort, *Riccia fluitans*, will provide all the plant material needed for a weekly feeding of a large marine system.

Dissolved Nutrients

Many marine invertebrates take up organic compounds dissolved in seawater. Which compounds are essential in what concentrations to which invertebrates is a subject for extensive research. A number of marine aquarium supply companies are now producing vitamin and organic compound mixtures for marine invertebrate tanks. Be sure such preparations are fresh. Judicious application of some of these products to marine invertebrate tanks is probably a good tactic, especially if B vitamins and potency protected vitamin C are included. The "wet thumb" of an observant, experimental, and analytical aquarist is of critical importance in this area. A vitamin preparation and a 10 % dextrose or glucose solution seems to be beneficial to filter feeders when added to particulate foods and fed on a weekly basis. Again, what works well for the reef system of one aquarist may not be helpful in another situation. Advertisers may tend to slightly exaggerate the claims for their products from time to time, I think this is called marketing. An aquarist should keep this in mind and evaluate nutrient products based on how they apparently help the animals in a particular system, rather than accept all claims at face value.

Light

High light levels are essential to the existence and growth of most marine algaes and invertebrates. The subject of light has been treated extensively in Chapters 2, 3, and 4. It is mentioned in this chapter on foods and feeding only to once again stress its importance in food production for corals and other "farmers" of the sea.

Part III

Marine Invertebrates

The organization of life in the sea

This section introduces the marine aquarist to the vast array of marine invertebrate and plant life.

Invertebrates come in many sizes, shapes, and colors. Some look reasonably like animals, at any rate they have legs and eyes; and others look more like plants, or monsters from outer space. A good invertebrate aquarium is a bewildering display of strange and fascinating creatures. Such an aquarium is great fun to watch and maintain, but in order to really appreciate marine invertebrates, it is important to have an understanding of the history of life on earth and how scientists classify the millions of different species of plants and animals that share our planet. An understanding of the scientific system of classification (Taxonomy) will also make identifications of invertebrates easier and more meaningful. Just as a biological filter is a tool to help the aquarist maintain marine invertebrates, the system of classification is a tool that helps the aquarist to understand the life forms in the aquarium. And with this knowledge comes an increased ability to care for the life in the aquarium.

Chapter 7

Classification and Development of Life

Common and Scientific Names

Identification of an organism consists primarily of giving it a name. There are many different ways to provide an animal or a plant with a name. Perhaps you have a hermit crab in your aquarium, a beautiful specimen of *Petrochirus diogenes*, that you affectionately call Herman. Herman the hermit crab, that's a nice name. Now you know who and what Herman is, and your friends may know also. However, if you start talking to someone you meet in the supermarket about how you have crabs and that you like to watch Herman drag his shell around, you may have a problem. Your identification of "Herman" doesn't mean very much without a lot of explanation. Obviously, we can't give animals any old name and expect people to know what we are talking about.

You could just call him a hermit crab and then most folks would have some idea of what you mean. Even so, you could be talking about a land hermit crab or one of dozens of species of hermit crabs that are found on sea bottoms all over the world or even an ordinary crab with antisocial habits. Calling it a hermit crab narrows the identification considerably, but still doesn't identify the species in question. You could call it the Giant hermit crab, an accepted common name for that species. But then someone who read a different book may call it the Conch hermit crab, also a common name used for that species, and there would still be confusion. There is always an element of doubt when common names are used because they can vary so much over time and geography.

Different common names may be applied to the same species in different geographical areas, and the same common name may be applied to different species from the same or different areas. And when creative efforts from collectors, pet shops, and hobbyists are tossed into the nomenclatural bag, there's no way one can know for sure what species is in the tank from the common name alone. Generally, however, people in one area use the same common name for a popular species, and confusion occurs mainly with geographical distance or as language changes over time. So common names are useful, especially in general conversation.

Obviously, however, if we want to seriously study the natural history and biology of a plant or animal, we have to be absolutely sure that the name we use refers to the same species wherever and whenever it occurs. This is where Carolus Linnaeus and the science of taxonomy come into the picture. (Taxonomy, incidentally, is not taxidermy, which is the art of preserving animals in life-like pose.) Taxonomy is the science of classification of plants and animals and incudes giving newly discovered species a scientific name. The word taxonomy comes from *Tasso*, meaning "arrange", and *Nomos*, meaning "law". The scientific name is used for only a single species, and that species is then recognized by that name alone by scientists throughout the world. Latin is the basic language of taxonomy. Latin is used only because Linnaeus and other early naturalists wrote in Latin, but this tradition is very useful since Latin is not a modern language and is not subject to changes in meaning due to current usage.

A species may have many common names, but it can have only one scientific name. For example, the scientific name of the Caribbean spiny lobster is *Panulirus argus* (Latreille). The binomial (two names) scientific name is made up of the genus and species name and is always printed in italics. The name of the author of the original description of the species, in this case

Latreille, follows the Latin name given to the organism. Parentheses around the author's name indicate that the organism is no longer classified under the genus of the original description. Sometimes the date of the original description (Latreille, 1804) follows the author's name.

It isn't easy to give an organism a scientific name. First, a detailed physical description of the new organism has to be written so that it can be recognized as a distinct species. Second, it has to given a name that will not change in meaning or use despite any changes in modern language, and third, a normal specimen of the new species must be designated as the type specimen and placed in a museum collection where it will be available for study next year or a hundred years later. Scientists have to be able to check up on one another's work. The scientific name and the description of the new species must also be published in the scientific literature and be accepted and used by modern science before the new species is considered valid.

Sometimes a scientist may write a description of a new species and give it a name without knowing that the "new" species had been previously described by someone else, or later research may show that the new species is just a different form of a previously described species. When this happens, and it is not an uncommon occurrence, the earliest name has precedence and is considered the valid name. Other scientific names that may have also been given to the species are considered synonyms. Taxonomists often spend many years working on a particular group of organisms and then publish a monograph that identifies all the species in the group, lists all their past scientific names, describes new species, and corrects past errors.

Problems due to name and species confusion were great in the 17th and 18th centuries because there was no universally accepted system for cataloging and naming plants and animals. In the 10th edition of *Systema Naturae*, published in 1758, Linnaeus defined the basic system (known as the Linnaean hierarchy) that we follow today in giving scientific names to all species of living things. In theory, every species known to science has one, and only one, accepted binomial scientific name. In practice, however, a couple of hundred years of developing names for newly discovered organisms, often with inadequate biological and geographical information and a lack of communication between scientists of different times and different places, has resulted in some confusion in the scientific names of certain groups of plants and animals. Despite occasional mixups, and frequently more than one name for the same animal, the Linnaean system brought order into the study of natural history and became one of the most important tools of modern biology. Taxonomic scientists are constantly striving to the put the attic of taxonomy into proper order.

The Linnaean hierarchy groups organisms into "taxons" based on their physical similarities, which reflects the closeness of their evolutionary relationship. Each level or grouping in the hierarchy is called a **taxon**. Linnaeus, of course, didn't know about evolutionary relationships since this information wasn't available in the 1750's, so he, and other naturalists of the 18th century, used only the general appearance and physical characteristics of the organisms to determine the levels and groups of the hierarchy system.

Even though we have a much greater understanding of the natural world today, the basic Linnaean system of classification reflects the structure of nature so well that it is still the basis of modern taxonomy. It is important to understand the structure of the higher taxons, the "Big Picture", for then the smaller groups—family, genus and species—make more sense. Think of the species as a shoebox, which is in a closet, in a house, in a neighborhood, in a city, in a county, in a state, in a country, and on a planet. To find the shoebox, you have to start with the right planet and go to the right place in each category before you can find the correct shoebox. If you look only for shoeboxes without finding the right city or house, there is little chance of finding the correct shoebox, or knowing which shoeboxes belong together.

The first few taxons (groups)—Kingdom, Phylum (Division), Class, Order—in this hierarchy are very large and include many organisms that are only distantly related. Each taxon is identified by a group of characteristics, however, that define the biological relationship at that level. For example, spiny lobsters, worms, fish, and horses are all in the Animal Kingdom, but when you get down to the Family and Genus level, other kinds of animals are eliminated and there are only types of spiny lobsters, worms, fish, and horses in each defined group.

The classification hierarchy listed below is very basic and has only seven levels. Most modern scientists use classification schemes that include intermediate taxons such as suborders, superfamilies, cohorts, and tribes—twenty one or more levels—to clearly define evolutionary separations. Not all taxonomists agree on how the various taxons should be established and it is not unusual to have two or more classification schemes for large and small groups in use at the same time. Eventually, however, enough scientific evidence for one classification is developed and scientists gradually accept the taxonomy that best fits the facts. Family names always end in *idae*, and some other taxons above the genus level also have specific endings. The groups get smaller as the levels descend toward the individual species, and the organisms in each group are more closely related. Thus, the family of spiny lobsters, Palinuridae, contains only animals that look like spiny lobsters, and when we get down to the genus, *Panulirus*, there are 19 species throughout the world that look very much alike.

The scientific names given to these groups have meaning and describe the taxon in some way. The last name, however, the species name, functions only to identify the species and may or may not be descriptive of the organism. It may refer to a physical characteristic of the organism or the geographical area the organism inhabits. The new species name may honor the individual that discovered the organism, or it may be named after another individual that the author wishes to honor for some other reason.

The seven basic levels of the classification of the spiny lobster is listed below.

Kingdom . **Animalia** (multicellular organisms that ingest food, have two equal sets of chromosomes, and reproduce through joining of different genetic material in sperm and egg)

Phylum . . **Arthropoda** (jointed feet)

Class . . . **Crustacea** (hard shelled)

Order . . . **Decapoda** (ten legged)

Family . . . **Palinuridae** (after *Palinurus*, the pilot of Aeneas. In Greek legend, Aeneas, a Trojan, the son of Aenus, escaped from ruined Troy and wandered for many years before finding Latium.)

Genus . . . *Panulirus* (an anagram of Palinurus. An anagram is a word made by transposing the letters of another word. Thus *Panulirus* may have been a mistaken spelling of Palinurus.)

Species . . *argus* (shining, bright. The giant *Argos* had a hundred shining eyes and upon his death, Juno placed them on the tail of a peacock.)

Thus if you know the classification and the scientific name of the Caribbean spiny lobster, you know that this particular organism is a hard shelled, invertebrate animal with ten jointed legs, a wandering habit, and bright, shining spots on its tail.

Now you probably know more about scientific names than you wanted to know, but it is important to have an understanding of how a scientific name is developed and what it means. Just knowing a name, scientific or common, however, is not a complete identification. It is only a foundation upon which to build a concept, a personal understanding, of a species. To really know an organism we should have some understanding of its ecological niche and its evolutionary history. A knowledge of the classification of an organism, from Kingdom down to Species, provides an understanding of how the organism fits into the structure of life that has been, and now is, on the Earth.

Development and History of Life

An animal or plant that is successful in the struggle for life and survives to reproduce before it dies is more than an individual organism. It is functioning part the gene pool of the species. A species is not just an individual or a group of individuals. A species is, fundamentally, a "pool" composed of all the genes of all the individuals that can successfully reproduce with each other. Each individual has some, but not all, of the genes that make up the totality of the species. The gene pool may be very small, such as the few ivory billed woodpeckers that still survive in the forests of Cuba, or very large, such as all the blue crabs in the Atlantic Ocean. The gene pool can also be severely restricted if all the individuals are very similar genetically, as in the African cheetah or clonal growth of certain grasses. In such genetically restricted populations, there may be many individuals, but relatively few genes, because all the individuals are expressions of the same genes. Fewer genes mean fewer possibilities for genetic interaction, less capacity for adaptive change, and a greater chance of extinction.

The textbook picture of evolution from Darwin through the 1970's was one of very gradual biological change; one species sequentially merging into other very similar species over millions of years, a process called phyletic evolution. Some evolutionary changes have occurred in this manner, but the main mechanism of evolution is speciation. This occurs when a reproductively isolated population responds to environmental changes; small genetic differences rapidly accumulate in a specific adaptive direction, and within a hundred thousand years or so, a new species comes into existence that is reproductively isolated from the parent species. If the gene pool can not adapt to changing conditions, it becomes extinct.

The history of a gene pool is often quite complicated since it may expand, contract, become extinct, change gradually or suddenly (gradually may be 50 to a 100 million years and suddenly may be only a few hundred thousand years), and often separate into different species. Only analysis of the fossil record, comparison of physical structures, and biochemical analysis of fossil and modern material give us an under-standing of the evolutionary history of a particular species. Each species now in existence, however, is at the end of an independent pathway that extends back through mists of unimaginable time to when the Earth was new and life began.

It is our perception of the history of life on Earth, through the process of evolution, that gives form and meaning to the classification of plants and animals. Whatever your beliefs about the origins of the Earth and its life, the intimate biological relationship of all forms of life can not be denied. The chemistry and molecular structure of bacteria, protozoa, plants, and animals result from the interaction of nucleic acids, amino acids, carbohydrates, and fats—a factor common to all life. The cellular organization and biochemistry of the genetic structure of all life from bacteria to whales is also a common thread. And within each phyla the similarities of sex, development, form, structure, and function in these often widely diverse species eloquently demonstrates their common ancestry.

To develop an overview of life on Earth we must begin at the very beginning. The oldest rocks known are about 3.8 billion years old. These ancient strata, found in Greenland, are so altered by heat and pressure that there is no evidence of any fossils that may have once been present. Fossil bacteria have been found, however, in rocks from South Africa that are 3.4 billion years old. Microscopic fossils in these early rocks show that simple life forms developed soon after the earth cooled and liquid water was present. For two billion years life on earth consisted only of simple cells similar to present day bacteria and bluegreen algae, the exclusive time of the kingdom of the

Prokaryotae. By the end of that unimaginably vast stretch of time called the Precambrian Era, eukaryotic cells had evolved and life had diversified first into nucleated, single celled plants (algaes) and animals (the Protoctista kingdom), and then into a limited number of soft-bodied animals, a few jellyfish, soft corals, and simple worms—the beginnings of the Animalia kingdom.

Then, at the beginning of the Cambrian Epoch, 600 million years ago, the development of life rapidly accelerated. It was as if a type of critical mass had been achieved and life suddenly exploded in a diversity of form and abundance. Within a short time—geologically speaking, only 10 to 20 million years— precursors of all the major phyla of invertebrates, and a few odd creatures that have no modern descendants, are present in the fossil bearing rocks. Even a lancelet-like animal, foreshadowing the cordates, has been found in mid-Cambrian rocks from the Burgess Shale deposits in Canada. This may represent a rapid flowering, an explosion of life as it has been termed, or it may be just a lucky find of a fossil "window" when unusual conditions allowed preservation and fossiliza- tion of a brief period in a long process of the development of varied life forms.

New fossil finds continue to broaden our knowledge of the development of early life forms. Jellyfish, worms, creatures similar to sea pens, and some strange forms with no modern affinities were discovered in 1947 in the Ediacara Hills of South Australia. There is no evidence of external skeletons or other hard parts in these abundant fossil remains. This find does indicate that life gradually developed over a 100 million years toward the complexity found in early Cambrian times. Fungi and higher plants also evolved from protocist ancestors, but the first representatives of these kingdoms do not appear in the fossil record until about 400 and 350 million years ago. To provide an illustration of the relative lengths of the geologic time periods, Figure 49 lays out the entire time line of Earth on the same linear scale. Although detail of the last 600 million years is lost in this presentation, it provides a clear perspective

Figure 49. The time line of Earth, 5 billion years.

of the total length of time between the formation of the Earth, the development of life, and relatively recent geologic times.

To say that the fossil record is imperfect, especially as far back as hundreds of millions of years, is quite an understatement. Despite the millions of fossils now in museums and laboratories, and more unearthed each year, we have relatively very few pieces of the "history of life" jigsaw puzzle. For the most part, only shallow water marine fauna can fossilize, thus we know very little about ancient deep water fauna from fossil evidence. Fossilization, especially of soft bodied organisms, is a rare event that occurs only when certain conditions are present. Thus our knowledge of the development of life and the construction of a meaningful taxonomy is dependent on information preserved in the fossil record and careful analysis of the physical and chemical characteristics of modern species.

Classification of Life

The reason that science works as well as it does is simply because its theories and concepts change as new information is developed and proven valid. New theories, if accurately based on solid evidence and reproducible experimental results, soon leave old ideas in the dust of the past. Our concepts of the development and relationships of life on Earth have had a volatile and impassioned history within and outside of the scientific community. Taxonomy is by nature conservative and the classification of organisms has often been at the root of many controversies. But as our scientific knowledge advances, the classification of organisms gradually changes to incorporate and accommodate new information.

Biological knowledge has exploded in the last quarter century. New tools and new techniques, knowledge building on knowledge, has given scientists a better understanding of the natural world. The electron microscope has given us a window to the molecular level of life and new biochemical and computer technologies have allowed research into the nature of genes, proteins, and enzyme systems that has produced information at an unimaginable pace. This knowledge has greatly advanced medicine and agriculture and has also given us greater insight on the origins and relationships of plants and animals. A better understanding of early bacterial evolution and electron microscope studies on the fine structures of microscopic organisms will continue to change our perceptions of the history of life on Earth.

At first, beginning with the ancient Greeks, there were only two Kingdoms: Plantae and Animalia. If it didn't eat, was usually green and stayed in one place, it was a plant. If it wandered around and ate things, then it was an animal. The nature of microorganisms added controversy to the subject after Antony van Leeuwenhoek and others observed them through primitive microscopes around 1675; but it wasn't until almost two centuries later that Louis Pasteur, in the 1860's, demonstrated that these "tiny animalcules" did reproduce and were not the product of "spontaneous generation". Gradually, then, the structure of the natural world was expanded to include microorganisms. Those that could make their own food through photosynthesis were included with the plants, and those that couldn't were considered animals. This was rather awkward in many instances, however; so in 1866 Ernst Haeckel proposed that a third kingdom, the Protista, be established to include the protozoa, fungi, algae, and bacteria. The only thing these groups of organisms have in common is their relatively simple biological organization, but even so, the third kingdom made sense, given the state of biological knowledge at the time; and mainstream biology had three kingdoms of organisms from the late 1800's up to about 1960.

As it turns out, however, the fundamental division in living organisms is not between the plant and animal lines—it is in the separation of the prokaryote and the eukaryote cell. These terms—**prokaryote**, meaning "before the nucleus", and **eukaryote**, meaning "true nucleus"—were coined by the French marine biologist Edouard Chatton in 1937. Bacteria and blue-green algae (cyanobacteria) have prokaryotic cells; all other organisms—fungi, animals, and plants—have eukaryotic cells. The differences between the two types of cells could fill a book, but basically, prokaryotic cells have no membrane contained nucleus and are very small. Many species are anaerobic (poisoned by oxygen), they have no mitochondria (a small "organelle" within a cell that produces energy), do not form tissues, and rarely transfer genetic material. Eukaryotic cells are more complex with distinct, membrane bound nuclei and large cells. They always require oxygen (rare exceptions) and contain mitochondria and other organelles. Multicellular forms and tissue formation is common in eukaryotic organisms, and sexual systems with equal contributions of genetic material are typical.

Prokaryotic cells developed early in the history of life, as evidenced by the 3.5 billion year old stromatolites found in Australia. Stromatolites are composed of mats of bacteria and blue-green algae that trap sand and sediments and eventually fossilize into rock. There are a number of theories on how eukarotic cells came into existence about 1.5 billion years ago. The symbiotic theory as described by Lynn Margulis (1982) of Boston University is a good possibility. **Symbiosis** is the biological term for two or more separate species living closely together to the mutual benefit of each participant. There are many examples of such a partnership in the natural world: lichens, plant/fungus associations, and corals with their *zooxanthellae* (single celled dinoflagellates in the genus *Symbiodinium* that live within their cells and produce energy for the coral polyp through photosynthesis) are well known symbiotic associations.

The symbiotic theory of eukarotic cell origin suggests that, among other changes, free living prokaryotic organisms entered into a symbiotic relationship with the ancestors of eukarotic cells and eventually became part of this new type of cell. One prokaryotic organism produced energy for the cell through generation of adenosine triphosphate (ATP) and became mitochondria, and another enabled a later cell line to produce its own food energy and became the photosynthetic plastids in plant cells. The complex flagella and cilia (undulipodia) found in many eukarotic cells may also have originated as a prokaryotic symbiont. Similarities between the genetic and molecular structure of present day prokaryotes and these eukarotic organelles provide evidence for this theory. This melding of different types of prokaryotic cells through symbiosis created the potential for growth and differentiation that made possible the development of the fungi, animals, and plants.

The five kingdom system of classification was first proposed by R. H. Whittaker in 1959 and, with a few modifications, is the taxonomic structure preferred by most modern biologists. The kingdoms are the basic taxons and they reflect the fundamental pathways of the development of life. The first two kingdoms trace the two separate paths of descent that single celled organisms followed after life first appeared over 3.5 billion years ago. The three kingdoms of more complex life forms follow the subsequent development of the three major linages of cellular organisms that developed from the eukaryotic cell line. The five kingdoms now recognized are **Prokaryotae**, the single celled bacteria and blue-green algae; **Protoctista**, the protozoa, nucleated algaes and slime molds; **Animalia**, the consumers; **Fungi**, the absorbers; and **Plantae**, the producers.

The phylum is the next major taxon under kingdom. It too reflects evolutionary separations that took place very early in the history of life. (Note: botanists often use the term Division in place of Phylum.) The ancestors of most phyla can be found in the ancient rocks of the early Cambrian era, over 550 million years ago. Some phyla have been very successful and have separated into millions of species, while others have maintained their existence with only a few species. Even though some of the species in a particular phylum may appear very different, such as the molluscan octopus and oyster, there is a constellation of characteristics in each phylum that undeniably disclose their common ancestry.

I have followed the classification presented by Lynn Margulis and Karlene Schwartz in their recent book *Five Kingdoms*

(Margulis and Schwartz, 1988). Their work generally reflects current thought and consensus in biology on classification at the kingdom and phylum level, although there are differences of opinion among experts on the structure and placement of certain phyla. In their book, Margulis and Schwartz have tried to make the level of phylum represent the same taxonomic concept in each kingdom, a sort of "common denominator" in the classification system.

The phylum level is very important to the marine aquarist for it represents the first level where common ancestry is usually very clear, and the organisms within each phyla have definitive common characteristics. It is also the basic taxon where identification is usually meaningful in popular language. Phylum level is often as precise an identification as a marine aquarist might get on an unusual or difficult to identify organism. Therefore, the arrangement of life in this book is based on the phylum taxon. Lower taxons such as class, order, and family, are, or course, used wherever they are meaningful to most marine aquarists.

In the past, a marine invertebrate aquarium was little different from an aquarium devoted to fish. The tank was generally set up and decorated with large, sterile display pieces of coral or rock, and particular large invertebrates—anemones, crabs, shrimp, mollusks, starfish, and sea urchins—were selected and placed in the tank. One knew pretty well what was in the tank. Nowadays, however, an invertebrate tank is likely to consist of live coral, bunches of wild algae, and "live rock"—rock taken right off the ocean floor with its load of macro and microscopic life. One never knows what may pop up in a modern marine invertebrate aquarium. Quite possibly animals new or very rare to science may appear. For this reason I have included all phyla of life in this book, briefly of course. The list of phyla is complete, and with a little luck and a hand lens you may be able to find the correct identification, at least to phylum level, for that strange little creature climbing up the wall of your aquarium.

The "trophic" nature and level of many of the taxa discussed is often used as an important descriptive characteristic. The group may be on a high or low **trophic level**; they may be autotrophs or chemotrophs or heterotrophs, or even chemoheterotrophs. This is confusing unless you know the terminology. The word trophic comes from *trephein* meaning "to feed" and describes how the organism gains nutrition. **Autotroph** means that the organism makes its own food, usually through photosynthesis, a photoautotroph in essence, "eats light". A **chemoautotrophic** organism takes up particular non organic chemicals in the presence of free oxygen, NO_2 (nitrite) for example, oxidizes it (adds an atom of oxygen) to make NO_3 (nitrate), and uses the energy released by the chemical reaction for its own metabolism. It "eats chemical energy" in other words. This is very important to marine aquarists as is the feeding activity of nitrifying bacteria that makes biological filtration work and makes a marine aquarium possible. *Hetero* means different or other and a **heterotroph** feeds on a variety of organic chemical compounds, free proteins, lipids, and carbohydrates and breaks them down into simpler chemical molecules. A **chemoheterothroph** (see phylum M-11, the Omnibacteria) uses certain chemical compounds, nitrate for example, and by reducing it in the absence of oxygen to nitrogen gas, it gains the energy to feed on various organic compounds. This process makes a "denitrifier" work, another important bacterial contribution to the marine aquarist.

Where the organism lives is also an important characteristic that is often used as part of the general description of a taxa. **Planktonic** refers to living among the plankton, free floating without attachment to bottom or shore. There are different categories of plankton, by size: macroplankton (larger than 1 mm), microplankton (1 mm down to 60 microns), the nanoplankton (tiny organisms between 60 and 5 microns), and the ultraplankton (organisms smaller than 5 microns). The zooplankton are the animals, including the larval forms of crustacea, mollusks, and other large species, and the phytoplankton are the photosynthetic organisms. **Pelagic** refers to living in the surface or upper waters of the sea but with powers of directed movement through swimming. Benthos and **benthic** refers to living on or under the bottom substrate, and **sessile** means that the organism is attached to the substrate. Algaes in particular attach to many types of substrates and can be described by this attachment. Epilithic algae are attached to rocks and stones; epipelic algae attach to soft substrates such as sand or mud; epiphytic algae attach to other plants; and epizoic algae attach to animals.

Note that viruses are not included in the classification of life. It's not that viruses aren't important. Fish can have many virus caused diseases such as lymphosystis (cauliflower disease) in tropical fish, infectious pancreatic necrosis (IPN) in salmon, trout, and other species, and even grunt fin agent (GFA) in grunts. Quite probably most of the organisms we keep in marine aquaria have their own constellation of viruses, and we know next to nothing about most of these little bits of "almost life". Viruses are not organisms composed of cells. They are bits of nucleic acid, either DNA or RNA, surrounded by a protein coat. They can exist outside of a host cell, but can only grow and reproduce within and through biological utilization of particular cells of a particular host organism. Viruses are apparently detached fragments of the genetic material of cellular organisms that acquired the ability to reproduce rapidly and independently of the genetic control of cell growth and to survive transmission from one cell to another. Their origin, then, is from within living organisms, and they are not a part of the line of life of independent cellular organisms.

The first step in identification is to place the organism in the proper phylum. The listing of the kingdoms and phyla in Chapter 8 serves as a brief summary of the characteristics of the organisms grouped in these taxons and a guide to the first step in identification of an organism. The brief description of the characteristics and the line drawings of the most common representatives of important phyla should help place the organism in the proper phylum. The expanded discussion for phyla of the most common organisms should help confirm and further define the identification to a lower taxon, even to species in some cases. Firm identification of all invertebrates and algaes to the species level is far beyond the scope of this book, indeed, beyond the scope of most libraries and marine science laboratories. Some additional popular books that are accurate, reasonably available, and that will aid the serious aquarist in identification of many more species of invertebrates are Colin (1978), George (1979), Kaplan (1988, 1982), Miner (1950), Voss (1976), Wall (1982), and Wood (1983). Banister and Campbell (1986) is also an excellent general reference, but is not a great help for specific identifications.

Chapter 8

A Concise Guide to the Phyla

The List of Life on Earth

Margulis and Schwartz (1988) list 92 phyla in five kingdoms, which includes all of the 10 to 20 million described and undescribed species of organisms that now exist on Earth. Their work is an excellent summary of current taxonomic thought and a sound working structure to the organization of life. A sixth kingdom consisting of noncellular organisms such as viruses is included in some classifications, but since most noncellular life seems to be derived from the genetic structure of cellular organisms, and since few viruses are encountered by marine aquarists, the sixth kingdom is not erected in this classification.

In the outline that follows, I have included *all* the phyla in the Margulis and Schwartz classification to provide a complete listing of life on Earth. However, only those phyla of particular interest to the marine aquarist—phyla that include species that always or only occasionally occur in a marine aquarium—have an expanded discussion. The list includes species that one can't see without a microscope as well as all the big familiar critters. Just because we can't see them with the naked eye doesn't mean they aren't there, and the presence, or absence, of microscopic organisms is often more important to the aquarium than the organisms we carefully select and culture. Of the 92 phyla defined by Margulis and Schwartz, 61 (66%) have marine species, and there is a reasonable chance for a representative of most of these marine phyla to occur in a marine aquarium. That's an amazing slice of life to keep in one's living room.

The letter and number before the name of each phylum is the designation used by Margulis and Schwartz (1988) to order and structure the phyla list. This gives each phylum a letter/number designation that allows quick reference to the kingdom and location of the phylum. An asterisk (*) after the phylum name indicates that the phylum may possibly (in some cases by a stretch of the imagination) be found in a marine aquarium. Two asterisks (**) indicates that the phylum is important to marine aquarists. The descriptive phrase that follows the phylum is the meaning of the scientific phylum name.

Kingdom Prokaryotae (Monera)

Bacteria and blue-green algae

The name **prokaryotae** means "before the nucleus", and this great kingdom includes all organisms that do not have a membrane around a cell nucleus. Cellular organelles such as mitochondria (energy engines) and chloroplasts (photosynthesis plastids) are also absent. The recent change in the name of this kingdom from Monera (established by the 19th century biologist, Ernst Haeckel) to Prokaryotae reflects the greater understanding that scientists have developed of the structure and relationships of living organisms. The linage of the Prokaryotae is the most ancient of living organisms and is numbered in billions of years. There are two basic groups, each considered a subkingdom: the Archaebacteria and the Eubacteria. Fundamental differences in biochemistry and genetics separate the two subkingdoms of bacteria. The **Archaebacteria** are the most primitive and are found in areas similar to the oxygen poor, earthly environments of over 3 billion years ago:

hot springs, sulphur laden deep sea vents, boiling muds, and waters of very high salt content. The vast majority of bacteria, however, are the **Eubacteria** that are found in all typical earthly environments, including most living organisms.

Over billions of years, great evolutionary changes have taken place in these two subkingdoms of bacteria. Many, many species have developed, some with generalized and some with highly specific environmental and nutritional requirements. Most distinguishing characteristics of bacteria are on the molecular level, unlike the large, easily observed structural variations of plants and animals. Various divisions and species of bacteria are based more on biochemical activity and molecular genetic structure than on visible physical characteristics.

A fundamental difference in the cell walls of bacteria was discovered in 1884 by Christian Gram, a Danish physician. Some bacteria (termed Gram-positive) retained a violet color during a particular staining process while others (Gram-negative) lost the violet stain. The retention or loss of this violet stain depends on basic differences in the structure of the cell wall, and it is a very important tool in identification and classification of bacteria. The four major divisions of bacteria are based on the structure of the cell wall. Bacteria in the Division **Mendosicutes**, the only division in the Subkingdom Archaebacteria, lack a thin, inner peptidoglycan layer of the cell wall and are Gram-negative. Division Firmicutes includes all Gram-positive bacteria, which have a thick peptidoglycan cell wall and no outer lipoprotein layer. Division **Gracilicutes** are Gram-negative with thin, rigid cell walls, and Division **Tenericutes** are Gram-negative with soft cell walls.

In number and mass, bacteria are the most abundant organisms on Earth. Bacteria are, in fact, responsible for the transformation of the Earth from a sterile, chemical planet 3400 million years ago to the dynamic, life laden world it has become. The existence of life on Earth, and also in a marine aquarium system, depends on the chemical cycling activity of bacteria.

Subkingdom Archaebacteria
Division Mendosicutes (Gram-negative)

M—1. METHANCRETICES* (creator)

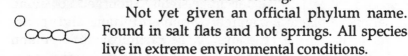

Methane producing bacteria, found in marine muds.

M—2. HALOPHILIC and THERMOACIDOPHILIC
BACTERIA (salt and hot acid loving)

Not yet given an official phylum name. Found in salt flats and hot springs. All species live in extreme environmental conditions.

Subkingdom Eubacteria
Division Tenericutes (Gram-negative)

M—3. APHRAGMABACTERIA (without fence)

Contained in a membrane, without typical bacterial cell walls. Found in low oxygen, fresh-water muds.

Division Gracilicutes (Gram-negative)

M—4. SPIROCHAETAE* (coiled, long hair)

Tightly coiled, very tiny cells. Many parasite and disease causing species (syphilis). Some species found in the crystal-line style of some mollusks.

M—5. THIOPNEUTES* (sulphur breather)

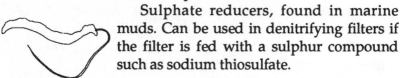

Sulphate reducers, found in marine muds. Can be used in denitrifying filters if the filter is fed with a sulphur compound such as sodium thiosulfate.

M—6. ANAEROBIC PHOTOTROPIC BACTERIA
(light feeder)

Found in some marine sediments where oxygen is low or absent, but light is present.

M—7. CYANOBACTERIA** (dark blue bacteria)

The **blue-green algae**. Tiny bacteria-like, photosynthetic cells very common in marine waters and in marine aquarium systems. Thousands of living species. Most abundant living organisms on the Earth from 2500 million years to 600 million years ago.

Filamentous forms

Cyanobacteria contain only chlorophyll *a*, but also have two other lipid soluble pigments, phycocyanin and allophycocyanin. The photosynthetic pigments are embedded in spherical structures called phycobilisomes that are bound to cell membranes. Chloroplasts, the pigment containing cellular organelles of eukaryotic cells, are not present. Cyanobacteria may be single cells (**Class Coccogoneae**) or filaments (**Class Hormogoneae**). The slimy dark green, black and red mats that form along the sides and over the bottom of tanks with low light levels and elevated nutrients are mostly composed of blue-green algae. Many species can fix nitrogen and are important in nutrient cycles in the sea. Some blue-green species enter into a symbiotic relationship with sponges and become a type of *zooxanthellae* to many species of sponges. Blue-green algae can utilize low light levels, so many sponges can live in deep water and still maintain *zooxanthellae* derived from Cyanobacteria.

M—8. HLOROXYBACTERIA* (yellow-green bacteria)

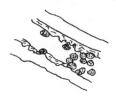

First described under the name Prochlorophyta in the 1960's. Cells with bacterial structure and some plant-like characteristics. They grow on the external and internal surfaces of tunicates. The nature of this association is unknown.

M—9. NITROGEN-FIXING AEROBIC BACTERIA

Rhizobiaceae, Azotobacteriacae, gram-negative, flagellated. Common in soil and water, their nitrogen fixing capability in plants makes agriculture possible.

M—10. PSEUDOMONADS** (false, single)

Gram-negative rods. Important disease causing, nitrate reducing, heterotrophic bacteria. Many thousands of species. Many species have the ability to metabolize a wide variety of organic compounds. Other species can respire anaerobically using nitrate as the terminal electron accepter and reducing it eventually to nitrogen gas. Common bacteria in denitrifying filters. Common bacteria in external bacterial infections of fish.

M—11. OMNIBACTERIA** (all gut)

Gram-negative. Huge group including single celled and aggregated bacteria. Most abundant life forms on Earth. Important disease causing, nitrate reducing, chemoheterotrophs. Includes intestinal (enteric) bacteria. Common in denitrifying filters.

M—12. CHEMOAUTOTROPHIC BACTERIA**

Gram-negative, shaped as rods, spheres and spirals. Includes nitrifying bacteria (*Nitrosomonas, Nitrobacter* and others) and the bacteria that are the base of life in the newly discovered deep sea, vent communities. These bacteria live on only air, salts, water, and the energy stored in inorganic compounds. The cycling of nutrients in the sea and terrestrial environments depends on the activity of these bacteria.

M—13. MYXOBACTERIA** (mucus bacteria)

Gram-negative, flexible rods. Cause of columnaris disease in fish. Most structurally complex of bacteria.

Division Firmicutes (Gram-positive)

M—14. FERMENTING BACTERIA*

 Gram-positive rods and spheres. Includes lactic-acid bacteria, clostridia, and peptococcaceae. Very important because of great fermenting capabilities. Some species are found in marine sediments. Some species are rarely implicated in fish disease, *Streptococcus*.

M—15. AEROENDOSPORA (air, seed within)

Gram-positive, spore forming, usually motile rods, mostly soil bacteria. Air borne spores spread these bacteria to all environments. Includes the wide spread genus *Bacillus*.

M—16. MICROCOCCI (small berry)

 Gram-positive, aerobic, spherical, important disease causing bacteria, *Staphylococcus*.

M—17. ACTINOBACTERIA** (ray bacteria)

Gram-positive, straight or curved rods, many filament forming fungus-like groups. One species of *Mycobacterium* causes fish tuberculosis and another causes human tuberculosis. *Streptomyces* produces streptomycin and other antibiotics.

KINGDOM PROTOCTISTA

Protozoa and nucleated algae

The Protoctista is the "catch all" group of this taxonomy. The kingdom is composed of all the organisms that are definitely not bacteria, fungi, true plants, or animals. The origins and relationships of many of these phyla are uncertain. They may be single celled or multicellular, phototropic or heterotrophic, microscopic or macroscopic; but all have eukaryotic, nucleated cells. The term protozoa (Kingdom Protista) has been generally used in reference to this group of organisms. The term "protozoa", however, typically applies to single celled organisms, and the concept of this kingdom, based on functional biology, includes multicellular as well as single celled organisms. The term "protoctist" refers to all the lower creatures, large or small, with animal-like and/or plant-like characteristics. This kingdom includes some of the largest (kelps) and smallest (single celled algae) organisms on earth.

The origins of some of these phyla are so ancient and their relationships to other phyla so obscure that some classifications elevate many of the protoctist phyla to kingdom or sub-kingdom level. Other classifications retain the single cell concept of the Kingdom Protista and scatter multicellular protoctist phyla to other kingdoms. Much basic biology in the disciplines of taxonomy, genetics, physiology, and biochemistry has yet to be accomplished with organisms in these phyla, and changes in classification will inevitably occur before science develops a general consensus on higher classification. But for now, this arrangement helps marine aquarists understand the life in a marine aquarium.

Pr—1. CARYOBLASTEA (nuclear bud)

A single species, *Pelomyxa palustris*. A giant celled, primitive amoeboid organism, freshwater.

Pelomyxa

PR—2. DINOFLAGELLATA** (whirling whip)

(Pyrrhophyta). Several thousand species of single celled, occasionally colonial, mostly marine planktonic forms. The cell wall (theca) is composed of cellulose divided into several hardened plates. Dinoflagellates may be armored when the plates are large and unarmored when the

Gymnodium, Gonyaulax

plates are small and imbedded in the cell membranes. The DNA structure in dinoflagellates is intermediate between prokaryotic and eukaryotic cells. The genera *Gymnodinium* and *Gonyaulax* have species that create the toxins that cause red tides. *Noctiluca* is the bioluminescent dinoflagellate that occasionally lights up the sea at night. *Amyloodinium* (*Oodinium*) is the most important parasite on tropical marine fish in marine aquariums. The dinoflagellate *Gymnodinium* (*Symbiodinium*) *microadriaticum* is the species that usually enters into a symbiotic relationship with corals. Termed *"zooxanthellae"*, these algal cells contribute food and oxygen (about 80 percent of their production) to the animal tissues and utilize ammonia and carbon dioxide from the animal host. Soft corals, hard corals, some clams (*Tridacna*), and anemones are all animals that utilize dinoflagellate *zooxanthellae*.

Pr—3. RHIZOPODA* (root foot)

Amoebas, five classes, some marine. Among the most simple in structure and life history of the organisms in this kingdom. Some marine species in the genera *Mayorella* and *Paramobea* of the **Class Conopodina** may occur in marine aquariums. Delicate cells observable only with a

Mayorella

microscope. Some amoebas construct tests of sand grains and other inorganic particles, and these tests are found in the fossil record of 500 million year old Paleozoic rocks.

Pr—4. CHRYSOPHYTA* (golden plant)

Single celled and colonial forms that contain plastids with golden yellow pigments. Many planktonic species form intricate tests of silica built from dissolved silica in ocean waters. The silicoflagellate group are common in all marine environments.

Marine forms

Pr—5. HAPTOPHYTA* (fastening plants)

Nannoplanktonic (very tiny), golden, motile cells, mostly marine. They produce coccoliths, microscopic discs of calcium carbonate that have formed great chalk deposits.

Coccosphere   Rhabdosphaera

Pr—6. EUGLENOPHYTA* (true eyed plant)

Flagellated protozoans with some characteristics of both plants and animals, 800 species, some marine. Most euglenoids are photosynthetic and have an eyespot and flagellum that allows them to move toward light. *Euglena* sp. are typical representatives of this phylum.

Euglena

Pr—7. CRYPTOPHYTA* (hidden plants)

Both animal-like (*Cyathomonas*) and plant-like (*Cryptomonas*) single celled protozoan forms. Found as clumps of gelatinous streamers in quiet, shallow marine waters (*Chrysophaeum talylori*).

Cyathomonas

Pr—8. ZOOMASTIGINA (animal whips)

Flagellated protozoans, mostly single celled, and important parasites. The Class Choanomastigotes may be ancestral to sponges.

Zoomastigna

Pr—9. XANTHOPHTA (yellow plants)

Colonial, photosynthetic, freshwater algae. Commonly seen as pond scum.

Xanthophyta

Pr—10. EUSTIGMATOPHYTA (true eyespot plant)

Photosynthetic, mobile, single celled algae. Important food chain base, mostly freshwater.

Phacus

Pr—11. BACILLARIOPHYTA** (little stick plant)

Lauderia (centric)

Tabellaria, Synedra (pennate)

The diatoms, encased in microscopic, two valved, frustules (shells) composed of clear silica. They are single celled and colonial photosynthetic algae with about 10,000 living species. The two major groups of diatoms are the **centric** (rounded, disc-like) and the **pennate** (elongated). Reproduction is usually mitotic, division of one cell into two daughter cells, although sexual reproduction does occur. The smaller half of the rigid frustule produces a smaller diatom after reproduction. Small diatoms produce auxospores, however, which grow into normal sized diatoms. Some species are planktonic, and some occur in bottom growths. Diatoms make up some of the golden brown encrusting growths that occur on rocks and sides of well lighted marine aquariums. The "lab-lab" growths that are fed to many bottom feeding fish and invertebrates are made up mostly of diatoms. Diatomaceous earth is composed of sediments made up from the ancient silica shells of diatoms and is widely used as a mechanical filter media. The tiny pores in the silica frustules are less than 5 microns and filter all but the tiniest particles. The tiny, microscopic shells (frustules) of some species are sculpted with fine patterns that are so precise that they are used to test the resolution of microscopes. Diatoms are common inhabitants of marine aquariums, especially older, well established aquariums, where they are active in detritus accumulations and algae encrustations.

Pr—12. PHAEOPHYTA (brown algae).

Padina

Dictyopterus

Sargassum

Large and small seaweeds, about 1500 species, including giant kelp and *Sargassum* weed. Only three freshwater species. Brown algae are thought to have evolved from the single celled chrysophytes, Phylum Pr—4. There are twelve orders of Phaeophyta, three previous class distinctions have been rescinded. Dawes (1981) presents a key to the twelve orders. Brown algae are highly variable in color, ranging from yellow to almost black depending on light intensity, size and age, and species. There are a number of species that may do well in modern marine aquarium systems if collectors and wholesalers bring them into the market. Some of these are *Dictyota* sp., *Padina* sp., attached *Sargassum* sp., *Turbinaria* sp., and many others. A variety of small tropical species may develop from spores in live rock.

Pr—13. RHODOPHYTA (red algae).

Large and small seaweeds, 4000 species, including ornamental and encrusting species common in marine aquariums. Red algae appear to be closely related to the prokaryotic blue-green algae, phylum M—7. The **Class Ban-**

giophyceae are the simplest forms. Most red algae are in the **Class Florideophyceae** and are more complex in structure. Red algae are usually some shade of red and often feel slippery or

slimy to the hand. There are many shallow water species including small, brittle, coralline species that grow from live rock. Calcium carbonate in the tissues forms a rigid, yet flexible, structure for the thallus. Red algae—*Chondrus* (Irish Moss), *Gigartina*, *Gracilaria*, and *Eucheuma*,—are sources of commercially

Gracilaria, Hypnea, Arochcetium

important agar, used in all sorts of industrial and food products. Several strains of tank raised *Gracilaria* are available to the marine aquarium market, and many other species find their way into marine tanks attached to live rock.

Pr—14. GAMOPHYTA (marriage of plants)

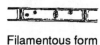

Conjugating green algae, mostly filamentous forms. Freshwater species only.

Filamentous form

Pr—15. CHLOROPHYTA** (yellow-green plant).

Green algae that form zoospores, about 5500 species including ornamental and encrusting species common in marine aquariums. About 90% are freshwater species. Green algae are almost always some shade of green. They contain pigments very similar to terrestrial green plants and are generally considered to be the ancestors of land plants. Three classes are recognized: **Chlorophyceae**, which is the largest group and contains the species important to marine aquarists, and the **Charophyceae** and the **Prasinophyceae**. The microscopic greens, unicellular and filamentous, often show up on live rock, but usually just blend in with the encrusting growths of blue-greens, diatoms, red algae and other organisms that appear.

Ulva lactuca

Acetabularia crenulata

Caulerpa racemosa

Caulerpa prolifera

Caulerpa floridana

The macroscopic green algae are the species most beautiful and most in demand for marine aquariums. The various species in the genus *Caulerpa*, in particular, *C. sertularioides, C. prolifera, C. racemosa,* and *C. taxifolia* are most common in marine tanks. Other green algae genera—*Halimeda* (calcareous), *Ulva* (sea lettuce), *Valonia* (green bubbles), *Bryopsis*, (feathers), *Codium* (green sponge), *Penicillus* (shaving brush), and many more—are common in reef type marine systems. Hair algae, *Enteromorpha* sp., may make a beautiful, thin hair-like growth on the bottom of a marine tank, or if light and nutrients are particularly favorable, may take over a tank with a thick, mat-like growth over all surfaces. Increase in redox potential and decrease in nutrients will reduce hair algae growth. A few algae eating sea urchins and/or mollusks may also keep hair algae in check and can be easily removed if they begin feeding on other algae. More information on green algae is found in Chapter 3.

Pr—16. ACTINOPODA* (ray foot)

Dictyophinus

Lithelius

The **Radiolaria**, almost entirely marine, planktonic, noncolonial protozoa. They have a radially symmetrical shell composed of strontium sulfate with numerous spicules extending outward all around the central shell. All radiolaria are pelagic and occur from the surface to depths of several thousand meters. They are able to move up and down in the water column by altering their specific gravity. Symbiotic haptophytes (Pr—5) in species that remain near the surface photosynthesize for the radiolarian. Some red clay marine muds are over 50% radiolarian shells.

Pr—17. FORAMINIFERA* (bearing little holes)

Marine, non colonial, protozoa with complex, pored shells composed of calcium carbonate granules, sand grains, or other bottom materials. These tiny protozoa live in marine sediments and algae growths, although two families are planktonic.

Pulvinulina

Pr—18. CILIOPHORA** (bearing eyelashes)

Cryptocaryon
(cyst and trophont)

Marine and freshwater single celled and colonial protozoa, about 8,000 species. Most ciliates are covered with cilia, short, whip-like flagella. Many species are common in marine aquariums, but observation and identification are difficult. *Cryptocaryon* is an important fish parasite and *Euplotes* is a useful larval food organism. Many marine ciliates can be grown on yeast suspensions, and some species may become important foods for larval

Tintinnopsis fish and invertebrates. Planktonic and benthic species are common. Reproduction is usually by mitotic division of the cell.

Pr—19. APICOMPLEXA* (embracing the apex)

Eimeria

Spore-forming, heterotrophic, microbial, internal parasites of animals. All cells have an apical complex of organelles at one end The coccidians (*Eimeria*) are widespread internal parasites of fish.

Pr—20. CNIDOSPORIDIA** (filament spore)

Heterotrophic, microbial, internal animal parasites with a polar filament or thread. Important internal parasites in fish and invertebrates.

Glugea

Pr-21. LABYRINTHULOMYCOTA*

(little labyrinth easily broken)

Heterotrophic, colonial protoctists that produce transparent colonies on marine grasses and algaes. Slime net "amoebas".

Labyrinthula

Pr—22. ACRASIOMYCOTA (bad mixture fungus)

Heterotrophic, amoeboid protoctists found in freshwater and damp terrestrial environments. Individual amoeboid cells aggregate into a slug-like and then a spore generating stage.

Dictyostelium

Pr—23. MYXOMYCOTA (mucus fungus)

Up to 500 species known, heterotrophic, amoeboid protoctists found in damp, woody terrestrial environments. Individual amoeboid cells aggregate into a plasmodium that produces stalked sporocarps.

Echinostelium

Pr—24. PLASMODIOPHOROMYCOTA

(multinucleate protoplasm bearing fungus)

Osmotrophic obligate plant parasites, 35 known species. Freeliving zoospore and parasitic multinucleate plasmodium stages. No marine species known.

Plasmodiophophora

Pr—25. HYPHOCHYTRIDIOMYCOTA (web pot fungus)

Fungus-like, but with flagellated (undulipodiate) cells. 15 known parasitic or saprobic species from soil and freshwater.

Hyphochytrium

Pr—26. CHYTRIDIOMYCOTA (pot fungus)

Fungus-like but with flagellated (undulipodiate) cells. Parasitic or saprobic microbes found in freshwater or soil. Cell walls *Blastocladiella* of chitin with hyphae and flagellated zoospores.

Pr—27. OOMYCOTA** (egg fungus)

Fungus-like but with zoospores with two flagella of unequal length. Damp terrestrial and freshwater environments, plant and animal parasites. Cause of the Irish potato famine. An *Saprolegnia* external parasite (*Saprolegnia*) on marine fish.
oogonium stage

KINGDOM FUNGI

The fungus phyla

Fungi are organisms with eukaryotic cells that form spores and lack flagella at all stages of the life cycle. They lack photosynthetic pigments and obtain nutrients by absorption of nutrients from living or dead organisms. They do not have true roots, stems, or leaves. Many fungi form root-like hyphae and rhizoids that grow into organic material, release powerful enzymes to digest it, and then absorb released nutrients. Out of 100,000 species, only 500 or so are marine. Most marine fungi are closely associated with a particular type of substrate or host organism. Many fungi enter into intimate association with algaes and form growths called lichens. The fungi provide a rigid support and store water. The algae photosynthesizes and produces food for itself and the fungus. Some very important diseases of algae, fish, and crustaceans are caused by marine fungi. The loss of the commercial sponge beds in Florida and the Bahamas in 1939 was caused by a water mold fungus, and another fungus, *Dermocystidium marinum*, devastates commercial oyster beds.

F—1. ZYGOMYCOTA** (pair fungus)

Ichthyosporidium

At least 600 species, no cross walls or septa. Many parasitic species including *Ichthyosporidium hoferi* (Ichthyophonus), an important internal parasite of marine fish.

F—2. ASCOMYCOTA* (bladder fungus)

Yeast cells

Yeasts and molds, thousands of species, all have an ascus reproductive structure. *Trichosporon* is parasitic on shrimp, and some yeast type ascomycota are parasitic on clams.

F—3. BASIDIOMYCOTA (small base fungus)

Coprinus

Mostly terrestrial mushrooms, 25,000 species. Rusts, smuts, and puffballs. They all contain a club-like reproductive structure, the basidium. Four species known from the marine environment. A smut, *Melanotaenium ruppiae*, attacks the sea grass, *Ruppia maritima*.

F—4. DEUTEROMYCOTA (second fungus)

Trichophyton
(athletes foot)

Fungi Imperfecti, about 25,000 species, no organs for sexual reproduction. Very important group including producers of penicillin and other antibiotics and some human parasites. The families Coelomycetidae and Hypomycetidae have marine species.

F—5. MYCOPHYCOPHYTA (fungus algae plant)

Cladonia

The **lichens**, about 25,000 species of algal/fungus partnerships, common in the salt spray coastal zones. Various species of fungi and algae can combine to form a lichen.

KINGDOM ANIMALIA

The Animals

Animals develop from the equal contributions of genetic material from an egg and a sperm. They are multicellular with differentiated cells organized into tissues and they obtain food from the environment rather than manufacturing it through photosynthesis. Most animals are mobile at some stage of life. Even sessile corals and sponges have larval stages that swim with the currents. Animals maintain a relatively constant internal environment with high levels of sodium chloride within cells and tissues and are usually responsive to the outer environment through a nervous system. Within the common characteristics that define animals, the diversity between and within phyla is astounding. Size varies from microscopic to whales, and complexity ranges from simple tissues to the mind of humans. The animal phyla developed many millions of years ago from various protoctist ancestors and subsequently, from various generalized animal ancestors.

Animals originated in the sea and most have remained there. Only a relatively few species of arthropods and chordates have become completely liberated from a moist, aquatic environment. We can observe and study many of the primitive and complex animals of the sea within the artificial environment of a modern marine aquarium system. The list of phyla begins with the simplest animals and moves toward the most complex. Complexity, however, is a judgement of the human mind, and who are we to say that the intricate and highly successful adaption of a coral species to life in a tropic sea is any less complex than the life of an aquarist in New York City. Anyway, we call it the way we see it, and to us, corals are simple and mammals are complex.

A—1. PLACOZOA* (flat animal)

Trichoplax

The simplest of animals, a single species phylum, *Trichoplax adhaerens*. An amoeba-like animal composed of a few thousand cells, all surface cells with cilia. Reproduces from eggs fertilized by sperm. First found on the walls of a marine aquarium in Austria in 1883 and always found in marine waters. Specimens have been taken only from marine aquaria containing rocks and invertebrates from coral reef areas.

A—2. PORIFERA** (bearing pores)

The sponges, the simplest tissue level of organization, two tissue layers, no organs, no symmetry. About 10,000 species, only 150 are freshwater. The sponges are named for the thousands of pores incorporated into their structure. Unusual among animals, they are without definite form or a particular symmetry. Although the cells that form sponges are organized into layers of particular cell types, these cell layers are not true tissues. The cells that make up some sponges can even be separated by forcing the sponge through a fine sieve and the cells will then reorganize themselves into a semblance of their original structure. The highly variable form and color of sponges makes identification difficult, even for experts. Often only the shape of the spicules, microscopic internal supporting structures, can identify the species.

Sponges are an ancient phylum. They have been found in fossils dated to over 550 million years ago. The form and mode of life of sponges has been so successful that few changes in structure and function have occurred through ages of evolution. Many sponges maintain a species of blue-green algae within their tissues that act as *zooxanthellae* and produce food for the sponge. Most of the nutrition of sponges, however, is obtained by filtering water through the outer pores to central chambers and then passing the filtered water from the sponge through large pores called oscules. Tiny organic particles including bacteria and other plankton are filtered and consumed by the sponge. Sponges are difficult to maintain in aquarium systems because of the need for tiny plankton, high water quality, and strong water movement. Many species require low light levels, more blue light, and do best under structures that shield them from direct light. A strong, healthy sponge has a clean surface and clear, open pores with no mucus, scum, or algae coating the surface. Other species do well under high light levels. Such species may have methods of preventing algal growth on their surfaces. Maintaining sponges in aquarium systems is still highly experimental. Proper light, strong water currents, and occasional feedings of very fine, particulate foods will help maintain sponges in the aquarium.

Haliclona (red sponge)

Callyspongia
(fluorescent sponge)

There are four classes within the phylum. **Class Calcarea** have calcareous, needle-like or rayed spicules and are relatively small, dull colored, shallow water sponges. **Class Hexactinellida** are vase shaped with six rayed, silica spicules. The dried skeleton looks like it is composed of glass fibers, which gives this class of deep water sponges the common name of glass sponge. **Class Sclerospongiae** are the coralline sponges and have a massive calcareous (calcium carbonate) skeleton with embedded silica spicules and an organic spongin network. They can be mistaken for corals because of the hard, massive (up to 1 meter) skeleton. The **Class Demospongiae** contains many species, over 9,000. Most are marine, but there are some freshwater species. The skeletal material is spongin (but many species also have spicules) and many varied sizes, shapes, and colors exist. Commercial sheepswool and yellow sponges and the ornamental sponges found in the marine tropical market are in this class. Many species of shallow coral reef sponges may grow from a tiny attachment on live rock if conditions of light and water quality are acceptable in the aquarium. The red finger sponge, *Haliclona rubens*, is one of the most common sponges available to the marine aquarist, but there are thousands of species of Demospongiae that may turn up in an aquarium. The boring sponges, *Cliona* sp., are common on live rock and will develop into a yellow or orange encrusting growth under favorable conditions. The fire sponge, *Taedania*, may also come in on live rock or algae rock and can cause a fiery stinging sensation on exposed skin.

A—3. CNIDARIA** (nettle hollow intestine)

The coelenterates—hydras, jellyfish, corals, and anemones—are the simplest animals with cells organized into true tissues. They are radially symmetrical, almost all marine, have two tissue layers, and have internal organs. The body forms are polyps and/or medusae and there are about 10,000 species. All have only one opening to the gut. All species also have nematocysts in the tentacles, which are small cells that shoot a "poisoned dart" into prey or predator. In most species (corals and anemones) this is little more than an annoyance to humans, but in others (the man o' war jellyfish and the cubomeduse), an encounter can be very painful and even fatal. (Don't rub a jellyfish sting. Sprinkle meat tenderizer on the area to break down the toxin.) Coelenterates take on two basic forms, the polyp and the medusa. Many species use both forms at different stages of the life cycle. The polyp is tubular (solitary or colonial) with one end attached to a substrate or embedded in secreted skeletal material, and has a ring of tentacles around the mouth or oral opening at the upper end. The medusa, the typical jellyfish, is the polyp flattened out and turned upside down. The oral opening and the tentacles extend downward and a smooth rounded dome forms the upper surface.

The common names for the corals typically found in marine systems are very descriptive and highly variable. There are no standard common names. Names of corals are often made up by wholesalers or retailers and are based only on appearance. Terms such as pink frilly, orange bush, green mat, mushroom, yellow finger, and green bubble are tacked onto a generic name like coral, anemone, or gorgonian. Although some of the common names of common species are fairly well established and can point one toward the right identification, an accurate identification down to family, genus, or possibly species requires spending some time with good reference books. Wood (1983) is a good reference to the structure and taxonomy of reef corals.

Depending on the classification one follows there are three to six classes of Cnidaria. The usual arrangement is three classes: **Hydrozoa** (hydras, fire corals and Portuguese man o' war), **Scyphozoa** (typical jellyfish), and **Anthozoa** (soft corals, stony corals and anemones). The sea wasp jellyfish, cubomeduse, are often taken from the Scyphozoa and elevated to class level, **Cubozoa.**

Physalia
(Portuguese man o' war)

Hydrozoons have the most primitive features in the phylum and are often found in reef tanks as tiny growths. They frequently form encrusting growths with many feather-like polyps. The fire corals, **Order Milleporina**, form hard, encrusting growths, some species with large flat upward projecting blades, and often enter marine systems as part of a live rock. Hydrozoons require light and abundant micro plankton to survive and generally do not do as well in marine systems as corals and anemones that can get by on mostly light.

Gonionemus (medusa)

The major life stage in the **Class Scyphozoa** is the medusa. These are the typical jellyfish such as the large moon jelly, *Aurelia aurita*, of the tropical Atlantic. Jellyfish are planktonic and drift with the currents, but do swim with rhythmic contractions of the oral ring. An exception to the typical planktonic jellyfish is the only jellyfish commonly found in marine aquariums. This is the bottom living *Cassiopea*, a brownish-green, shallow water jellyfish that rests "upside down" on the bottom with its tentacles extended upward. It captures planktonic organisms with its tentacles and contains *zooxanthellae* in its tissues.

The **Class Anthozoa** has over 6,500 species and contains two subclasses. Here is where we find most of the animals that occupy reef tank systems.

Cnidarians in the **Subclass Alcyonaria (Octocorallia)** have eight tentacles and this includes the orders: **Alcyonacea** (soft corals), **Gorgonaceae** (sea fans, sea fingers, and gorgonians), **Coenothecalia** (blue corals) and **Pennatulacea** (sea pens).

Briareum
(sea fingers)

The **Subclass Zoantharia (Hexacorallia)** have tentacles in sets of six and includes the orders: **Actinaria** (anemones), **Scleractinia** (massive stony corals), **Ceriantharia** (tube anemones), **Zoanthidea** (colonial anemones), **Antipatharia** (black corals), and **Corallimorpharia** (flattened coral-like anemones, (false corals) corallimorpharians). The corals and anemones most kept in marine reef systems are members of this class.

The large Pacific anemones (Actinaria) in the genera *Radianthus* (long tentacled) and *Stoichactis* (carpet) are very popular in reef systems. These are the anemones that most commonly host clownfish. The Atlantic anemones in the genus *Condylactis* (pink tipped) are also familiar and do very well in most well lit, low nitrate aquariums. Many other

Condylactis
(sea anemone)

genera of anemones are common, such as *Anthopleura, Tealia, Adamsia, Calliactis*, and the tube anemones *Cerianthus*. Friese (1972) is a handy popular reference to anemones.

A popular soft coral group are the alcyonacean tree corals in the genus *Dendronephthya*. These small soft corals are highly branched and brightly colored and can reproduce asexually in good reef system tanks. Although small in the aquarium, they can reach heights of one meter on Pacific reefs. The soft corals in the genus *Anthelia* are popular and do well in good reef system tanks. A variety of colorful gorgonians, sea fans, sea whips, and sea fingers are available. They require relatively strong currents and planktonic food to do well in marine systems. Many of the soft corals can begin new colonies from small sections that are fastened in favorable locations in reef systems. Usually, sea anemone and coral gametes develop directly within the tissues that line the gastric area. Eggs and sperm are released into the gastric cavity and into the sea. In some species, however, the gametes are released through pores in the tentacle tips or at the base of the polyp (Campbell, 1974). Delbeek and Burleson (Delbeek, 1989) recently photographically documented tentacular release of eggs in the soft coral *Anthelia*. A few of the sea pens, particularly the sea pansies, *Renilla*, are occasionally available. The sea pansies show bioluminescence when disturbed in a darkened tank.

Most of the large, stony, reef building (hermatypic) corals (Scleractinia) such as brain coral, star coral, and pillar coral are seldom seen in reef systems. They are illegal to collect in some areas (Florida) and do best in systems that generate strong water surges through the coral formations. Home aquarists have so far had the best success

Oculina (bush coral) with anthozoan corals and anemones that favor strong lighting and protected habitats on the reef. Small solitary corals in this order, however, are popular in marine reef systems. The Suborder **Caryophylliina** includes the bubble corals in the genera *Pterogyra* and *Physogyra*, such as *Physogyra liechtensteina* (try saying that with a mouthful of soda crackers). The bubbles that surround the polyps during the day are thought to protect the polyps. The bubbles retract at night, and the tentacles of the polyps then expand to collect plankton and even large organisms. Some bubble corals are fed pieces of shrimp or even small goldfish and guppies. The flower corals of the genus *Euphyllia*, Family Caryophyllidae, with their short, bulbus, green, bluish or brown polyps that fill large, strongly ridged cups are popular corals in this group.

The solitary and colonial corals of the Suborder **Dendrophylliina,** Family Dendrophylliidae, are frequently found in marine reef systems. Clumps of these coral polyps packed in rounded orange colonies (*Dendrophyllia gracilis* is a common species) form delicate growths in reef tanks. The individual coral polyps have solitary skeletal cups (calices) that are fragile and are easily damaged during collection and handling. Handle all corals with great care. Hitting or crushing the colony may break a few polyp skeletons and these will not survive when placed in the tank. The damaged polyps die and decay and the bacteria may even spread to healthy polyps near the damaged ones. A strong current of water over the colony helps clean the damaged and decaying tissues from the around the healthy polyps.

Also in this suborder, the colonies of bright orange polyps of sunflower corals, *Tubastrea,* are striking in reef tanks. The

 bright orange color indicates a liking for low light and deep water, so it is best not to expose these corals to the brightest lit areas of the tank. Corals that occur as solitary polyps and some large colonial polyps are in the suborder **Fungiina.**

Manicina (rose coral)

The solitary mushroom corals, *Fungia,* and rose coral, *Manicina,* are common examples. These corals do well under brighter light. The popular *Goniopora* coral colonies are in the family Poritidae. They form large rounded colonies of large polyps that are 2 to 5 mm diameter and 2 to 4 cm in length. The polyps are usually extended during the day and a good colony of *Goniopora* makes a spectacular addition to a reef tank. These corals are difficult to keep more than six to eight months, although many colonies may survive for well over a year. Proper lighting is very important to these and other corals, since light is critical to the well being of the *zooxanthellae* in the corals tissues. The *zooxanthellae* are not only important in food production through photosynthesis but also contribute to removal of CO_2 from the coral's tissues and to calcification of the stony skeleton of the coral. *Goniopora* are one of the corals that benefit greatly from a wave surge system in a reef tank. It is also important to keep phosphate in inorganic and organic form at very low levels in the system water. As with other corals, maintain a space of three to four inches between colonies to prevent "aggression" and stress caused by coral colonies warring for their ecological niche.

The **zoanthids** are small, mostly colonial corals that look much like small anemones. Many are brightly colored, orange and red, although some are brownish or green, and they occur in colonies of many individuals. The species *Zoanthus sociatus* from the tropical Atlantic forms extensive green mats of small, circular polyps about a centimeter across and can do well in reef systems.

The **Corallimorpharia**, including the mushroom and elephant ear anemones, are very popular in reef systems. They are hardy, generally easy to care for, live well and even reproduce easily in marine systems that have the proper conditions of light and water quality. The corallimorpharians are a

wide variety of mostly colonial coral-like anemones, large and small, most with bulbous tips on the end of the tentacles. Many small species accompany live rocks into marine systems. The genus *Ricordea*, colonies of small green disks several centimeters across with bubble-like tentacles, and *Rhodactis*, more solitary polyps, are

Ricordea
(mushroom anemone)

common Caribbean species. Many Pacific species are also becoming available. They depend greatly on *zooxanthellae* for nutrition, but many of the species with large tentacles feed actively on plankton and small benthic organisms. After feeding, the anemone folds up into a ball or cup shape while digesting the food organism. Like other cnidarians, mushroom anemones should not be kept close to other corals or anemones. Mushroom anemones prefer low current situations so don't place them directly in the surge pattern or in the direct line of the pump discharge. Keep about three inches between specimens to avoid "combat" and possible loss of one

specimen. Delbeek (1987) discusses maintenance of corallimorpharians in marine systems.

A—4. CTENOPHORA* (bearing combs)

Comb jellies or sea walnuts are biradial-
ly symmetrical, and are all marine, 90
species. All but a few species, such as the
bottom creeping *Coeloplana*, are planktonic.
Transparent, with true muscles, they have
eight bands of paddle-like comb plates
along the length of the animal. Ctenophores
have the appearance of small, transparent
blobs of jelly as they float in the sea. They
can not be easily collected and do not appear in marine
aquariums. It is possible, however, for ctenophores to develop
and live in larval rearing systems that are fed on wild plankton.

Mnemiopsis
(sea walnut)

A—5. MESOZOA* (middle animals)

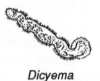

About 90 species of worm-like, urinary
tract parasites of shallow water marine invertebrates. They have only two tissue layers
and one organ, a gonad. Hosts are flatworms,
polychete annelids, cephalopods, and
echinoderms. There is alternation of sexual and asexual genera-
tions.

Dicyema

A—6. PLATYHELMINTHES** (flat worm)

Soft bodied, ribbon shaped, bilaterally
symmetrical animals with two tissue layers,
about 15,000 species. Both free living and
parasitic species. They are the simplest
animals with distinctive anterior and
posterior ends and upper and lower sur-
faces. Most are very small and seldom seen. The classes **Ces-
toda** (tapeworms) and **Trematoda** (flukes) are both totally
parasitic. Both groups have species that are important parasites
on marine fish. The **Class Turbellaria** has the free-living flatworms. Live rock may contain a few small flat worms when
introduced into the aquarium, but these seldom survive for

Callioplana

long. The **Order Polycladida** contains a number of brightly colored, large (2 to 3 inch long) flatworms with undulating fringes that may occasionally be found in shops. Little is know about the biology of these species but they are thought to prey on tiny organisms present in detrital accumulations. A few species can capture larger soft bodied invertebrates. They have a chance to survive in older, well established reef tanks. Most are in the Family Pseudocerotidae, genera *Pseudoceros* and *Thysanozoon*.

A—7. NEMERTINA** (sea nymph)

About 900 species of ribbon worms. Unsegmented, fragile, flat worms with a long anterior proboscis that may be extended
Nemertina   three times the length of the body. Simplest animals with both mouth and anus. Nemertians are carnivorous. Pelagic and benthic species. Some Pacific species occasionally enter the marine tropical trade.

A—8. GNATHOSTOMULIDA* (jaw mouth)

About 88 species of tiny, less than 1 mm long, marine worms that live in sediments and on the leafy parts of marine plants. They
Problognathia   are bilaterally symmetrical and transparent, the jaws are the only hard parts. Specimens are difficult to preserve.

A—9. GASTROTRICHA* (stomach hair)

About 400 species of lobed headed, bilaterally symmetrical, flattened worms 1/2 to 4 mm in length with some bristles
typical form   and scales. Freshwater and marine species. Their unsegmented bodies cling to vegetation with adhesive tubes that project from their bodies. They are an important food source for many tiny marine predators.

A—10. ROTIFERA** (wheel bearers)

About 2,000 species (50 marine species) of tiny, bilaterally symmetrical animals (they may superficially appear radially

Brachionus
(marine rotifer)

symmetrical) with a crown of cilia. The body is enclosed in a layer of chitin called a lorica. There are free-living, planktonic, benthic, and parasitic species. Rotifer cysts of various species undoubtedly enter marine systems with live rock, and some must survive in detrital accumulations in marine reef systems. Unless the aquarist spends time with a microscope, the presence of these little "wheel animalcules" is seldom noticed. The main importance of these animals to the marine aquarist is to culture them as marine plankton for feeding to larval fish and invertebrates or as live planktonic food for reef tank systems. The species *Brachionus plicatilis* is most commonly cultured for this purpose.

A—11. KINORHYNCHA* (snout movers)

Echinodorella

About 150 species of tiny, unsegmented (but metameric with 14 metameres) marine worm-like animals. The head is retractile with stout recurved spines, and the body is covered with bristles. They move by pulling themselves along with their head spines. They feed on diatoms and organic matter and are food to many other marine animals. May be found in the detritus of marine aquarium systems.

A—12. LORICIFERA* (girdle bearing)

Nanaloricus

About 10 species of very tiny marine animals, less than 1/3 mm long, with spiny heads and girdle of spiny plates, a lorica, around the abdomen. The phylum is newly described in 1983. They live in marine substrates and have been taken from 15 to 480 meters.

A—13. ACANTHOCEPHALA* (thorn head)

About 600 species of spiny headed, parasitic worms, mostly vertebrate parasites. The extendable proboscis has sturdy hooks that attach the parasite to the walls of the intestine. Some species, *Neoechinorhynchus*, are *Leptorhynchoides* parasitic in marine fish.

A—14. ENTOPROCTA* (inside anus)

Mat animals, about 150 species of stalked, colonial, marine (one freshwater species) animals. Most are sessile (attached to the substrate) and have 6 to 36 tentacles at the end of the stalk. They are individually small (1 to 2 mm) filter feeders. The anus

Barentsia

opens within the ring of tentacles. The colony is often visible as a mat or network. Superficial appearance similar to ectoprocts, see phylum A—17.

A—15. NEMATODA** (thread)

The roundworms, 80,000 species described with perhaps a millon total. Free-living and parasitic species worms covered

Thoracostema

with a transparent cuticle and with three tissue layers. They range in size from very tiny, 1/10 mm, to almost 1 m. They move by flipping and bending rather than by extending and contracting. Tiny free-living species are common in the detritus of marine aquariums.

A—16. NEMATOMORPHA* (thread form)

The horsehair worms, about 240 species of long (10 to 70 cm), wiry, unsegmented worms. Few marine species. They do not eat, but absorb nutrients through the body

Nectonema

walls.

A—17. ECTOPROCTA** (outside anus)

Bugula

The moss animals **(bryozoa).** About 5,000 species, all but 50 are marine. They are individually small, usually colonial, with a true coelom (body cavity) and lophophore. The anus is located outside of the horse shoe shaped, tentacled organ, the lophophore, that surrounds the mouth. Bryozoa form extensive hard or gelatinous mats on bottom substrates. They are easily confused with algal growths, but close observation reveals the polyp-like zooid. Growths on live rocks in marine aquariums are common. There are two marine classes. The **Class Stenolaemata**, about 1000 species, contains marine bryozoans with calcified colonies and terminal, circular openings for the zooids. The **Class Gymnolaemata**, about 4000 species, have uncalcified zooid walls, and the zooid openings have a closing apparatus. Some species form crispy mats and others form knobby growths that mimic corals. Species identification is difficult without microscopes and special laboratory techniques. The common bugula, *Bugula neritina*, in the family Bugulidae forms an erect, bushy, reddish brown colony in shallow, tropical Atlantic waters and may find its way into marine systems on live rock.

A—18. PHORONIDA* (nest bearing)

Phoronis

The horseshoe worms, about 10 to 15 species of small, marine, sessile worms that produce leathery cases. The long tentacled lophophore extends from the case in a spirally coiled, horseshoe shaped, double ridge and functions as a plankton filter. The worm tubes are usually colonial and form dense, spaghetti-like masses attached to rocks and hard substrates. They feed on plankton, organic compounds, and even detritus. They are small and not likely to be noticed, but may occasionally show up in marine reef systems.

A—19. BRACHIOPODA* (arm foot)

Lingula

Crania

The lamp shells are about 335 species of clam-like, solitary, bilaterally symmetrical, marine animals with two hard valves (shells) and attach to the substrate by a flexible stalk or burrow into sediments. The valves of brachiopods are dorsal and ventral; the valves of bivalve mollusks are right and left. They bear a lophophore and are filter feeders. Their fossil history, *Lingula* in particular, extends back 400 million years. Not common in marine aquariums.

A—20. MOLLUSCA** (soft)

A vast and successful phylum, about 120,000 species including bivalves (clams), univalves (snails), nudibranchs (slugs), and cephalopods (squid and octopus). They are complex, bilaterally symmetrical, soft bodied animals, most with a hard external or internal shell and a fold in the body wall (a mantle) that lines and secretes the shell (snails and clams) or enfolds the body in a muscular sac (squid and octopus). Mollusks have a gut with a mouth and anus, a blood system, a reproductive system, an excretory system, and a nervous system. Fossil mollusks date back 530 million years to the Cambrian period. The annelids, phylum A—24, and the mollusks are thought to have a common origin somewhere in the Precambrian.

Depending on the classification one follows, there are five to eight classes. Molluskan classification is uncertain at this time and a variety of classification schemes are in the recent literature. When eight classes are defined, they are **Monoplacophora** (one shelled, deep sea), **Aplacopora** (the solenogasters and chaetoderms), **Caudofoveata** (shell-less and worm-like), **Polyplacophora** (the chitons), **Gastropoda** (Univalvia—snails, slugs and sea hares), **Pelecypoda** (Bivalvia—clams and oysters), **Scaphopoda** (tusk, tooth shells), and **Cephalopoda** (squid and octopus). Of these eight classes, four are important to marine aquarists.

The chitons, **Class Polyplacophora**, often called the "coat-of-mail" shells, are small, primitive, oval shaped, marine mollusks with a broad, strong foot and a shell composed of eight overlapping plates. The girdle that extends beyond the shell may be smooth or covered with hairy projections. They cling

tenaciously to rocks and feed by rasping algae from the rocks. Because they cling so tightly to rocks, small specimens may accompany live rock into marine reef systems. Some species of chitons are found in very shallow tidal areas. A few species are large, 2

Chiton
(squamose chiton)

to 3 inches, and colorful enough to be occasionally available as individual specimens.

The **Class Gastropoda** is largest and most diverse class of mollusks. Some gastropods, Order Stylommatophora, live in trees (tree snails) and gardens (garden snails and slugs) and many live in fresh and brackish water, but the vast majority are marine. Most are univalves with a single coiled shell, but there is one order of bivalve gastropods, Sacoglossa, and a few orders without shells in the adult stages. Classification is based on twisting of the body (torsion), presence and type of shell, type of respiratory organ, and many other characteristics. There are three subclasses.

The **Subclass Prosobranchia** exhibits pronounced torsion to the point that the gills and anus are located in front of the viscera. The shells are coiled in a spiral. The abalones, turban shells, and limpets of the Order Diotocardia; the wrinkles, slipper limpets, conch shells, cowries, and moon shells of the Order Mesogastropoda; and the whelks, drills, olive, tulip and cone shells (Don't handle live cone shells, their sting can be fatal!) of the Order Neogastropoda are in this subclass. The carnivorous snails in this group, such as the flamingo tongue, *Cyphoma gibbosum*, do well in marine systems if the proper food is available. Flamingo tongues feed only on gorgonians, and unless they are fed these soft corals, they do not survive for long. Strombid conchs, such as the Queen conch, *Strombus gigas*, are herbivores and do very well in systems with a variety and abundance of algae. Tank raised queen conchs are now available to marine aquarists. Carnivorous snails, such as the tulip

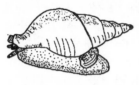

snail, *Fasciolaria tulipa*, do well on small pieces of shrimp, squid, scallop, and other seafoods. But beware, tulip snails are determined predators. Other mollusks are not safe in the same tank with a tulip snail. Cowries generally hide during the day and are active at night.

Charonia (trumpet triton)

The shells are beautifully colored, smooth and lustrous, and are kept that way by the strong, membranous mantle that usually completely envelops the shell. The white spotted, dark, fist-sized deer or spotted cowrie, *Cypraea cervus*, from the tropical Atlantic is frequently found in aquarium shops as is its smaller cousin, the measled cowry, *C. zebra*. The feeding habitats of cowries, and many other mollusks, are not well known and the observant aquarist has an opportunity to contribute much new information on these animals.

The mollusks in the **Subclass Opisthobranchia** have "untwisted" and show various degrees of detorsion. The shell is reduced and may be absent in the adults. The mantle cavity and gills may be reduced or lost, and various respiratory structures may be developed on the dorsal surface. The bubble, lobe, and canoe shells of the Order Bullomorpha; the pyramid shells, Order Pyramidellomorpha; the sea butterflies and pteropods in the orders Thecosomata and Gymnosmota; the sea hares in the Order Aplysiomorpha; and the shell-less sea slugs in the **Order Nudibranchia** are all in this subclass.

The nudibranchs (naked gills) are among the most spectacular of marine animals. Kerstitch (1988) presents a beautiful pictorial essay on many of the nudibranches available to the

marine aquarist. Nudibranchs are sea slugs with exposed gills (cerata) and no shells. Most live among shallow, tropical bottom growths, but a few burrow into the bottoms and a couple of species are pelagic. They are mostly carnivorous and feed upon sponges, corals, detrital

Hermissenda (sea slug)

animals, and even each other. Some species require a very specific diet, but others feed more widely. In some nudibranchs the intestinal wall of the mid gut extends in long pocket-like projections into the cerata along the dorsal surface of the slug. When the slug feeds on coral polyps, the stinging cells are passed undigested and fully functional into the dorsal surface tissues of the slug. The protective function of these cells is then passed on to the nudibranch, and any animal that disturbs the slug is stung by the nematocysts that were stolen by the nudibranch from the coral polyp. The Atlantic lettuce slug, *Tridachia crispata*, is a farmer. It feeds on algae and removes the chloroplasts (entire and fully functional) from the algae cell, transfers them to an area just under the transparent skin of its dorsal projections, and encourages them to survive and photosynthesize—but now for the benefit of the slug and not the algae. Two species with the common name Spanish shawl, *Coryphella iodenia* and *Chromodoris quadricolor*, from the Philippines, and the Spanish dancer, *Hexabranchus sanguineus*, are often available in aquarium shops. As some of these common names imply, the swimming motions of these nudibranchs are spectacular displays of motion and color. The mantle rim is extended outward in all directions and undulating waves move along the brilliantly colored mantle as the animal slowly swims through the water. This gloriously display of color and motion may be a warning to predators that the dancer is unpalatable.

The **Subclass Pulmonata** contains mostly terrestrial species in the orders Systellommatophora, tropical slugs; Basommatophora, pond and marsh snails; and Stylommatophora, land and tree snails and slugs.

The bivalves, **Class Pelecypoda**, have species common to fresh, brackish, and marine waters. Clams, oysters, scallops,  and mussels are typical bivalves. A dorsal and ventral valve or shell hinged at the rear is characteristic of this class. The mantle and foot are modified according to the life mode of the species. The foot is

Pecten (scallop)

strong and muscular in burrowing

species such as clams and greatly reduced in species that remain cemented to one location such as oysters. The adductor muscles hold the shells together. Scallops (**Order Anisomyaria**) are the most mobile of the bivalves and swim by compressing water between the valves with strong contractions of the adductor muscles. The mantle shapes this flow into a directional water jet. The flame scallop, *Lima scabra*, is popular with marine aquarists. Common oysters, *Crassostrea* and *Ostrea*, are also in this order as are the thorny oysters, *Spondylus*, which are often found firmly attached to coral rock. The **Order Heterodonta** contains the giant clams *Tridacna crocea* and *T. gigas* that do well in reef tanks, especially since they have *zooxanthellae* in the exposed mantle and are thus able to provide much of their own nutrition under the proper lighting. Many coral rocks contain rock boring mollusks, or the remains of their shells. There are a variety of species of bivalves in the Order (or subclass) Heterodonta, piddocks and others, that bore deep into rocks and can not be removed unless the rock is broken open. These rock borers usually die in the collection and transport of live rock unless special care is taken. The Order Adepedonta includes the razor shells and the Family Teredinidae, genera *Bankia* and *Teredo*, the wood boring shipworms. The Order Taxodonta includes the ark shells and the Order Mytiloida includes the pen shells and mussels.

The **Class Cephalopoda** includes the **Subclass Nautiloidea**, the fabled chambered nautilus, *Nautilus* sp. Four

living species occur in the south western Pacific. These are the only surviving cephalopods with external shells. Once very rare in the marine tropical industry, *Nautilus* are now very occasionally found in the tanks of wholesalers. The **Subclass Coleoidea** includes the bottle-tailed squids and cuttlefish, **Order Sepiodea**, and the octopuses, **Order Octopoda**. Nautilus and squid are pelagic animals and not easy to keep in marine aquarium systems. Large tanks are necessary, of course, and

Nautilus
(chambered nautilus)

these animals are usually only found in public aquariums. They are carnivorous animals and are used to live prey, but

Octopus

may be trained to take small fish and shrimp in captivity. There are many species of octopus, and small specimens are often found in shops. Octopuses are also carnivorous and feed well on small shrimp, crabs, and fish. They are mostly nocturnal and are good occupants of night systems. The blue-ringed octopus, *Hapalochlaena maculosa*, is sometimes found in the trade, but be very careful; the bite of this species can be fatal. *Octopus vulgaris* (meaning common, not vulgar) is the common Atlantic species, but many small species in the genus *Octopus* are available. The female lays eggs, takes care of the young until hatching, and then dies. Octopuses can be kept in fairly small tanks, but the tank must be tightly covered for they can, and often do, squeeze out of the tank and wander around the room.

With the development of marine reef aquarium systems, it is possible for the marine aquarist to keep many new species of mollusks. The feeding patterns of mollusks are as varied as their forms and colors, and for the most part, little is known about the life and habits of many mollusks.

A—21. PRIAPULIDA* (little penis)

Tubiluchus

Only 8 species of small (5 to 200 mm), unsegmented, mud living, marine worms. Characterized by a straight gut, large body cavity, superficial segmentation with spines and warts on the body surface, and a short, spiny proboscis (presoma).

A-22. SIPUNCULA* (little pipe)

Paraspidosiphon

The peanut worms, about 300 species of marine, unsegmented, bilaterally symmetrical worms with a true coelom (body cavity), no circulatory or respiratory organs, and a very contractile body. Fully contracted, the body is pulled into a knot resembling a peanut. The worm burrows by extending the forepart of the body (the introvert) into the sediment, expanding its tip, and then drawing its rear forward. They range in size from 2 or 3 cm to over a meter long.

A—23. ECHIURA* (snake tailed)

The spoon worms, about 140 species of soft, plump, unsegmented marine worms with a rough, prickly surface. They range in size from 2 or 3 mm to 400 mm. The proboscis (spoon) of some species, *Bonellia*, can be enormously extended to over a meter in length, is bifurcated at the end, functions as gill, and may be regrown if lost.

Bonellia

A—24. ANNELIDA** (little ring)

The segmented worms, about 11,500 species including earthworms, polychetes (marine bristle worms), and leaches. They are segmented, bilaterally symmetrical, with a true coelom and chitinous bristles. There are a few planktonic species, but most are burrowing forms. Many species, such as the marine fanworms, build tubes and use a spread of tentacles to filter food organisms from the water. Most marine annelids feed on plankton and detritus, although some species are carnivorous and some of these feed on corals. There are three classes: the earthworms, **Oligochaeta**; the leeches, **Hirudinea**; and the largest group, **Polychaeta**, which contains 8000 species including the marine ragworms, lugworms, bristleworms, and fanworms. Some polychaetes reproduce asexually, but most favor sexual reproduction. Some species brood eggs and larvae and can reproduce in aquariums. Some build tubes and are sessile, but many are free living. Most marine aquariums, especially reef systems, probably contain many polychates that never come to the attention of the aquarist. They remain hidden in sediments and under rocks, although some may come into the open during night hours. The **bristleworms** or fireworms, **Order Amphinomida**, Family Amphinomidae, and the **feather duster** and **Christmas tree worms**, Families Sabellidae and

Serpulidae in the **Order Sabellida,** are most common to marine aquarists.

The bristleworms are not called fireworms just because of their bright orange and red colors. The fine, needle-like bristles are hollow and contain a potent venom. The stings caused by these worms feel like fire and last a long time. Don't handle them with bare hands. The common Caribbean species *Eulalia* (bristleworm) is the fireworm, *Hermodice carunculata,* in the family Amphinomidae. Several other species of fireworms in this family may occasionally show up in marine tanks, and all are dangerous. The orange bristle worm, *Eurythoe complanata,* is common in rocks around coral reefs. It is a long, segmented orange worm with a line of short white bristles on each side. This species can easily reproduce in marine aquariums, and rocks and filter beds may develop large populations of this polychaete bristleworm. Many polychaetes reproduce with a modified trochophore larvae that spends a short time in the plankton and subsists on yolk during the entire pelagic planktonic stage. These species can reproduce easily in marine systems.

The fan worms, feather dusters and Christmas tree worms, on the other hand, are beautiful, shy, and harmless. They are sessile and feed on plankton and organic particles with a fan of tentacles derived from the gill structures. These orange, red, green, or blue feathery structures gather food and serve as respiratory organs for the worm encased in the rigid tube. Food particles trapped in the feathery crown are moved down to the mouth by the action of tiny cilia. Fine plankton particles are important to these worms. Brown eye spots on the crown are connected to enormous nerve fibers that extend along the entire body of the worm. Changes in light intensity on the crown, such as a passing fish or diver, stimulate a startle response that retracts the crown in the blink of an eye, an effective response to a potential predator. The worm can, and occasionally does, shed its crown. The worm is not necessarily dead and can grow a new crown of tentacles.

Sabellastarte
(feather duster fan worm)

The feather duster fanworms of the **Family Sabellidae** are familiar to aquarists as individual tubes with flowering crowns. The tubes are membranous or built of sand grains, are often attached to rocks, and may be entwined with each other. The genera *Sabella* and *Sabellastarte* are common.

Spirobranchus
(Christmastree fan worm)

The spiral structure of the crown is most evident in the Christmas tree worms of the **Family Serpulidae**. The tubes of these worms are calcareous, are usually embedded in coral rock, and are seldom visible. The beautiful red, orange, white, and brown crowns occur in pairs, usually embedded in coral rock. The Atlantic species *Spirobranchus giganteus* is most common in marine aquariums. Serpulids have true pelagic trochophore larvae and the relatively long planktonic stage is a barrier to reproduction in marine systems.

A—25. TARDIGRADA* (slow step)

Batillipes (water bear)

The water bears are tiny (1/20 to 1.2 mm), arthropod-like, bilaterally symmetrical animals with four pairs of stumpy legs ending in claws or adhesive disks. They have oral stylets and a suctorial pharynx for feeding and are without circulatory or respiratory systems. Only 25 marine species. One species, *Demodex folliculorum*, lives in the hair follicles of humans.

A—26. PENTASTOMA (five mouth)

Lingulataua
(tongue worm)

The tongue worms are about 70 species of flattened, bilaterally symmetrical, vertebrate parasites. They are unsegmented but have 90 or so external rings.

A—27. ONYCHOPHORA (bearing claws)

The velvet worms, about 80 species of small worms with 14 to 43 pairs of unjointed hollow legs. They have

Peripatus (velvet worm) characteristics of both of the great phyla Annelida (A—24) and Arthropoda (A—28) and may represent an ancient link between them.

A—28. ARTHROPODA** (jointed foot)

The most successful phylum of animals contains over a million species and includes the insects, crustaceans (lobsters, crabs, shrimp), millipedes, spiders, and many other groups. They have segmented bodies, usually divided into head, thorax, and abdomen; jointed legs; and bodies covered with a chitinous exoskeleton. Size varies from 1/10 mm to 60 cm. Arthropods have characteristics in common with annelids (phylum A—24) and probably originated from an ancient polychete stock. The modern velvet worms, phylum A—27, show characteristics of both phyla. The extinct trilobites, Subphylum Trilobitomorpha, are the most primitive arthropods. Over 3900 fossil species of trilobites have been described. They were extinct by the end of the Paleozoic era, 180 million years ago. There are three great living groups in this phylum: the **Uniramia**, millipedes, centipedes, and insects; the **Chelicerata**, sea spiders, horseshoe crabs, scorpions, spiders, mites, and ticks; and the **Crustacea**, water fleas, copepods, ostracods, barnacles, shrimps, lobsters, and crabs. Some taxonomists are of the opinion that these three groups developed independently and that each group should be raised to phylum level. Here they are considered as subphyla. The Uniramia have no truly marine species even though the phenomenally successful Class Insecta is a member of this subphylum.

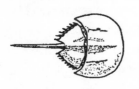

The **Subphylum Chelicerata, Class Merostomata**, Order Xiphosura, contains the horseshoe or king crabs that are familiar to most marine aquarists. One species of these dome shaped crabs with

Limulus (horseshoe crab) the long spiked tails and book shaped gills, *Limulus polyhemus*, is found in shallow waters of the Atlantic, and three species are found in the West Pacific. Small specimens may swim upside down using their page-like gill lamellae as paddles. They are carnivores and scavengers and feed on clams, worms, and whatever small animals they can catch and tear apart. Horseshoe crabs first appeared in the Devonian period, 400 million years ago, and they have changed very little throughout time, a true living fossil species. The Atlantic species is most common in marine aquariums. The blood of horseshoe crabs has become so valuable in laboratory research that a small industry has developed catching, collecting blood, and then releasing the crabs back to the sea. The **Class Pycnogonida** contains about 600 species of sea spiders. Shallow water sea spiders are very small and delicate and are seldom seen in marine aquaria.

The **Subphylum Crustacea** has the most interest for marine aquarists. There are about 39,000 species in ten classes. If insects dominate the land, then crustaceans dominate the sea. Few plankton tows or hauls of dredge or net are without some species of crustacean. And crustaceans, as invited and uninvited guests, grace most marine aquariums. Crustaceans have a hard, external skeleton that protects them and supports the muscles and other soft parts of their body. They can only grow by shedding the old, hard external shell and expanding the new shell before it hardens. This is the process known as molting (the technical term is ecdysis). The molted shells are often perfect except for a small slit in the rear where the animal exited from the old shell. When the molt is discovered, many an aquarist has assumed that their favorite shrimp or crab has died, or that an identical animal has miraculously appeared in the tank overnight. The molts need not be removed from the tank since it is usually rapidly consumed by the animals in the system.

The **Class Cephalocarida** was discovered only as recently as 1955 and contains but 8 species of small shrimp-like animals that live at great depths and feed on detritus.

The **Class Branchiopoda** contains about 800 species of small shrimp-like creatures that are mostly freshwater dwellers. This class would scarcely be worthy of mention to marine aquarists except for one genus in the **Order Anostraca**, *Artemia* sp. These are brine shrimps which are so important as food organisms to commercial and hobby aquaculturists. They are discussed in Chapter 6, and Moe (1982) and Florida Aqua Farms (1987) contain instructions on hatching and rearing brine shrimp for home marine aquaria.

The **Class Remipedia** has only one species which is blind and lives deep in marine caves.

The **Class Tantulocarida** has only four species. They are very tiny ectoparasites on deep water crustaceans. Not likely to be found in marine aquaria.

The **Class Mystacocarida** has ten species in the family Derocheilocaridae. They are very tiny crustaceans that live between sand grains in shallow marine waters and feed on detritus.

The **Class Branchiura** is not popular with aquarists. This class contains 150 species of fish lice, external parasites on freshwater and marine fish, including the genus *Argulus*.

The **Class Copepoda** is familiar to many aquarists as the "little white bugs" that crawl over the inside surfaces of aquariums. Although some species of copepods are parasitic, the species that are found living free in aquaria are seldom harmful to fish and invertebrates. When found feeding on a

 dead or dying fish, they are just taking advantage of the carcass and did not cause the death of the animal. There are over 8,000 species of copepods, mostly planktonic. In fact, copepods are the most abundant animals in the plankton and form a very

Cyclopoid copepod

important link in the food chains of the sea. The **Order Calanoida** contains most planktonic species. The **Order Cyclopoida** (one eye, of course) contains planktonic marine and freshwater species and some benthic species. The **Order Harpacticoida** contains mostly benthic species that live in sediments and muds. The harpacticoid copepods are the ones that can reproduce most easily in marine aquaria. They make good fish food and can even be cultured for feeding to larval marine fish and invertebrates. See Chapter 6.

The **Class Cirripedia** are the barnacles, which are of great importance to boat operators, but less so to marine aquarists. There are four orders with about 1000 species. Some species are tiny and parasitic and others, such as the goose neck bar-

Balanus
(typical barnacle)

nacles, are large, colorful and occasionally show up in marine aquariums. The

Lepas
(gooseneck barnacle)

gooseneck barnacles, *Lepas* sp., are in the order Thoracica and are often mistaken as mollusks. Two shell-like formations, actually the highly calcified cuticle or exoskeleton of the head, are on the end of a long slender stalk that looks like the neck of a goose. The legs of most barnacles are modified into feathery cirri that rapidly stroke the water and filter out planktonic organisms for food. If planktonic food is available, many species are not difficult to keep in aquaria.

The **Class Ostracoda** contains five orders of mussel shrimps and seed shrimps, about 2000 species. Most species are small bottom dwellers and probably show up as rarely seen, uninvited guests in many marine aquaria. They have an extensive fossil record, 500 million years, and ostracod fossils are often found in oil bearing rocks.

The **Class Malacostraca** has 3 subclasses, 14 orders, 359 families, and about 23,000 species. To the casual observer, all we are talking about in this class are shrimps, crabs, and lobsters. There is, however, much more in this huge group then meets the casual eye. The animals that belong in this class are so diverse and so abundant that they do not fit neatly into one obvious taxonomy. Various classifications that use different higher taxons—subclass, superorder, order, suborder, infraorder, and superfamily—have been constructed to describe relationships of groups within the class. Much more information on genetic structure, ecology, reproduction, and biochemistry will be developed in future years, and a consensus on a taxonomy will eventually be established. I have followed the classification presented in Banister and Campbell (1986) for this class.

The **Subclass Phyllocarida** contains only one family, Nebaliidae, with 25 species. These small, marine "bugs" are mostly bottom living in muds and seaweeds. They represent a primitive group with a fossil record that extends back 300 million years.

The **Subclass Hoplocarida** has one order, **Stomatopoda**,

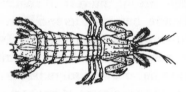

Squilla (mantis shrimp)

with 12 families. These are the infamous mantis shrimps or "thumb splitters" as they are called by commercial shrimp fishermen. They are long, shrimp like crustaceans with sharp spines on the tail, and long claws that fold neatly out of sight under the head. They feed on various fish and invertebrates and are fast and very efficient predators. The long, large, sharp, and strong toothed claws unfold and impale their prey in the blink of an eye. Many an unwary hand has suffered a mean gash when a thumb splitter is unwittingly picked up. Some species are small, less than 4" total length, while others reach a total length of about 12".

The larger species are favored as food shrimp in many coastal areas. They live on the bottom in small holes in rocks or burrowed into the bottom sediments. Small specimens hidden deep in holes can easily accompany live rock into marine reef tanks where they feed on valuable fish and invertebrates as they mature. The Atlantic species, *Squilla empusa*, is the most common uninvited invader of marine reef systems. They are most active at night, but can often be seen during the day as a small, green shrimp-like creature scuttling between rocks. They can be removed from the tank if the aquarist is lucky enough to see in which hole in which rock the mantis shrimp has hidden.

This rock can then be removed from the tank and placed in bucket of seawater. A coathanger or other long flexible implement inserted into the holes in the rock should drive the thieving thumb splitter from its lair out into the bucket. (It can then be sold to some novice marine aquarist for big money. Just kidding, please don't do such a thing!) Some brightly colored Pacific species such as *Odontodactylus scyllarus*, however, are often offered to marine aquarists and make interesting additions to the right type of invertebrate tank.

The **Subclass Eumalacostraca** has 4 superorders. The superorders Syncarida and Pancarida contain only a relatively few species of small, bottom living, detritus eating crustaceans. Most live in fresh water and none are of interest to marine aquarists. The **Superorder Percarida** has 6 orders, 5 listed below, with few species that show up in marine aquarium systems, but many that are of general interest to marine aquarists. The **Superorder Eucarida** has only 3 orders but one of these is the **Decapoda** which contains almost all the crustaceans of real interest to marine aquarists.

Superorder Percarida

The **Order Mysidacea** has 6 families and about 780 species of opossum shrimps. These are small crustaceans, mysid shrimps, that are often found in swarms in protected areas of coral reefs. Most are filter feeders and live in the plankton. Not found in marine aquariums.

The Order Cumacea are small marine and brackish water crustaceans that live in burrows and feed on detritus. They have a very large head and narrow abdomen.

The Order Tanaidacea are very small, mostly marine crustaceans that live in burrows, feed on plankton or detritus, and extend from shallow water to great depths. A few species may show up in marine aquariums, but would be difficult to see and identify.

The **Order Isopoda** is a large group of crustaceans, 4000 species in 100 families, that has species common in marine, freshwater, and terrestrial environments. These are the common sow bugs, pill bugs, woodlice and sea slaters, and sea roaches. Most are small and harmless and feed on detritus and vegetation, but a few deepsea species may reach 12 inches in length. The common sea roaches, *Ligia* sp., seen about docks and boats are intertidal isopods. They may be interesting inhabitants of tidal or marsh type marine aquarium systems. A few isopods are predators on small animals and one, *Limnoria quadripunctata*, the gribble, causes great damage. This is an isopod less then 4 mm long that burrows into marine timbers and even submarine cables. Some small aquatic species of isopods may enter marine systems along with algaes and live rock. The young remain in the brood pouch of the female for some time so reproduction in marine aquaria is possible. Isopods would look like large copepods to most marine aquarists. They would be most open and active at night.

The **Order Amphipoda** contains about 6000 species in 96 families that are mostly free living marine crustaceans, although some live in fresh water, and a few are external parasites on whales and fish. Amphipods are small, from only a tenth to half an inch long, and are known as beach fleas, sand hoppers, and skeleton shrimps. Most feed on plant and animal detritus, but a few are filter feeders, algae eaters, and predators. They are common shallow water marine crustaceans and may often enter marine systems on algae and live rocks. The female broods the young, so some reproduction in favorable marine systems can be expected. The curved body shape generally separates the amphipods from the flattened isopods.

Superorder Eucarida

The **Order Euphausiacea** has 85 species in two families of small, pelagic, filter feeding shrimps generally called krill. The euphasid shrimps are generally reddish in color, especially northern deep water species, although tropical species are greenish. They swim in great swarms and are an important food source for whale and other large plankton feeders. The larvae of krill and decapods hatch into nauplii and go through a planktonic stage. Some krill is harvested directly for human food and some is a valued food for aquarium fish, rich in important minerals and pigments. *Euphausia superba* is the whale krill and is one of the main species now harvested.

The Order Amphionidacea contains only one marine species, a free swimming form about 3 cm long.

The **Order Decapoda** is the major order of marine crustaceans. These are shrimps, lobsters, and crabs that are familiar on the dinner table and in the aquarium. And there are many of them, 10,000 species in 105 families. There are two suborders: **Dendrobranchiata (Natantia)**, the shrimps and prawns (these terms are interchangeable, shrimp is most widely used), and **Pleocyemata (Reptantia)**, the lobsters, hermit crabs, squat lobsters and true crabs. All have ten legs as the name *deca* (ten) and *poda* (foot) implies. The former names of these suborders, Natantia and Reptantia, divided the group into swimmers (shrimps) and crawlers (lobsters and crabs). Recent classifications rely on more fundamental biological characteristics. Dendrobranchiates (shrimps) have many branched gills and release eggs that are pelagic and hatch into tiny nauplii larvae. Pleocyemates (lobsters and crabs) have gills formed as plates or filaments and hold their eggs (which hatch out as large zoeae larvae) under their abdomen during early development.

Most decapod crustaceans are not difficult to keep in marine aquaria. They are usually compatible with tank mates of marine species other than themselves and feed well on particulate food placed in the tank. Some species, however, will feed on corals and anemones so caution is advised. An aquarist interested in decapod crustaceans should acquire the book by Debelius (1984).

Shrimps of the **Suborder Dendrobranchiata** (Natantia) have an elongated shape, usually compressed on the sides, usually have a long spine extending forward between the eyes (a rostrum), usually have pinching claws on the first three pairs of legs, and have gills with many branches. The family Penaeidea contains the commercial shrimps. These are the pink, brown, and white south Atlantic shrimps in the genus *Penaeus*, as well as many other important food shrimps throughout the world. The pink shrimp, *Penaeus duorarum*, is a very important food and bait shrimp in Florida and is often found in the tanks of marine wholesalers and retailers as well. These commercial shrimps do well in marine systems and are easy and interesting to keep.

The **Suborder Pleocyemata** contains crustaceans with very variable body forms—lobsters, crabs, and hermit crabs for example—but all have gills that are either plate-like or filamentous, not branching.

The **Infraorder Stenopodidae** has one family of cleaner  shrimps, Stenopodidae, also known as boxer shrimps, that are very familiar to marine aquarists. They can be easily separated from other shrimps because the side plate of the first abdominal segment overlaps the side plate of the second segment. The red and white banded coral shrimp, *Stenopus hispidus*, with its long curved white antennae, are very popular in marine tanks. They almost always occur in pairs hidden under rocks or in shallow caves in the tropical Atlantic. Unpaired coral banded shrimp are not compatible and will fight fiercely if kept in a single tank. *Stenopus scutellatus*, the golden cleaner shrimp, and *Microprosthema semilaeve*, the scarlet cleaner shrimp, are two other Atlantic species in this family that are common in marine aquariums. They are easy to care for and generally do well in aquaria. Well fed *Stenopus* molt regularly in aquaria. The old shell is quickly disposed of by bacteria and other marine organisms in the tank. It is not unusual for these shrimp to lose claws or legs during the molt. This is not cause for great alarm, however; the lost appendages will be regenerated in the next molt. Continued loss of appendages during molting, however, indicates poor water quality.

Stenopus
(banded coral shrimp)

Because they form strong pairs and are easy to feed, these popular cleaner shrimps spawn easily in aquaria. The first sign of impending spawning is when the ovaries under the carapace along the back of the female begin to turn green. The male must mate with the female for the eggs to be fertile. The male performs a courtship ritual and "dances" for the female before mating. After ovulation, the female holds the green eggs under her abdomen for two to three weeks while they go through early development. The eggs hatch out into well developed, pelagic zoeae larvae. The larvae swim about the tank and are soon eaten by other tank inhabitants or consumed by the filtration system. It is possible for a diligent aquarist to rear the larvae since they will feed on rotifers and brine shrimp, but this must be done in a separate larval rearing system. The reproduction of other small shrimps, lobsters, and crabs in the Suborder Plecyemata is much the same as *Stenopus*.

The **Infraorder Caridea** contains 22 families of small shrimps, including the pistol shrimps. The tiny shrimps that ride on floating sargassum weed and prance delicately on the tentacles of sea anemones are also members of this infraorder, as are a number of other cleaner shrimps. All members of this infraorder have the side plate of the second abdominal segment overlapping the side plate of the first segment. The cleaner shrimps in the genus *Lysmata* of the family Hippolytidae are well known to marine aquarists. These typical shrimp-shaped cleaners are usually colored some combination of red, orange, yellow, and white. *L. amboinesis* with its longitudinal red and centered white stripes and long white antennae are common in marine systems. These cleaners will work on many fish in marine aquarium and will also pair and spawn in aquaria. The marbled shrimp are also in the family Hippolytidae. *Saron marmoratus* is the common species of marble shrimp imported from the Indo-Pacific. This is a large species, up to 9 cm, and is only active in movement and feeding during dark. The peppermint shrimp are in the family Rhynchocinetidae. The Indo-Pacific peppermint shrimp, *Rhynchocinetes uritai*, are frequently found in marine systems. They are a common shallow water species, occurring in small groups, and do well in marine systems. They feed actively on corals, however, and are not good additions to tanks with hard and soft corals.

The family **Palaemonidae** contains the **anemone shrimps**. These small, transparent shrimps, such as *Periclimenes brevicarpalis*, a Pacific species with vivid violet spots on the abdomen and intense white bands on the carapace and purple bands on the claws, live within the tentacles of sea anemones. It feeds on all types of particulate food and, as with other cleaner species, it does best when it is able to perform its cleaning behavior. The shrimps found in *Sargassum* weed and colored like the weed, *Leander tenicornis* and *Hippolyte acuminata*, for example, are also found in this family as are the small shrimps that live on the spines of sea urchins. The snapping shrimp or pistol shrimp are in the family Alpheidae. These shrimp have one large claw that can make a very loud snap when closed. The shock of the loud snap stuns small fish and invertebrates and allows the shrimp to capture them. They are usually found in soft sediments around rocks and reefs. A diver or snorkler can sit very still on soft, grassy bottoms and hear the snaps and pops of these shrimp on distant reef formations. It has been said that the noise produced is so loud that it can break the glass of a marine aquarium. (I'm not sure I believe this.)

The incredibly beautiful Pacific **harlequin shrimp,** *Hymenocera picta,* is in the family Gnathophyllidae. The thin flaps on the head, large flat claws, and brilliant white with intense reddish purple spots makes it easy to identify shrimps of this genus. The harlequin shrimp feeds on starfish, including the notorious crown-of-thorns starfish that destroys so much coral on Pacific reefs. They require starfish when kept in aquaria, but this is not as great a problem as it may appear. Starfish easily regenerate their arms, and several starfish may be kept in a separate aquarium and fed well on clams or oysters. An arm removed every 8 to 10 days and fed to a pair of harlequin shrimp will not kill the starfish (which go on to regenerate the lost arm), but will keep the shrimp nicely fed. Starfish in the genus *Linkia* are preferred by the shrimp above other species. The harlequin shrimp will spawn in marine aquaria when kept well fed and under good water quality.

The **Infraorder Astacidea** contains five families of lobsters and lobster-like crustaceans. The American lobster, *Homarus americanus*, and a number of species of small deep sea lobsters, are in the family Nephropidae, as are the freshwater crayfish. Although American lobsters are common in refrigerated tanks in supermarkets and restaurants, they are not common in home marine aquariums. These lobsters are fierce predators and can destroy many other species in marine systems.

There are five families of spiny, Spanish, and slipper lobsters in the **Infraorder Palinura**. The spiny lobsters, Family

Panulirus
(spotted spiny lobster)

Palinuridae, have long, spiny antennae and no claws. A few species such as the Spanish lobster or spotted spiny lobster, *Panulirus guttatus*, (so named because of the abundant small, white spots over the body) are found off the Florida Keys and in the Caribbean and are not uncommon in marine aquaria. The painted rock lobster, *P. versicolor*, and the ornate spiny lobster, *P. ornatus*, are Pacific species that are small and very colorful and often enter the marine live specimen trade. Large spiny lobsters are very effective at capturing fish at night and should not be kept with small fish.

Justitia
(long armed lobster)

The long armed spiny lobster, *Justitia longimanus*, is found in deeper tropical Atlantic waters. It is bright red and the male has false claws on the elongated arms that develop from the first pair of walking legs. The family Scyllaridae contains the slipper lobsters, which are also called Spanish lobsters, shovel-nosed lobsters, sand lobsters, and "bulldozers". *Arctides regalis* is a small Pacific slipper lobster that is brightly colored with red margins around the flat, shovel-shaped antennae, and this species is sometimes found in marine

tanks. As are most decapods, these tropical lobsters are nocturnal and usually roam the aquarium during the night hours. The
larval form of these lobsters is known as a phyllosome larvae—
a very flattened, long legged larvae. These larvae drift in
oceanic currents for as long as 6 to 9 months before settling out
as tiny lobsters. This extended larval stage makes rearing spiny
lobsters a very difficult undertaking.

The **Infraorder Thalassinidea** contains seven families of

mud shrimps and mud lobsters. The
Family Axiidae includes the lobster-like
shrimps generally called the reef
lobsters. *Enoplometopus occidentalis* is the
small, bright red, hairy Pacific lobster
with equal claws that is often found in
marine aquaria. A rare Atlantic species,
Enoplometopus antillensis, has recently
been found in some numbers in deep
water offshore of West Palm Beach,
Florida. Members of the Family Cal-
lianasidae, the mud shrimps, build burrows in soft sediments and are rarely

Enoplometopus
(flaming reef lobster)

found in marine aquaria.

The **Infraorder Anomuran** has 13 families of quite diverse
decapod crustaceans. These include the hermit crabs,
Diogenidae, Coenobitida, and Paguridae; the squat lobsters,
Galatheidae; the porcelain crabs, Porcellanidae; and the mole
crabs, Hippidae. These groups have long antennae and well
developed abdomens. They are in-between the lobsters and
crabs and have some of the characteristics of both. The land
hermit crabs, such as the common Caribbean species, *Coenobita
clypeatus*, spend most of their life on land near the sea and
return to the sea only to spawn. The larvae pass several weeks
in the plankton, settle out on the bottom, pick up a small snail
shell, and crawl out on land.

Most hermit crabs in marine aquarium systems are in the
Family Paguridae. They all use the empty shells of marine
snails to guard their soft abdomens. The end of the abdomen

has strong recurved hooks that attach to the inside of the shell and keep the crab securely fastened within the shell. The crab can release the hooks and switch shells when it encounters a more suitable home. The claws of many species are formed to completely block the entrance to the shell when the crab retracts, thus providing complete protection from predators. Hermit crabs are easy to keep in low nitrate systems and will feed on whatever can be scavenged from the tank bottom. Large hermit crabs, such as the Caribbean conch hermit crab, *Petrochirus diogenes*, are very strong and can move rocks and decorations about the tank. Perhaps because of their protection, hermits are active during daylight hours and are very interesting inhabitants in marine systems. There are many, many species of hermit crabs, 80 or more just in Florida waters, so identification of individual species is difficult. The small, red-legged Caribbean hermit, *Paguristes cadenati*, is a common hermit in marine systems. The Pacific hermit, *Dardanus megistos*, has red hairy legs with numerous black outlined white dots and is also common in marine systems.

The squat lobsters are seldom found in marine aquaria, although some species are very numerous in the natural environment. The vast numbers of "lobster krill" of northern waters are two species of squat lobster in the genus *Munida*. The porcelain crabs are more common to marine aquarists. Several species live commensally with sea anenomes and sea urchins. *Neopetrolisthes ohshimai* is a purple and white Pacific species of porcelain crab that lives with the giant carpet anemone, *Stoichactis kenti*. The porcelain crabs are filter feeders and require some planktonic food to survive in marine systems. Feeding planktonic particles to anemones as described in Chapter 6 does double duty if a porcelain crab lives with the anemone. Mole crabs are also filter feeders. The most familiar mole crabs live in beach sand in the intertidal areas and filter water from receding waves. They are not kept in marine aquaria.

The true crabs are in the **Infraorder Brachyura**. There are about 4,500 species of crabs in 47 families. A crab's body is

Libinia (spider crab)

flattened from top to bottom, the carapace is large, and the abdomen is small and tightly tucked under the carapace (thorax). The antennae are usually very small. Crabs have developed into many ecological niches and exhibit a wide variety of adaptations. Some feed on algae, some are carnivores, and some are scavengers. Some burrow, some are pelagic, and some live commensally in the mantle cavities of mollusks. There are very large spider crabs and very small pea crabs. Some are deep water marine and some live part of their lives in fresh water. Many different species of crabs find their way into marine aquarium systems. Marine aquarists are familiar with some species while others are just small, nondescript crabs that hide and wander the bottom with the aquarist wondering exactly where they came from.

The **Family Dromiidae** contains the sponge crabs, *Dromia*

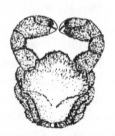

Dromidia (sponge crab)

sp. These small crabs hold sponges and other growth on their backs with their modified rear legs. The sponges help conceal the crab from predators. The box crabs, **Family Calappidae**, have a domed carapace with depressions for the claws and legs which gives the crab a smooth, box-like shape when everything is retracted. The shame faced or shy crabs in this family, *Calappa* sp., are common in Caribbean waters. They are called shy or shame faced because the claws completely hide the face of the crab.

Most crabs introduced into marine aquarium systems are

Stenorhynchus
(arrow crab)

spider crabs, **Family Majidae**. The arrow crab, *Stenorhynchus seticornis*, with its long jointed legs and the long rostrum that points to the sky is frequently seen wandering over the rocks and anemones in reef tanks. They are opportunistic feeders and do well on particulate food in the aquarium. Also in this family, the small, usually hairy and green, species in the genus *Mithrax* are common in aquaria. The largest Caribbean

species in this genus, the giant spider crab, *M. spinosissimus*, is frequently available in a small size of several inches across the carapace. Like the sponge crabs, many small species of spider crabs are "decorator crabs", for they encourage the growth of sponges, anemones, and algaes on their backs to camouflage their presence.

Stenocionops
(decorator crab)

The crabs of the **Family Portunidae** are the swimming crabs such as the Atlantic blue crab, *Callinectes sapidus*, which is an important commercial food species. The rear legs of the swimming crabs are modified into paddles and they will quickly swim to the surface for food when they are kept in aquaria. Their claws are also very sharp and they do not hesitate to pinch an unwary finger. Many crabs in the **Family Xanthidae** are popular aquarium species. The small stone crabs in this family hide deep in reef formations. The Atlantic spray or urchin crab, *Percnon gibesi*, is a small shore crab in the **Family Grapsidae** that makes a hardy and interesting addition to a marine tank. The carapace is square and flattened with a sharp yellow or greenish line around the front beneath the eyes; the legs are brown and long with bright yellow spots at the joints; and it moves very fast. Another grapsid group, the boxing crabs in the genus *Lybia* are fascinating in marine displays. Crabs of this genus carry a small anemone firmly grasped in each claw. The crab protects itself from predators by thrusting

the anemones toward the danger just as a boxer protects himself with his gloves. Other familiar crabs such as ghost crabs, fiddler crabs, coral crabs, and coconut crabs are in families in this infraorder. The interested aquarist has worlds of crabs to explore.

Percnon (spray crab)

A—29. POGONOPHORA (beard bearing)

beard worm

The beard worms are about 100 species of deep sea, sessile worms with no gut that form upright chitin tubes. They were first discovered in 1900 off Indonesia. Long beard-like tentacles on the head or cephalic lobe give this phylum its name. Even though they are exclusively marine, they live at such depths that occurrence in a marine aquarium is not expected.

A—30. ECHINODERMATA** (sea urchin skin)

About 6,000 species of brainless, headless, unsegmented, radially symmetrical animals compose the echinoderms. They have a unique water vascular system that functions in locomotion, feeding, and respiration. The tube feet are part of the water vascular system. Each tube foot has a suction disk on the outer end, has its own internal water reservoir (ampulla), and functions independently to help move the animal about. Small shells, bits of algae, and pebbles are often held to the surface of sea urchins by their tube feet. The madreporite is the "valve" to the water vascular system. It is external in basket stars, brittle stars, and starfish and internal in sea cucumbers. The radial body plan is usually formed into five sections or rays. Larval echinoderms are bilaterally symmetrical. The typical radial symmetry does not appear until the larvae settle and metamorphose into the adult form. The echinoderm skeleton is made up of calcite crystals formed around the tissues in an open lattice work structure. This makes a strong, very light weight skeletal support.

Echinoderms have evolved to fill many ecological niches. The digestive system is simple, but complete. Most species have a mouth and anus with a digestive track between them. Some are filter feeders; some ingest sediments and digest the organic matter in muds, silts, and sands; some are grazers or predators; and some can absorb nutrients from the water through their skin. The fossilized primitive ancestors of modern echinoderms are present in pre-Cambrian rocks over

530 million years old. Echinoderms and chordates evidently had an ancient common ancestor because the pattern of early development (radial cleavage of the egg, formation of the anus from the blastopore), development of a true body cavity, and presence of three basic tissue layers are fundamental characteristics of both groups.

Echinoderms do best in marine aquarium systems where water quality is high and there is little nitrate. There are three living subphyla: **Crinozoa**, the sea lilies and feather stars; **Asterozoa**, the brittle stars, basket stars, and starfish; and **Echinozoa**, the sea urchins and sea cucumbers.

There are about 650 species of sea lilies and feather stars in the **Subphylum Crinozoa, Class Crinoidea**, Order Articulata.

Marine aquarists are most familiar with the **feather stars**. These fascinating crinoids have long arms that extend upward with many feathery lateral projections, a small central disk, and a number of downward projecting arms (cirri) that are modified for grasping the substrate. The feathery arms are extended, usually at night, and capture planktonic organisms from the seawater. Most species can move at will across the bottom by walking with the cirri, and some species are even good swimmers. The number of arms is usually some multiple of five. Some species are beautifully colored in red and orange, and others are dressed in browns and grays. The Caribbean *Nemaster rubiginosa* in the family Comasteridae is an orange species that is occasionally found in marine systems, as are other species in this genus. Pacific species in the families Himerometridae, Mariametridae, and Colobometridae are also found in the trade.

Heterometra
(feather star)

The **Subphylum Asterozoa** has two great classes: **Asteroidea**, the **starfish**, and **Ophiuroidea**, the **brittle stars** and **basket stars**. Starfish are familiar to almost everyone, marine aquarist or not. They are common to shallow seas everywhere, and the five armed shape is practically the universal symbol of the marine invertebrate. There are about 2,000 species of starfish, in two subclasses, Somasteroidea and Euasteroidea, and five orders. Most have five arms, although a number of species have many more arms. The infamous crown-of-thorns starfish, *Acanthaster planci*, that feeds exclusively on coral polyps has 9 to 23 arms. The small circular "valve" to the water vascular system is on the dorsal surface of the disk of starfish and on the ventral surface of the brittle star disk.

Echinaster (starfish)

Starfish can be quite large, such as the giant Caribbean sea star or cushion star, *Oyreaster reticulatus*, and quite small, such as some Indo-Pacific species in the genus *Patiriella*. Coloration, size, and structure vary greatly among the many species of starfish. Some Pacific species common in marine aquaria are the blue star, *Linckia laevigata*; the spiny star, *Amphiaster insignis;*, the red spine star, *Protoreaster lincki*; the bat star, *Patiria miniata*; and the smooth star, *Dermasterias imbricata*. Common Atlantic species are the banded star, *Luidia alternata*, the thorny star, *Echinaster sentus*; and the orange star, *Ophidiaster guildingii*. The common Atlantic comet star, *Linckia guildingii*, is dull red to purple, often has only one or two arms, and is in the process of regrowing the other arms. Starfish in the genus *Astropecten* usually have pronounced marginal plates along the edge of the arms.

Most starfish are predators on other invertebrates—worms, clams, other mollusks—and even other echinoderms. Some species such as the red spine star are slow, but gluttonous predators. They attack and consume anemones, tube worms, small mollusks, other echinoderms, and almost all small animals that can not escape the slowly moving predator. Small pieces of shrimp, squid, and clam are appropriate foods for most starfish. Most starfish are easy to keep in marine aquaria when fed on relatively large particulate foods. Although starfish are hardy animals, water quality is important, especially for new acquisitions. Beware of starfish that are sunken in on the central disk or along the edge of the arms. The tube feet should also retract slowly, but firmly when the animal is disturbed. A starfish that is not in good condition or that is transferred to a system high in nitrates may die and decompose in a few days.

The 1600 species of **brittle stars** and **basket stars** in the **Class Ophiuroidea** are not noticed as often as starfish because they are not active during daylight hours, and brittle stars spend most of their time under rocks or deep in the reef structure. The three orders are Oegophiurida, Phrynophiurida (serpent stars and basket stars) and Ophiurida (brittle stars). The arms of brittle stars move sinuously and rapidly in a serpent-like manner. In fact the name is derived from the Greek term *Ophis*, which means snake. The **Order Phrynophiurida** contains the Family Asteroschematidae, the serpent stars; and the **Family Gorgonocephalidae,** the basket stars. Both are groups of very odd creatures. The arms of the serpent stars are very long and flexible. They wind themselves in very tight coils around the branches of soft corals. They may feed on small invertebrates or detritus. Aquarists seldom encounter serpent stars unless a small specimen is carried coiled about a soft coral. Basket stars are also associated with soft corals. They are frequently found attached to the upper structure of sea fans or gorgonians. During the day the basket star is simply a fist sized mass of fibers, but at night it unfurls into a glorious fine meshed net. The arms that compose the net are flexible and fast, and even small fish and shrimp can be caught if they blunder into an extended basket star. The common Atlantic species is *Astrophyton muricatum*, and *Astroboa nuda* is common in the Indo-Pacific. Small basket stars may be kept in marine aquaria, but they must be fed at night when they are expanded. Small pieces of shrimp or fish placed in the "basket" may be sufficient.

The brittle stars are so named because they easily break off arms when handled. The arms are rapidly regenerated, however, and the loss of these appendages is apparently a defensive

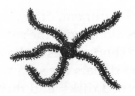

Ophiocoma (brittle star)

capability of the brittle star. Brittle stars are large and small, hairy and smooth, colorful and drab. Most can move very rapidly when necessary. A slow brittle star that is exposed in daylight hours is a sign of high nitrate or otherwise poor water quality in a marine system. There are over a thousand species of brittle stars in at least 10 families, and there are probably a good number of undescribed tropical species. It is quite likely that undescribed species are quietly living somewhere in some hobbyist's systems. Some species of brittle stars, such as the Caribbean sponge brittle star, *Ophiothrix suensonii*, are filter feeders. They hide during the day and then find a spot at night where they can extend their arms with the very long, thin bristles into the night currents that are rich in plankton. A few species of brittle stars such as *Ophioplocus japonicus*, internally incubate their young through the larval stages, and then release tiny, fully formed brittle stars into the environment. Such species should be easy to rear in marine systems. Two common Caribbean brittle stars in marine systems are the giant red brittle star, *Ophiocoma wendti*, that has long arms with strong bristles, hides under rocks, and is totally a deep reddish black. The banded brittle star, *Ophioderma brevispinum*, is also common and has long, sinuous arms that are alternately banded dark grey and white and do not have noticeable bristles. The red bristle star feed well on dead particulate food in marine aquaria. The brittle star hides between rocks and extends one long arm out into the tank to capture food. The tube feet hold the food within a bend on the bottom of the arm, and as the bend moves toward the disk, the particle is rapidly passed up the arm to the mouth of the brittle star.

The **Subphylum Echinozoa** has two classes. The **Class Echinoidea** contains about 800 species of sea urchins, sand dollars, sea biscuits, and heart urchins, and the **Class Holothuridea** holds about 900 species of sea cucumbers. Many of the echinoids in the Superorder Gnathostomata, the heart urchins and sand dollars, burrow deeply into sand or silt bottoms and feed directly on vast amounts of sediment, digesting the live or dead organic matter that enters along with the sediment. The heart urchins are covered with short spines and are compressed from top to bottom. The sand dollars are so compressed that they have the shape of flattened disks, and their spines are very small and fine. These burrowing species are difficult to keep in marine systems unless special care is taken to develop a deep, oxygenated sediment.

The **sea urchins** are generally spherical in shape and have pronounced spines and long tube feet that project outward between the spines. There is great variation in color and spine structure as well as mode of life in sea urchins. One of the most infamous sea urchins is the long spined *Diadema antillarum* of the Caribbean. The long brittle spines may be over a foot long (30 cm) and are very sharp with a thin poisonous skin. The pain from a puncture is quite intense. An aquarist should be very

Eucidaris
(slate pencil urchin)

careful when handling any sharp spined sea urchin. Other common Atlantic sea urchins are the variegated urchin of the Family Arbaciidae, *Lytechinus variegatus*, common in the grass flats around coral reefs, and the slightly smaller *L. williamsi* found on coral reefs. They are colored green to white, with purple to pink short, stout spines. The slate pencil urchin, *Eucidaris tribuloides*, in the **Family Cidaridae** is very popular in marine systems since it is not dangerous and survives very well. The rock boring sea urchin in the **Family Echinometridae**, *Echinometra lucunter*, is small, dark purple with a flaming red center, feeds on algaes, and also does very well in a marine aquarium system. A number of algae eating sea urchins in a marine system may be too destructive of the macro algaes, but one or two may help keep unwanted hair algaes in check. There are many beautiful Indo-Pacific species of sea urchins such as another slate pencil urchin with massive brown spines, *Heterocentrotus mamillatus,* and some colorful species of the long spined urchins in the genus *Diadema.*

Pseudocolochirus
(sea apple)

The **sea cucumbers** in the **Class Holothuridea** are not easy to keep in marine aquaria. These echinoderms have a leathery skin, and most have the appearance of giant worms. Some feed by ensnaring plankton or other prey organisms in the feeding tentacles, modified tube feet, that surround the mouth. Others ingest bottom sediments and detritus to digest the organic matter included in the sediment. The tube feet are usually arranged in five rows that run long the length of the body. Some sea cucumbers can eject their internal gut and respiratory trees when disturbed, which are toxic and may kill fish and other organisms in the tank. The most common sea cucumber in marine systems is the brilliantly colored sea apple, *Pseudocolochirus axiologus*. This filter feeding holothuridean usually orients upright and has a crown of feeding tentacles about the mouth. Five broad, bright red stripes outlined in yellow along the body mark the location of the tube feet. Other small, similar species are sometimes available, but identifications often depend on the shape of the spicules in the skin and are difficult to determine. Particulate planktonic food must be available, mostly at night, for filter feeding echinoderms to do well in marine aquaria.

A—31. CHAETOGNATHA** (hair jaw)

Sagitta (arrow worm)

The arrow worms are about 100 species of small (1/2 to 15 cm), planktonic, predatory, worm-like animals. They are bilaterally symmetrical, transparent with lateral fins, and have strong, movable hooks about the head that catch and hold small prey. They are hermaphroditic (both sexes present in one individual) and reproduce easily in aquaria set up for larval rearing where planktonic food is available. Larval rearing tanks fed wild plankton may be overrun with arrow worms within 20 to 30 days, and loss of valuable larvae may be very high.

A—32. HEMICHORDATA* (half cord)

The acorn and tongue worms are about 90 species of unsegmented, bilaterally symmetrical, worm-like animals that live in U shaped burrows in muddy marine bottoms. They range from 2.5 to 250 cm long, and have gill slits and a stomachord; which is a short anterior projection of the mouth that extends into the proboscis. It was once thought to be a notochord. The muddy, burrowing habitat makes it unlikely that hemichordates will be kept in marine aquaria.

Chiridota (acorn worm)

A-33. CHORDATA** (cord)

The chordates are about 45,000 species of bilaterally symmetrical animals that are defined by the presence of an internal supporting structure (a notochord), a dorsal nerve cord, and gill slits in the throat or pharynx. These characteristics can occur at any time in embryonic or larval development and need not be present in the adult animal. This phylum includes the acraniate (without a brain) tunicates of the **Subphylum Tunicata**, sessile marine animals when adult; and the lancelets of the **Subphylum Cephalochordata**, small scaleless, fish-like animals. Also in this phylum are the craniate (with a brain) animals of the **Subphylum Agnatha**, fish without jaws such as the lampreys and hagfish, and the **Subphylum Gnathostomata**, all the cordates with brains and jaws. The sharks, skates and rays are in the **Class Chondrichthyes** and the bony fish are in the **Class Osteichthyes**. The remaining chordate classes are the amphibians, **Class Amphibia**; the reptiles, **Class Reptilia**; the feathered reptiles or birds, **Class Aves**; and the mammals, **Class Mammalia**.

There are about 2000 species of tunicates in 3 classes and 7 families. Of the three classes: **Ascidiacea**, Thaliacea (the planktonic salps), and Larvacea, marine aquarists will generally only encounter the ascidian **sea squirts**. These are solitary or colonial **tunicates** that are attached to the bottom and live as sessile adults. The dorsal

Halocynthia (solitary tunicate)

nerve cord that marks them as cordates is present only in the larval stage. Ascidians have a tunic, a tough, cellulose covering that surrounds, protects and supports the animals. Colonial tunicates have an extensive common tunic, while solitary tuni-

cates have individual tunics. Two tubes, the inhalant and the exhalent siphon, extend from each animal. The bright colors—yellow, orange, red, pink and even blue—and encrusting habit of some colonial tunicates give an appearance more like a coral or sponge than a complex chordate, but the twin siphons extending from each animal

Distomus
(colonial tunicate)

identify them as tunicates. Water is rapidly drawn into the inhalant siphon and passed through a basket-like, mucus covered pharynx wall that filters plankton and other organic matter from the water. The water then exhausts out the exhalent siphon. Small species of solitary and colonial tunicates often enter marine systems along with live rock and are very interesting to observe while they live. Abundant small, planktonic particles are necessary to maintain tunicates in marine systems, and they will survive only if special care is taken in food and feeding. *Clavelina* is one genus of small, colonial tunicates that are not uncommon in reef areas. Much work has yet to be done on the taxonomy of tropical tunicates.

The lancelets or "amphioxus" of the **Subphylum Cephalochordata** are about 25 species of small, colorless, fish-like creatures that are not vertebrates, al-

Branchiostoma (lancelet)

though they do have a dorsal notochord. They have no jaws but do have a large pharynx with gill like slits that lead into an internal exhalent chamber. Water passes through the pharynx where food is filtered and respiration occurs. Lancelets are found in the shell and sand sediments of shallow tropical seas. The species *Branchiostoma lanceolatum* is common in Florida waters and may possibly turn up in a marine aquarium system.

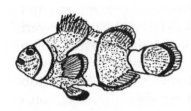

Amphiprion (common clownfish)

Of the other chordates, only fish are found in marine aquarium systems (unless you're partial to penguins), but with about 25,000 species there are far too many fish for inclusion in this book. Fish are classified in two subphyla, Agnatha (the jawless fish) and Gnathostomata (the jawed fish). The superclass **Pisces** includes the class **Chrondrichthyes** (sharks and rays) and the class **Osteichthyes** includes all the bony fish.

KINGDOM PLANTAE

The true plants

The true plants are relatively late arrivals on the Earth. They evolved from the green algaes, Chlorophyta (Pr—15), and first appear in the fossil record in the Devonian Period only about 400 million years ago. True plants all develop from embryos that result from sexual reproduction and are multicellular with eukaryotic cells. Most plants are sessile with roots, stems, and leaves, and almost all manufacture their own food through photosynthesis, although a few highly modified species are not photosynthetic. Plants also have cellulose cell walls and chlorophyll, which animals do not. Note that the chlorophyll in corals is contained in their algal symbionts and that the cellulose in tunicates is not in the form of cell walls. The term Division is often used by botanists to define groups that are conceptually the same as Phylum. There are very few true plants that are entirely marine.

Pl—1. BRYOPHYTA (moss plant)

Porella

There are about 24,000 species in three classes in this phylum of small, primitive moist environment plants. They are nonvascular and without true roots (liverworts, hornworts and mosses). No marine species.

Pl—2. PSILOPHYTA (smooth plant)

Psilotum

Only four living species, 2 genera, *Psilotum* and *Tmesipteris*, of primitive, leafless, fern-like plants. May be representative of the first land plants of 400 million years ago. No marine species.

Pl—3. LYCOPODOPHYTA (wolf foot plant)

Lycopodium

The club mosses, about 1000 species in 5 genera of primitive vascular plants with simple leaves and unjointed stems. Club mosses and quillworts. No marine species.

Pl—4. SPHENOPHYTA (wedge plant)

Equisetum

The horsetails, many extinct species and about 40 living species. Leaves are small and simple, arranged in whorls, stems joined. No marine species.

Pl—5. FILICINOPHYTA (fern plant)

Dryopteris

The ferns, Pteridophyta, about 12,000 living species of vascular land plants with large, complex leaves and reproduction by spores. No marine species.

Pl—6. CYADOPHYTA (palm plant)

About 100 species of palm-like tropical plants. Small shrubs to trees. No marine species.

Cyadophyta

Pl—7. GINKGOPHYTA (silver apricot plant)

One living species, the maidenhair tree. Exclusively cultivated, no wild specimens, not marine.

Ginkgo

Pl—8. CONIFEROPHYTA (cone bearing plant)

The conifers, softwoods or evergreens, have simple, needle-like leaves, and reproductive structures are usually in hard cones. The largest living organism, the giant sequoia, and the oldest, the bristlecone pine, are in this group. No marine species.

Araucaria

Pl—9. GNETOPHYTA (gnetophyte plant)

About 70 species of cone bearing, desert living plants. Similar in some respects to both conifers and seed bearing plants. No marine species.

Welwitschia

Pl—10. ANGIOSPERMOPHYTA** (little case seed plant)

The most advanced and largest phylum of plants, at least 250,000 species. All have flowers. The two basic groups, **dicotyledons** and **monocotyledons**, are separated by the number of seed leaves, mono (1) and di (2), that appear when the seed sprouts. The flowering plants have expanded over all the earth, yet they are the youngest plant group, only 150 million years old. They apparently evolved from the seed ferns. There are only 49 truly marine species, all monocots. These are the seagrasses, and they are of great importance in the marine environment. Turtle grass, *Thalassia testudinum*, and the north-

Halophila
(star seagrass)

ern eelgrass, *Zostera marina*, are most well known. Seagrasses are very important in the marine environment. They stabilize sea bottoms by trapping sediments, are important primary producers of organic material, remove nutrients from coastal waters, are important food sources and marine nursery areas, and even serve as substrate for many tiny plants and animals. Star-grass, *Halophila engelmannii*, covers vast areas of soft sediments of the south west coast of Florida. With its small, star-shaped leaves, this attractive species may be a good candidate for culture in marine aquarium systems. Growth of seagrasses in aquaria is possible, but not common.

REFERENCES

Axelrod, R. and L. P. Schultz. 1955. Handbook of Tropical Aquarium Fishes. McGraw-Hill Book Company, Inc., New York, NY, USA. 718 pp.

Baker, D. E. Jr. 1983. My Natural System Marine Aquarium. Tropical Fish Hobbyist: Vol. 31, No. 7: pp 9-21.

Banister, K and A. Campbell (Editors). 1986. The Encyclopedia of Aquatic Life. Facts on File Publications. New York, NY, USA. 349 pp.

Bardach, J. E., J. H. Ryther and W. O. McLarney. 1972. Aquaculture. John Wiley & Sons, New York, NY, USA. 868 pp.

Barghoorn, E.S. and D.H. Linder. 1944. Marine fungi: their taxonomy and biology. Farlowia, 1(3): pp 395-467.

Belorusky, Jr., W. 1988. How to build a living reef system. FAMA (Freshwater and Marine Aquarium Magazine): Vol. 11, No. 6: pp 106-107, 110-111.

Birdsill, B. 1988. Over the Counter. FAMA (Freshwater And Marine Aquarium Magazine): Vol. 11, No. 6. pp: 60-61.

Birdsill, B. 1985. Doing Saltwater Up Small. FAMA (Freshwater and Marine Aquarium Magazine): Vol. 8, No. 1: pp 22-27.

Blackburn, W. 1988. The Ecological Use of Live Rock. FAMA (Freshwater And Marine Aquarium Magazine): Vol. 11, No. 8: pp 8-11.

Blasiola, G. C. 1984. Protecting Aquarium and Pond Fish from the Danger of Chloramine. FAMA (Freshwater And Maine Aquarium Magazine): Vol. 7, No. 4. pp: 10-12,78-83.

Blogoslawski, W.J. and R.G. Rice 1975. Aquatic Applications of Ozone. International Ozone Institute. Syracuse Univ., Syracuse, N.Y. 226 pp.

Blok, J. 1986. Biological Filtration for the Marine Aquarium. Part Four: The Anaerobic Denitra Filter. FAMA (Freshwater And Marine Aquarium Magazine): Vol. 9, No. 12: pp 6-7.

Bogorad, L. 1962. Chlorophylls. in Physiology and Biochemistry of Algae. R.A. Lewin, Ed., Academic Press, New York, NY, USA. pp 385-408.

Bower, C.E. 1983. The Basic Marine Aquarium. Charles C. Thomas, Publisher. Springfield, IL.: 269 pp.

Bower, C.E., and D.T. Turner. 1981. Accelerated nitrification in new seawater culture systems: effectiveness of commercial additives and seed media from established systems. Aquaculture. Vol. 24, pp: 1-6.

Breck, W.G. 1974. Redox Levels in the Sea. *in* The Sea. Ideas and Observations on Progress in the Study of the Seas. Vol. 5. Marine Chemistry. Edward D. Goldberg, Ed. John Wiley & Sons. New York, NY, USA. pp 153-179.

Burleson, J. 1989. Reef tips. FAMA (Freshwater and Marine Aquarium Magazine): Vol. 12, No. 4. pp: 120-121.

Burleson, P. 1988. Burleson's Living Reef. FAMA (Freshwater and Marine Aquarium Magazine): Vol. 11, No. 1. pp: 48-49.

Burleson, J. 1987. Miniature Reef Aquarium Lighting. SeaScope, Vol. 4. pp 1 and 2.

Campbell, R. D. Cnidaria. *in* Reproduction of Marine Invertebrates, Vol. 1. Giese, A. C. and J. S. Pearse, Ed., Academic Press. New York, NY, USA. pp:133-199.

Colin, P.L. 1978. Caribbean Reef Invertebrates and Plants. T.F.H. Publications, Inc., Neptune City, NJ, USA. 512 pp.

Dawes, C. J. 1981. Marine Botany. John Wiley & Sons, New York, NY, USA. 628 pp.

Dawson, E. Y. 1956. How to Know the Seaweeds. WM. C. Brown Co., Dubuque, IA, USA. 197 pp.

de Graaf, F. 1973. Marine Aquarium Guide, (English translation, Dr. Joseph Spiekerman). The Pet Library, LTD., Harrison, NJ 284 pp.

Debilius, H. 1984. Armoured Knights of the Sea. Quality Marine (English Edition), Los Angles, CA, USA. 120 pp.

Delbeek, C. 1989. Soft Corals Spawn in the Aquarium. FAMA (Freshwater and Marine Aquarium Magazine). Vol. 12, No. 3. p: 128.

Delbeek, C. 1987. The care and feeding of mushroom anemones. FAMA (Freshwater and Marine Aquarium Magazine). Vol. 10, No. 10. pp: 4-6.

Delbeek, C. 1986. Construction and Implementation of an External Protein Skimmer. Atoll (Marine Aquarium Society of Toronto). Vol. 4, No. 4. pp: 6-11.

Dewey, D. (Editor) 1986. For What It's Worth, Vol. 1. *FAMA Anthology Lib. Ser.* R/C Modeler Corp. Sierra Madre, CA, USA 271 pp.

Editor, 1983. A critique of: The removal of dissolved inorganic and organic substances from freshwater and seawater by two commercial filtrants, Poly-Filter and Chemi-pure. FAMA (Freshwater and Marine Aquarium Magazine). Vol. 6, No. 1. pp: 4-7, 91-94.

Ewing, C. 1987. On the Removal of Nitrate from Marine Aquaria. Atoll (Marine Aquarium Society of Toronto). Vol. 2, No. 2. pp: 14-17.

Florida Aqua Farms. 1987. Plankton Culture Manual. Fla. Aqua Farms, 5532 Old St. Joe Road, Dade City, FL 33525, USA. 53 pp.

Fox, D. L. 1957. Particulate Organic Detritus. Geol. Soc. America. Memoir 67, Vol. 1. pp 383-390.

Friese, U. E. 1972. Sea Anemones. T.F.H. Publications, Inc., Neptune City, NJ, USA. 128 pp.

Galtsoff, P.S., F.E. Lutz, P.S. Welch, and J.C. Needham. 1937 Culture Methods for Invertebrate Animals. Dover Edition, 1959. Dover Publications, Inc., New York, NY, USA. 590 pp.

George, David and Jennifer. 1979. Marine Life. An illustrated encyclopedia of invertebrate life in the sea. John Wiley & Sons, New York, NY, USA. 288 p.

Gieskes, J. M. 1974. The Alkalinity — Total Carbon Dioxide System in Seawater. in The Sea. Ideas and Observations on Progress in the Study of the Seas. Vol. 5. Marine Chemistry. Edward D. Goldberg, Ed. John Wiley & Sons. New York, NY, USA. pp 123-151.

Giovanetti, T.A. 1988. Protein Skimmers and Ozone in Marine Aquaria - Their Use and Maintenance. FAMA (Freshwater And Marine Aquarium Magazine): Vol, 11. No. 5. pp: 74-78, 80, 122.

Greco, F. 1987. The Living Reef. Part One: Protein Skimming and Ozonation. FAMA (Freshwater And Marine Aquarium Magazine): Vol. 10, No. 9. pp: 52-53, 58-61.

Greco, F. 1987. The Living Reef. Part Two: The mechanics. FAMA (Freshwater And Marine Aquarium Magazine): Vol. 10, No. 10. pp: 80-85, 106-107.

Greco, F. 1988. The Living Reef. Part Seven: power skimmers and trickle filters. FAMA (Freshwater and Marine Aquarium Magazine): Vol. 11, No. 7. pp: 45-47, 49.

Gunter, G. 1957. Temperature. Geol. Soc. America, Memoir 67, Vol.1 pp 159-184.

Harvey, H. W. 1963. The Chemistry and Fertility of Sea Waters. Cambridge University Press. London, England. 240 pp.

hEOCHA, C.O., 1962. Phycobilins. in Physiology and Biochemistry of Algae. R.A. Lewin, Ed., Academic Press, NY, USA. pp 421-435.

Homes, R.W. 1957. Solar Radiation, Submarine Daylight, and Photosynthesis. in Geol. Soc. America, Memoir 67, Vol. 1, Chap. 6. pp 109-128.

Kaplan, E. G. 1988. A Field Guide to Southeastern and Caribbean Seashores. Houghton Mifflin Company, Boston, MA, USA. 425 pp.

Kaplan, E. G. 1982. A Field Guide to Coral Reefs, Caribbean and Florida. Houghton Mifflin Company, Boston, MA, USA. 289 pp.

Kerstitch, A. 1988. Living Rainbows of the Sea. FAMA (Freshwater and Marine Aquarium Magazine): Vol. 11. No. 3. pp: 15-19.

Kingsford, E. 1975. Treatment of Exotic Marine Fish Diseases. The Palmetto Publishing Company. St. Petersburg, FL, USA. 90 pp.

Lamm, D. R. 1988. Culturing Copepods: A food for marine fish larvae. FAMA (Freshwater and Marine Aquarium Magazine): Vol. 11, No. 10. pp: 98-99, 102-104, 110.

Lerman, M. 1986. Marine Biology - Environment, Diversity and Ecology. Benjamin/Cummings Publishing Co., Inc. Menlo Park, CA. 534 pp.

Lundegaard, G. 1985. Keeping Marine Fish. Blandford Press, Dorset, England. 94 pp.

Lutz, F. E., P. S. Welch, P. S. Galtsoff and J. G. Needham, Chairman. 1937. Culture Methods for Invertebrate Animals. Dover edition (1959). Dover Publications,Inc., New York, N.Y. USA. 590 p.

Margulis, L. 1982. Early Life. Science Books International, Inc. MA, USA. 160 pp.

Margulis, L. and K. Schwartz. 1988. The Five Kingdoms. W.H. Freeman and Company, NY., USA. 376 pp.

Melzak, M. 1984. The Marine Aquarium Manual. ARCO Publishing, New York, NY, USA. 175 pp.

Miner, R.W. 1950. Field Book of Seashore Life. G. P. Putnam's Sons, New York, NY, USA. 888 pp.

Moe, M.A. Jr. 1982. The Marine Aquarium Handbook - Beginner to Breeder. Green Turtle Publications. Plantation, FL, USA. 170 pp.

Morin, L. G. 1983. A Primer on Aquarium Filtration, Part One. FAMA (Freshwater and Marine Aquarium Magazine): Vol 6, No. 4. pp: 19-23, 59-62.

Nakayama, T.O.M., 1962. Carotenoids. in Physiology and Biochemistry of Algae. R.A. Lewin, Ed., Academic Press, NY, USA. pp 409-420.

Neelon, M. 1987. How to Build a 100 and 240 Gallon Plywood Tank. FAMA (Freshwater And Marine Aquarium Magazine). Vol. 10, No. 6. pp: 66-67.

Osborne, K. 1983. Full Spectrum Lighting in the Planted Aquarium. Part 2. FAMA (Freshwater And Marine Aquarium Magazine): Vol. 6. No. 1. p: 8.

Osborne, K. 1982. Full Spectrum Lighting in the Planted Aquarium. Part I. FAMA (Freshwater And Marine Aquarium Magazine): Vol. 5, No. 12. p: 14.

Paletta, M. 1988. The Relationship of Redox Potential to Micro Algae. Sea Scope, Vol. 5: pp 1 and 4.

Siddall, S. E. 1973. Recent research in biological filtration. The Marine Aquarist. Vol. 4, No. 1: pp 6-13.

Siddall, S. E. 1974. Studies of closed marine culture systems. Prog. Fish Culturist. Vol. 36, No. 1: pp 8-15.

Sieswerda, P. L. 1977. Grow Some Rotifers. The Marine Aquarist, Vol. 8, No. 4. pp: 6-15.

Simkatis, H. 1958. Salt-Water Fishes for the Home Aquarium. J.B. Lippincott Company, New York, NY, USA. 254 pp.

Smit, G. 1986. Marine Aquariums, Part one: Is it time for a change? FAMA (Freshwater and Marine Aquarium Magazine): Vol. 9, No. 1. pp: 35-42, 84-85.

Sorgeloos, P., E. Bossuyt, E. Lavina, M. Baeza-Mesa, and G. Persoone. 1977. Decapsulation of *Artemia* cysts: A simple technique for the improvement of the use of brine shrimp in aquaculture. *Aquaculture* 12: pp 311-315.

Spotte, S. 1970. Fish and Invertebrate Culture: Water Management in Closed Systems. John Wiley & Sons. NY, USA. 145 pp.

Spotte, S. 1973. Marine Aquarium Keeping. John Wiley & Sons. NY, USA. 171 pp.

Spotte, S. 1979. Seawater Aquariums, The Captive Environment. John Wiley & Sons. NY, USA. 413 pp.

Sprung, J. 1989. Reef Notes. FAMA (Freshwater and Marine Aquarium Magazine): Vol. 12, No 5. pp: 70, 74-75,78.

Stopka, K. 1975. European and Canadian Experiences with Ozone in Controlled Closed Circuit Fresh and Salt Water Systems. in, Aquatic Applications of Ozone. Blogoslawski and Rice, ed., International Ozone Institute. Syracuse Univ., Syracuse, NY, USA: pp 170-175.

Straughan, R. P. L. 1964, 1969 (Revised). The Salt-Water Aquarium in the Home. A. S. Barnes and Company, Inc., Cranbury, NJ, USA. 360 pp.

Tamura, T. 1970. Marine Aquaculture. Translation through The National Technical Information Service. National Science Foundation, Washington, DC, USA. 1000 + pp.

Taylor, W. R. 1960. Marine Algae of the Eastern Tropical and Subtropical Coasts of the Americas. University of Michigan Press. Ann Arbor, MI, USA. 870 pp.

Thiel, A. 1988. The Marine Fish and Invert Reef Aquarium. Aardvark Press, Bridgeport, CT, USA. 278 p.

Thiel, A. 1989. Advanced Reef Keeping I. Aardvark Press. Bridgeport, CT, USA. 440 p.

Tommasini, R. 1988. The Year of the Mini Aquarium. FAMA (Freshwater and Marine Aquarium Magazine). Vol. 11, No. 1: pp 38-46, 126-128.

Turner, D. T. and C. E. Bower 1983. Removal of some inorganic and organic substances from fresh water and artificial seawater by two commercial filtrants. Jour. Aquariculture and Aquatic Sci., Vol. 3, No. 4. pp: 57-63.

Vecellio, M. 1987. How to Build a Canister Filter. FAMA (Freshwater And Marine Aquarium Magazine): Vol. 10, No. 11. pp: 35-38.

Voss, G. L. 1976. Seashore Life of Florida and the Caribbean. Banyan Books, Inc., Miami, FL, USA. 199 p.

Walls, J.G. (Ed.) 1982. Encyclopedia of Marine Invertebrates. T.F.H. Publications, Inc., Neptune City, NJ, USA. 736 pp.

Weast, R. C. 1987. Chief Editor. Handbook of Chemistry and Physics. CRC Press, Inc. Boca Raton, FL, USA.

Wilkens, P. 1973. The Saltwater Aquarium for Tropical Marine Invertebrates. 2nd Extended Edition. (English Translation). Engelbert Pfriem, Wuppertal-Elberfeld, Germany. 216 pp.

Wood, E.M., 1983. Reef Corals of the World, Biology and Field Guide. T.F.H. Publications, Inc. Neptune City, NJ, USA. 256 pp.

Appendix

Perodicals of interest

Aquarium Fish Magazine. Fancy Publications, Inc. 3 Burroughs, Irvine, CA. 92718

Freshwater and Marine Aquarium. R/C Modeler Corp. P.O. Box 487, Sierra Madre, CA. 91024

Journal of Aquariculture and Aquatic Sciences. The Written Word. 7601 E. Forest Lakes Dr. NW, Parkville, MO. 64152

Marine Fish Monthly. Publishing Concepts Corp. Main Street, Luttrell, TN. 37779

Marine Reef. Aardvark Press. 575 Broad Street, Bridgeport, CT. 06604

Today's Aquarist Newsletter. Pisces Publishing Co., Suite 2-155, 548 Naugatuck Ave., Devon CT 06460

Tropical Fish Hobbyist. T.F.H. Publications, Inc. One TFH Plaza, Neptune City, NJ. 07753

Special organizations

ANAI, inc.
1176 Bryson City Road
Franklin, NC 28734

International Marinelife Alliance (IMA U.S.)
94 Station Street
Hingham, MA 02043

The International Oceanographic Foundation
(publishers of *Sea Frontiers*)
3979 Rickenbacker Causeway
Virgina Key, Miami, FL 33149

National Audubon Society
Membership Data Center
P.O. Box 2666
Boulder, CO 80322

Marine Aquarium Societies. Check your local aquarium shop for the names and addresses of local aquarium societies and clubs. Freshwater societies often have internal marine groups. If you have no local society, join a society in a nearby city or start a new society with a few like minded friends.

Symbols, Measures, and Conversions

Abbreviations

Selected chemical symbols

Aluminum	Al	Hydrogen	H	Rubidium	Rb
Arsenic	As	Iodine	I	Potassium	K
Barium	Ba	Iron	Fe	Silicon	Si
Boron	B	Lead	Pb	Silver	Ag
Bromine	Br	Magnesium	Mg	Sodium	Na
Calcium	Ca	Manganese	Mn	Strontium	Sr
Carbon	C	Molybdenum	Mo	Sulphur	S
Chlorine	Cl	Mercury	Hg	Tin	Sn
Cobalt	Co	Nitrogen	N	Vanadium	V
Copper	Cu	Oxygen	O	Zinc	Zn
Fluorine	F	Phosphorus	P		

Selected chemical compounds

Ammonia, NH_3

Ammonium, NH_4^+

Bicarbonate, HCO_3-

Calcium carbonate, $CaCO_3$ (chalk, calcite, aragonite)

Carbon dioxide, CO_2

Carbonate, CO_3^{2-}

Carbonic acid, H_2CO_3

Hydrogen sulfide, H_2S

Magnesium carbonate, $MgCO_3$

Nitrate, NO_3^-

Nitrite, NO_2^-

Sodium bicarbonate, $NaHCO_3$ (baking soda, bicarbonate of soda)

Sodium carbonate, dry, Na_2CO_3 (soda ash)

Sodium carbonate, crystalline, $NaHCO_3$ (washing soda, sal soda)

Sodium chloride, $NaCl$ (table salt, rock salt)

Sodium thiosulfate, $Na_2S_2O_3,5H_2O$ (hypo, dechlorinator)

Water, H_2O

Light

1 foot candle = 1 lumen
1 candle power = 12.56 foot candles
1 Lux = 0.0929 foot candles (or lumens)
1 lumen = 10.76 Lux
1 nanometer (nm) = 10 Angstroms (Å)

Temperature

Fahrenheit scale: (°F) water freezes 32 °F, water boils 212 °F.
Centigrade (Celsius) scale (°C): water freezes 0 °C, water boils 100 °C.
Kelvin (Absolute) scale (°K): water freezes 273 °K, water boils 373 °K.
To convert °F to °C.   (°F - 32) divided by 1.8 = °C
To convert °C to °F.   (°C x 1.8) + 32 = °F

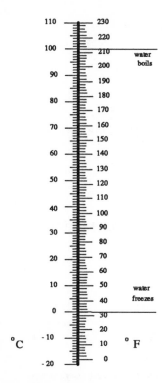

Liquid measure

1 cubic centimeter (cc) = 1 ml, approximately 20 drops
1 milliliter (ml) = 1 cc, 1/1000 l
1 liter (l) = 1000 ml, 1.06 qt, 2.1 pt
20 large drops or 25 small drops = approximately 1 ml
1 teaspoon (tsp) = 5 ml, 1/6 fl oz
1 tablespoon (tbsp) = 3 tsp, 1/2 fl oz, 15 ml
1 fluid ounce (fl oz) = 2 tbsp, 6 tsp, 29.6 ml
1 cup = 8 fl oz, 236.8 ml
1 quart (qt) = 32 fl oz, 2 pt, 946.3 ml, 0.95 l
1 gallon (gal) 128 fl oz, 8 pt, 4 qt, 3.8 l, 231 in^3
1 part per million (ppm) = 1 ml or mg per l (ml/l), 3.78 mg/gal

Length

1 micron ( ) = 1/1000 mm
1 millimeter (mm) = 1/10 cm, 1000 microns, 0.039 in
1 centimeter (cm) = 10 mm, 0.39 in
1 meter (m) = 1000 mm, 100 cm, 39.37 in, 3.28 ft
1 inch (in) = 25.4 mm, 2.54 cm
1 foot (ft) = 12 in, 30.48 cm, 0.3 m
1 yard (yd) = 3 ft, 91.44 cm, 0.91 m

Weight

1 milligram (mg) = 1/1000 g
1 gram (g) = 1000 mg, 15.4 gr, 0.035 oz
1 kilogram (kg) = 1000 g, 35 oz, 2.2 lbs, one l pure water
1 grain (gr) = 0.65 g
1 ounce (oz) = 28.35 g
1 pound (lb) = 16 oz, 454 g, 0.45 k

Surface area (square measure, length X width)

1 square centimeter (cm^2) = 0.155 in^2
1 square meter (m^2) = 10,000 cm^2, 10.764 ft^2, 1555 in^2
1 square inch (in^2) = 0.007 ft^2, 6.45 cm^2
1 square foot (ft^2) = 144 in^2, 929.03 cm^2
1 square yard (yd^2) = 1296 in^2

Volume (cubic measure, length X width X height)

1 cubic centimeter (cm^3) = 0.061 in^3
1 cubic meter (m^3) = 11.77 ft^3, 1.31 yd^3
1 cubic inch (in^3) = 0.00058 ft^3, 16.387 cm^3
1 cubic foot (ft^3) = 1728 in^3, 0.765 m^3
1 gallon = 231 in^3

Formulas and data

1 ft^3 of seawater = 64 lbs, 29.02 k, 7.5 gal, 28.4 l, 1728 in^3, 3785.4 cc

1 gallon of seawater = 8.5 lbs, 3.86 k, 231 in^3

To find the number of gallons in a rectangular or square tank
Multiply length X width X height in inches and divide by 231.

To find the number of gallons in a cylindrical tank
Multiply the diameter squared x 0.8 X the height in inches and divide by 231.

To find the number of gallons in a hexagon, octagon or other multi sided tank with sides of equal width, measure the total perimeter and multiply by the width of a single side. Then divide by 2, multiply by the height in inches, and divide by 231 to get the number of gallons.

To find the number of gallons in a spherical tank, measure the radius (distance from the center to the edge of the sphere) in inches and cube this measurement (times itself by 3). Multiply this figure by 3.1416 (pi) and multiply the result by 1.33. Divide by 231 to get the volume of a sphere and again by 2 to get the volume of half a sphere.

Full salinity seawater contains 35 to 37 parts per thousand (ppt, o/oo) salt. This is 35 to 37 grams per kilogram or liter, 4.7 to 5 oz per gal, and 2.9 to 3.1 lbs per 10 gal. *Approximately* 2.7 to 3 lbs of artificial sea salts make up 10 gal of full salinity seawater.

True specific gravity (sg) of full strength seawater (35 o/oo) is 1.0260. A standard hydrometer calibrated at 59 °F (15 °C) reads 1.0234 sg at 77 °F (25 °C). Seawater at a salinity of 30 o/oo has a true specific gravity of 1.0222. A standard hydrometer reads 1.096 sg at 77 °F.

Index

S

About the Author

Martin A. Moe Jr. has been working with marine fish and marine aquarium systems since 1960. He holds a masters degree from the University of South Florida and has worked as a fishery biologist, marine biologist, ichthyologist, and commercial marine fish culturist for almost 30 years. His scientific and popular articles on fish and marine biology date back to 1962 when he worked as a marine biologist for the State of Florida. He entered the private sector in 1969 and developed the basic technology for breeding Florida pompano in 1970. The first commercial scale production of clownfish was accomplished in Moe's garage in late 1972. Over the years, he has reared over 30 species of marine tropical fish including spawning, rearing, and even hybridizing French and grey Atlantic angelfish in 1976. He founded Aqualife Research Corporation in 1973 and Green Turtle Publications in 1982. He still keeps his thumb wet as a consultant for Aqualife, but he and his wife Barbara now work more at writing and publishing than breeding marine fish.

Books for the saltwater aquarist by Martin Moe

The Marine Aquarium Handbook
Beginner to Breeder

A practical handbook on the theory and methods of keeping and breeding marine tropical fish. Everything you need to know to set up and maintain a successful saltwater aquarium.
176 pages
ISBN 0-939960-02-8
LC 87-30174
$12.95

The Marine Aquarium Reference
Systems and Invertebrates

A major reference for the modern aquarist. This book contains 512 pages of text, tables, figures, and drawings that clearly and simply explain the techniques and technology of modern marine aquarium systems, including reef systems. It also introduces the aquarist to the latest classification of invertebrates and other living organisms, with expanded discussions of the invertebrate groups most important to marine aquarists.
This new book is a companion volume to *The Marine Aquarium Handbook* and contains new (not duplicated) information.
512 pages
ISBN 0-939960-05-2
LC CIP 89-7554
$21.95
You can borrow these books from your local library.
You can purchase them at your local pet\aquarium shop that carries saltwater fish and at many public aquariums.
If you can not find them locally, send your order to Green Turtle Publications, P.O. Box 17925, Plantation, FL 33318 and include $2 for shipping. Florida residents please include the appropriate sales tax.